# REIMAGINING INTERNATIONAL TAXATION

# REIMAGINING INTERNATIONAL TAXATION

*Navigating through the crises of pandemic, lack of consensus and retrospective taxation*

**2021**

*Edited by*

Parthasarathi Shome

*Foreword by*

Leandro M. Passarella
Maria Celina Valls

ITRAF
INTERNATIONAL TAX RESEARCH AND ANALYSIS FOUNDATION

OakBridge

*Published by*
OakBridge Publishing Pvt. Ltd.
M 35, 1st Floor, Old DLF, Gurugram, 122001, Haryana, India
Tel.: +91 124 4305970, E-mail: info@oakbridge.in
www.oakbridge.in

---



ISBN: 978-81-949911-7-5

Printed and bound at Saurabh Printers Pvt.Ltd.

# Foreword

This foreword is written in Buenos Aires, Argentina, some 15,000 kilometers away from ITRAF in Bangalore, India. While this may seem curious to this volume's readership, this is one of the few positive outcomes of the ongoing COVID-19 pandemic crisis that has stopped the world on its heels: It has brought people with common interests closer, although being apart (and, in this case, quite apart!), through the advances in technology. Since March 2020, videoconferences have become a part of our daily lives as more people have become connected in real time all around the world more often through different platforms.

In the past, such connections would have been possible during in-person conferences, seminars or congresses. This may no longer be the case because, in December 2019, a minuscule life form-a coronavirus—appeared on our human world. Since then, it has silently spread using human beings and their advances in technology as means of transportation. Nowadays, coronavirus is an uninvited guest in our lives and looms everywhere, yet human beings cannot see it or detect it before its unsettling presence becomes real—once it has already infected human beings, jeopardizing their lives.

Governments initially reacted to the spread of the virus requesting citizens, or directly requiring us, to retreat to our homes, disrupting our normal lives. Borders were closed, planes were grounded; we cannot move far from our places of residence and, if we do, in many cases we are required to comply with a preventive quarantine. We live very much as if we were characters of a science-fiction novel. Any similarities between our current lives and the life on Solaria that Isaac Asimov imagined in 1957 when writing THE NAKED SUN—the third book of his "Robot Series"—is pure coincidence.[1] The main difference is that we are now more than 7 billion people, while only 200,000 Solarians existed in Asimov's book. Just like us, Solarians practiced social distancing, communicating with each other, and even sharing meals, through screens. However, they had the help of millions of robots, which we do not have ... yet.

Until getting back to "normal", human beings continue to be pushed to transform our lifestyles. This transformation includes the way in which we do business. Social distancing is now the rule, and electronic commerce is widespread. Everything is delivered to our doors or screens, and this behaviour will very likely remain once we learn to coexist with the pandemic. If we change the way we do business, this for

1. Isaac Asimov, *The Naked* Sun, Bantam (1957). Needless to say, Asimov's Spacers (i.e., humans living in Outer Worlds conquered with robots) wore filters in their nostrils when meeting with Earthmen because of their fear to infections. Any similarity with our current face masks may also be pure coincidence.

sure will have, and already has, tax implications. Indeed, the COVID-19 pandemic has wreaked havoc on even the most stable economies. So far, governments have used tactics and tools already known to them to deal with this pandemic's effects on their countries' economies, and their long-term results are uncertain.

In this context, during the first series of worldwide lockdowns in 2020, we contacted Dr Partho Shome—among other scholars from around the world—to invite him to participate in "UTDT Global Tax Talks", an initiative of our University (Universidad Torcuato Di Tella). "UTDT Global Tax Talks" is a platform fostering an interdisciplinary dialogue on a single, hard tax topic among faculty members from all continents, as well as tax policymakers. Based on a common questionnaire, tax law professors, economists and political scientists share their views on the same issue, offering the audience a comprehensive analysis. Last year, we discussed several unsolved issues of the international tax system that the COVID-19 pandemic crystallized.[2]

Several of these issues are covered in ITRAF's fifth volume, which were presented at ITRAF's fifth annual (webinar) conference held on 4-5 December, 2020. They reflect the main debates around how to frame the new international tax order in four different parts. There are contributions from various specialists which make up a general overview of crucial tax debates stemming from the stressful time our world has been living in over the last two years.

As Dr Shome contends in Chapter 1, advanced and emerging economies alike have had to spend so much during the COVID-19 pandemic in 2020 that they have reached unprecedented fiscal deficit ratios of 10-16 percent of GDP. With this background, tax policy changes must be made in an innovative way so as not to disrupt productive activities (Shome). In this pandemic scenario, the discussion on new international tax rules has come to the fore and indeed exacerbated the need to revisit and re-design the international tax architecture.

There, Dr Shome sets the stage, by summarizing the issues that India is facing as a result of the pandemic and proposing tax reforms (especially targeted on the wealthy and superhigh-income earners, rather than increasing consumption taxes) to bring additional revenues, as well as the implementation of recommendations to reform India's tax administration. Mukesh Butani's rejoinder to Shome's chapter offers an additional perspective to the same issues, pointing out that speedy resolution of pending tax litigation may help India's revenue coffers, affected by the pandemic. Once the stage is set, it is time to discuss the crisis, considered also as an opportunity to change, which is the purpose of the following chapters.

2. The playlist of talks is available and can be accessed at https://www.youtube.com/playlist?list=PLmZkgXYrGwgjLtF0z62Thp1_My9OZyqU9.

Based on a historical analysis, Prof. Eduardo Baistrocchi describes that the International Tax Regime has been evolving along a spiral trajectory correlated to two global power shifts in Chapter 2. Firstly, a power shift from the U.K. to the U.S. in the 1930s and then, an emerging power shift from the U.S. to China beginning in the early 21st century.

Then, Prof. Philip Baker introduces the concept of a new international tax architecture, but not in terms of new rules or principles. Rather, in his concise chapter, Prof. Baker explains why he considers that the OECD is not the appropriate intergovernmental organisation in international tax because of its lack of democratic legitimacy or comprehensive agenda, and that the UN should claim that relevant position. In his rejoinder to this Chapter, Dr Shome asks whether a global tax organization or a world tax authority, as proposed by Vito Tanzi, would be a more suitable entity for that purpose.

The following two chapters discuss the well-known Vodafone case. Dr Nigam Nuggehalli's chapter comments on the retrospective taxation issue and its role in framing future tax law with a rejoinder by Dr Shome on the issue. On the other hand, Mr Hans Mooij analyses the case and reaches the conclusion that there is an urgent need for tax treaty arbitration as an effective mechanism to resolve cross-border tax disputes. An interesting discussion complements Mr Mooij's Chapter with Mr Butani's rejoinder, Prof. Baker's comment and Mr Mooij's addendum.

Then, Part 3's focus is on international consensus. Under the premise that the allocation of taxing rights should be interpreted uniformly, Messrs Sumeir Ahuja, Mukesh Butani and Riya Gupta discuss the nexus-based issues in their Chapter on "Profit Attribution: Approaches and Conflicts". They focus specifically on Indian domestic law and tax treaties. They offer a comprehensive picture of the different proposals currently under discussion in relation to nexus. Taking the three main kinds of permanent establishment (PE) as recognized by Indian tax treaties (fixed place of business, agency PE and service PE) as a framework, they analyze the effects of the Indian tax treaty network and the related judicial cases. They comment on the impact of MLI provisions on India's tax treaties. Their Chapter is followed by an interesting rejoinder by Mr P V Srinivasan.

Next, Messrs Hitesh D. Gajaria, Radhika Karadkar and Jitesh Golani present a noteworthy overview of OECD's Pillar One and Two. They address the possible implications for countries such as India in terms of expected revenue and implementation aspects. Then, Messrs Padamchand Khincha, Neha Khincha, and Priya Kothari refer to "Source and Nexus of Income" in their Chapter, elaborated further by Mr K R Sekar in his rejoinder.

Then, it is time to consider the income tax implications of cryptocurrencies. In their Chapter, Messrs K R Sekar and Alok Prasanna Kumar present India's institutional responses to the cryptocurrency phenomenon, while analysing the issues and challenges that, dealing with mining and transacting cryptocurrencies, may arise under current Indian tax laws. Their views are complemented by a rejoinder by Prof. Rohit Roy.

Last, but not least, ITRAF's volume ends with an issue that will remain very relevant for the times to come. With governments' pressing needs to collect tax revenues to afford the economic crisis caused by the COVID-19 pandemic, a taxpayer's charter of rights is crucial. In the last chapter, Mr K R Girish highlights the need for tax authorities to create mutual trust with their taxpayers by implementing and applying a taxpayer's charter. After providing historical background, Mr Girish summarizes the charters of rights and obligations in several countries and their impact before analysing the situation in India.

After reviewing the chapters that comprise this volume from ITRAF, we found that its selection of chapters has a very comprehensive coverage of all the topics the authors have dealt with. The rejoinders in this volume assist the reader to have a quick comprehensive picture of each topic while airing the different views on the same issue which reflect the intense debate posed by this pandemic environment.

This book is an important contribution to the current discussion of proposals to substantial changes to the international tax rules. It highlights the geopolitical, historical and technical differences that need to be bridged to arrive at a consensus on a new all-encompassing international tax architecture.

Buenos Aires
Spring 2021

Leandro M. Passarella
María Celina Valls

# Preface

This is the fifth edited volume on prevailing issues in international taxation that ITRAF has produced in its five years of existence. Each volume has emphasized particular areas, for example, a range of existing and continuing challenges in international taxation in the first volume, international tax base erosion through multinational profit shifting (BEPS) in the second volume, an array of issues from the taxation of charitable entities to cryptocurrency as well as taxpayer's rights in the third volume, and international taxation in the digital era, control instruments against tax avoidance, including GAAR and POEM, legislative over-activism and tax treaties in the fourth volume.

The present, fifth volume presents a collection of papers in the form of the main chapters accompanied by rejoinders. To begin, it imparts a sense of crisis and the need for an urgent reform in India's tax structure (Shome with a rejoinder by Butani). This is of particular relevance in the prevailing economic environment and fiscal deficit situation exacerbated by the ramifications of the yet uncontrolled COVID-19 pandemic. The volume then presents prevailing challenges in international taxation, including follies in setting up locations for the international taxation portfolio in international organizations (Baker, with a rejoinder by Shome), the history of how those biases gathered force over the past century (Baistrocchi, with a rejoinder by Shome), nagging issues in the taxation of the digital economy (Sekar and Prasanna Kumar, with a rejoinder by Roy, and Gajaria et al., with a rejoinder by Shome) and, relatedly, to the attribution of profits (Ahuja and Gupta with a rejoinder by Srinivasan) and the source versus nexus controversy (Khincha et al. with a rejoinder by Sekar). In an environment of what may be perceived as excessive taxpayer exposure, the final chapter takes up the issue of a taxpayer's charter (Girish, with a rejoinder by Chaudhary).

One of the major challenges facing international taxation in India spread over the past decade has been between the Indian government and foreign investors in India who have faced retrospective application of tax law for revenue collection by the tax authorities. This has led to long, drawn-out litigations through the high courts, the Supreme Court, and international arbitral tribunals. Cases pertain to Vodafone International Holdings, Vedanta Resources, and Cairn Energy and related companies. Two—Vodafone and Cairn—have ended in favour of the foreign investor and against the Indian government. The decision on Vedanta is awaited. A sense of urgency has led to the reference to retrospectivity in the title of this volume.

There are many lessons to be learnt from these experiences, and a range of authors takes up the issue of legislating and applying tax law retrospectively. Accordingly, the volume contains an exhaustive treatment of the relevant issues and controversies with respect to retrospective taxation (Nigam, with a rejoinder by Shome) and the role of arbitration (Mooij, with rejoinders by Baker and Butani). Based on the analyses of the five authors who have contributed directly to the topic in this volume—while other authors, including Girish and Khincha have also mentioned retrospectivity in a selected context—it may be concluded that retrospectivity, as is being formulated and applied in Indian tax law, is of considerable concern to domestic and international tax experts alike.

Indeed, previous work and roles of some of the authors have been referred to widely in subsequent academic works and court judgments, including in the just published Cairn arbitral award, Baker receiving seven citations and Shome receiving sixteen citations either directly or through committee or commission chairmanships. Therefore, the analytical work on this crucial issue cannot cease until an appropriate resolution is arrived at. For, otherwise, its deleterious ramifications on lowering investment and, thus, setting back GDP growth are likely to continue.

The ten chapters in this volume have been written by seventeen authors encompassing tax practitioners from tax advisory firms and independent practitioners, as well as academicians in tax law and economics. This volume is truly international in that the authors are from Argentina, the Netherlands, the United Kingdom and, of course, India. Thus, the knowledge of ITRAF's work has been spreading rapidly across continents. ITRAF's fourth volume was released in the tax law department of the London School of Economics, UK, in March 2020, while this fifth volume takes one step further in ITRAF's global reach.

Most of the chapters in this fifth volume of ITRAF were initially presented in ITRAF's fifth annual conference in December 2020, which had more than a hundred participants. An innovation in this volume, as mentioned above, is that the main chapters are accompanied by rejoinders from those who provided comments on the papers during or after the conference. This has added a supportive yet alternative stance to the view expressed in the main chapter. The variety in perspectives should make the volume interesting to read. The ability to publish this volume in particular during the global pandemic reflects ITRAF's resolve to move forward with its research and dialogue in the area of international taxation and its global dissemination.

I appreciate the contributions from all authors who have given valuable time in drafting their well-delineated chapters and for taking into consideration my comments and guidance on their earlier drafts. I especially appreciate the contributions of international authors from the London School of Economics, Oxford University, Tribute, Netherlands, and Universidad Torcuato Di Tella (UTDT), Buenos Aires. I particularly appreciate Professors Leandro Passarella and Maria Celina Valls of UTDT for writing the Foreword that entailed not only participation in the ITRAF conference but also perusing the various subjects contained in the volume.

Rohitash Chaudhary provided valuable assistance in formatting the chapters. Shreesh Chandra has continued to publish ITRAF's volumes at high production standards, this being ITRAF's third annual volume from Oakbridge. I would like to recognize the excellent copy-editing by the editorial team of Oakbridge. Needless to say, all contents related to the chapters and rejoinders, including the views expressed in them, are the sole responsibility of the authors and should not be attributed to ITRAF, or the editor of this volume, or its publisher.

**Parthasarathi Shome**

London
Spring 2021

Editor and
Chairman, ITRAF

# About the Contributors

*(in order of appearance)*

**Dr Leandro M. Passarella** is a founder partner and the tax practice leader of Passarella Abogados, a boutique Argentine tax law firm, where he focuses his practice on advice for inbound and outbound investments. He is also the professor of Personal Income Taxation at the Masters programs in Tax Law of Universidad Torcuato Di Tella (Buenos Aires, Argentina), where he also coordinates UTDT Global Tax Talks, a platform fostering an inter-disciplinary dialogue among faculty members, global tax policymakers and practitioners on hard tax topics of international taxation. He holds a JD degree (with honors) from Universidad de Buenos Aires, as well as the LL.M. degree from Harvard Law School, jointly obtained with the Harvard International Tax Program certificate. He has contributed chapters in several books, the latest being the Argentine chapter for "Taxation of Crypto Assets" (Wolters Kluwer, 2020).

**María Celina Valls** is professor of Corporate Income Taxation and director of the Masters degree in Tax Law and LLM in Tax Law at Universidad Torcuato Di Tella (UTDT), Buenos Aires, Argentina. She is a partner of the Tax Law Department at O´Farrell Law firm (Argentina). She leads complex tax disputes relating to transfer pricing. She earned a Masters degree in Law and Economics with an emphasis in Taxes from UTDT and an LLM from Universitat Pompeu Fabra, Spain. She was appointed as co-chair of the committee of "Transfer Pricing" at Asociación Argentina de Estudios Fiscales (the recognized branch of IFA in Argentina).

**Dr Parthasarathi Shome** is Chairman, ITRAF, Bengaluru, and Senior Visiting Fellow, London School of Economics. Earlier, he was Adviser (Minister of State) to the Indian Finance Minister, and chaired the Tax Administration Reform Commission (TARC). Before that, he was Chief Economist, UK Revenue and Customs; Chief of Tax Policy, IMF; and Professor, American University, Washington DC. He chaired India's Ninth and Tenth Five Year Plan Task Forces on tax policy and administration. He received Brazil's highest civilian honour, *Commander of the Order of the Southern Cross,* for his contributions to Brazilian fiscal reform, and the Jeanne S. Mattersdorf Award of the National Tax Association of America as "an outstanding student in the field of taxation and public finance" for his Ph.D. thesis on the incidence of the corporation income tax. He is widely published and is invited to speak across the globe.

**Mukesh Butani** is a Founder Member of ITRAF and the Managing Partner of BMR Legal. He is a Chartered Accountant, has a law degree and practices as an advocate in various Tribunals, High Courts and the Supreme Court of India. He is President, International Fiscal Association (IFA), India. He represents the International Chamber of Commerce (ICC), Paris, on the Ministry of Finance (MoF) Standing Committee on TDS and Foreign Tax Credit. He has served as member, Expert Task Force on International Tax and Transfer Pricing, MoF, in July 2012. He was member of the Tax Bureau of OECD – BIAC, Permanent Scientific Committee of IFA and is presently Vice Chairman of Taxation Commission of ICC. He was member of the Focus Group on Administrative Practices on tax disputes at the Tax Administration Reform Commission (TARC) set up in August 2013 by the MoF.

**Dr Eduardo Baistrocchi** is Associate Professor of Law at the London School of Economics and Political Science. He studied law at the Universidad de Buenos Aires before obtaining an LLM at Harvard Law School and later an LLM on Tax Law at LSE. He has been a Fulbright Scholar and a Chevening Scholar. He has also been a Distinguished Visiting Professor in Brazil (FGV Direito Sao Paulo), Canada (University of Toronto) and the United States (Northwestern University). His research and publications are focused on international taxation, with a particular emphasis on tax treaty disputes in the G20.

**Dr Philip Baker** is Queen's Counsel, Field Court Tax Chambers, Gray's Inn, London, and Visiting Professor at the Law Faculty, University of Oxford. He has a Ph.D. from the London University. He specializes in international tax issues, with a particular interest in double tax conventions, EU tax law, and taxation and human rights (especially the European Convention on Human Rights). He has appeared in a significant number of cases before courts and tribunals at the highest level, including the European Court of Justice.

**Dr Nigam Nuggehalli** is Dean of the School of Law at BML Munjal University, Gurugram. Previously, he was a Visiting Professor at the National Law School, Bangalore and an Associate Professor at Azim Premji University, Bangalore. He holds a DPhil in Law from Oxford University and an LLM (Taxation) from New York University School of Law. Prof. Nuggehalli also taught at BPP University, London, for several years, where he led a team of academics in delivering undergraduate programmes in jurisprudence and post graduate programmes in commercial law and international tax law. Prior to joining academia, Prof. Nuggehalli was an international tax lawyer working in New York, USA. Prof. Nuggehalli is presently completing a monograph on international taxation from an Indian perspective.

**Hans Mooij** is an independent tax counsel specializing in international tax compliance and controversy. He assists corporate clients as well governments. As tax treaty consultant he has worked for various international organizations including OECD, United Nations, and IMF. He is a Visiting Professor at the International Tax Centre (ITC) Leiden, and at the University of Amsterdam School of Law. He served the Netherland's Government as tax treaty negotiator, as Competent Authority in tax treaty matters, as prime litigator in tax treaty and EU law cases before the Dutch Supreme Court and the Court of Justice of the European Union, and as delegate to the OECD Working Party No. 1 on the Model Tax Convention and member of its Steering Group. He chairs the TRIBUTE organization, an independent, global initiative of leading experts in international taxation, which seeks to spread awareness of tax arbitration and tax mediation among the global tax community and avails experts for appointment as arbitrator, mediator or technical advisor in disputes on tax treaty or cross-border tax issues.

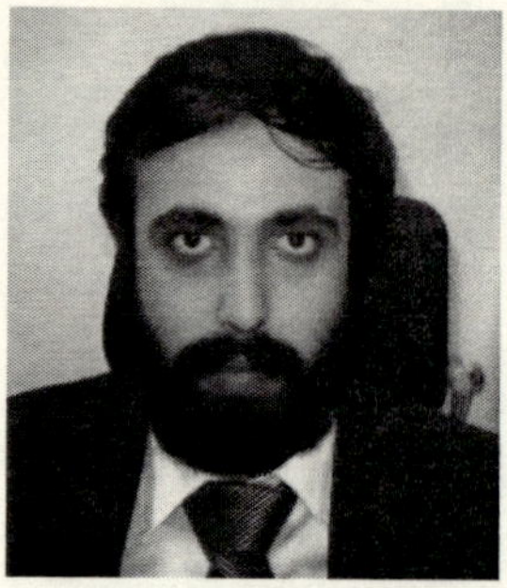

**Sumeir Ahuja** is a lawyer and holds an advanced LLM in International Tax Law from Leiden University, Netherlands. He has experience in the field of international tax and transfer pricing. Having contributed to several research projects and tax policy prescription; one of his contributions on digital tax, titled, 'Removing roadblocks in taxing business income in the digital era', received appreciation from Director-General, Taxation and Customs, European Commission. He is currently working in the international tax services & transfer pricing practice of BMR Legal, New Delhi.

**Riya Gupta** holds a bachelor's degree in law from O.P. Jindal Global Law School, Haryana, India. She specializes in domestic corporate and international tax and has contributed to several research projects. She has also represented India in the Global Tax Treaties Commentaries competition organized by International Bureau of Fiscal Documentation (IBFD) in Amsterdam and qualified as the winner.

**P. V. Srinivasan** is a Chartered Accountant and a Member of the Institute of Chartered Accountants of India (ICAI), New Delhi. He is engaged as a corporate advisor on global taxation and corporate law matters. His experience is in manufacturing and information technology industries with regard to corporate tax compliances across tax jurisdictions. He headed the Corporate Tax function at Wipro, Bangalore. He was a member of Emerging Issues Task Force on Non-Resident Taxation of Ministry of Finance, and the working group on transfer pricing. He is the Chairman of the Indirect Taxation Committee of Bangalore Chamber of Commerce and Industry (BCIC). He has been a visiting faculty at Training Institute of Income Tax Department, ICAI, and Institute of Company Secretaries of India.

**Hitesh D. Gajaria** is Senior Partner with the tax practice at KPMG India with more than three decades of tax, transfer pricing and regulatory consulting experience. Prior to his role as the Senior Partner, Hitesh led the Industrial and Consumer Manufacturing Sector Corporate Tax practice, and has also co-led KPMG in India's Transfer Pricing practice. He has co-authored BCAS' publications - 'Taxation of Non-Residents, FERA / FEMA' and 'Transfer Pricing Manual' and was Country Reporter for India at IFA international conference. He is also a mentor at KPMG in India's, Enactus initiative, guiding college students in developing socially sustainable community projects. He is a Fellow Member of ICAI.

**Jitesh Golani** is a Manager with the Corporate and International Tax practice at B S R & Associates LLP. He is a fellow member of the ICAI, securing all-India rank at Intermediate and Final level. He has more than 5 years of professional experience of advising clients on domestic/ international tax matters, and cross-border transactions. He is an avid reader of OECD's tax initiatives and global developments. He has also authored/co-authored articles on the OECD Pillar One on national platforms (i.e., Taxsutra and the Chamber of Tax Consultants).

**Radhika Karadkar** is a Manager with the Tax Advisory practice at B S R & Associates LLP. She is a Chartered Accountant and a LLM graduate in International Taxation from Leiden University, Netherlands. As a tax professional, she has experience in domestic and international tax, tax treaties, BEPS, MLI, cross-border transactions & structuring. She has a keen interest in research and academics. Extracts of her Masters research paper on BEPS Action 6 have been published as an article by IBFD in the Bulletin for International Taxation. She has also co-authored an article on Place of Effective Management (published in the journal of Chamber of Tax Consultants).

**H. Padamchand Khincha** is a Founder Member and Director on the Board of ITRAF. He is a partner in H. C. Khincha & Associates, Bangalore. He advises on tax structuring, due diligence, transfer pricing and compliance aspects. He has represented large corporates in high-profile cases before Income-tax tribunals and is associated with landmark decisions. He has deposed before several high-level government committees. He has many books and articles to his credit. He lectures on income tax issues, including at IIM, Bangalore, ICAI, and Direct Taxes Training Institute of the Income Tax Department. He is a 1982 Chartered Accountant securing 25th rank. He is a member of ICAI's Committee for preparing a paper on Income Computation and Disclosure Standards.

**Neha P. Khincha** is a Chartered Accountant working with H. C. Khincha & Co. for the past 8 years. A young professional with many degrees and accolades, Neha holds a bachelor's degree in Law and Commerce, a diploma in fashion styling from Instituto Marangoni, Italy, is a registered Ashtanga Yoga teacher and is currently pursuing a degree in sports fitness and nutrition. Neha, an avid fitness enthusiast and a yogi, juggles her time writing tax articles, running obstacle course races, and practising acroyoga. Apart from various tax articles and opinions, Neha has co-authored, with CA H. Padamchand Khincha, a handbook analysing and decoding the various sections of DTAA, published by the Bombay Chartered Accountants' Society. She also co-authored, along with CA H. Padamchand Khincha and CA Priya Kothari, "The Taxpayers Rights in International Exchange of Information", in *Challenges in Domestic and International Taxation: Emerging Indian Experience,* OakBridge publication for ITRAF as well as an analysis of the "Concept of real income - Section 5" in the publication titled 101 Supreme Court Landmark Judgements published by The Chamber of Tax Consultants.

**Priya Kothari** is a young professional working with H. C. Khincha & Associates. She is a commerce graduate from the Bangalore University. She is an Associate member of the ICAI enthusiastically obtaining insights in the field of direct taxes. She also holds a bachelor's degree in Law. Priya has participated and won accolades including "Best Lady Advocate" and "Winners" at National Moot Court competition and intra-college competitions. She has co-authored with CA. H. Padamchand Khincha and Neha Khincha, an analysis "Concept of Real income – Section 5" in the publication titled "101 Supreme Court Landmark Judgements" published by The Chamber of Tax Consultants. She has also co-authored for ITRAF in respect of "The Taxpayers Rights in International Exchange of Information", in *Challenges in Domestic and International Taxation: Emerging Indian Experience*, OakBridge publication.

**Alok Prasanna Kumar** is Senior Resident Fellow and Team Lead, Vidhi Karnataka. His areas of research include Judicial Reforms, Constitutional law, Urban Development, and Law and Technology. He graduated with a B.A. LL.B. (Hons) from the NALSAR University in 2008 and obtained the BCL from University of Oxford in 2009. He writes a monthly column for the Economic and Political Weekly and has published in the Indian Journal of Constitutional Law and National Law School of India Review apart from media outlets such as The Hindu, Indian Express, Scroll, Quint and Caravan. He has practiced in the Supreme Court and Delhi High Court from the chambers of Mr. Mohan Parasaran, and currently also co-hosts the Ganatantra podcast on IVM Podcasts.

**K. R. Sekar** is a Founder Member and Director on the Board of ITRAF. He is a Tax Partner with Deloitte and leads Deloitte Private for Deloitte India. He has more than 30 years of experience in the field of direct taxes, mergers and acquisitions, international taxation and transfer pricing. His client portfolio includes leading companies in technology, media, telecommunications, manufacturing and engineering. Sekar's key areas of expertise include inbound structuring, litigation support and advising on cross-border tax issues. He advises inbound global companies coming into India on entry strategy, inbound structuring and assists them on mitigating tax risks. He is also associated with many landmark litigation cases for global companies. He was recognized as one of the leading tax controversy leaders by *International Tax Review*, UK.

**Dr Rohit Roy** is Assistant Professor of Law at Christ (Deemed to be University), Bengaluru. He has a Ph.D. in International Environmental and Trade Law and Policy and a Masters in International Commercial Law, both from Cardiff University, UK. His current research interests are in the field of climate change and the regulation of displaced persons, as well as in various aspects of international taxation. His areas of teaching comprise environmental law (domestic and international), international taxation and food security policy. Prior to teaching, he worked as a Tax Research Consultant at ITRAF, Bengaluru.

**K. R. Girish** is a Founder Member and Director on the Board of ITRAF. Previously he was a Senior Tax Partner and National Head of Tax Litigation and Disputes Resolution practice in KPMG. After 20 years, he took an entrepreneurial step and set up his own practice under K. R. Girish & Associates, specialising in direct tax and regulatory issues. He was a president of the Bangalore Chamber of Industry and Commerce (2009-10) and continues to be Chairperson of the Finance Committee of the Chamber. He is fellow member of ICAI and an Associate member of the Australian Taxation Institute. He is a regular faculty member of ICAI Diploma in International Tax programme. He has Law degree from the Karnataka State Law University.

**Rohitash Chaudhary** is Research Associate at ITRAF, Bengaluru. Earlier he served as Research Consultant, Tax Administration Reform Commission (TARC), Government of India, New Delhi and as Research Associate, National Council of Applied Economic Research (NCAER), New Delhi. He has an M. Sc. in Financial Economics from the Madras School of Economics and B. Tech. in Computer Science and Engineering from Uttar Pradesh Technical University. His areas of research interest include macro-economics, socio-economic issues, poverty, wealth & income distribution, and domestic & international taxation matters.

# Brief Contents

# Detailed Contents

## SETTING THE STAGE



## A SENSE OF CRISIS—GLOBAL POWER SHIFTS, TAX ARCHITECTURE, AND RETROSPECTIVITY

## IN SEARCH OF INTERNATIONAL CONSENSUS

## ADMINISTRATIVE INNOVATION

# SETTING THE STAGE

CHAPTER 1

# India in a Global Pandemic—Macro-Economic and Tax Considerations

**Parthasarathi Shome**

## 1. Introduction

Advanced and emerging economies alike have had to spend so much during the COVID-19 pandemic in 2020, and continuing, that they have reached unprecedented fiscal deficit ratios of 10-16 percent of GDP. This deficit level is higher than during the 2008-09 global economic crisis. It, therefore, calls for extraordinary tax measures since cutbacks in expenditure are unlikely in the face of a heightened need for socio-economic expenditure in particular.[1] The International Monetary Fund (IMF) estimated that India's general government[2] fiscal deficit would reach 13 percent of GDP in Financial Year (FY) 2020-21, primarily due to weak tax revenue.

In the last two decades, India's GDP growth rates increased until 2010 but steadily declined after that (Table 1). 2020 has been estimated as a significantly negative growth year reflecting both an already declining trend and the deleterious economic ramifications of the COVID-19 pandemic. The high GDP growth rate projected for 2021 merely reflects a high rate on the low 2020 GDP base.

A comparison of India with China has remained of interest to analysts. Though both India and China have enjoyed high growth rates, China's GDP growth rate has been above that of India for most of the past four decades. India's gross capital formation was 30 percent of GDP during 2010–18 while China's hovered just below 50%. There is little doubt that, to recuperate GDP, India needs significant injections of investment, including foreign direct investment (FDI), perhaps in particular from the US.

India's FDI increased from $27 billion to $51 billion during the 2010-2019 period, but its scale was a quarter of China's. India struggled to provide ultra-modern economic infrastructure through vehicles such as Special Economic Zones (SEZ). It introduced SEZs through an Act of Parliament in 2006, but performance

1. Parthasarathi Shome. 2012. Rebalancing and Structural Policies—An Indian Perspective, *Oxford Review of Economic Policy*, Volume 28, Number 3, pp 587–602.
2. General government comprises all—central, state and local—levels of government.

has trailed that of China. While China's SEZ's are mammoth but less than 20 in number, India approved some 160 of them, even some single buildings being designated as an SEZ, reflecting an intrinsic failure in its SEZ policy.

**Table 1: Real GDP Growth**
**(annual percent change)**

| Year | India | China |
|---|---|---|
| 1995 | 7.6 | 10.9 |
| 2000 | 4.0 | 8.5 |
| 2005 | 9.3 | 11.4 |
| 2010 | 10.3 | 10.6 |
| 2015 | 8.0 | 6.9 |
| 2019 | 4.2 | 6.1 |
| 2020* | -8.0 | 2.3 |
| 2021** | 11.5 | 8.2 |
| 2022** | 6.8 | 5.6 |

*Source:* IMF Database and World Economic Outlook Update, IMF, January 2021.[3]

* Estimate, ** Projections

**Note:** For India, figures are presented on FY (April 1- March 31) basis. Based on the calendar year, India's growth is estimated at -7.6 percent for 2020 and projected at 11.0 percent for 2021.

Another limitation on FDI is India's overall stance on international taxation policy. To expect FDI to occur on a large scale while a regime of retrospective application of tax law rages on multinational enterprises (MNEs) is folly. Unless this policy is reined in through changes in the law and only prospective application of tax changes is assured, the tax will continue to determine GDP, rather than tax collection being the outcome of GDP and GDP growth (Shome Rejoinder to Nigam, Chapter 4).

In terms of non-tax policy, China attracts foreign investors because of its disciplined labour force, among other things, that India has not been able to offer. Foreign investors continue to go to China despite stringent pre-conditions such as technology transfer and a minimum length of stay for foreign investors. Such long-term strategic benefits that China enjoys have not accrued to India.

China's growth strategy has rested on an export push while maintaining tight control on imports through a long-term policy of undervalued currency. India's

3. IMF. 2021. World Economic Outlook Update, January 2021: Policy Support and Vaccines Expected to Lift Activity. https://www.imf.org/en/Publications/WEO/Issues/2021/01/26/2021-world-economic-outlook-update, (last accessed on January 28, 2021).

currency was historically over-valued thus restricting export growth. China's undervalued currency began to unravel recently under international pressure. Nevertheless, in 2019, China's exports remained 18% of GDP (19 percent for India). But India imported more. Thus, overall, India suffered a trade deficit of 2 percent of GDP while China enjoyed a trade surplus of 1 percent of GDP.

India's needed tax reforms have to be seen in light of this overall macro-economic and fiscal situation that has deteriorated sharply during the COVID-19 pandemic.

## 2. Needed Tax Reforms

Tax policy changes must be made innovatively so as not to disrupt productive activity. Thus, they should increase individual income and wealth taxes, which are low by global standards while rationalising the corporate income tax without touching its basic rate structure. The sharp edges of the Goods and Services Tax (GST) need to be smoothened quickly to reduce evasion and facilitate compliance. Crucial GST measures include the introduction of auto-population of tax return forms in order to check tax evasion, rather than increasing GST rates since it would hurt the common consumption basket.

Short term international taxes such as the Equalization Levy on the digital economy have to stay to garner and protect revenue from this sector in the absence of progress in its taxation mechanisms in multilateral discussions and despite unilateral measures by the US against every country that has introduced it. Last but not the least, rapid reform of tax administration, with a customer focus and away from retrospective application of taxes, is imperative to push up investment and GDP growth.

### 2.1. Taxes on Wealth and Very High Incomes

Countries have reduced corporate income tax rates for reasons of international competitiveness, and these lower rated structures cannot be again scaled up easily. While that is the prevailing reality in the corporate sector, global indicators reveal a shocking increase in the income gap and income and wealth concentration in all country income-groupings. Yet countries have abolished or reduced wealth taxes for reasons including tax avoidance, tax evasion, and limits to the ability of tax administration. Nevertheless, in a search for a tax base of unproductive assets in the ongoing economic crisis, a wealth tax is appropriate since it would have little adverse effect on productivity and provided that the design of its structure is simple and, commensurately, its administration is effective.

To elaborate, a wealth tax is justifiable because of the following reasons. (1) Wealth building in recent years has not been through economic fundamentals but based on destabilizing speculation such as the financialization of global commodity markets that have had little to do with their actual market demand and supply. (2) Tax administration capability has improved in emerging economies to better track and cover wealth in the tax base. (3) Global indicators reveal a significant increase in the wealth gap and wealth concentration in all country categories. (4) Accumulated wealth is often economically unproductive. And (5) with international tax harmonization by means of double taxation avoidance arrangements (DTAAs), foreign tax credit for wealth tax is possible.

While wealth tax should include both real and financial wealth, it is important: (1) to not have prohibitive rates; and (2) to have a high threshold so that only the significantly wealthy come under the tax.

Perhaps the most crucial need for wealth taxation in India arises from India's racing wealth & income concentration. In India, where 0.001% of the top income cohorts are enjoying the most rapid increase in wealth concentration in the entire world, a tax on wealth is imperative for equity and growth. If well conceptualised and fairly implemented, it should also generate good revenue.

Thus, there is room in India for reintroducing a wealth tax on all assets. The net wealth definition should ensure that all assets — real and financial — are included, keeping the tax rates low, say 0.25% between Rs 0.5 billion[4] and Rs 1 billion, and 0.5% above Rs 1 billion. The tax rate needs to be very low so that the wealth tax is successful both in compliance by taxpayers and revenue collection by the administration.

India also needs to introduce higher tax rates on the incomes of the super-rich. The prevailing income tax rates in India are 5, 10, 12, 20, 25, 30 percent, a structure that is among the lowest in the world (even on a $ to $, rather than a PPP[5], basis). Therefore, an income tax on the super-rich should be introduced at 40% for incomes above Rs. 1 billion. After all, it cannot be denied that India is among the very poor countries of the world, and its income and wealth distribution and growing concentration continue to draw the surprise and shock of much of the world if not to Indians in the uppermost income groups themselves.

## 2.2. Corporate Income Tax

India's main corporate income tax (CIT) rate was reduced to an average of 27.69% from FY 2019-20 through a Taxation (Amendment) Ordinance[6] on September 20, 2019. A special taxation regime was introduced:

---

4. On 19 March 2021, US$ 1 = Rs 72.49, and UK£ 1= Rs 101.07.
5. PPP is purchasing power parity. It indicates not just a nominal $ but what is the value of a basket of goods that a $ could buy in India.
6. An ordinance is defined as an authoritative order, or a decree or law promulgated by a state or national government without the consent of the legislature. It includes examples such as collecting revenue through new taxes or harnessing resources during an emergency or threat. For an ordinance to be enforced effectively, it must not be in conflict with any higher law such as state or national law or constitutional provisions.
   http://www.legalservicesindia.com/article/1820/Ordinances-in-India.html#:~:text=The%20term%20%22ordinance%22%20is%20defined,during%20an%20emergency%20or%20threat.

- For existing manufacturing companies (under Section 115BAA) the CIT rate was reduced to 25.17%. (22% + 10% SC + 4% HEC); and
- For new manufacturing companies (under Section 115BAB) the CIT rate was reduced to 17.16%. (15% + 10% SC + 4% HEC).[7]

These rates are comparable with advanced economy rates currently. For example, a range may be surmised from 27% in the US, 25% in China and Netherlands, 19% in the UK, and 12.5% in Ireland.[8] Therefore, there is little room for India to increase corporate income tax rates at this time.

However, what can and should be done is to freeze tax incentives for 5 years to increase neutrality across the corporate sector and protect tax revenue. The focus should, instead, be on improving the ease of paying taxes, a criterion in which India ranks lower (115) than China (105) in a cross-country comparison (Table 2).

**Table 2. Ease of Paying Taxes (EPT): Cross Country Comparison 2020**

| Country | Tax contribution rate (% of profit)[2/] | Payments (number/ year)[3/] | Paying taxes (hours/ year)[4/] | Post-filing index (0-100)*[5/] | Overall EPT rank (of 190)[6/] |
|---|---|---|---|---|---|
| **UK** | 30.6 | 9 | 114 | 71.0 | 27 |
| **US** | 36.6 | 11 | 175 | 94.0 | 25 |
| **South Africa** | 29.2 | 7 | 210 | 60.8 | 54 |
| **Russian Federation** | 46.2 | 9 | 159 | 77.8 | 58 |
| **India**[1/] | **49.7** | **11** | **252** | 49.3 | **115** |
| **China** | **59.2** | **7** | **138** | 50.0 | **105** |
| **Brazil** | 65.1 | 10 | 1501 | 7.8 | 184 |

* Doing Business 2017-20 methodology.

*Source:* Doing Business Report-2020, World Bank.

1/ The Indian numbers relate only to the cities of Delhi and Mumbai.

2/The "tax contribution rate" measures the amount of taxes and mandatory contributions borne by the business in the second year of operation, expressed as a share of commercial profit. The total amount of taxes and contributions borne is the

7. Surcharge (SC) and Health and Education Cess (HEC).
8. See Corporate Tax Rates for 2010-2020, KPMG. https://home.kpmg/xx/en/home/services/tax/tax-tools-and-resources/tax-rates-online/corporate-tax-rates-table.html, (last accessed on January 5, 2021)

sum of all the different taxes and contributions payable after accounting for allowable deductions and exemptions. The taxes withheld (such as personal income tax) or collected by the company and remitted to the tax authorities (such as VAT, sales tax, or goods and service tax) but not borne by the company are excluded. The taxes included are: profit or corporate income tax, social contributions and labour taxes paid by the employer, property taxes, turnover taxes, and other taxes (such as municipal fees and vehicle taxes.

3/The tax payments capture the total number of taxes and contributions paid, the method of payment, the frequency of payment, and the frequency of filing. It includes taxes withheld by the company, such as sales tax, VAT and employee-borne labour taxes.

4/The time to comply with tax laws measures the time taken to prepare, file and pay three major types of taxes and contributions: the corporate income tax, value added or sales tax and labour taxes, including payroll taxes and social contributions.

5/The post filing index is based on four components—time to comply with VAT refund, time to obtain VAT refund, time to comply with a corporate income tax correction and time to complete a corporate income tax correction. The score for post filing index benchmarks economies with respect to the regulatory best practice on the indicator. The score is indicated on a scale from 0 to 100, where 0 represents the worst regulatory performance and 100 the best regulatory performance, and is computed based on the methodology in the DB17-20 studies.

6/The ranking of economies on the ease of paying taxes is determined by sorting their scores for paying taxes.

Points to note from Table 2 include:

- EPT measures the payments, number of payments, time taken to pay, and post-filing convenience for a firm to comply with all tax regulations.[9]
- India's components of the index—number of tax payments per year (11) and time taken for paying taxes (252 hours) have improved though the total tax to be paid as percent of profit (49.7) has worsened over recent years.[10]
- On examination, India's overall sharp improvement is due to a 44.8 point gain on the post-filing index – a new component included in 2017 to measure "ease of doing business" in which India scored 49.3 out of 100 in 2020 compared to 4.5 in 2017. (Note: higher numbers are better).

9. World Bank. 2019. Doing Business 2020. https://www.doingbusiness.org/en/reports/global-reports/doing-business-2020, (last accessed on January 6, 2021).
10. For 2017 the figures were: number of tax payments per year (33), time taken for paying taxes (251 hours) and total tax to be paid as percent of profit (56.2). Note that number of hours went up in 2020 compared to 2017.

- Thus it is the experience of companies operating in India "after" the filing of corporate income tax returns that is driving its EPT score.
- India's improvement is primarily the result of enhanced electronic tax payment mechanisms, and due to the speeding up of the post-filing processes — where one-to-one contact between the taxpayer and the tax official has been reduced.
- Interestingly, China's tax contribution rate is higher than India's; nevertheless, its FDI is higher. This clearly reflects greater certainty in China's business environment as argued before.
- India's overall EPT ranking (115 in 2020) has improved (172 in 2017, 119 in 2018, and 121 in 2019).
- The Indian finance minister said in October 2019 that,

  till now, two cities have been covered. For a large country with regional diversity being very distinct, we have been impressing upon the World Bank that having just two cities, Delhi and Mumbai, may not be adequately representative…from the coming year, Kolkata and Bengaluru will be added to the list of cities surveyed.[11]

## 2.3. Goods and Services Tax (GST)

The introduction of GST was the outcome of a decade-long effort. It is now more than three years old. Several points of required improvement have emerged including the need to streamline tax compliance further.

Urgent administration reform required include:

- Reduce the number of rates and classifications. The voluminous list of the GST tariff structure indicates its departure from global norms and makes GST compliance challenging for taxpayers. In turn, the likelihood of continuing high incidence of litigation as in the previous domestic indirect tax regime, continues.
- Step back from the newly introduced rule that a dealer or trader can be picked up for audit in any state, making post-tax compliance onerous for taxpayers. This practice was not prevalent under the previous state-level VAT.
- Replace the joint administrative powers of the centre and states over the same taxpayer even at low turnover levels. Currently, this comprises a heavy

11. Quoted in Subhayan Chakraborty and Arup Roychoudhury. 2019. India Rises 14 Places to 63rd in Global Ease of Doing Business Rankings, *Business Standard*, October 24. https://www.business-standard.com/article/current-affairs/india-rises-14-places-to-63rd-in-global-ease-of-doing-business-rankings-119102400190_1.html, (last accessed on January 5, 2021).

compliance burden on taxpayers who have to face and deal with the central level tax administration plus the state level administrations where he is trading. Instead, information exchange among various tax administrations should be carried out more intensively to reduce the high incidence of tax evasion in specific sectors and in particular regions.

- Introduce auto-population of return forms connecting output tax and input tax. Without it there is no automatic cross-check, and the essence of GST is absent. The three GST Forms—1M, 2A, and 3B—were intended to be electronically linked, but they are not. Form 3B should have been automatically (electronically) populated as soon as the GST number of a taxpayer is entered in Form 1M or 2A. Ideally, there should be no requirement or possibility for a taxpayer to enter information into the three forms separately. This has led to GST evasion since carrying out manual cross-checks of all related return forms is impractical.

There are fundamental changes needed in the overall GST structure. To note are:

- The crux of a GST is to have a broad base that, in turn, enables a low tax rate to yield the same tax revenue.
- Petroleum products contribute one-fourth to half of the different states' revenues. The states have been opposed to including it in the GST base to maintain their hold over this stream of revenue.
- Keeping petroleum out leads to *double cascading*: petroleum users cannot take the input tax credit (ITC), and the petroleum sector itself cannot take ITC for its inputs. Therefore, the petroleum sector causes significant distortions in the allocation of resources across the supply chain in the economy as a whole.
- The GST Council which is the Centre-State policy making body comprising policymakers at the ministerial level retains an enabling provision to tax petroleum, and the Centre prefers to include petroleum in the GST base. But states have been steadfast in their resistance to do so. This has to be reconsidered and there should be a via media for petroleum to be included in the GST base.
- Stamp duty on immovable property is also excluded from the GST base. This leads to cascading generated in the construction sector.

If the required structural changes are made, the GST should be more revenue productive since resource misallocation would be reduced and that would generate higher GDP growth and, therefore, more revenue. Revenue needs cannot be minimized in the prevailing pandemic environment.

Finally, a sustained increase in selective excises on conspicuous consumption comprising extreme luxury goods that has become the wont of the super-rich should be introduced rather than increasing excises on domestic gas and petroleum consumption that hits the middle class badly and benefits a small class of super-rich rich suppliers.

### 2.4. Taxpayer Reaction

While some of the suggested reform measures will improve the ease of tax compliance, others will lead to higher revenue contribution. Realistically, taxpayers may react adversely to those increases. However, it has to be understood that there remains no alternative to tax increases for, after all, their impact would be confined primarily to very high-income earners and wealth owners. Obviously, those increases must be considered in light of not depending on any increase in the overall corporate tax burden—except for non-neutral tax incentives that should be removed—in order to obviate any further adverse ramifications for an already diminished economy with dormant capital, low bank lending, and high under- and un-employment.

Thus, an increased tax burden has to be borne by the rich, on both wealth accumulation and super-high incomes, and on conspicuous consumption. There could be some unwillingness but a realistically designed wealth tax and increase in the income tax must proceed given India's highest rate of growth of income concentration compared to the rest of the world.

## 3. Tax Administration Reform

India's Tax Administration Reform Commission (TARC), 2014-15, was the first government established commission—as opposed to a committee—that spanned two government administrations and issued the most voluminous recorded report that made an exhaustive list of recommendations for tax administration reform. Among them remain several that are yet to be implemented. It is crucial that they are addressed without delay. They can enhance the ease of compliance while enabling the monitoring of taxpayers and cross-checking of tax returns. At the same time, such reforms can generate additional revenue. The most important of these are:

- Consolidate into one the two departments of Central Board of Direct Taxes (CBDT) and the Central Board of Indirect Taxes and Customs (CBIC). Currently, in a cross-section of countries, only India administers the two branches—direct tax and indirect tax—separately for tax purposes. Consolidation will save scarce public resources, give better access to taxpayers for tax payment, and improve the ability of the tax administration to cross verify the compliance behaviour of taxpayers. Details of a proposed consolidated structure is provided in the TARC Report.

- Fifty countries have introduced Large Taxpayer Units (LTUs) that enable large enterprises to establish tax relations with the tax administration at a single window. Usually, LTUs are segmented by economic sectors such as oil and gas, banking, insurance, telephone and telegraph, and others. This encourages the specialisation of tax officers in particular sectors who develop knowledge of the characteristics of individual sectors and how they are functioning at a particular point in an economic cycle. India started late on establishing LTUs in 2006, and, even after they were introduced, they stagnated in application and enthusiasm to come up to global standards, reflecting the changing whims of policymakers. The process has to be speeded up now and completed without delay.
- TARC emphasised the fixing of accountability on the tax administration in completing scrutiny and audit; and that, if not completed within a fixed period, it should conclude in the taxpayer's favour. It also recommended that scrutiny should be the responsibility of a tax officer even if he is transferred before the scrutiny is completed. This is an important element to be introduced to improve the ease of taxpayer compliance and assign appropriate responsibility on tax officers. Fixing accountability follows international norms and needs to be established as soon as possible.
- The current Indian authorities introduced a system of faceless assessment in 2020 in which any face-to-face encounter between the taxpayer and the tax officer is removed. It is too early to conclude how faceless assessment will be accepted by tax officers and taxpayers alike since there are inconveniences attached to both. There have been fears that an assessment file from a major metropolitan city could be assigned to a small tax office somewhere across the country. The system could also be vitiated if demands are made on taxpayers for excessive document submission unrelated to the scrutiny itself.

Indian tax experts are already pointing to shortcomings in the implementation of the faceless assessment system. Sinha (2020) quoted several experts to say,[12]

- The scheme was launched with good intentions, but now that aim appears to be going off track.
- The faceless scheme was supposed to be a post office through which one sends a letter and gets a response, but even the process of getting a response from assessees is not so simple.

12. Shishir Sinha. 2020. Faceless Schemes of Direct Taxes Creating More Problems than Solutions, *Business Line*, December 29. https://www.thehindubusinessline.com/news/national/faceless-schemes-of-direct-taxes-creating-more-problems-than-resolutions/article33445675.ece#, (last accessed on January 9, 2021).

- Questionnaires are being prepared without application of mind. Many details are being asked which are not required.
- There are cases of pick and choose.
- An officer doing peer review may not go against the ruling given by another officer, fearing vigilance enquiry at a later stage. Therefore, peer review should be carried out by independent panels of tax experts.
- Communication gaps should be resolved, and the possibility of personal hearings should be introduced in case of complex issues.

Therefore, for the system to be successful, there is an urgent need for a clearer indication from the authorities regarding how the system is operating and how it will be modified to reflect meaningful views being expressed by India's tax experts. Unless improvements are introduced on a real-time basis, the complex faceless assessment system is likely to end up with some notoriety.

Another measure of 2020 that the Indian authorities have taken is the introduction of a taxpayer's charter in Indian tax legislation. (See Girish, Chapter 10) This is the first time that a charter has become law as opposed to an administrative declaration of intentions. In that, it can be an important step forward if the law is implemented seriously and for the protection of good taxpayers by making tax law predictable and compliable. The charter is an opportunity to build trust between the taxpayer and the tax administration. Of course, the obligations of the tax administration to enforce the law, and meeting legitimate expectations of taxpayers from the charter, are a difficult balance to achieve.[13]

In the end, the tax administration measures taken in 2020 by the authorities can be a significant advance in reforming administrative implementation. On the other hand, as pointed to earlier, they may be subverted if the administration demands voluminous documentation or those unrelated to the main purpose of an assessment. Such demands counter the objectives enshrined in a charter. Thus, the success of the measures will depend on the cooperation received from the tax administration for, ultimately, only that can ensure the desired outcomes of the reforms.

## 4. International Taxation

### 4.1. Permanent Establishment and Source Versus Residence

Some changes that have been occurring in recent years with the advance of digital access, accelerating during the pandemic, is remote operation without any local presence while maintaining management functions in more than one jurisdiction.

---

13. Mukesh Butani and Shreyash Shah. 2020. Taxpayer Charter: A Roadmap for Mutual Trust and Respect, *Financial Express,* August 21. https://www.financialexpress.com/opinion/taxpayer-charter-a-roadmap-for-mutual-trust-and-respect/2061181/, (last accessed on January 9, 2021).

The spread of the "home office" has been significant. Many employees seem to prefer it. Some multinational enterprises (MNEs) have cut back on local presence. In this light, the concept of "permanent establishment" (PE) may need to be revisited and redefined. The question arises as to whether such changes should apply exceptionally to certain industries or become the general rule[14]

The emphasis of the OECD to move towards source from residence through its tax base erosion and profit shifting (BEPS) project has to continue since it attempts to reassign tax revenue allocation among trading countries in the right direction.[15] In the 1990s, the US changed its rules and allowed such related foreign companies to be de-linked from their US parent by 'ticking the box' - a set of loose criteria - resulting in a lack of relationship for tax purposes. That is, if they did not bring back profits to the US, there was no tax to be paid which was 'deferred'. This destabilised the parent-PE relationship.

India and several emerging economies had steadfastly argued well before the BEPS project that tax revenue must justly accrue in source jurisdictions where value-added was created in the international supply chain of a commodity or service. By and large, advanced economies had ignored this stance, their position being that revenue should accrue where risk-taking and management decisions were made and where capital resided. However, with the collapse in advanced economy revenue with the onset of the 2008 global economic and financial crisis, advanced economies began to realise the potential revenue benefits of applying the source principle due to the limits of international capital movements.[16] (See Baistrochhi, Chapter 2)

Thus, the source principle should assume permanence in international tax rules: it is rational; both emerging and advanced economies other than the US have been progressing towards acceptance of the ramifications of the source principle. (See Khincha et al., Chapter 8, for their views) The debate over the OECD's Pillar I and Pillar II that has emerged in the digital economy taxation context indicates that the US continues to be reluctant when it comes to its MNEs to be taxed in source jurisdictions. It continues to insist that tax revenue should accrue to the US where digital companies are headquartered. (See Gajaria et al., Chapter 7) Baker

14. This was a question put to this author in a Q&A by Leandro Passarella, professor of tax law, and María Celina Valls, director of graduate tax law programme, "Global Tax Talks 2020", Conference Hosts, Universidad Torcuato Di Tella (UTDT), Buenos Aires, on September 2, 2020. https://www.youtube.com/watch?v=wmrP8z-TiSI&list=PLmZkgXYrGwgjLtF0z62Thp1_My9OZyqU9&index=3&t=0s, (last accessed on January 6, 2021).

15. Parthasarathi Shome (edited). 2016a. *Base Erosion and Profit Shifting (BEPS): The Global Taxation Agenda*, ITRAF, Wolters Kluwer, Bangalore.

16. P. Shome (edited). 2014. *The G20 Macroeconomic Agenda: India and the Emerging Economies*, Cambridge University Press, New Delhi.

commented in a nutshell,[17] "The MNE tax avoidance problem could be linked primarily to those MNEs with headquarters (HQs) in the US."

Regarding whether the PE concept should be redefined, the OECD's original 2014 proposal of a 'permanent virtual establishment' (PVE) was not a poor one. Once an MNE's sales reach a certain level in a jurisdiction, it would be deemed to have a PE in that jurisdiction. In that case, profits from the MNE attributable to the virtual PE could be taxed by the source jurisdiction.

In effect, providing a healthy customer base should suffice to entitle a source state with the right to tax profits arising in (or from) that state. Such a concept would operate based on the continuous and commercially significant business activity of a non-resident enterprise in the source country. This idea matches the fundamentals behind source-based taxation. In practice, whether a sufficiently high sales revenue creates a legal right for a country to claim the ability to tax an enterprise (other than VAT or GST, of course) is, however, not accepted by all, as is evident from ongoing international deliberations.

The OECD's PVE discussion draft in fact states that varieties of a 'virtual' presence PE are included 'only for the sake of completeness.' Perhaps 'for the sake of completeness' means that the OECD is not proposing to move forward with these suggestions at least at this time. It reflects a lack of enthusiasm for these alternatives as pointed out by experts such as Girish[18] and others.

To sum up, countries have expressed increasing keenness that the international taxation regime (ITR) be designed to attribute revenue among tax jurisdictions fairly. As a backdrop, it has to be recalled that the ITR was not fair over the past century. This was because value-added was not recognized as an appropriate criterion, but capital ownership was. That is, tax revenue never accrued to those countries *to which* capital was exported and where value-added was created, but to those countries *from where* capital was exported.

That convention and practice reflected the pattern of the global colonial past though, unfortunately, it continued even after colonies vanished. It reflected the predominance of the OECD, an advanced economy group, that remained powerful in consolidating its interests. But the BEPS project is challenging that pattern due to the broader inclusion of countries in the G20. Ironically, today the US appears to be the sole visible adherent of the exclusivity of the residence principle.

---

17. Philip Baker. 2016. 'BEPS: Emergence of International Tax Law and Future Direction,' in P. Shome edited, *Base Erosion and Profit Shifting (BEPS): The Global Taxation Agenda*, ITRAF, Wolters Kluwer, Bangalore.
18. K. R. Girish, 'A Comprehensive Overview of Shifts in International Taxation,' in Shome P (ed), *International Taxation in the Digital Era*, (OakBridge 2020).

### 4.2. Arm's Length Pricing

The pandemic has affected the comparability of an MNE's intercompany transactions. This has led to particular challenges in determining the arm's length range during the associated economic downturn. For setting any arm's length or transfer pricing, mark-ups are usually set up when economic conditions are good.[19] Usually, 10-12 % mark-ups are common.

However, during the pandemic, all sectors have suffered. Neither manufacturing nor services sectors are enjoying mark-ups in that range; far from it. Therefore, much lower mark-ups that reflect the prevailing conditions of sector-specific economic activity must be used. This may need market search in sectors. It is the responsibility of tax administrations to carry out this task meaningfully.

## 5. Non-Tax Measures

Countries can supplement several non-tax measures to tax reform. One measure is to impose severe penalties including confiscation of assets on big industrial houses for failure to service or amortise debt. Banks should refrain from pursuing medium-sized industry borrowers who have fallen in the cracks of government's shifting subordinate legislation and its bureaucratic implementation. Accurate accounts of bank and non-bank credit, by sector (agricultural, non-agricultural, services, others) and by income deciles, should be developed and published to gauge the size and location of the problem correctly.

Central banks could make credit available through commercial banks, which could then lend to the economy. But the problem with issuing massive debt is that it cannot be done beyond a point because just lending money without solid take-up and productivity catching up will lead to high or hyper-inflation. Thus, this is not always a safe route to adopt. And India has a severe non-performing assets (NPA) problem.

One method would be for governments to issue bonds. If there is little take-up, central banks can issue bonds directly. However, government debt cannot just build up since it passes the repayment burden to posterity.

Under the COVID-19 related extreme economic decline in 2020, poorer countries may wonder if there is any "claim" that they may possess over advanced economies in terms of income transfers during and after this period. But both advanced and emerging economies are in an exceptionally vulnerable position brought on by the pandemic. It is unrealistic to expect, at this time, that a significant amount of direct transfers from richer to poorer countries would occur. All countries essentially have to find solutions on their own to come out of the pandemic's effects.

19. P. Shome (edited). 2016b. *Insights into Evolving Issues of Taxation: Existing and Continuing Challenges*, ITRAF, Wolters Kluwer, Bangalore.

However, multilateral channels are available for the redressal of economic pain through selected transfer mechanisms. These include the collaboration among IMF member countries to increase funding through IMF (macro-economic and structural) and World Bank and its affiliates (sectoral) lending through their crisis windows. Of course, there are economic conditions to loans that are challenging, yet they are essential.[20]

If the pandemic continues and leads to the collapse of the poorest economies, then intense global collaborative post-crisis solutions would be needed. A group of individual advanced countries could form a consortium that would garner resources for a single country in a deep economic crisis. Loans would be made to it on easy terms, at a low interest rate, and with a long amortisation period. Some economic conditions would eventually have to be built in so that the recipient country could emerge from its crisis condition in the medium term, but those conditions should be as soft as possible, meaningfully allowing for socio-economic recuperation. The number of such groups would reflect the number of countries in crisis. The IMF has also had a window in which it has managed funds from such donor consortia. The activity of that window can be strengthened.

## 6. Concluding Remarks

To sum up, there is no way out from the pandemic except through a carefully designed increase in taxes. That solution lies in a wealth tax and super-rich income tax while cutting back on incentives from the corporate income tax complemented by tax administration reform and, in the area of international taxation, pushing for fairness in revenue sharing among tax jurisdictions. The poorer countries can also approach multilateral institutions for loans on easy terms that are designed in particular to address crisis conditions. Ironically, it would not be entirely surprising even for advanced economies to approach the IMF for loans to help ease their economic distress.

Humankind has faced enormous challenges through the course of history and has, thus far, survived them. On a philosophical note, Tanzi[21] has recently said,

> .... the ongoing pandemic has exposed some major weaknesses that may exist in the competitive, democratic system that we as economists have admired and have promoted, over the years. It is not easy to think of satisfactory alternatives to that system. However, it is easier to argue that, in a world in which major disasters and pandemics exist, and may become more frequent, because of

---

20. Note that a multilateral tax-based measure would be the switching from residence to source-based taxation that would imply transfer from richer to poorer countries.
21. Vito Tanzi. 2021. Perfect Markets, Perfect Democracies and Pandemics. Transformation, Integration and Globalization Economic Research Working Paper Series No. 142.

> climate change and other developments, we will need some new thinking, that might suggest some desirable ways to change the modus operandi that we have admired up to now. That thinking should suggest ways to still promote efficiency, an objective that cannot be abandoned, and democracy. But the new ways should do a better job in dealing with major shocks, including pandemics, and **with equity consideration of economic policies** (emphasis added) that often receive little attention in mainstream economics. As Rita Levi Montalcini wrote four decades ago, let us hope that some good may come from the difficult moment that we are experiencing.[22]

Tanzi goes on to quote Montalcini,[23]

> It is imperfections—not perfection—that is the end result of the programme written into the formidable complex engine that is the human brain, and of the influences exerted upon us by the environment and whoever takes care of us during long years of our physical, psychological and intellectual development.... don't fear difficult moments, [because] the best comes from them.

It is hoped that the COVID-19 pandemic is drawing together invaluable lessons from which humankind can take strong and meaningful action. Internationally, a global carbon tax to arrest climate change could be employed if a push can be made using a tax instrument. Easing international trade rather than putting barriers on it, with powerful countries standing back from hegemonic positions and obstacles should also comprise a step forward. Domestically, all countries should enhance equity in their taxation systems for the pandemic has resulted in a rapidly worsening income distribution. Emerging economies, in particular, should improve tax administration to remove barriers to investment and enable recovery of economic growth by making the tax responsibility easier to comply with. A new era cannot emerge without such fundamental steps that have always been easy to perceive though difficult to achieve. The human race is at this doorstep. A forward step has to be taken globally, together and as a whole. It has to be complemented with resolute action by individual nations to buttress the global socio-economic condition.

22. Rita Levi Montalcini, an Italian biologist, won the Nobel Prize in medicine in 1996.
23. See Rita Levi Montalcini. 1988. *In Praise of Imperfections: My Life and Work,* Basic Books, New York.

## REJOINDER

### Mukesh Butani

## 1. Introduction

The COVID-19 pandemic and associated lockdowns have prompted unprecedented fiscal actions that amounted globally to $11.7 trillion, or close to 12 percent of global Gross Domestic Product (GDP), as of September 11, 2020. Half of the fiscal actions consisted of additional spendings or forgone revenue, including temporary tax cuts, and the other half liquidity support, including loans, guarantees, and capital injections by the public sector. This forceful response by governments has saved lives, supported vulnerable people and firms, and mitigated the fallout on economic activity. However, the consequences of the crisis for public finances, combined with the revenue loss from the output contraction, have been massive. In 2020, government deficits were set to surge by an average of 9 percent of GDP, and global public debt is projected to approach 100 percent of GDP, a record high.[24] As against this, India's debt is pegged at approximately 89.3% of GDP in 2020 (72.3% in 2019).[25]

Views are divided amongst economists if nations should pursue an expansionary fiscal stance and allow widening of their deficit in the wake of contracting GDP growth and mismatching revenue collection and expenditure(fiscal stimulus) due to the COVID-19 pandemic. Whereas the prescriptions would vary for each jurisdiction, depending on the peculiarities of its economy, it is clear that government revenues from tax and non-tax would continue to receive greater attention in national budgets. Ideally, increasing taxes or levying additional taxes must be considered only if the government exhausts all other options to bridge the fiscal deficit gap.

## 2. India's Selected Tax Options

### 2.1. Tax Structure and Revenue Contribution

Levy of additional tax on individuals and/or businesses and implications, would pose interesting perspectives. An analysis of taxpayer data released by the Government of India for the assessment year 2018-19, reveals as under:[26]

- Only 75 out of 55.3 million individuals offer returned income higher than Indian rupees (Rs) 1 billion; their share in the total income returned by individuals is 0.51%. Thus, increasing the tax burden on this class of taxpayers will not have any material impact for augmenting resources, as it

24. International Monetary Fund (IMF). 2020. *Fiscal Monitor: Policies for the Recovery.* Washington, October. p x.
25. https://www.business-standard.com/article/economy-policy/india-s-public-debt-to-gdp-likely-to-reach-record-high-of-90-in-2020-120102201553_1.html.
26. https://incometaxindia.gov.in/Documents/Direct%20Tax%20Data/IT-Return-Statistics-Assessment-Year-2018-19.pdf.

comprises 0.0001% of total individual taxpayers. Action to impose three rates of super-rich surcharge pushing the maximum marginal rate of tax for individual income earners above Rs. 5 crores as part of the 2020 Finance Act, has met with mixed feedback. Historical data suggests a direct correlation between rates of tax and generation of parallel economy and non-compliance.

- Taking taxpayer segmentation forward, 1,504 out of 0.84 million companies (0.17%) returned income in excess of Rs. 1 billion. However, their contribution to the total returned income of corporates is 71.6%.
- When the then finance minister of India repealed wealth tax in his budget announcement of 2015, he announced that it would instead be replaced with a surcharge of 2% on individuals earning over INR 10 million. To quote his budget speech,

  > ...further, to track the wealth held by individuals and entities, the information regarding the assets which are currently required to be furnished in wealth-tax return will be captured in the income tax returns. This will ensure that the abolition of wealth tax does not lead to escape of any income from the tax net.

  Currently, individuals earning over Rs. 5 million pay surcharge in the range of 10% to 37% depending on their slab. Thus, the reintroduction of wealth tax may also not be a viable option.
- Additionally, individual taxpayers across the board pay a surcharge of 4% in health & education cess. Thus, introducing an additional health cess ought to be an avoidable option.
- Besides, India's annual budget approach as an avenue for levy of cess collections has been questioned by States, under the constitutional framework, given that its devolution is unclear, and the utilization of such levy is seldom transparent. Cess levy for health-related situations ought to follow a consumption (GST) approach and not taxed directly. Given that the rates of the Goods and Services Tax (GST) are at the highest slab, coupled with compensation cess, any further burden could disrupt the GST design, which based on the recent Centre-State spat suggests that the GST cess would stay for meeting the Center's constitutional obligation.

Speedy resolution of cases embroiled in tax controversy could significantly ramp up tax collection. Though one needs to see the outcome of the 2020 tax settlement scheme, *Vivad-se-Vishwas,* this would be a one-time bounty not sustainable in the future. However, given the historically low ratio of cases resolved in the income tax department's favour, a long-term approach is to carry out legislative changes for compromise or settlement of cases; merit-based decisions to not file an appeal at a higher appellate forum is also recommended by the prevailing Direct Tax Code (DTC) drafting group of the Indian government.

### 2.2. Taxing Digital Economy

While unilateral levies by countries on digital companies remain a reality across the world, it may be helpful if the Indian government comes out with adequate guidance on its levy. A recent report from the Office of the United States Trade Representative under Action 301 of the US Trade Act of 1974, irrespective of its merits, has initiated action.[27] A reasonable ask from the US technology giants is to clarify nuanced aspects of the law. This would cut down on ambiguity and may potentially augment the collection of the levy. India should continue its alignment with the OECD/G20 BEPS Inclusive Framework to augment international tax revenues.

### 2.3. Mutual Agreement Procedure (MAP)

Based on the peer group feedback, administrative announcements made by the Central Board of Direct Taxes (CBDT) in its May[28] and August[29] communique shall go a long way to seek speedy resolution of MAP cases. A medium-term tax treaty policy stance to not adopt mandatory arbitration needs to be considered, particularly with select treaty partners, given the government's commitment to adopt minimum standards under Base Erosion and Profit Shifting (BEPS) Action 14 with regard to the resolution of disputes under its tax treaties.

### 2.4. Multilateral Instrument

It may also be helpful if administrative guidance is provided on the applicability of the 'principal purpose test' as laid out in the Multilateral Instrument (MLI) under Action Plan 15 of the OECD/G20 BEPS Inclusive Framework, to which India is a signatory. In the absence of such guidance, India is opening itself to significant disputes on the availability of tax treaty benefits, which could result in clogging the dispute resolution machinery. This, coupled with amendments such as the one under Section 254(2A) of the Income-tax Act (ITA), whereunder even stay of demand has been made conditional on mandatory payment of 20 percent of taxes, is viewed as curbing the independence of the Tribunal as a judicial forum, besides impacting India's attractiveness as a business-friendly jurisdiction.

## 3. Non-performing Assets (NPAs)

An area of focus could be NPAs, especially of public banks, which will come under greater focus, given the recent report of the Reserve Bank of India (RBI) in its Financial Stability Report, which has signaled a surge in the NPAs.[30] Indian banks

27. https://ustr.gov/sites/default/files/enforcement/301Investigations/Report%20on%20India's%20Digital%20Services%20Tax.pdf.
28. S.R.282 (E) dated May 6, 2020.
29. F.No. 500/09/201 6-APA-I.
30. https://www.rbi.org.in/Scripts/BS_PressReleaseDisplay.aspx?prid=50949.

have been struggling to deal with bad debts and the provisioning, given tighter regulatory norms resulting in erosion of its capital. This has pushed many state-owned banks' capital adequacy ratio below the regulatory threshold, forcing the government to step up the capitalization of these banks to ensure that they are well above the regulatory capital requirements. Consolidation of PSU banks shall ensure better utilization of such capital infusion.

While the RBI did change the policy for NPA recognition in 2020,[31] even in pre-COVID times, India has had a poor track record for NPAs. The 2019 IMF data ranks India 33 among 137 nations with a bad NPA ratio in descending order. Of the 32 countries with a worse ratio, 16 are in Africa, and the rest are spread across Asia, Europe and the Caribbean. The lowest NPA ratio was reported by Canada at 0.4 percent, followed by South Korea at 0.5 percent, and Switzerland at 0.6 percent.[32] Overhauling India's NPA regime with consolidation is a long-term reform to augment government resources and reduce public capital inflow into capitalizing banks.

## 4. Growth, Investment and Deficit

Medium to long-term prospects on growth driven with short-term expansionary stance seems to be a viable option. Empirical estimates based on a cross-country data set and a sample of 400,000 firms show that public investment can have a powerful impact on GDP growth and employment during periods of high uncertainty—which is a defining feature of the current crisis. For advanced and emerging market economies, the fiscal multiplier peaks at over 2 in two years. Increasing public investment by 1 percent of GDP in these economies would create 7 million jobs directly, and between 20 million and 33 million jobs overall when considering the indirect macroeconomic effects.[33]

Targeting the fiscal deficit in the medium to long term shall assume center-stage in the coming central government budget (Finance Bill). It is increasingly clear that a new roadmap has to be laid out given that the longstanding medium-term target of 2.5-3% of GDP as prescribed under the Fiscal Responsibility & Budget Management (FRBM) Act is unlikely to be met. A government-appointed committee's recommendations on fiscal consolidation to bring down the deficit to 3.1% of GDP in Fiscal 2022-23 could be difficult to meet given the present situation. Hence, the writing on the wall is that, to enable the fiscal deficit to widen, the government is likely to propose an amendment in FRBM in the forthcoming budget.

31. https://www.rbi.org.in/Scripts/bs_viewcontent.aspx?Id=3853.
32. https://theprint.in/economy/india-has-the-second-worst-npa-ratio-among-large-economies/195844/.
33. International Monetary Fund (IMF). 2020. *Fiscal Monitor: Policies for the Recovery.* Washington, October. p xii.

## 5. Conclusion

With the use of economic diplomacy, a clearer articulation of free trade agreements and the government's investment oriented Atmanirbhar (self-reliance) approach, India should continue to receive a fair share of foreign direct investment (FDI) and foreign institutional investment (FII) flows into emerging markets. The government could further build upon its recent initiatives such as the taxpayers' charter, the faceless assessment scheme, and India's alignment with globally recognized international standards such as those proposed under the OECD/G20 BEPS Inclusive Framework. This coupled with a categorical announcement to not introduce retrospective laws, which are not taxpayer friendly, could significantly improve taxpayer confidence and boost India's image as a business-friendly destination, which would further attract FDI and FII. Raising corporate taxes to bridge the fiscal deficit gap could only upset the apple cart.

# A SENSE OF CRISIS—GLOBAL POWER SHIFTS, TAX ARCHITECTURE, AND RETROSPECTIVITY

CHAPTER 2

# The International Tax Regime and Global Power Shifts

**Eduardo Baistrocchi**[1]

## 1. Introduction

The world has experienced three globalization booms and four busts over the last two centuries. The first boom, the Concert of Europe system, began in 1815 following Napoleon's defeat and lasted until the beginning of First World War (WWI). The second boom, the League of Nations system, ranged from the end of WWI until the Wall Street Crash in 1929. The third boom, the United Nations system, started at the end of Second World War (WWII) and persisted until about 2015 with the emergence of disruptive forces, including the trade war between China and the United States, the shifting locus of economic activity, and the fourth industrial revolution.[2] The years before, in-between, and after the three globalization booms have been ones of geopolitical conflicts, major wars, and anti-globalization backlashes.[3]

---

1. Associate Professor of Law, London School of Economics. This chapter has benefited greatly from the comments by John Avery Jones, Reuven Avi-Yonah, Alejandro Chehtman, Tsilly Dagan, Steven Dean, Martin Hearson, Emer Hunt, Martin Hevia, Pablo Ibañez Colomo, Liliana Lerchundi, Ezequiel Monti, Leandro Passarella, Ian Roxan, Mitchell Kane, David Kershaw, Pasquale Pistone, Eduardo Rivera López, Partho Shome, Andrew Summers, Suranjali Tandon, Emmanuel Voyiakis, participants in the 2019 Global Tax Symposium, Universidad Torcuato Di Tella Law School Faculty Workshop, and the London School of Economics Faculty Workshop. It has also benefited from excellent research assistance by Patricio Castells and Aiden Hepworth. Views, errors and omissions remain my own. The full version of this chapter will appear in the Virginia Tax Review in Volume 40, Number 02, Winter 2021.
2. Richard Dobbs, James Manyika, & Jonathan Woetzel, No Ordinary Disruption: The Four Global Forces Breaking All the Trends (2015), Part 1: The Four Disruptive Forces.
3. Michael J. Mazarr, Jonathan Blake, Abigail Casey, Tim McDonald, Stephanie Pezard, & Michael Spirtas, Rand Corp., Understanding the Emerging Era of International Competition: Theoretical and Historical Perspectives 6–11 (2019), www.rand.org/content/dam/rand/pubs/research_reports/RR2700/RR2726/RAND_RR2726.pdf. *See also* Jeffrey G. Williamson, *Winners and Losers over Two Centuries of Globalization*, (Nat'l Bureau of Econ. Rsch., Working Paper No. 9161, 2002), www.nber.org/papers/w9161.

One consequence of the globalization booms was the emergence in the late 19th century of a novel strategic problem among countries: how the international income tax base should be allocated to avoid international double taxation given the lack of a higher authority.[4] Since the end of WWI, countries have been involved in a strategic interaction in pursuit of a solution. The international tax regime (ITR) has emerged as a global legal system that aims to work out the double taxation problem.[5] The ITR is

4. *See* Werner Haslehner, *Tax Treaty Disputes in Germany*, *in* A Global Analysis of Tax Treaty Disputes 290, 299–300 (Eduardo Baistrocchi ed., 2017). Haslehner's analysis includes the beginning of double taxation relief in the German-speaking area of pre-WWI Europe (1869–1912). The oldest of such tax treaties is between Prussia and Saxony in 1869. The words "countries" and "jurisdictions" are used as synonyms in this paper.

5. The literature on the ITR is broad and deep. Excellent surveys on the ITR include the following: (1) Reuven S. Avi-Yonah, *The Structure of International Taxation: A Proposal for Simplification*, 74 Tex. L, Rev. 1301 (1996); (2) Michael J. Graetz & Michael M. O'Hear, *The "Original Intent" of U.S. International Taxation*, 46 Duke L, J, 1021 (1997); (3) Nancy H. Kaufman, *Fairness and the Taxation of International Income*, 29 L. & Pol'y Int'l Bus. 145 (1998); (4) John F. Avery Jones, *Are Tax Treaties Necessary?* , 5 Tax L. Rev. 1 (1999). (5) Frans Vanistendael, *Impact of European Tax Law on Tax Treaties with Third Countries*, 8 E.C. Tax Rev. 163 (1999); (6) H. David Rosenbloom, *International Tax Arbitrage and the "International Tax System,"* 53 Tax L. Rev. 137 (2000); (7) Victor Thuronyi, *International Tax Cooperation and a Multilateral Treaty*, 26 Brook. J. Int'l L. 1641 (2001); (8) Yariv Brauner, *An International Tax Regime in Crystallization*, 56 Tax L. Rev. 259 (2003); (9) Mitchell A. Kane, *Strategy and Cooperation in National Responses to International Tax Arbitrage*, 53 Emory L.J. 89 (2004); (10) Reuven S. Avi-Yonah, *International Tax as International Law*, 57 Tax L. Rev. 483 (2004); (11) Yoshihiro Masui, *International Fiscal Association 2004 Vienna Congress, General Report: Group Taxation*, 89b Cahier de Droit Fisc. Int'l 21 (2004); (12) Allison Christians, *Sovereignty, Taxation and Social Contract*, 18 Minn. J. Int'l L. 99 (2009); (13) Ruth Mason, *Tax Expenditures and Global Labor Mobility*, 84 N.Y.U. L. Rev. 1540 (2009); (14) J. Clifton Fleming, Jr., Robert J. Peroni, & Stephen E. Shay, *Worse Than Exemption*, 59 Emory L.J. 79 (2009); (15) Wolfgang Schön, *International Tax Coordination for a Second-Best World (Part I)*, World Tax J. 67 (Sept. 2009); (16) R. Vann, *Taxing International Business Income: Hard–Boiled Wonderland and the End of the World*, 3 World Tax J. (2010); (17) Neil Brooks & Thaddeus Hwong, *Tax Levels, Structures, and Reforms: Convergence or Persistence*, 11 Theoretical Inquiries L. 791 (2010); (18) Adolfo Martín Jiménez, *Beneficial Ownership: Current Trends,* World Tax J. 35 (Feb. 2010); (19) Edward D. Kleinbard, *Stateless Income*, 11 Fla. Tax Rev. 699 (2011); (20) Daniel Shaviro, *The Rising Tax-Electivity of U.S. Corporate Residence*, 64 Tax L. Rev. 377 (2011); (21) Jinyan Li, *The Great Fiscal Wall of China: Tax Treaties and Their Role in Defining and Defending China's Tax Base*, 66 Bull. for Int'l Tax'n, 452 (2012); (22) Hugh J. Ault, *Some Reflections on the OECD and the Sources of International Tax Principles*, 70 Tax Notes Int'l 1195 (2013); (23) Ian Roxan, *Limits to Globalisation: Some Implications for Taxation, Tax Policy, and the Developing World* (L., Soc'y & Econ., Working Paper No. 3, 2012), https://ssrn.com/abstract=1995633; (24) Edoardo Traversa, *Interest Deductibility and the BEPS Action Plan: Nihil Novi Sub Sole?,* 2013 British Tax Rev. 607 (2013); (25) Yariv Brauner & Pasquale Pistone, *BRICS and the Future of International Tax Coordination*, *in* BRICS and the Emergence of Tax Coordination (Yariv Brauner & Pasquale Pistone eds., 2015); (26) Michael P. Devereux & John Vella, *Are We Heading Towards a Corporate Tax System Fit for the 21*[st] *Century?*, 35 Fisc. Stud. 449 (2014); (27) Michael Lang, *BEPS Action 6: Introducing an Antiabuse Rule in Tax Treaties*, 74 Tax Notes Int'l 655 (2014); (28) Tsilly Dagan, International

**[Footnote Nos. 5 & 6 contd.]**

based on a legal technology first suggested in the 1923 Economists' Report to the League of Nations (LN).[6]

The ITR is now encapsulated in the OECD Model Tax Convention on Income and on Capital (OECD Model).[7] The OECD Model is a soft law that served as the template for over 3,000 bilateral tax treaties linking most countries from all continents.[8] Since the 2015 Base Erosion and Profit Shifting Reports to the OECD and G20 (BEPS Reports), the ITR aims to mitigate not only international double taxation but also international non-taxation problems after public outrage over aggressive corporate tax planning schemes on all continents.[9]

The ITR is a decentralized network market that has set jurisdictions in competition for capital, residents, and tax revenue.[10] The ITR is enforced via a decentralized network of local courts that may have the incentive to interpret and apply the ITR strategically to favor the positions of their own jurisdictions *vis a vis* competing jurisdictions.[11]

---

**[Footnote Nos. 5 & 6 contd.]**

Tax Policy: Between Competition and Cooperation (2017); (29) Miranda Stewart, *Redistribution Between Rich and Poor Countries*, 72 Bull. for Int'l Tax'n 297 (2018); (30) Philip Baker, *The League of Nations' Draft Convention for the Allocation of Business Income Between States – A New Starting Point for the Attribution of Profits to Permanent Establishments*, 2018 British Tax Rev. 514 (2018); (31) Sol Picciotto, *International Tax, Regulatory Arbitrage and the Growth of Transnational Corporations*, 25 Transnat'l Corps. 27 (2018); (32) Itai Grinberg, *International Taxation in an Era of Digital Disruption: Analyzing the Current Debate* (Scholarship at Geo. L. Work in Progress 2018), https://ssrn.com/abstract=3275737; (33) Sunita Jogarajan, Double Taxation and the League of Nations (2018); (34) Peter Harris, International Commercial Tax (2d ed. 2020).

6. *See Report on Double Taxation*, League of Nations Doc. E.F.S.73. F.19 (1923), http://adc.library.usyd.edu.au/view?docId=split/law/xml-main-texts/brulegi-source-bibl-1.xml;chunk.id=item-1;toc.depth=1;toc.id=item-1;database=;collection=;brand=default. The members of the committee were Prof. Bruins (Commercial University, Rotterdam), Prof. Luigi Einaudi (Turin University), Prof. Seligman (Columbia University, New York), Sir Josiah Stamp (London University). *See also* Edwin R. A. Seligman, Double Taxation and International Fiscal Cooperation (1928).
7. *See* Org. for Econ. Co-operation & Dev. [OECD], *Model Tax Convention on Income and on Capital: Full Version* (Nov. 21, 2017), https://doi.org/10.1787/g2g972ee-en.
8. *UN Primer on Double Tax Treaties*, United Nations: Dep't Econ. & Soc. Affs., https://www.un.org/esa/ffd/capacity-development-tax/primer-dtt.html (last accessed on October 27, 2020).
9. Jannick Damgaard, Thomas Elkjaer, & Niels Johannesen, *The Rise of Phantom Investments. Empty Corporate Shells in Tax Havens Undermine Tax Collection in Advanced, Emerging Market and Developing Economies*, Fin. & Dev., September 2019, at 11. *See also* A Global Analysis of Tax Treaty Disputes, *supra* note 4.
10. Eduardo Baistrocchi, *The International Tax Regime and the BRIC World: Elements for a Theory*, 2013 Oxford J. Legal Stud. 1 (May 10, 2013). *See also* Dagan, *supra* note 5, at 12–14.
11. Eduardo Baistrocchi, *The Use and Interpretation of Tax Treaties in the Emerging World: Theory and Implications*, 2008 British Tax Rev. 352, 354 (2008).

The global economy's center of gravity is moving along an east–southward trajectory. The average location of economic activity across geographies worldwide has shifted from a point in the mid–Atlantic (between the U.S. and Europe) in 1980, to a location east of Helsinki and Bucharest in 2008.[12] Developing and emerging countries like China are, in fact, returning to the role they had for most of history. Before technological innovation gave Britain its industrial lead in the 19th century, today's developing and emerging economies dominated the global output. It has been estimated that in the eighteen centuries prior to 1820, they had produced, on average, around 80% of the global total. The consolidation of Europe's Industrial Revolution, however, left behind today's developing and emerging countries. By the early 20th century, their share in global output had fallen to about 40%.[13] Yet as of the early 21st century, developing and emerging countries have been making a comeback in this area. For example, China's economy was larger than the U.S.'s in 2014.[14] Developing and emerging countries contributed again to over 50% of the global output, in purchasing power parity terms, as was the usual case before the Industrial Revolution.[15] As Danny Quah argues, if soft power mirrors but lags behind economic power, then the source for global and political influence will be similarly shifting gradually east.[16]

This chapter offers the first historical analysis of the correlation between global power shifts and innovation at the technological and financial regulatory levels on the evolution of the ITR since its emergence in the 1920s. This analysis is relevant because it offers normative lessons that could contribute to solving the new challenges that the ITR is facing in the early 21st century: the increasing difficulties countries are facing in reaching consensus on how to deal with emerging issues. Taxation of global digital commerce is a case in point.

This chapter is organized into five sections. After this introduction, Section 2 presents a theoretical framework grounded on the dynamics of hegemonic orders and the rule–standard regulatory spectrum ("the spectrum"). The spectrum offers a framework to illuminate the evolving legal architecture of the ITR and its correlation with shifting hegemonic orders. Section 3 provides a concise structural description of the history of the ITR in the light of the dynamics of hegemonic orders and the spectrum. It illustrates the ITR evolution in the G20 along a spiral trajectory

12. Danny Quah, *The Global Economy's Shifting Centre of Gravity*, 2 Glob. Pol'y 3, 3 (2011).

13. *Emerging Economies: Climbing Back*, Economist (January 19, 2006), https://www.economist.com/finance-and-economics/2006/01/19/climbing-back.

14. In 2014, the IMF estimates the size of the U.S. economy at USD17.4 trillion, and the size of China's economy at USD17.6 trillion. *See* Keith Fray, *China's Leap Forward: Overtaking the US as World's Biggest Economy*, Fin. Times (October 8, 2014), https://www.ft.com/content/166230a2-a18c-38f1-bcac-cbbdd495503a

15. *See* Angus Maddison, The World Economy, Volume 1: A Millennial Perspective 126–27 (2007).

16. Quah, *supra* note 12, at 3.

encapsulated in Figure 1, revealing an ITR spiral evolution crystallizing in three sequential eras of regulations: from a standard-based legal system to a rule–based regime and then back to a standard-based legal system over 111 years running from 1908 to 2019. The three eras, in turn, are divided into 63 stages representing the rise, decline, and fall of the relevant era. Section 4 assesses the spiral evolution theory against empirical evidence and its normative implications. Section 5 concludes.

## 2. The Theoretical Framework

### 2.1. The Dynamics of Hegemonic Orders and the Rule–Standard Spectrum

A rule-based international tax system is a global public good, in the same way the rule-based international monetary and trade systems are public goods. International relations scholars have long argued that such systems are only stable under conditions of hegemony, in which a predominant power ensures the supply of these public goods.[17] The gold standard of 1880–1914 marked the peak of an open trading system under British hegemony and the Bretton Woods system of 1945-1971 marked the peak of a fixed exchange rate system under U.S. hegemony. The World Trade Organization (1948-2017) is another example of a rule–based global public good with one peculiarity: it was originally proposed and then blocked by the same country, the U.S., with its "America First" policy on the assumption that the WTO no longer serves U.S. interests.[18]

The hegemon ensures the provision of global public goods that are needed to maintain, for example, an open world trading system, including a stable currency system and a stable international tax regime. A hegemonic regime also needs a purpose, which after WWII has been "embedded liberalism" subsequently replaced by neoliberalism.[19] The hegemon's role in the international tax sphere is to provide some underlying purpose and coherence. The hegemon, which is normally the

17. *See, e.g.*, Robert O. Keohane, After Hegemony: Cooperation and Discord in the World Political Economy (1984); David A. Lake, *Leadership, Hegemony, and the International Economy: Naked Emperor or Tattered Monarch with Potential?*, 37 Int'l Stud. Q. 459 (1993); Robert W. Cox, *Gramsci, Hegemony and International Relations: An Essay in Method*, *in* Gramsci, Historical Materialism and International Relations (Stephen Gill ed. 1993); 4 Charles P. Kindleberger, The World in Depression, 1929–1939 (1986); Robert W. Cox, *Social Forces, States and World Orders: Beyond International Relations Theory*, 10 Millennium 126 (1981); Stephen D. Krasner, *State Power and the Structure of International Trade*, 28 World Pol. 317 (1976). Please note that global hegemon, global power and ruling power are synonyms in this paper.
18. Martin Wolf, *Martin Wolf on Bretton Woods at 75: Global Co-Operation under Threat*, Fin. Times (July 10, 2019), https://www.ft.com/content/e82a1f48-a185-11e9-a282-2df48f366f7d.
19. John G. Ruggie, *International Regimes, Transactions, and Change: Embedded Liberalism in the Postwar Economic Order*, 36 Int'l Org., 379, 393, 414–15 (1982).

major capital exporter, is really pursuing the interests of the hegemon's capital, and it uses the ideas and a sense of purpose to generate consent for its hegemony. The hegemon has the incentive to pursue the interests of its multinationals, and it uses the income allocation norm as a tool through which it persuades other countries to accept a set of rules that makes it harder for them to tax the hegemon's capital.

In this section, I introduce a sequential model to explain the evolution of the ITR. It maintains that the rule–standard spectrum offers a framework to illuminate the evolving legal architecture of the ITR and its correlation with hegemonic orders. International hegemony is defined here as "the mobilization of leadership" by a predominant power in order to create an international order. An international order is manifest in the settled regulations and arrangements between jurisdictions that define and guide their interactions.[20]

Definitions of the rule and standard concepts are in order. A jurisdiction can give content to norms *ex-ante* (via rules) or *ex-post* (via standards). Examples of rules and standards can be found in many settings. For instance, a norm that demands "no driving in excess of 55 miles per hour" is a rule, because violations are proscribed *ex-ante* and no judgment is required by the subject of the regulation. The trigger in a rule is mostly empirical, rather than evaluative.[21] Conversely, a norm to "drive carefully" is a standard, because it requires judgment from the subject and precise prohibitions are determined *ex-post* through case law or a functional equivalent.[22]

Rules and standards differ in at least one important dimension: the distribution of power within a legal system. Whereas rules are usually a creation of the legislative branch of government or a functional equivalent, standards are a decentralized creation of the law through, paradigmatically, the judiciary or a functional equivalent.[23] The standard "drive carefully" is a case in point; it allocates a relatively wide power to courts to provide an *ex-post* meaning to this standard. Conversely, the rule "no driving in excess of 55 miles per hour" keeps the power centralized under the rule setter's control. So, the rule conveys a relatively narrow power to the judiciary or a functional equivalent because the trigger in a rule is only empirical.

---

20. G. John Ikenberry & Daniel H. Nexon, *Hegemonic Studies 3.0: The Dynamics of Hegemonic Orders*, 28 Sec. Stud. 395, 411–12 (2019).
21. Pierre J. Schlag, *Rules and Standards*, 33 UCLA L. Rev. 379, 382–83 (1985).
22. The theoretical framework of this article is grounded on the law and economics literature on the rules and standards concepts. *See* Louis Kaplow, *Rules Versus Standards: An Economic Analysis*, 42 Duke L.J. 557 (1992). *See also* Isaac Ehrlich & Richard Posner, *An Economic Analysis of Legal Rulemaking*, 3 J. Legal Stud. 257 (1974). On the rule and standard framework in international taxation from a legitimacy perspective, *see* Steven A. Dean, *Neither Rules nor Standards*, 87 Notre Dame L. Rev. 537 (2013).
23. *See* Kaplow, *supra* note 22, at 608–11.

In sum, under conditions of hegemony, a rule–based ITR normally emerges as a global public good. When this hegemony breaks down due to shocks, the ITR legal architecture drifts towards the standard–based end of the continuum because the hegemon is no longer able to enforce participation in a rule–based system.

It is now time to explore the rules and standards spectrum from a static and dynamic perspective.

## 2.2. Rules and Standards as a Spectrum: Its Static Dimension

The rules and standards concepts are opposing ends of a spectrum. Indeed, a pure rule is on one end and a pure standard is at the other end. A number of hybrid regulations are in–between the opposing ends of the continuum.

There is a myriad of patterns of regulations in the rule–standard spectrum. The OECD Model is used here as a case study. An instance of a pure rule is the term "national," in relation to a contracting State. National means "[…] any individual possessing the nationality or citizenship of that Contracting State."[24] So the OECD Model provides an *ex-ante* meaning to the term "national," where just having the, say, French passport implies that the individual should be deemed as a French national within the terminology of the OECD Model (Pattern #1: A Pure Rule).

An example of a pure standard is the Principal Purpose Test (PPT). The PPT is an anti-avoidance regulation to deter tax treaty shopping. The PPT regulation provides the following:

> [...] a benefit under this Convention shall not be granted in respect of an item of income […] if it is reasonable to conclude, having regard to all relevant facts and circumstances, that obtaining that benefit was one of the *principal purposes of any arrangement* […] that resulted directly or indirectly in that benefit, unless it is established that granting that benefit in these circumstances would be in accordance with the object and purpose of the relevant provisions of this Convention (emphasis added).[25]

The PPT is a pure standard because it lacks an *ex-ante* meaning. This includes the lack of the *ex-ante* meaning of the words *principal purpose of any arrangement*. The meaning of these words can only be provided *ex-post* through case law or a functional equivalent (Pattern #6: A Pure Standard).

Hybrid regulations in–between the pure rule and pure standard, the opposing ends of the spectrum, include the following four patterns. First, the advance pricing agreement (APA) is an example of an *ex-ante* procedural regulation. It provides a

24. OECD, *supra* note 7, at M-10.
25. *Id.* at M-80–81 (emphasis added).

procedural framework in which the contracting States may provide an *ex-ante meaning* to the material regulations of the jurisdictions involved before the taxpayer makes the relevant cross–border investment. The APA norm is as follows: "The competent authorities of the Contracting States shall endeavour to resolve [*ex-ante*] by mutual agreement any difficulties or doubts arising as to the interpretation or application of the Convention. They may also consult together for the elimination of double taxation in cases not provided for in the Convention."[26] The APA is not a pure rule because contracting states are not obliged to agree on the *ex-ante* meaning of the material set of regulations. So, APA is an example of a regulation that is closer to the pure rule end than the pure standard end of the spectrum because APA may provide an *ex-ante* meaning of the pertinent set of norms (Pattern #2: *Ex-ante* Procedural Regulation).

Second, a rule can be embedded in one or more standards. For example, a standard (e.g., "a fixed place of business through which the business of an enterprise is wholly carried on is a permanent establishment") is subject to a rule (e.g., a place of extraction of natural resources).[27] So the OECD Model deems that a place of extraction of natural resources is a fixed place of business for permanent establishment purposes (Pattern #3: A Rule Embedded in One or More Standards).

Third, a standard can be embedded in one or more rules. For example, the rule (undefined terms must be defined by contracting states' domestic laws) is subject to a standard ("unless the context otherwise requires").[28] So, for example, the undefined term "law" in Article 3.2 of the OECD–based tax treaty signed between Chile and the United Kingdom shall be defined according to Chilean domestic law, unless the context requires otherwise (Pattern #4: Standards Embedded in One or More Rules).

Fourth, tax arbitration is an example of an *ex-post* procedural regulation. The relevant provision states the following:

> Where, […] a) a person has presented a case to the competent authority of a Contracting State on the basis that the actions of one or both of the Contracting States have resulted for that person in taxation not in accordance with the provisions of this Convention, and b) the competent authorities are unable to reach an agreement to resolve that case […], any unresolved issues arising from the case shall be submitted to arbitration if the person so requests in writing.[29]

26. *Id.* at M-68.
27. *Id.* at M-19.
28. *Id.* at M-11.
29. *Id.* at M-68–69.

Tax arbitration is an example of a regulation that is closer to the standard end rather than the rule end of the spectrum. This is so because tax arbitration is an *ex-post* procedural regulation: it provides an *ex-post* meaning to the material regulation that is *after* rather than *before* the cross–border investment has been made (Pattern 5: *Ex-Post* Procedural Regulation).

Table 1 crystallizes examples of the rule–standard spectrum along the six different patterns of regulations outlined above.

**Table 1. The Rule–Standard Spectrum**

| | Patterns | Examples |
|---|---|---|
| #1 | Pure Rule | The term "national" |
| #2 | *Ex-ante* Procedural Regulation | APAs |
| #3 | A Rule Embedded in One or More Standards | A Place of Extraction of Natural Resources |
| #4 | A Standard Embedded in One or More Rules | Tax Treaty Interpretation |
| #5 | *Ex-post* Procedural Regulation | Tax Arbitration |
| #6 | Pure Standard | Principal Purpose Test |

Patterns #1, #2 and #3 crystallize a rule–based legal system because they provide an *ex-ante* meaning of the relevant regulatory framework with a decreasing degree of clarity. Pattern 1 (a pure rule) provides the clearest possible *ex-ante* meaning. Conversely, patterns #4, #5 and #6 encapsulate a standard–based legal system because they provide an *ex-post* meaning to the regulatory framework with a decreasing degree of clarity. Pattern #6 (a pure standard) lacks an *ex-ante* meaning; only case law or its functional equivalent can provide an *ex-post* meaning.

In sum, patterns #1 and #6 are on the opposing ends of the spectrum. There are at least four hybrid patterns of regulations in–between the opposing ends: patterns #2 to #5. The hybrid patterns are closer to one or the other end of the spectrum; for example, Pattern #5 (*ex-post* procedural regulation like tax arbitration) is closer to Pattern #6 (pure standard), instead of Pattern #1 (pure rule), because tax arbitration can only provide an *ex-post* meaning to the relevant set of norms. It is now time to explore the rule–standard spectrum from a dynamic rather than static perspective.

## 2.3. The Rule–Standard Spectrum: Its Dynamic Dimension

Rules and standards may change over time: a rule can evolve into a standard (and vice versa). This evolution may be triggered, for example, by exogenous forces such as shifts in foreign direct investment (FDI) bilateral flows, case law with public good features and/or technological innovation.

### *2.3.1. A rule may evolve into a standard*

Let us begin with an example of a rule becoming a standard due to shifts in bilateral FDI flows. The U.K. persuaded the Irish Free State (IFS) to accept the exclusive residence jurisdiction rule for solving the double taxation problem in their tax treaty during the interwar period. The Agreement between the British Government and the Government of the Irish Free State in respect of Double Income Tax was signed on April 14, 1926 (the IFS-UK DTC).[30] It provided the following no–source taxation rule:

> [...] Any person who proves to the satisfaction of the Revenue Commissioners that for any year he is resident in Great Britain [...] and is not resident in the Irish Free State shall be entitled to exemption from Irish Free State income tax for that year in respect of all property situate and all profits or gains arising in the Irish Free State, and to exemption from Irish Free State super-tax for that year [...].[31]

So, U.K. resident companies were exempt from Irish income taxes (and vice versa). The corporate residence test, in turn, provided the following:

> For the purposes of this Agreement a company, whether incorporated by or under the laws of Great Britain [...] or of the Irish Free State or otherwise, shall be deemed to be resident in that country only in which its business is managed and controlled [the 1926 residence test].[32]

The IFS-UK DTC was an asymmetric tax treaty because it is assumed here that virtually all inward FDI into the Irish Free State originated in the U.K. by 1926.[33] Thus, the 1926 residence test is closer to the pure rule end, instead of the pure standard end, for contextual reasons: the asymmetric FDI flows between the IFS and the U.K. The 1926 residence test was a rule–based regulation because it provided an *ex-ante* meaning: all companies doing business in the IFS were U.K. residents in the 1926-27 fiscal year, so they were exempt from the Irish tax.[34]

---

30. Finance Act 1926 (Act No. 35/1926) (Ir.), http://www.irishstatutebook.ie/eli/1926/act/35/enacted/en/print.
31. *Id.*, 1st sched., pt. I, § 1(b).
32. *Id.*, § 4.
33. Ireland was part of the U.K. until 1922, and the only industry in the IFS was agriculture (as opposed to Northern Ireland, which was relatively industrialized). In 1924, imports into the IFS were vastly from the U.K., and exports from the IFS almost solely went to the U.K. The name IFS disappeared in 1937 with the adoption of a new constitution, and the state henceforth became known as the Republic of Ireland. *See* Frank Barry & John Bradley, *FDI and Trade: The Irish Host-Country Experience*, 107 Econ. J., 1798 (1997).
34. There was no TP regulation in the 1926 IFS/UK DTC. So, the rule/standard spectrum analysis is applied here to the closest available regulation dealing with the double taxation problem: the residence test.

Interestingly, the residence test in force in the DTC between the Republic of Ireland and the U.K. in 2017 is similar to the 1926 residence test. The 2017 residence test provides the following:

> Where [...] a person other than an individual is a resident of both Contracting States, then it shall be deemed to be a resident of the Contracting State in which its place of effective management is situated [the 2017 residence test].[35]

Unlike the 1926 scenario, FDI flows between the Republic of Ireland and the U.K. were broadly symmetrical by 2017. For example, the outward FDI flows from the U.K. to Ireland were USD 2,068.7 M; and the inward FDI flows from Ireland to the U.K. were USD 3,373.9 M.[36] Moreover, FDI from the U.K. to Ireland was just 7.7% of the total FDI to Ireland by 2017.[37]

So, the residence test that by 1926 was a rule–based regulation because virtually all inward FDI to Ireland came from the U.K., by 2017 had become standard–based because of a substantial shift in FDI flows between Ireland and the U.K. Hence, the application of the 2017 residence test now requires what is usual in any standard–based regulation: a case–by–case analysis of the place of effective management of the relevant corporation. Unlike what happened in the 1926-1927 fiscal year, the place of corporate residence for Ireland/U.K. DTC purposes could have been either the Republic of Ireland or the U.K. in the fiscal year 2017-2018.

In sum, the test of residence in the Ireland-U.K. tax treaty network is an example of a regulation evolving from the rule end towards the standard end of the spectrum

---

35. Convention Between the Government of the United Kingdom of Great Britain and Northern Ireland and the Government of the Republic of Ireland for the Avoidance of Double Taxation and the Prevention of Fiscal Evasion with Respect to Taxes on Income and Capital, U.K.-Ir., November 4, 1998, Art. 4,
https://assets.publishing.service.gov.uk/government/uploads/system/uploads/attachment_data/file/822648/Synthesised_text_of_the_Multilateral_Instrument_and_the_1976_Ireland-UK__Double_Taxation_Convention____in_force.pdf.
36. *See* Org. for Econ. Co-operation & Dev. [OECD], *Benchmark Definition, 4th Edition (BMD4): Foreign Direct Investment: Financial Flows by Partner Country (Edition 2017)*, https://doi.org/10.1787/10707ea6-en (last accessed on October 17, 2020).
37. Data on main investing countries in Ireland in 2017 is as follows:

| Main Investing Countries in Ireland | 2017 (in %) |
|---|---|
| United States | 23.8 |
| Offshore Centers | 19.0 |
| The Netherlands | 13.3 |
| Luxembourg | 12.2 |
| Switzerland | 9.9 |
| United Kingdom | 7.7 |

*See Foreign Direct Investment*, An Phríomh-Oifig Staidrimh: Cent. Stat. Off. (November 1, 2018), https://www.cso.ie/en/releasesandpublications/er/fdi/foreigndirectinvestmentannual2017/.

over the course of almost a century (1926-2017). This evolution is due to contextual forces: a shift in the FDI flows between Ireland and the U.K.

### *2.3.2. A standard may evolve into a rule*

It is time to offer an example of a regulation evolving from the standard end towards the rule end. The doctrine of good faith performance establishes a standard for contract interpretation in the U.S. The good faith concept is now encapsulated in the Uniform Commercial Code. It is defined as "[...] honesty in fact and the observance of reasonable commercial standards of fair dealing."[38] Over the last century, case law with public good features has enriched the concept of good faith so that it is now possible to infer a number of rules.[39] The judicial test that distinguishes good faith performance from bad faith performance, and the examples identified by case law, is an example. The good faith standard has eventually turned into a constellation of rule–based regulations in certain areas of U.S. contract law because of a myriad of judicial decisions applying the good faith concept to a wide range of factual scenarios. Case law with public good features has been mutating the good faith concept's original character from the standard–based regulation end towards the rule–based end in certain areas.

In sum, rules and standards may change over time due to, for example, exogenous forces such as substantial shifts in bilateral FDI flows[40] or case law with public good features. In the next Section I will provide an account of the evolution of the ITR and show that it can be explained by the theoretical framework just outlined.

## 3. The Spiral Evolution of International Taxation: The Three Eras[41]

This section offers a diagrammatic exposition of a spiral evolution of international taxation over 111 years (Figure 1). The first ITR standard–based era (the first era) lasted 25 years (1908-33). It began with the emergence of the first profit allocation

38. Steven J. Burton, *Breach of Contract and The Common Law Duty to Perform in Good Faith*, 94 Harv. L. Rev. 369, 376 n.35 (1980) (quoting U.C.C. § 1-201(19) (Am. L. Inst. & Unif. Comm'n 1977)).

39. Case law is a public good if it allows a representative person to predict the probable outcome of a court's future decision. The predictive function of case law is normally desirable in the rule of law because it minimizes transaction costs. *See* James M. Buchanan, The Limits of Liberty: Between Anarchy and Leviathan 107–09 (1975) (arguing that a legal precedent is a form of social capital having public good characteristics). *See also* William M. Landes & Richard A. Posner, *Legal Precedent: A Theoretical and Empirical Analysis*, 19 J. L. & Econ. 249, 250 (1976) (arguing that "the body of legal precedents [is] a capital stock that yields a flow of information services.").

40. *See supra* Section 2.3.1.

41. The details of the three eras appear in Baistrocchi, Eduardo A., The International Tax Regime and Global Power Shifts. LSE Legal Studies Working Paper No. 20/2020, Available at SSRN: https://ssrn.com/abstract=3744992 or http://dx.doi.org/10.2139/ssrn.3744992. Note that all references to Section 3 and its subsections that appear in the footnotes in this chapter refer to the earlier paper of Baistrocchi (2020) provided in the link.

dispute in the world involving Germany and the U.K. (that was solved in the light of two pure standards: the separate entity approach and the sham doctrine)The First era ended with the publication of the Carroll Report to the LN suggesting what was then a rule–based legal system for solving the profit allocation problem: the arm's length price (ALP). The first era consists of the 11 stages shown in Figure 1 below.

The second rule–based era (the second era) lasted 82 years. It began in 1933 with the publication of the LN Carroll Report, which shows the nascent influence of the U.S. in global tax policy making. It ended in 2015 with the publication of the OECD/G20 BEPS Reports that were drawn up in the context of an emerging power shift from the West to Asian economies, particularly China and India.

The second era began in a turbulent global context, including WWII. It then experienced consistent geopolitical stability and economic growth under the third globalization boom (the UN system) until 2015. The second era consisted of 43 stages as shown in Figure 1 below.

The third, standard–based, era is running from 2015 to the present (the third era). It kicked off with the publication of the 2015 OECD/G20 BEPS Reports offering a new version of the ALP as a standard–based legal system.

The context of the third era of the ITR is a period in–between the demise of the third globalization grounded on the UN system (1945-2015) and the emergence of a still elusive fourth globalization. Therefore, the current period has some features of the times in between two globalizations: geopolitical disruptions, anti-globalization backlashes and nationalism.

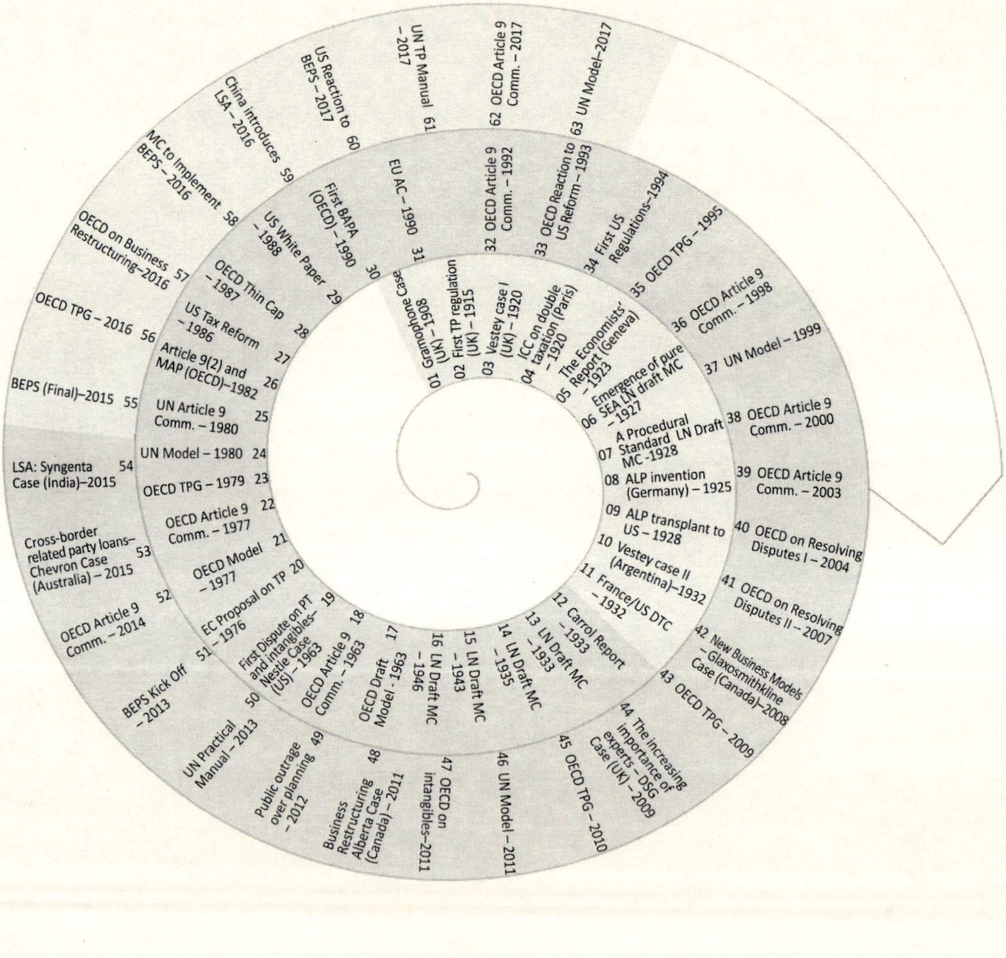


*Figure 1.* The Allocation Norm: A Spiral Evolution 1908-Present

## 4. The Spiral Evolution: Analysis and Implications

This Section offers an analysis of the spiral evolution and its implications in the light of the theoretical framework outlined in Section 2 above. The analysis focuses on two issues: 1) An assessment of the theory against empirical evidence; and 2) The implications of the spiral evolution, using global digital taxation as an example.

### 4.1. Assessing the Theory against Empirical Evidence

The history of international taxation outlined in Section 3 suggests that the hegemon normally prefers a rule–based system over a standard–based one given the ITR's decentralized competitive structure.[42] Indeed, the former limits the decentralization of power within the ITR more than the latter does to a growing, decentralized global network of countries.[43]

ITR evolution from 1933 to 1963 is an example of this rule–based ITR preference under the then U.S. hegemony. When external shocks (such as technological and/or regulatory innovation) emerges, making the rule–based ITR unworkable, there seems to be no better option for the hegemon than to accept an ITR shift towards the standard–based end of the spectrum, ideally under the hegemon's control. ITR evolution from 1963 to 2015 is an example of the gradual movement towards the standard–based end of the spectrum under U.S. control via the transplant of U.S. domestic law and case law to the OECD Guidelines and their regular updates.[44] The U.S. eventually lost control of ITR evolution since 2015 onwards, which is correlated with the gradual rise of China and the publication of the BEPS Reports (a constellation of standard–based regulations). The value creation principle is an example of this constellation of norms without an ex-*ante* meaning. This pattern of evolution of the ITR legal architecture seems consistent with the hegemon literature.[45]

The hegemon's role in the international tax sphere has been to provide some purpose and coherence, which the U.S. has done from 1933 until 2015 through, for example, its support for the ALP. The hegemon, which is normally the major capital exporter, is really pursuing the interests of the hegemon's capital, and it uses the ideas and the sense of purpose to generate consent for its hegemony. For example, the U.S. has been pursuing the interests of U.S. multinationals in the period from 1933 to 2015, and the ALP has been a tool through which it persuaded other countries to accept a set of regulations that made it harder for them to tax U.S. capital. For

42. *See supra* Section 2.2 (offering definitions and examples of rule-based and standard-based legal systems).

43. *See supra* Section 2.1 (describing the impact of the rule and standard spectrum on the distribution of power within a legal system).

44. *See supra* Section 3.2.

45. *See supra* note 17 (providing examples of the hegemony literature).

instance, the crucial 1933 Carroll Report to the League of Nations was funded by the Rockefeller Foundation.[46] The foundation had begun under Standard Oil owner John D. Rockefeller on 1913. Standard Oil was then the largest U.S. MNE. The funding arrangement of the Carroll Report suggests that the interests of the U.S. and U.S. MNEs were aligned when a solution to the problem of the allocation norm was being discussed and agreed at the League of Nations in the early 1930s.[47]

The Carroll Report was criticized for understating the extent to which formula apportionment methods were actually in use in order to strengthen the case for the solution that was actually preferred by the U.S.: the arm's length principle.[48] Presumably the U.S. was against the formula apportionment method in 1933 because it would have given a broader taxing jurisdiction than the ALP to the material countries of source.

A new database shows that the U.S. strategy of supporting the ALP at the League of Nations in the 1930s ultimately proved successful for the interest of US MNEs. Indeed, the proportion of tax treaty cases in the G20 won by the US MNEs has steadily increased since the 1940s and has been consistently greater than 50 percent since the 1980s.[49]

### *4.1.1. Why the evolution has been spiral?*

There are structural similarities between the first and third eras of the allocation norm regarding the profits of associated enterprises; namely, they both are legal systems that are closer to the standard end, instead of the rule end, of the regulatory spectrum as defined in Section 2.1 above. The central difference is that the standard–based legal system encapsulated in the third era exhibits increasing levels of complexity *vis a vis* the first era consistent with the growing complexity of international trade itself.

Table 2 below offers an example of the growing complexity of standard–based regulations in the ITR. Indeed, the 2016 version of the OECD Multilateral Instrument (MLI) includes a range of ex-post procedural regulations that are

---

46. A grant of $ 90,000 was secured by T.S. Adams to assist the Fiscal Committee in its work on double taxation. The plan was for the League of Nations Secretariat to hire some specialist staff to research existing laws, country practices, and accounting methods. The scope of the work was to include an analysis of the methods of separate accounting and fractional apportionment. *See* the 1930 Report to the Council (n. 91), at 7–8. *See* also R. S. Collier and J. L. Andrus, *Transfer Pricing and the Arm's Length Principle after BEPS*, (Oxford University Press, 2017), sec. 1.64.
47. *See supra* Section 3.2.1.
48. Spain, Switzerland and some U.S. states are cases in point because these jurisdictions were using formula apportionment methods when the Carroll Report was published in 1933. Stanley I. Langbein, *The Unitary Method and the Myth of Arm's Length*, 30 Tax Notes 632, 634 (Feb. 17, 1986).
49. *See* Eduardo A. Baistrocchi & Martin Hearson, *Tax Treaty Disputes: A Global Quantitative Analysis, in* A Global Analysis of Tax Treaty Disputes 1512, 1529 (Eduardo A. Baistrocchi ed., 2017), https://ssrn.com/abstract=3045917.

functionally similar to Article 5 of the LN Draft Model (1928) but more complex. Whereas the 1928 version of the allocation norm consisted of a sentence–long *ex-post* procedural regulation, the 2016 version of the allocation norm provides a constellation of *ex-post* procedural regulations. The two–page Article 17 of the MLI, dealing with dispute resolution regarding corresponding adjustments, is a case in point.

**Table 2. *Ex-post* Procedural Regulations in the First and Second Eras**

| | **1928** | **2016** |
|---|---|---|
| **LN Draft Model, Art. 5** | "The competent administrations of the two Contracting States shall come to an [*ex-post*] arrangement as to the basis for [income] apportionment." | |
| **OECD MLI, Art. 17(3)(b)(ii)** | | "[I]ts competent authority shall endeavour to resolve the [corresponding adjustment] case under the provisions of a Covered Tax Agreement relating to mutual agreement procedure [governed by article 25 of the OECD Model]." |

The similarities between the 1928 and 2016 standard–based provisions listed in Table 2 above are meaningful. They both are *ex-post* procedural regulations. They can only provide an *ex-post* meaning to the relevant norms, that is, *after*, instead of before, cross–border investment has been made. The greater complexity of the standard–based legal system emerging in the third era as compared with the first era explains why the evolution of the ITR has been spiral rather than circular.

The ITR evolution may be represented through graphical formats different from a spiral. This includes a pendulum and a straight, horizontal line (line). A pendulum swinging from the rule end to the standard end is an appealing option, but it does not reflect the increasing complexity of the third era *vis a vis* the first era. Hence, a pendulum is a model that would over–simplify the ITR evolution.[50] A line would be as good as a spiral in this area; however, the spiral is preferred here because it can crystalize substantial amounts of data in a more concise and aesthetic way than a line.

50. Compare Adam Watson's "pendulum" model or long–cycle theory. *See* Adam Watson, The Evolution of International Society (1992).

Hence, the spiral seems to be the best available format to represent the ITR's centennial evolution due to its stronger explanatory power, efficiency, and aesthetic considerations in relation to a circle, pendulum, and straight, horizontal line.

#### *4.1.2. The ALP evolution: from the rule end toward the standard end of the spectrum*

As shown in Section 3.2 above, the ALP has been involved in a creeping evolution since its inception in 1933. From 1933 to 1963, the ALP was a regulation close to the pure rule end of the spectrum; it then gradually moved to the pure standard end from 1963 to 2019, as defined in Section 2.2 above.

The ALP evolution has been correlated with technological innovation, such as the international trade of intangibles seen in disputes like *Nestle* in the U.S. in 1963,[51] *GlaxoSmithKline* in Canada in 2008 and *DSG* in the U.K. in 2009. There has been a correlative decision of the U.S., then accepted by the OECD, to increasingly embed a range of standard–based norms into the ALP to adapt it to technological innovation. The five OECD transfer pricing methods introduced in the OECD Guidelines in 1979 and 1995 are a case in point. These OECD standards include the profit split and transactional net margin methods.

The ALP evolution seems to be from the rule end towards the standard end of the spectrum by means of provisions like Pattern #4 regulations, as defined in Section 2.2 above; that is, a constellation of standards embedded into a rule–based legal system that eventually transforms the system into a standard–based one.[52]

Both the LN and OECD have implicitly acknowledged this ALP evolution. For example, while both international institutions considered the ALP as a concept with an *ex-ante* meaning in 1933 and 1963, the OECD considered the ALP as a concept largely without an *ex-ante* meaning by 2017. Table 3 below reflects the ALP evolution during a period of 83 years (1933–2019).

**Table 3: Evolution of the ALP from the Rule End toward the Standard End of the Spectrum**

| ALP | *Ex-ante* Meaning | No *Ex-ante* Meaning |
|---|---|---|
| **1933** | "[...] the conduct of business between a corporation and its subsidiaries on the basis of dealings with an independent enterprise **obviates all problems of allocation** [...]."[53] | |

51. *See supra* Section 3.2.2.

52. *See supra* Sections 3.2, 3.3.

53. The *Carroll Report*, para. 628, at 177 (emphasis added).

| ALP | *Ex-ante* Meaning | No *Ex-ante* Meaning |
|---|---|---|
| **1963** | "[...] Article [9] seems to call for very little comment."[54] | |
| **2017** | | "[TP] disputes may arise even though the guidance in these Guidelines is followed in a conscientious effort to apply the arm's length principle. It is possible that taxpayers and tax administrations may reach differing determinations of the arm's length conditions for the controlled transactions under examination given the complexity of some transfer pricing issues and the difficulties in interpreting and evaluating the circumstances of individual cases."[55] |

The initial absence of disputes dealing with the meaning of the ALP suggests that the ALP was a largely rule–based regulation from 1933 to 1963. Indeed, the predicated ALP starting point as a rule in the 1930s is grounded on the lack of transfer pricing disputes in the G20 triggered by the lack of comparable transactions until the emergence of the *Nestle* case in the U.S. in 1963.[56]

In sum, there is a striking similarity in the evolution of the ALP from 1933 to 1963 and the Ireland–U.K. test of corporate residence from 1926 to 2017.[57] Both regulations are examples of rules that eventually evolved as standards due to exogenous forces: technological innovation in the ALP arena[58] and changes in the flows of bilateral FDI in the Ireland–U.K. test of residence.[59]

#### *4.1.3. The spiral evolution, global political shifts and innovation*

Global power shifts and innovation at the technological and financial regulatory levels have probably been two central driving forces in the evolution of the allocation norm regarding the profits of associated enterprises since its origin in the early 20th century. These two elements will be addressed independently.

54. Org. for Econ. Co-operation & Dev. [OECD], *Draft Double Taxation Convention on Income and Capital*, OECD Doc. No. C(63)87, at 93 (1963), https://www.oecd-ilibrary.org/taxation/draft-double-taxation-convention-on-income-and-capital_9789264073241-en.
55. OECD TPG (2017), ch. IV, sec. D, para. 4.1.
56. *See supra* Section 3.2.2. *See also* Resolving Transfer Pricing Disputes: A Global Analysis, chapter 21, (Cambridge University Press, 2012).
57. *See supra* Section 2.3.1.
58. *See supra* Section 3.2.2.
59. *See supra* Section 2.3.1.

The transitions from the first era to the second era and from the second era to the third era correlate with power shifts in the world. The transition from the first era to the second era correlates with the power shift from the U.K. to the U.S. in the 1930s. Likewise, the transition from the second era to the third era correlates with an emerging power shift from the West to the East, mainly China, since the early 21st century.[60] Emerging countries again contribute over 50% of global economic output in purchasing power parity terms, as was the case before the first Industrial Revolution.[61] The Cold War (1947–1991) did not have any relevant impact on the evolution of the allocation norm, given the limited role of the Soviet Union in global trade.[62]

The U.K. did not persuade the LN on using a rule–based regulation to solve the emerging international double taxation problem after WWI: the exclusive residence taxation (the U.K. rule). The U.K. rule was only accepted by the Irish Free State in its tax treaty with the U.K. signed in 1926.[63] So the U.K. did not disrupt the standard–based character of the first era of the ITR (1908-1933).

On the global stage, *ex-post* procedural regulations emerging in the first and third eras (1908 to 1933 and 2015 to 2019, respectively) have been the central allocation norm. This is probably so because key countries in international trade have been unable to agree on a rule to solve the allocation problem.[64] By contrast, the second era of the allocation norm (1933 to 2015) represents a period of relative geopolitical stability in the international tax arena. The U.S. was certainly the global hegemon regarding the allocation norm during the second era. For example, the U.S. induced the LN to adopt the ALP as the allocation norm in 1933 (first element) and the U.S. then influenced the OECD on how to adapt the ALP to technological innovation from 1979 onwards (second element).[65]

The 1933 Carroll Report is an example of the first element, as this report is the core source for Article 5 of the LN Draft Model (1933), which, in turn, is a core source for Article 9 of the OECD Model as of 1963 to the present.

Section 482 of the U.S. Internal Revenue Code (IRC) is an example of the second element, as these U.S. regulations were key sources for both the 1979 and 1995 OECD TP Guidelines. In effect, the *OECD Transfer Pricing Report* (1979) and the 1995 OECD TPG are grounded in the 1968 and 1994 versions, respectively, of IRC

---

60. Baistrocchi, *supra* note 10, at 733.
61. 'Emerging Economies; Climbing Back' *The Economist* (London, January 21, 2006) 71.
62. *See* Irina Dmitrieva, *Tax Treaty Disputes in Russia,* in A Global Analysis of Tax Treaty Disputes 905, *supra* note 4, at 911–16.
63. *See supra* Section 2.3.1.
64. For example, countries were unable to agree on how to deal with the TP problem in the early 1920s. *See* M. B. Carroll, 'Taxation of Foreign and National Enterprises', in *Methods of Allocating Taxable Income*, (LN, 1933) [Carroll Report], IV, at 15, 17.
65. *See* OECD, *supra* Section 3.2.

Section 482 regulations.[66] These two OECD documents address similar issues and, in most instances, reach the same conclusions as the IRC regulations do.[67]

The convergence of the OECD Guidelines and the U.S. IRC Section 482 regulations is no coincidence. Rather, it is the result of long–standing U.S. tax policy, aimed at exporting the IRC Section 482 regulations to OECD member countries and beyond, with a view to creating an international consensus for applying the ALP under U.S. control, on the one hand, and adapting the ALP to technological innovation, on the other.[68] The OECD Guidelines probably make more effective U.S. influence on OECD soft law than the Commentary on Article 9 of the OECD Model. This is so because OECD member countries cannot introduce observations or reservations on the OECD TPG, as they can when dealing with the wording of Article 9 of the OECD Model or its Commentary.[69]

The global transplanting of the ALP shows U.S. dominance in this area during the second era. The ALP was first transplanted from the U.S. to Europe via France in 1936, then to Latin America via Argentina in 1943, to Australasia via Australia in 1946, subsequently to Asia via Japan in 1986, and, finally, to Africa via South Africa in 1995.[70]

The global transplant of the ALP has normally been a direct consequence of waves of foreign U.S. direct investment (FDI) to the relevant countries and/or regions. For instance, the transplant of the ALP from the U.S. to France in 1932, implemented via the France–U.S. Tax Treaty (1932), was the result of the increasing expansion of American MNEs into France after WWI.[71] The ALP has been gradually transplanted worldwide, normally on the basis of a two–stage dynamic: first, from a model tax treaty to treaty law; and second, from treaty law to domestic law. The U.K. is an early representative example. Indeed, the U.K. and the U.S. signed their first comprehensive tax treaty, which incorporated the ALP, in

66. *See supra* Section 3.2.2.1.

67. *See* J. Wittendorff, "The Arm's Length Principle and Fair Value: Identical Twins or Just Close Relatives?" *Tax Notes International*, 223 (April 18, 2011), at 38–39.

68. *See* Wittendorff, *Id.*, at 38. *See* S. S. Surrey, "Secretary Surrey Reports on Developments in Treasury's Foreign Tax Position," *Journal of Taxation*, 24 (54) (1966), 56. Surrey writes on the influence of the U.S. in the OECD:

> The United States believes that the OECD Fiscal Committee is the proper body to undertake the task of establishing the allocation standards to guide countries in reaching accommodations with each other. The OECD Fiscal Committee appointed a Working Party for this purpose. We intend, as a measure of assistance to that Working Party, to lay before it our proposed Section 482 regulations as they are developed. […] these regulations may represent a more structurally developed and detailed framework of allocation rules than has been formulated elsewhere […].

69. Wittendorff, *supra* note 67, at 122.

70. Eduardo Baistrocchi, *Transfer Pricing Dispute Resolution: The Global Evolutionary Path,* in Resolving Transfer Pricing Disputes: A Global Analysis 835, 837, https://ssrn.com/abstract=2337717.

71. *Id.*

1945.[72] The U.K. introduced the ALP into its tax treaty law immediately after WWII and domestic regulations were issued a few years later, in 1951.[73]

Most countries explored in this chapter followed a similar evolutionary path to dealing with the TP problem, starting at different points in time and going along the path at different paces. The U.S. and China are clear examples. Whereas the U.S. took 94 years to complete the full cycle, as from 1918, when U.S. income taxation was first introduced, China achieved this in just 30 years, from the inception of a Western–style income tax in China in 1980.[74]

The emerging power shift that has triggered the third era of the allocation norm (2015-present) implies a return to the standard–based approach of the first era (1908-1933). China and India have an increasingly relevant say in comparison with the U.S. since 2013. Just as the U.S. has been using the OECD Guidelines to export IRC Section 482 regulations to the OECD Model and beyond as of 1979,[75] China and India now seem to be willing to use the UN Transfer Pricing Manual to export Chinese and Indian domestic law on TP to the UN Model and beyond as of 2013.

LSAs appear to be one major innovation proposed by China to the OECD. The OECD has accepted the LSA concept as compatible with the ALP in 2017, after its original rejection before the publication of the BEPS Reports.[76] This OECD acceptance of the LSA is a pragmatic decision. It embeds an additional standard to the ALP within the wording of Pattern #4 (a standard embedded in one or more rule) in the rule–standard spectrum.[77] This embedding of a new standard aims to adjust the ALP to the demands from countries like China to expand the concept of jurisdiction to tax.

Correlated with the emerging power shift from the U.S. to China, the ITR is seemingly heading back to an ecosystem similar to the early stages of the first era, in which there will probably be competing, incompatible regulations. The ongoing clash between the orphan approach, defended by the U.S., and the family approach, sponsored by China and India, is a case in point.[78]

#### *4.1.4. The spiral evolution, countries and MNEs*

Since the 1960s the ITR has grown strongly. Moreover, since the 1980s international investments has increased steeply. Much of this economic internationalization has occurred within transnational business structures. Global estimates indicate that roughly 7,000 MNEs were counted in 1970. From 1990 to 1998 the number

72. Double Taxation: Taxes on Income, U.K.-U.S., April 16, 1945, 60 Stat. 1377.
73. Baistrocchi, *supra* note 70, at 837.
74. *Id.* at 837–38.
75. *See supra* Section 3.2.2.1.
76. *See, e.g.*, OECD TPG 2010, paras 6–7.
77. *See supra* Section 2.2.
78. *See* Reuven S. Avi-Yonah & Ajitesh Kir, A Break in the Dam? India's New Profit Attribution Proposal and the Arm's Length Standard (July 8, 2019) (U. Mich. L. & Econ. Rsch. Paper), https://ssrn.com/abstract=3414266.

increased from 35,000 to 53,607.[79] By 2006 there were 78,000 parent companies with at least 780,000 affiliates.[80]

Rixen has developed an illuminating but incomplete account of the history of international tax governance and offered a rationalist reconstruction of its trajectory.[81] His paper argues that as an unintended consequence of its institutional setup, the ITR, which originally only dealt with double tax avoidance, produces harmful tax competition. Despite this negative effect there are only incremental and partial changes of the regime, which are insufficient to curb tax competition. He argues that this development can be explained by considering the properties—and the sequence in which they come up—of the collective action problems inherent in double tax avoidance and tax competition. First, in double tax avoidance, a coordination game with a distributive conflict, governments did not want to endanger the solution they had institutionalized long before tax competition became virulent. Second, governments are unable to resolve the emergent asymmetric prisoners' dilemma of tax competition due to conflicts of interest among big and small country governments and successful lobbying of corporate capital. As a result, the institutional trajectory is characterized by the simultaneous occurrence of stability in the core principles and indirect and incremental changes of the regulations in the form of norm stretching and layering.[82]

Rixen's account is illuminating but incomplete because it bypassed the larger picture: the impact of external shocks on the ITR legal structure over time and space. Indeed, external shocks such as global power shifts and technological and financial regulatory innovations have been correlated with the evolution of the ITR legal architecture from the rule end to the standard end of the spectrum, as defined in Section 2.2 above. For example, the *Nestle* case decided in the U.S. in 1963 marks the decline of the second rule–based era of the ITR and the emergence of international tax competition among jurisdictions for capital in the context of an increasingly standard–based regulatory framework. The *Nestle* case is an example of a technological innovation impacting the structure of the ITR: the international trade of intangibles that has been facilitating international double non-taxation cases since the 1960s.[83]

This strategic scenario has been reinforced with external regulatory innovation like the end of exchange controls since the 1980s,[84] which, in turn, induced the

79. Rixen, Thomas "From Double Tax Avoidance to Tax Competition: Explaining the Institutional Trajectory of International Tax Governance", *Review of International Political Economy*, 18 (2), 2011), 197-227, 212, at 207.

80. Org. for Econ. Co-operation & Dev. [OECD], *Multinational Enterprises in the Global Economy*, at 6 (May 2018), https://www.oecd.org/industry/ind/MNEs-in-the-global-economy-policy-note.pdf.

81. Rixen, *supra* note 79, at 197.

82. *Id.*

83. *See supra* Section 3.2.2.

84. James E. Croning, Global Rules: America, Britain and a Disordered World 138 (2014).

emergence of non-G20 hubs as locations for intermediate holding companies;[85] indeed, this scenario has encouraged MNEs to strategically locate intangibles in non-G20 hubs, grounded on the separate entity approach introduced in the ITR in the early years of its second era, to minimize the effective tax rates of MNEs.[86] The corporate tax planning schemes that triggered public outrage in 2012 are cases in point.[87]

As shown elsewhere, the ITR is a network market implemented via a two–sided platform.[88] The platform is now the OECD Model and related soft laws. The OECD–based platform, in turn, has two distinct users, MNEs on one side of the platform and countries on the other side. The ITR platform has been having the net effect of minimizing the tax entry and exit costs to the relevant jurisdictions. Examples of strategic interaction between G20 countries and non-G20 hubs to attract FDI include the interaction between Argentina and Chile; Brazil and The Netherlands; Canada and The Netherlands; China and Hong Kong; India and Mauritius; Indonesia and The Netherlands; Mexico and Switzerland; Russia and Cyprus; South Africa and Switzerland; South Korea and Belgium; Turkey and The Netherlands; and the U.S. and The Netherlands.[89]

---

85. A new logic has been emerging in the strategic interaction among G20 countries and non-G20 country hubs since the emergence of international tax competition in the 1960s. G20 countries increasingly compete against each other for capital, just as private firms compete for market share. The ITR has been facilitating this new logic. In bilateral tax treaties that G20 countries conclude with country hubs, the latter serve as outlets for the bundled products that G20 countries offer to multinational enterprises (MNEs). One component of the bundle is the tax treaty network in its interaction with the relevant domestic laws, which is a vehicle to minimize the tax entry costs and/or tax exit costs. Eduardo A. Baistrocchi & Martin Hearson, *Tax Treaty Disputes: A Global Quantitative Analysis, in* A Global Analysis of Tax Treaty Disputes (Eduardo A. Baistrocchi ed., 2017), at 1513. This logic illustrates the marketization of international taxation: a growing number of countries deem taxes as negotiable with MNEs as a price for attracting capital. So countries have been increasingly unable to use their tax systems for income redistribution in a context of increasing inequality within local societies.
86. Jannick Damgaard, Thomas Elkjaer, & Niels Johannesen, *The Rise of Phantom Investments. Empty Corporate Shells in Tax Havens Undermine Tax Collection in Advanced, Emerging Market and Developing Economies*, Fin. & Dev., September 2019, at 12.
87. Aidan Regan, *Apple Won't Have to Pay Nearly $15 Billion in European Taxes,* Wash. Post (July 15, 2020), https://www.washingtonpost.com/politics/2020/07/15/apple-wont-have-pay-nearly-15-billion-european-taxes/. *See also* Joined Cases T-778/16 & T-892/16, Ireland v. Comm'n (July 15, 2020), http://curia.europa.eu/juris/document/document.jsf;jsessionid=2E4EB3A000A2F5962C8B2F3F07745969?text=&docid=228621&pageIndex=0&doclang=EN&mode=lst&dir=&occ=first&part=1&cid=10005665.
88. Eduardo Baistrocchi, *The International Tax Regime and the BRIC World: Elements for a Theory,* 2013 Oxford J. Legal Stud. 1 (May 10, 2013), at 740.
89. Eduardo A. Baistrocchi & Martin Hearson, *Tax Treaty Disputes: A Global Quantitative Analysis, in* A Global Analysis of Tax Treaty Disputes (Eduardo A. Baistrocchi ed., 2017), at 1540–41.

In sum, the ITR two–sided platform has been indeed resilient. It has adapted to global power shifts and technological and regulatory innovation by gradually evolving from the rule end to the standard end of the spectrum since the emergence of the second era.[90] The ITR evolution has implicitly allocated increasing power to a decentralized network of local courts, which in turn, have facilitated the strategic interpretation and application of tax treaty law by countries and MNEs as an attempt to maximize the flow of inward capital and minimize the MNEs effective tax rate, respectively.[91] And G20 countries have been unable to reform the ITR to effectively address the double non–taxation problem because of increasing collective action costs.[92]

## 4.2. Implications: A Default Rule–based ITR to deal with Opportunistic Behaviour and Inequality

It is now time to explore some implications of the spiral evolution theory in new problem areas. The international taxation of global digital commerce is a challenge the ITR is currently facing.[93]

G20 countries have been unable to reach a consensus on how to solve this problem. The OECD has painfully acknowledged this lack of global consensus: "There is no consensus on… [the] importance to the location of value creation and the identity of the value creator."[94] This issue has been transformed into what has been aptly named as a global tax war: the battle over taxing global digital commerce.[95]

In the context of the third standard–based era, countries are now experimenting with unilateral, incompatible regulations to deal with this issue. This experimentation is uncoordinated in a manner similar to that seen before the publication of the Four Economists' Report to the LN in 1923. The tax conflict between the U.K. and France on the one hand and the U.S. on the other in digital taxation is a case in point.[96]

---

90. *See supra* Section 3.2.
91. Eduardo Baistrocchi, *The International Tax Regime and the BRIC World: Elements for a Theory*, 2013 Oxford J. Legal Stud. 1 (May 10, 2013).
92. Rixen, *supra* note 79, at 201–02.
93. Org. for Econ. Co-operation & Dev. [OECD], *OECD/G20 Base Erosion and Profit Shifting Project: Addressing the Tax Challenges of the Digital Economy, Action 1, 2015 Final Report*, para. 2 (Oct. 5, 2015), https://doi.org/10.1787/9789264241046-en.
94. Org. for Econ. Co-operation & Dev. [OECD], *OECD/G20 Base Erosion and Profit Shifting Project: Tax Challenges Arising from Digitalisation, Interim Report 2018*, para. 36 (Mar. 16, 2018), http://dx.doi.org/10.1787/9789264293083-en.
95. Arthur J. Cockfield, *Tax Wars: The Battle over Taxing Global Digital Commerce*, 161 Tax Notes 1331, 1331–32 (Dec. 10, 2018).
96. Chris Giles & Claer Barrett, *UK Braves US Ire by Pressing Ahead with Tax on Tech Companies: Move Comes Hours after Washington Threatened Sanctions against France for Similar Levy*, Fin. Times, (July 11, 2019), https://www.ft.com/content/41069548-a3d8-11e9-974c-ad1c6ab5efd1.

The OECD and the IMF are exploring the possibility of introducing multilateral rule–based regulations to resolve the–digital taxation problem in the hope of setting the foundations of a new fourth rule–based era. The exploration includes the global formulary apportionment concept. It is a formula grounded on objective, rather than subjective, elements such as sales, for the allocation of the international tax base to the relevant countries.[97]

The spiral evolution framework suggests the following point. It is unlikely that a multilateral rule–based resolution to the digital taxation problem will emerge in the context of the third era. This era has emerged after the collapse of the third globalization outlined in Section 1 above. It shares some elements of the previous periods before and in–between the first and second globalizations: geopolitical tensions, major wars, and geopolitical disruptions. Moreover, there is no jurisdiction or group of jurisdictions so far with global influence in global international tax policy comparable to the influence of the U.S. during the second era.

So, the question now is what policy options can be drawn from the ITR spiral evolution that may be relevant for solving the digital taxation problem. A potential response to this question can be crystallized in a two–step approach. While exploring rule–based regulations such as those suggested in the Carroll Report in 1933 or the OECD Program of Work to Develop a Consensus Solution to the Tax Challenges Arising from the Digitalization of the Economy,[98] standard–based regulations are also worth exploring, such as those attempted by the LN in 1928. The two–step approach may be organized, for example, along with the following two elements:

1. *Default Procedural Rule*: If the G20 is unable to solve the digital taxation problem in the near future, the E.U. could work as a laboratory for the creation of a default income allocation formula in the area of digital taxation, taking into account the interest of China and India in this area or vice versa. A minimum global corporate tax rate could be an example of a default rule–based ITR to deal with opportunistic behavior and inequality, i.e., two fundamental problems seen in the second era of the ITR.[99] So, for example, the local legislature, or its functional

97. OECD (2020), *Tax Challenges Arising from Digitalisation – Report on Pillar One Blueprint: Inclusive Framework on BEPS*, OECD/G20 Base Erosion and Profit Shifting Project, OECD Publishing, Paris, https://doi.org/10.1787/beba0634-en.

98. Org. for Econ. Co-operation & Dev. [OECD], *OECD/G20 Base Erosion and Profit Shifting Project: Programme of Work to Develop a Consensus Solution to the Tax Challenges Arising from the Digitalisation of the Economy*, paras. 28, 30, 40 (May 2019), https://www.oecd.org/tax/beps/programme-of-work-to-develop-a-consensus-solution-to-the-tax-challenges-arising-from-the-digitalisation-of-the-economy.htm.

99. The OECD has suggested a minimum corporate income tax rate. *See* Org. for Econ. Co-operation & Dev. [OECD], *Global Anti-Base Erosion Proposal ("GloBE") (Pillar Two), Public Consultation Document*, paras. 7–8 (December 2, 2019), http://www.oecd.org/tax/beps/public-consultation-document-global-anti-base-erosion-proposal-pillar-two.pdf.pdf.

equivalent, should have the duty to review the minimum corporate tax rate and local spending policy on a regular basis when the local Gini coefficient does not meet the desirable figure.[100] Then, this default rule–based regulation could be submitted to the OECD-G20 for consideration as an addition to the Multilateral Convention to Implement Tax Treaty–Related Measures to Prevent BEPS (the Multilateral Instrument).[101]

2. *Regulatory Framework for the Transition Period*: The MAP procedure, including tax arbitration, could work as a laboratory for the creation of norms with precedential value for the crucial transition period. So, until a consensus is reached on a global regulation to the digital taxation issue, the OECD may use the MAP and arbitration decisions in such a way as to allow the OECD to identify global and/or regional trends in disputes dealing with central issues in the digital taxation arena. They include nexus and profit allocation.[102] Then the OECD could transform these ever–changing trends into, for example, commentaries to Article 5, 7 and 9 of the OECD Model.[103] The ingenuity of the decentralized network of courts, and its functional equivalent, interpreting and applying tax treaty law to the digital global commerce, could create new regulations with global impact in this area.

The *Nestle* and *DuPont* cases are examples of innovative concepts created by local courts with an impact on ITR evolution worldwide. The *Nestle* case invented the commensurate–with–income principle in the area of valuation of intangibles;[104] the *DuPont* case created, in turn, the Berry ratio as a TP methodology to determine the proportion of gross profit to operating expenses in cross–border supply chains.[105] Both local judicial inventions have had a lasting global impact.

## 5. Concluding Remarks

The theory expounded in this chapter predicates that there is usually a correlation between global power shifts and the evolution of the ITR. The theory maintains that the hegemon normally prefers a rule–based system over a standard–based one given the ITR's decentralized competitive structure. The hegemon's preference is based on

---

100. This rule may work as follows: A country should have the duty to recalibrate its taxing and spending policy when the local Gini coefficient reaches a certain level. This may include, for example, raising the minimum corporate tax rate and spending allocation on education and health care. OECD (2020), Income inequality (indicator). doi: 10.1787/459aa7f1-en (last accessed on November12, 2020).

101. *OECD Multilateral Convention to Implement Tax Treaty Related Measures to Prevent BEPS* (Nov. 24, 2016), Treaties IBFD, at 1.

102. OECD (2019), Programme of Work, para. 7.

103. Org. for Econ. Co-operation & Dev. [OECD], *Model Tax Convention on Income and on Capital, Condensed Version*, at 92, 130, 181 (July 22, 2010), http://dx.doi.org/10.1787/20745419.

104. Nestle Co. v. Commissioner, 22 T.C.M. (CCH) 46 (1963); *see also supra* Section 3.2.2.

105. E.I. DuPont de Nemours & Co. v. United States, 608 F.2d 445, 456 (1979).

the assumption that the former limits the decentralization of power within the ITR more than the latter does to a growing, decentralized global network of countries. When external shocks (such as technological and/or regulatory financial innovation) emerges making the rule–based system unworkable, there is normally no better option for the hegemon than to accept an ITR shift towards the standard–based end of the spectrum, ideally under the hegemon's control until the hegemon's collapse.

The hegemon's role in the international tax regime is usually to provide some underlying purpose and coherence, which the U.S. has done from 1933 until 2015 through, for example, its support for the ALP. The hegemon, which is normally the major capital exporter, is really pursuing the interests of the hegemon's capital, and it uses the ideas and the sense of purpose, to generate consent for its hegemony.

In 1725, Giambattista Vico theorized that history can be reconstructed as a spiral (*corsi e recorsi storici*).[106] In a similar vein, this chapter shows that the history of the ITR can be reconstructed as a spiral in which its central driving forces are shocks impacting the ITR architecture.[107] Indeed, the ITR found itself in the midst of a three–era spiral evolution: from standards (1908-1933) to rules (1933-2015) and then back to standards (2015 to the present). The spiral trajectory correlates to two global power shifts: first, a power shift from the U.K. to the U.S. in the 1930s and then, an emerging power shift from the West to the East (mainly from the U.S. to China) beginning in the early 21st century.[108]

Strikingly, considerations of global tax justice have been largely irrelevant in the evolution of the ITR over the period covered here.[109] For example, the global tax justice problem was bypassed in both the Economist Report submitted to the League of Nations in 1923[110] and the OECD BEPS Reports submitted to the G20 in 2015.[111]

The spiral evolution of the ITR will not necessarily end in the third standard–based era. The evolution may move back to a rule–based fourth era if certain conditions are met, such as those seen in the second era (1933-2015). This includes

---

106. Giambattista Vico, The New Science of Giambattista Vico (Thomas Goddard Bergin & Max Harold Fisch trans., 3d ed. 1948). *See also* Isaiah Berlin, *Corsi e Ricorsi*, 50 J. Mod. Hist. 480, 480 (1978).

107. The spiral seems to be the best available format to represent the centennial evolution of the ITR. Indeed, the spiral offers a number of advantages *vis a vis* three alternative formats: i) a circle, ii) a straight line, and iii) a pendulum..

108. *See supra* Section 3.

109. On global tax justice, see, for example, Adam Kern, *Illusions of Justice in International Taxation*, 48 Phil. & Pub. Aff. 153, 155, 184 (2020). *See also* Tsilly Dagan, *International Tax and Global Justice*, 18 Theoretical Inquiries L. 1, 2 (2017).

110. *See supra* Section 3.1.1.

111. *See supra* Section 3.3.1.

the still unforeseeable emergence of a hegemon powerful enough to create and enforce a new rule–based normative system.[112]

It is important to recognize the possibility of a more complex, pluralistic dynamic emerging in the ITR than a hegemonic torch passed on from Europe to the U.S. and soon to China. Less optimistically, it is believed that future research in this area should focus on, for example, the following crucial questions: i) If China doesn't fill the U.S.'s hegemonic shoes, will there be a problematic power vacuum?; ii) Can international organizations like the OECD and G20 buffer the increasing tension between the U.S. and China in the search for multilateral resolutions?; iii) Given increasing global inequality between and within countries, can countries and international organizations take global tax justice seriously when discussing the future of the ITR?[113]

Two centuries ago, Napoleon is said to have warned, "Let China sleep; when she wakes, she will shake the world."[114] Napoleon was indeed correct in this prediction. Today China has awakened, and the world is beginning to shake.[115] This chapter offers the first analysis of the impact of geopolitics in international taxation. It focuses on the clashes between ruling and rising powers and their impact on the evolution of the ITR since its emergence in the early 20th century. It also shows that history is to shed light on promising ways for the ITR in the 21st century.

---

112. *See supra* Section 3.2.1.

113. *See World Inequality Database*, WID.WORLD, https://wid.world/world/#sptinc_p99p100_z/US;FR;DE;CN;ZA;GB;WO/last/eu/k/p/yearly/s/false/5.070499999999999/30/curve/false/country (last accessed on October 26, 2020).

114. The quote "Quand la Chine s'éveillera, le monde tremblera" is attributed to Napoleon, but he never actually wrote it in any of his texts. He is said to have pronounced these words in 1816, during his exile in Saint Helena, after he read narratives of Lord Macartney, the British Ambassador to China in 1792–93. It was later used as the title of a famous essay written by Alain Peyrefitte, the French statesman. See Alain Peyrefitte, Quand la Chine s'éveillera...: ... Le monde tremblera (Français) Broché –1980.

115. Graham Allison, Destined for War: Can America and China Escape Thucydides's Trap? VII (2017).

## REJOINDER

### Parthasarathi Shome

The characteristic of the chapter by Baistrocchi that stands out is its innovation in perceiving international taxation over centuries as a "spiral" trajectory that has moved through several focal geographical locations, primarily, from the UK to the US and, as of now, inexorably towards China. Of course, in a sense, China represents the emergence of new economies such as Brazil and India that are also having an increasing say in the patterns of international taxation. From this, a re-arrangement from purely residence-based cross-country revenue allocation towards a more source-based allocation is clearly observable. Baistrocchi emphasizes the shift of the international tax regime from a hegemonic order of capital ownership to one based on the generation of income or value-added. He provides comprehensive historical justification to demonstrate his point and concludes by predicating that there is a correlation between global power shifts and the evolution of the international taxation regime.

There appears to be an element of inevitability in these developments such as the rapid spread of the digital economy in which emerging economies are contributing a big share of the value-added. Indeed, their contribution to global capital is also becoming increasingly visible. Their interests, therefore, are naturally having to be recognized and reflected in the work that is being carried out at multilateral organizations such as the OECD. He points out that this work was ushered in at the behest of the G20 group of countries that includes several emerging economies over and above major OECD members.

Baistrocchi points to technological and financial innovation as external shocks that are necessarily leading to a movement away from hegemonic rules once controlled and implemented exclusively by a hegemon such as the US. To some extent, perhaps, it reflects the reality that the US is no longer the only major capital exporter, with China coming up as an important international investor. He optimistically asks if it would be too surprising if a "more complex, pluralistic dynamic emerges in the international taxation regime (ITR) than (just) a hegemonic torch (being) passed on from Europe to the US and soon to China." Less optimistically, he asks, if China cannot become a powerful enough hegemon and cannot mirror the US, would it lead to a power vacuum and, continues somewhat rhetorically, whether international organisations such as the OECD can buffer the increasing tensions between the US and China including in the international taxation regime.

Baistrocchi's chapter is unique in its historical depiction and analysis of the ITR over the past centuries through a cogent and incisive presentation. It is a must- read for any student or researcher in international taxation.

# CHAPTER 3

# THE NEED FOR A NEW INTERNATIONAL TAX ARCHITECTURE

Philip Baker

## 1. Introduction

My topic is 'the need for a new international tax architecture'.[1] By architecture, I am referring to the structure of organizations involved in international tax.[2] I am not concerned with the rules or principles of international taxation concerning jurisdiction or nexus: that is a different type of architecture. The architecture I am concerned with is the institutional architecture: the OECD, the UN, the IMF, the World Bank, and other bodies. I am going to argue that the current architecture is disorganized and, to a certain extent dysfunctional. In particular, one of the problems lies with the OECD. I am going to discuss what is wrong with the OECD as the leading intergovernmental organization (IGO) in international tax. I am then going to speculate about the future.

## 2. Flawed Architecture

The current structure is disorganized. A clear architecture is needed to effectively develop international tax rules and principles, with cooperation between governments on taxation and fiscal policy, capable of producing solutions to recommend to countries – solutions to both domestic and international tax

---

1. This is a transcribed and corrected version of the talk given at the ITRAF conference on December 4, 2020. As a talk, it does not offer a full, academic treatment of the subject matter, which would require a much lengthier chapter. Footnotes and some references have been added, but not full sources for all statements.
2. There are several excellent articles discussing the need to reconsider the existing structure of organizations. Also, see, Sieb Kingma, *Inclusive Global Tax Governance in the Post-BEPS Era* (2020, IBFD), which contains a very full explanation of the current activities and constitution of the main intergovernmental organizations involved in tax matters. See also Allison Christians, *International Tax Organisations* in Y. Brauner (ed), *Research Handbook on International Taxation* (2020, Edward Elgar), 29-43, which contains a shorter review of the activities of IGOs.

problems. – The solutions need to be coherent, workable, and appropriate for all countries. They should have democratic support: they should be seen to achieve objectives supported by the people of the countries concerned and be the product of a transparent process that has allowed effective participation both by affected governments and affected groups in society. They should be legitimate and be seen and accepted as legitimate. They also need to be innovative as we are dealing with new situations that have not been faced before, and lastly, the solutions should be effective.

I can probably be criticized that some of those adjectives overlap, and it looks like I have opened a thesaurus to find them. However, those are the criteria that need to be met by the international tax architecture. I do not consider that our present architecture meets all (or even many) of these criteria.

## 3. History Behind OECD's Emergence

To a certain extent, our current architecture is the result of historical accidents. You can only explain the role of some organizations by explaining the history. History has produced a network of largely overlapping, and sometimes competing, organizational jurisdictions that cannot move forward at the pace that the world needs. I will try to make good this comment by looking at the current structure.

I must start with pride of place given to the OECD because the OECD often refers to itself as the leading organization in international taxation, and I think we would probably accept that at present, it is the leading organization. But this was not inevitable. The role of the OECD is primarily a historical accident. It was never intended that the OECD should become the leading international organization when it was established.

The history here takes us back, if you like, to the 1920s when much of the development of our rules for international tax was carried out through the League of Nations in Geneva, which was the precursor of the United Nations and was the first attempt to establish an international body capable of developing common rules for taxation around the world.[3] The League of Nations was wound up after the Second World War, and it was replaced by the United Nations. In the same way that there had been a League of Nations Fiscal Commission, which had carried out the work between the 20s and the 30s, the UN set up a Fiscal Commission. If the Commission had not stopped functioning in 1954, it would be the leading body now and it is reasonable to speculate that our rules on international tax would be very different from what they are now.

3. For an excellent history of the work of the League, see Sunita Jogarajan, *Double Taxation and the League of Nations* (2018, Cambridge).

## 3.1. The OECD's Emergence over the UN

Unfortunately, the Fiscal Commission set up in 1948 was wound up after six years in 1954. It was wound up partly because there was a cost- saving exercise that the UN was going through at the time, and partly because it had become mired in Cold War arguments. It was the height of the Cold War, and the communist countries were arguing with the capitalist countries, which stalled any progress in tax work. In what was, I think, a fateful decision, the UN closed down the Fiscal Commission. Therefore, no organization was there to work on international taxation for some time, resulting in a void. In that void, a couple of former delegates to the UN Commission contacted one another. If you go to the UK National Archives, you can see the correspondence: essentially, they needed a location where they could meet to talk about international tax rules. The UN was no longer an option, but what about this new organization in Europe called the OEEC, the Organisation of European Economic Cooperation, set up as part of the Marshall plan? They put together the idea of meeting under the aegis of this Paris-based organization, which, at the time, consisted only of Western European capitalist countries: America, for example, was not a member at the time, nor were other countries outside of Western Europe. The OEEC was receptive to the idea, and in time it set up a fiscal committee, and, as they say, the rest is history. The fiscal committee later developed into the OECD Committee on Fiscal Affairs, and eventually the Centre for Tax Policy and Administration, which oversees the OECD's tax work that we know at present.

The OECD is still, of course, at root a membership organization. At its core are 37 member countries: the Western European countries plus the US, Canada, Australia, New Zealand, Japan, Singapore, and a small number of other countries, including Chile and Colombia. India is not, for example, a member of the OECD.

## 3.2. OECD's Expansion into Inclusive Framework

In recent years, partly because of criticisms that the OECD is an organization with restricted membership, it has established the IF, the Inclusive Framework on BEPS, originating from the BEPS project in the last seven years. It is part of the implementation of that project from 2016. It now has 125 countries, which are associate members for this purpose. Countries must agree to the BEPS principles and the BEPS minimum standards, to join the group. So it is a way of encouraging countries to participate: to agree to accept the BEPS outcomes. Other international organizations, some of which I will mention, are observers. The work of the IF, in principle, is limited to BEPS, which is focused very largely on the direct taxation of multinational corporations. So, in principle, it is not a group looking at all issues on tax; it is focused on the BEPS issues. BEPS, of course, seems to be broadening almost day by day to cover wider and wider matters, but the IF is not a general agenda organization; its agenda is focused on BEPS.

### 3.3. The Re-Emergence of the UN

The UN came back to the tax issue in the 1960s, and in 1968 set up an ad hoc committee on tax treaties with developing countries; the present UN Committee of Experts grew from that. In 2004 it became a permanent committee. It consists of 25 experts. Virtually all of them are government officials who are put up for election. They serve in their personal capacity. India has always had a member on the committee. It reports to the Economic and Social Council of the United Nations and works within the Department of Economic and Social Affairs, but it has limited resources, unfortunately, and, as a result, a limited mandate. Its work is focused essentially on developing countries. It has become more active in the last ten years. Prior to that, it met once a year (and before that once every two years). Now it operates through working groups, and it has started to produce a greater output. However, it is limited by the lack of resources and by the fact that its mandate is focused on developing country issues.

## 4. Intergovernmental Organizations

There are two other major intergovernmental organizations currently active in the field. The IMF has a wide membership, and a relatively small Fiscal Affairs Department of individual experts. It provides technical advice and training. It is significant in what it does, but it does not have the same type of country participation in meetings that, say, the UN has. The World Bank Group also has a tax programme, and it provides development finance and assistance to countries on tax and fiscal matters. It too has a wide membership, and it has access to funding to support those programmes.

These four intergovernmental organizations have come together in the last few years to form a Platform for Collaboration on Tax.[4] This is a new institution. On the one-hand it can be seen as an attempt to coordinate the activities and the agendas of the four major organizations. Another view is that it is an attempt by the OECD to control the other three, and to stop the other three from growing and working on areas that the OECD considers are its domain. The Platform has started producing a small number of toolkits for the assistance of governments, mainly in developing countries. For example, it has a toolkit that it eventually adopted in 2020 on the taxation of gains from the indirect disposals of assets.[5]

Aside from those organizations mentioned above, there are a plethora of other organizations or groupings, some of them operating under the aegis of, or administered by, the OECD. These include: The Global Forum on Transparency

4. For information on the Platform, see Who We Are | Platform for Collaboration on Tax (tax-platform.org) (last accessed on January 14, 2021).
5. See https://www.tax-platform.org/sites/pct/files/publications/PCT_Toolkit_The_Taxation_of_Offshore_Indirect_Transfers.pdf (last accessed on January 14, 2021).

and Exchange of Information; the Forum on Tax Administration, which brings together heads of tax authorities; Tax Inspectors without Borders – the tax equivalent of *Medicins sans Frontieres* (doctors without borders) which sends tax officials to countries to provide assistance. There are various regional organizations, of which perhaps the most active is the European Commission.

Overall, there is a lack of coherent structure. There is a clear overlap between the agendas of different countries. There appears to be at least some element of organizational rivalry, and one can almost see the UN, the IMF, and the World Bank sitting in the wings waiting for the OECD to collapse over BEPS, and they are ready to step in. There is unnecessary complexity: one suspects that those who work in tax policy in many countries must get very confused about the number of different emails and documents they receive every week from various organizations.

## 5. Why is OECD the Wrong Organization

So that brings us to my question, "What is wrong with the leadership by the OECD?". The OECD has become the leading organization in the last 60 years, so what is wrong with it? There are lots of things wrong with this: at its core it is still a membership organization of (now) 37 countries. Within the Inclusive Framework, other countries join as associates, but they join essentially for work related to BEPS. With 60 years of history, unfortunately, the OECD carries a great deal of baggage. Many of its concerns are the concerns of its earlier members, the Western European and North American, wealthy countries. For example, its focus is on direct taxation, with limited work on indirect taxes, although indirect taxation is often much more important for developing countries. It focuses significantly on transfer pricing. It appears wedded to the arm's length principle. The idea of formulary apportionment still seems to be anathema to the OECD.[6] It has a legacy of involvement with some of the world's major tax havens. For many years its active members included countries frequently found in lists of tax havens contained in books on the subject; it is not entirely surprising that it is only in the last twenty years or so that the OECD has become committed to greater transparency and exchange of information.

### 5.1. Lack of Democratic Legitimacy

Perhaps most important, the OECD lacks democratic legitimacy. Government officials are sent from their tax departments to OECD meetings; many of the meetings are private and not open to observers. There is little scrutiny of its work, either at the international level or at the national level, and the outcome of discussions at the OECD are seldom debated. In part, the OECD develops soft law through the Model Tax Convention and its Commentaries and through the

6. Though the recent work on BEPS 2.0 contemplates at least some degree of apportionment.

Transfer Pricing Guidelines, which are implemented by countries without any real democratic overview.

The OECD operates as a consensus organization, seeking the agreement of all its members. While at first blush it may seem attractive that international tax policy changes should only proceed through consensus, this has a severe limitation: developments can be blocked by members. Access to bank information for tax purposes was blocked by Switzerland and Belgium up until the late 1990s. Countries know that they can block developments through the OECD. If they are willing to do so, individual countries can block progress through the OECD, and the US has been willing to prevent consensus on issues that were perceived not to be in its interests: that makes the work of the OECD particularly susceptible to the US electoral cycle.

## 5.2. Stalling of Digital Economy Taxation

At the timing of writing, the OECD is in the state of stasis or suspended animation. It cannot move forward on its Pillar 1 and Pillar 2 proposals until the new US administration has decided who is going to represent the US and what position it is going to take on those pillars. Everything is in waiting; the whole international tax world is waiting for the US to arrive and produce white smoke or black smoke. This is not the first time this has happened. It happened in 2000-2001 when a new US administration came in. Work was under way on harmful tax competition, which effectively stopped until the new US administration came in and said yes to the project, but only on its terms.

This element of working through consensus in practice gives huge power to individual countries, particularly the US, to determine the agenda, the direction, and the speed of progress. It is reasonable to say, writing at the start of 2021, that the international tax rules we will have in a year's time will effectively be those that the US is prepared to agree to once the new administration has people appointed to decide on the direction they will take.

## 5.3. Lack of a Full Agenda

The OECD as a tax organization also lacks a full agenda. Specifically, the OECD has no human rights agenda, unlike say the UN or the European Union. It does not have a department or commissioner for human rights. It is not particularly focused on developing rights for taxpayers or the public generally. The OECD does not particularly have a focus on development issues for non-member countries. To be fair, a significant part of its work now does have an aspect of helping developing countries, but at origin it was Western European/North American organization and it does not have a specific mandate to assist developing countries.

In tax matters, to a large extent, the OECD determines its own agenda. There is something of a pretense that its agenda is mandated to it by the G20. However, the reality would seem to reflect that it is more a process by which the OECD proposes its agenda to the G20; this seems to have been particularly true in connection with the original mandate to carry out the BEPS project. The notion of focusing on base erosion and profit shifting comes from the OECD itself. The OECD determined that BEPS should be the focus of its activities, not the full range of countries around the world.

Unlike bodies like the UN, the OECD lacks the structure for full participation by civil society groups. The UN, and specifically the functional commissions under ECOSOC, has detailed rules for the recognition and participation of non-governmental organizations. UN documents are publicly available. The OECD, because it was never intended to be a public participation organisation, does not have the required structure; the OECD lets the public into its discussions only when it wants to do so. This usually happens when key decisions have already been taken, and only certain documents are cleared for public dissemination and comment.

### 5.4. Inability to Move Forward

This chapter is only a summary of some of the reasons why the OECD is the wrong organization to be the leading body on international tax. At the time of writing, the fiscal situation in many countries is entering a critical phase because of the impact of the COVID-19 pandemic. However, the leading inter-governmental organization has fixed its principal focus on an issue that relates to only a category of multinational companies which, if adopted, would make a relatively small difference to the taxes collected in most countries. Even on this, cannot move forward until the US has concluded which position it will support. Everything in the BEPS 2.0 project (and other major work of the OECD, for that matter) is tied to the US electoral cycle.

## 6. Why the UN is the Preferred Location

If one looks to the future, the only body that realistically has the widespread membership of countries, the structure, the internal rules for participation and for transparency, and real legitimacy is the UN.[7] However, definitely <u>not</u> the UN Tax Committee as it is currently constituted. The 25 members of the UN Tax Committee are an impressive group and are mostly government representatives appointed as experts; it would form an excellent sub-commission on tax treaties and transfer pricing. But what is needed is a new structure, and the UN may draw on experience from the past.

---

7. This short chapter is by no means the only call for a new international, organizational architecture – see especially, Sieb Kingma, op. cit., at 415- 428.

### 6.1. Need for an Expanded Commission

There needs to be an inter-governmental commission: that is, a commission of a sufficiently large number of governments – probably 40 to 50 governments in rotation – to be able to represent the constituencies of the world and for coalitions to form between groups of governments to push forward the agenda. The UN works in many areas not through consensus but coalition-building. If there is a sufficiently wide coalition for a proposal, it will progress, even if, ultimately some countries are persistent objectors. If consensus was needed, many of the UN's most important achievements would never have reached a conclusion.

Below that inter-governmental commission, we need various expert sub-commissions coming up with new ideas, new proposals, new developments; some of them focusing on developing countries; some of them on indirect taxes; and a range of groups coming up with ideas for the inter-governmental commission to consider.

### 6.2. Secretariat and Dispute Resolution Panel

The UN-based structure might even involve a dispute resolution panel, perhaps somewhat like an international tax court. There is much to be said for the idea that we now need a dispute resolution panel for international tax issues.

The UN as the future leading body on international taxation needs a secretariat and it needs the sort of funding which is currently being spread between different organizations (with the UN currently getting very little funding and the OECD getting a much larger element of funding). The current OECD funding needs that to be transferred to the new, UN structure.

### 6.3. Full Tax Agenda

This new structure will cover the full tax agenda, have no baggage of history, follow the UN rules on transparency and participation, have clearer legitimacy, and avoid the problems presently stalling the OECD. It is rational and desirable. So, how do we get to that point? That is the question.

We may have to start with academics and others discussing this question of a new architecture. It would be sad if we had to wait until the OECD is seen by everyone to have failed before governments are prepared to move. However, we may not be very far from that point. The OECD has essentially failed to deliver on the key point of BEPS, Action Point no. 1 on taxation of the digitalized economy. If there is no agreement on Pillar 1 and Pillar 2 then the OECD knows it will have failed spectacularly. If that happens, then there will be stronger calls for a better and new architecture. Even if an agreement is reached, questions still need to be asked whether this direction of travel is the right one for all countries, and whether it is worth the effort.

## 7. Concluding Remarks

It would be rather sad to have to put off a logical development unless and until the OECD is seen to have failed; hopefully, wiser heads will say we need a better architecture. Peoples and governments must see that the current architecture is failing them. COVID-19 may be the catalyst for this to happen. Around the world, governments are incurring high levels of debt in order to deal with the COVID-19 crisis. They will need to raise large amounts of tax revenue to repay those loans and, in particular, to fund better healthcare in going forward. While governments are trying to prepare for this, the OECD is presently stuck in trying to progress its flagship project. It cannot move forward. It is waiting for the US. And when it does move forward, it will be moving forward on two pillars which involve only a limited increase in the amount of tax revenue: a few percentage points added to corporate tax revenue for countries around the world – that is the overall result of the current work.

So, are we moving towards a new world tax organization under the aegis of the UN? Potentially, yes. We need to start asking questions about the new architecture, accepting that the OECD was an historical accident, it has real limitations, and the world deserves a better international tax architecture going forward.

# REJOINDER

## Parthasarathi Shome

### 1. Introduction

The points that Baker has made in a nutshell in this excellent chapter are well-taken. He expresses concern about the dispersion of the prevailing international taxation architecture (ITA), which is currently spread across the OECD, UN, IMF and World Bank. He makes a well-considered point that the OECD's emergence as the flag holder over the UN in this field was almost an accident. His critique is regarding the OECD's so-called "consensus approach," which limits the possibilities of arriving at meaningful solutions to any issue, even while, as an organization, it possesses little democratic legitimacy. His most crucial conclusion is that, even in the G20 initiated BEPS project of the OECD, the project has been found to be focussed on and biased in favour of advanced economies. In the final analysis, it is found to be led by a single country, thus jeopardising the ITA.

Baker concludes with his view that the correct location for the ITA would be the UN, where the interests of all countries could be appropriately represented. However, Baker himself comments that there would have to be fundamental reforms within the UN structure for it to take over the function of the ITA meaningfully.

Further, the question must be asked whether, at this moment, there is any critical mass of agreement or financing to move the location of the ITA to the UN. Indeed, there is little evidence of a tight organization for moving the issue forward successfully.

### 2. Inclusive Framework and Tax Havens

Therefore, in the interim, some interesting questions and issues comprise:

(1) In what ways should the OECD's approach, style, and emphasis on functioning be changed, indeed, reformed?

(2) Can the OECD's Inclusive Framework (IF), comprising 135 countries, that was formed to take forward its work on BEPS, be useful in insisting on and initiating reform?

(3) What actions can the IF take as a single body, for example, in a composite approach, to the fifteen Actions for BEPS that the OECD proposed?

(4) Can the IF target the tax havens operating under the umbrellas of selected OECD countries themselves by openly pointing out their deleterious role in protecting international tax avoidance? It must be admitted that the European Union (EU) has been issuing lists of tax havens of its member countries; therefore, essentially, this work can and should be taken further forward by a group comprising the majority of nations such as the IF.

(5) There is some multilateral action being taken on tax havens. "The EU has taken up the tax havens issue directly over 2016-19 by issuing a code of conduct, drawing up a blacklist[8] and a grey list of offenders. Yet, not surprisingly, Oxfam, an NGO that fiercely tracks MNC misbehaviour, has given their view on it, raising issue with the EU as to why some countries were in the latter list and not the former, and why some had not been included in either list. Nevertheless, it has to be recognised that the EU is at least addressing the issue."[9]

(6) Enhanced action against tax havens would comprise bringing the entire tax haven matter into the open by the global economic community so that the role of selected OECD member countries appears in full view of the emerging economies. Otherwise, such advanced countries can continue to hide behind projects such as BEPS while effectively enabling pervasive international tax avoidance. In such a scenario, there is little bite in calling for action against tax avoidance through limited efforts such as BEPS.

In this backdrop, while awaiting cross-country agreement regarding the location of the ITA at the UN, can a global fiscal/tax organization be designed, and can the IF take the formulation of such an organization forward? Indeed, a concept has been discussed since the 1980s, one of the initiators being Tanzi.[10] Subsequently, Shome also elaborated on the concept of international tax organization.[11]

## 3. Global Tax Authority

Tanzi (1988) mooted the idea of a Global Tax Authority (GTA) some time ago. Thus, it is not altogether a new idea. But, at that point in time, the required commitment from nation-states would be enormous since it would indeed imply an intrinsic change in the ways in which governments of different political persuasions function, that is, some sacrifice of individual country sovereignty for the sake of the global good.

8. Oxfam names 18 jurisdictions that are likely to comprise the EU's updated blacklist totaling 23. They are worth identifying, namely, American Samoa, Bahrain, Cape Verde, Cook Islands, Dominica, Fiji, Grenada, Guam, Marshall Islands Morocco, Nauru, New Caledonia, Niue, Oman, Palau, Saint Kitts and Nevis, Samoa, Trinidad and Tobago, Turkey, Turks and Caicos Islands, the UAE, the US Virgin Islands, Vanuatu.

9. Parthasarathi Shome. 2019. Tax Havens and Sovereignty, *Business Standard*, November 20. https://www.business-standard.com/article/opinion/tax-havens-and-sovereignty-119112000013_1.html, (last accessed on January 8, 2021).

10. Vito Tanzi. 1988. "Forces that Shape Tax Policy," in *Tax Policy in the Twenty-First Century*, edited by Herbert Stein. New York: John Wiley and Sons.

11. Parthasarathi Shome. 1996. 'A 21st Century Global Carbon Tax', Bulletin for International Bureau of Fiscal Documentation (IBFD), Vol 50, No. 11/12, pp 481-89, November/December.

Prevailing conditions have changed in the face of repeated global economic, financial and fiscal crises. A GTA is essential now because of the proliferation of varieties of tax evasion modes, and the need to consolidate the exchange of information among tax authorities. An important advantage of such a consolidated approach would be that of the designated vehicle in the form of a GTA rather than dependence exclusively on bilateral treaties or individual countries being thrust upon with the responsibility to carry out the task for a global objective.

Evasion has continued to take various forms, including: (1) failure to file information, reports, or returns; (2) 'daisy chain' schemes involving the use of dummy companies that could claim to have paid the tax through a chain of complex paper transactions; (3) failure to pay taxes that have been already assessed or agreed upon by, say, setting up dummy corporations showing little assets; (4) filing false returns by claiming excessive use of inputs; and (5) exacerbating evasion associated with fuel excise taxes.[12] A GTA would be more able to address them based on more comprehensive information.

Therefore, a GTA would have to employ several methods both in direct and indirect tax areas. To cite a few: (1) improving regulations for screening, licensing, and bonding of taxpaying entities; (2) introducing innovative measures such as exclusive fuel colouration, in the case of fuel exports and imports,; (3) enforcing cross-border invoice requirements more thoroughly than currently; (4) developing a mechanism for carrying out selective cross-country audits; (5) continuously monitoring and practising modes of inter-administration cooperation; and (6) enforcing criminal penalties where appropriate. Though BEPS Action 13 deals with the above-mentioned (5), consolidating it under a GTA would provide a much more effective instrument for achieving it.

While it would have obvious pecuniary and opportunity costs, higher expenditure of global monies, and another international bureaucracy, its benefits should over-compensate the costs. Existing multilateral institutions whose mandates mainly comprise international monetary stabilization should not be burdened with additional tasks given the phenomenal increase in the complexities in world financial markets. A new, autonomous, and streamlined GTA deserves serious consideration.

Tanzi (2016) has continued to write on the matter, indicating that the time may have arrived for establishing a GTA that would monitor tax developments that have global implications. He elaborates on the role such an institution could play. He also

12. Arlee T. Reno, 1990. 'Measures to Curtail State Fuel Tax Evasion', National Cooperative Highway Research Program Paper No. 164, Transportation Research Board, National Research Council, Washington, DC, October.

mentions the obstacles to creating such an institution and the shape it might realistically take under the prevailing global environment.[13]

Tanzi clarifies that,

> .... a GTA would not collect taxes, although a time might come for such a role to finance global "public goods", but that would help bring order in the tax policies of countries, especially in those that have cross-countries' implications. In the absence of such an institution, some of the problems connected with unfair tax competition, with international tax avoidance, and with the "poaching" of other countries' tax bases are likely to intensify, contributing to progressively more serious macro-economic difficulties for some countries and to the reduction of some governments' ability to deal with domestic social problems.

## 4. Conclusion

To conclude, it is needless to say that immense multilateral efforts and agreements would be needed to successfully establish a GTA but, under the prevailing global, pandemic-driven fiscal crisis, there could be no better moment for all concerned countries to push in this direction. The outcome would be the reform of the ITA through a multilateral tax organization, reducing international tax avoidance, enabling the rationalisation of tax structures and promoting more efficient and streamlined country tax administrations. In turn, the reformed ITA would likely lead to improved global revenue generation that is needed to move towards closing the significant fiscal gaps prevailing in most countries.

13. Vito Tanzi. 2016. "Lakes, Oceans, and Taxes: Why the World Needs a World Tax Authority," in *Global Tax Fairness*, edited by Thomas Pogge and Krishen Mehta. Oxford Scholarship Online: Oxford University Press.
https://oxford.universitypressscholarship.com/view/10.1093/acprof:oso/9780198725343.001.0001/acprof-9780198725343, (last accessed on January 8, 2021).

# CHAPTER 4

# Retrospective Taxation and the Vodafone Case

Nigam Nuggehalli

## 1. Introduction

In 1980, the Indian government faced a peculiar situation concerning a set of tax provisions it had administered for a long time. In order to encourage industrial activity, the government had issued rules that allowed tax deductions to companies as a percentage of their deployment of capital in industrial activities. The rules laid down various conditions for the eligibility of deductions. One of these conditions stated that borrowings would not form part of the invested capital for the purpose of tax deductions (hereafter the 'no borrowing rules'). Presumably, the government did not want some clever tax planning to result in capital without real investment. Further, the government might have intended that only self-generated capital investment must be incentivized. In any case, the rules restricted borrowings from being included in the meaning of capital for purposes of the tax deductions available for industrial investment.

Unfortunately for the government, many years after the no borrowings rule was issued, some High Courts invalidated it on the basis that the rule went beyond the mandate of the parent section in the Income-tax Act, 1961 (hereafter 'the ITA') under which it was issued. The government amended the ITA to include the no borrowing rules in the parent section itself so that there was no doubt going forward. In order to sanctify its revenue assessments in the past, the amendment was made retrospective to 1972.

## 2. Retrospectivity and the Supreme Court

The retrospective nature of the amendment was challenged in the Supreme Court on the grounds that it violated the constitutional right to equality under Article 14 and the constitutional right to trade under Article 19(1)(g) of the Constitution.[1]

1. *Lohia Machine Tools v. Union of India*, MANU/SC/0153/1985.

Article 19(1)(g) prohibits the state from imposing unreasonable restrictions on a person's trade or business. The majority judgment resolved the retrospective legislation issue by denying it. They held that the rules issued under the ITA did not trespass beyond the legislative mandate of the ITA and therefore, the so-called retrospective amendment was merely clarificatory in effect.

The minority judgment written by Justice Sen addressed the retrospective issue squarely. Justice Sen held that the rules went beyond the mandate of the parent statute. Having decided that the restriction on capital investment in the rules was invalid, the follow-up question that arose was whether the curative amendment to the ITA could have a retrospective effect. Justice Sen analysed the judgments in this area which held that while the legislature was competent to enact retrospective legislation, it could not violate the fundamental rights of the taxpayers.

As stated above, there were two obvious candidates for violating fundamental rights: Article 14 and Article 19(1)(g). Justice Sen did not undertake a forensic examination of the two sections. Instead, he restricted himself to asking whether the legislative measure was unreasonable. In answering this question, Justin Sen went through a conspectus of case law that provided a facts and circumstances test in deciding whether a particular retrospective measure was unreasonable. These included the period of retrospection (indicative but not decisive), the financial hardship that the taxpayer would suffer as a result of the law turning back time, the purpose of the retrospective legislation (is the retroactive feature meant to better effectuate the objective of the statute?), and the effect of the retrospective legislation (will denying the retroactivity lead to a massive loss of government revenue).[2]

After analysing the case law, Justice Sen concluded that the tax statute in question was unreasonable. While it deprived the taxpayers of a legitimate tax deduction based on a plain reading of the statute (Justice Sen had already concluded that the parent tax statute clearly allowed the investment of borrowed capital), the state would not lose much tax revenue if the statute was applied only prospectively. Justice Sen was in the minority, but his analysis showed that a number of factors are involved in determining reasonableness in the issue of retrospective taxation, including a consideration of who is the bigger loser-the state or the taxpayer, if the legislation were to be applied retrospectively. The analysis in the *Lohia case*[3] has

2. *ibid* para 70-76. The cases referred to included *Epari Chinna Krishna Moorthy, Proprietor Epari Chinna Moorthy and Sons, Berhampur, Orissa v. State of Orissa*, MANU/SC/0256/1964, *Rai Ram Krishna and Ors v. State of Bihar* MANU/SC/0031/1963, *Jawaharlal v. State of Rajasthan and Ors*, MANU/SC/0268/1965, *Assistant Commissioner of Urban Land Tax v. The Buckingham & Carnatic Co., Ltd.* MANU/SC/0068/1969, *Krishnamurthi & Co. etc. v. State of Madras and Anr*, MANU/SC/0550/1972, *Hira Lal Rattan Lal etc. v. State of U.P.*, MANU/SC/0553/1972 and *State of Gujarat v. Ramanalal Keshuve Lal Soni*, MANU/SC/0346/1983.

3. *Lohia Machine Tools v. Union of India*, MANU/SC/0153/1985.

been followed in other cases, including, most prominently, *R.C. Tobacco Pvt. Ltd. v. Union of India.*[4]

In what follows, Section 3 of this chapter provides a context to the retrospective taxation debate through an analysis of the Vodafone case culminating in the Vodafone arbitration decision handed down by the Permanent Court of Arbitration in Hague, where the merits of retrospective legislation became a major point of consideration. The issue is complicated because the arbitration decision was based on the wording of a bilateral investment treaty (BIT) between India and The Netherlands. Section 4 analyses retrospective taxation from a comparative judicial perspective, taking into account representative judicial decisions in the United Kingdom and the United States. Section 5 concludes the discussion and points out that the peculiar circumstances of the post Vodafone retrospective legislation make for a strong case for invalidating the legislation because it was unreasonable and arbitrary.[5]

## 3. The Vodafone Case

The Indian income tax legislation taxes non-residents on a source basis, i.e., non-residents are taxed only on income with an Indian source.[6] The connection between taxability and source is meant to underscore the point that a country must have a territorial nexus with an item of income before asserting its right to tax that income. Indian source income can be uncontroversial in some instances, such as when a foreign person earns rental income from immovable property in India. But in many other instances, it is not clear if a certain item or income has an Indian source. In order to provide clarity in such cases, Section 9 of the ITA has introduced certain deeming provisions that determine whether certain items of income are Indian source income or not.

Section 9 deeming rules are synced with the scheduler system of taxation that forms the basis of the ITA. There are separate sourcing rules for business income, capital gains, and salaries. The sourcing rule for capital gains states that any income accruing or arising, whether directly or indirectly, *through* the transfer of a capital asset *situated* in India, would be deemed to have its source in India. The key phrase here is the requirement that the capital asset must be situated in India for any

4. MANU/SC/0581/2005.

5. This chapter uses 'retrospective' to refer to legislation that goes back in time. In the United States, such legislation is usually termed as 'retroactive'. In this chapter, there is no distinction made between 'retrospective' legislation and 'retroactive legislation'. The UK Chartered Institute of Taxation (CIOT) makes a distinction between these two terms on a technical basis that is not relevant to the discussion in this chapter. See Retrospective Taxation: A CIOT Discussion Paper, November 18, 2010, available at http://notoretrotax.org.uk/public-documents/F005-Notes%20on%20Retrospective%20taxation%20and%20tax%20policy%20making%20CIOT.pdf.

6. Section 5, ITA.

associated capital gain to be considered as Indian source income. A small cottage industry of tax planning was built around the idea of an asset situated in India.

To put it in a nutshell, non-residents sold shares of foreign companies (companies incorporated outside India) owning Indian companies (which in turn held significant assets in India) and claimed in their income tax returns that any capital gains accruing, as a result, did not have an Indian source because what was being transferred was a capital asset (shares in a foreign company) that was not situated in India. The argument had some plausibility because shares of foreign companies have conventionally been considered as situated outside India. However, it does look like a stretch when a foreign company holds only or substantially Indian assets, and yet a transfer of its shares is not considered as resulting in Indian source income.

When the Hutchison group sold its Indian communications business to Vodafone, the tax planning mechanism described above was adopted. Instead of Indian assets being transferred directly, what was transferred was the share capital of a Cayman Islands company that controlled the Indian assets. The Vodafone tax planning was not unusual at that time. Several multinationals had participated in similar tax planning arrangements. When the Revenue challenged Vodafone's interpretation of Section 9, the ensuing tax dispute wound itself through the Indian courts, eventually landing in the Supreme Court, the highest court of the land.[7]

The Supreme Court agreed with the interpretation preferred by Vodafone and decided that Section 9 did not allow for a territorial nexus to tax capital gains when there was a transfer of shares of a foreign company by a non-resident even if the foreign company primarily owned assets situated in India. The sum involved in the dispute was a large amount for a single taxpayer; $3.79 billion, including interest and penalties. The government was not happy with this decision and immediately brought forth legislation that overturned the Vodafone decision by adding certain 'explanations' to the ITA. These explanations, even though termed as such, were, in reality, detailed amendments to the ITA. The explanations were deemed to be part of the ITA from its inception, thus clothing them with a retrospective character even though they were supposedly explanations of extant law. The legislation also contained a validation clause that legitimatized the revenue assessment of Vodafone.[8]

Vodafone did not return to the Supreme Court to challenge the retrospective amendment. Instead, it filed an arbitration case with The Permanent Court of Arbitration (PCA) in Hague under the India-Netherlands BIT. Section 4 of the India-Netherlands BIT contains a non-discrimination clause. The clause states that 'investments of investors of each Contracting Party shall at all times be accorded fair

7. *Vodafone International Holdings B.V. v. Union of India and Anr*, [2012] 1 SCR 573.
8. For a detailed guide to the amendments, see Nikhil Mehta, 'Vodafone, Hydra and Hercules' Second Labour Revisited', GITC Review, Vol XI, No. 2 (December 2012) 83.

and equitable treatment and shall enjoy full protection and security in the territory of the other Contracting Party'. The PCA concluded that the enactment of the retrospective legislation that overturned the Vodafone decision violated the fair and equitable treatment that investors were entitled to from the Indian government. The Vodafone retrospective tax debate can be understood better through a comparative survey of the judicial treatment of retrospective taxation in the United Kingdom and in the United States, which is the subject matter of the discussion below.

## 4. Representative US and UK Case Law

Much like the *Lohia* case discussed above, the courts in both the United States and the United Kingdom adopt a facts and circumstances test that balances the hardship to the taxpayer with the public finance needs of the state. A representative case in the United States is the Supreme Court case of *Welch v. Henry*.[9] The State of Wisconsin used to allow taxpayers to deduct dividends received from corporations whose principal business was attributable to Wisconsin (on the principle that the dividends were paid out of money that had already been taxed by Wisconsin). However, subsequently, the Wisconsin legislature, in 1935, imposed a retrospective tax on these deductible dividends that had been received in 1933. The retrospective legislation was assailed on the ground that it denied equal protection (it targeted only dividends and no other types of income), and it was a violation of due process.

The Supreme Court rejected both these grounds of challenge. The equal protection argument was rejected because 'the equal protection clause does not require a State to maintain rigid rules of equal taxation, to resort to close distinctions, or to maintain a precise scientific uniformity.'[10] On the due process challenge, the Supreme court began by making the following comment on retrospective taxation:

> Taxation is neither a penalty imposed on the taxpayer nor a liability which he assumes by contract. It is but a way of apportioning the cost of government among those who in some measure are privileged to enjoy its benefits and must bear its burdens. Since no citizen enjoys immunity from that burden, its retroactive imposition does not necessarily infringe due process, and to challenge the present tax it is not enough to point out that the taxable event, the receipt of income, antedated the statute.[11]

9. 305 US 134 (1938). For an overview of the constitutionality of retrospective taxation in the United States, see Erika Lunder et al, Constitutionality of Retroactive Tax Legislation, Congressional Research Service 7-1500 (October 25, 2012).
10. *ibid* 145.
11. *ibid* 146-147.

The court went on to state that 'in each case it is necessary to consider the nature of the tax and the circumstances in which it is laid before it can be said that its retroactive application is so harsh and oppressive as to transgress the constitutional limitation.'[12] Considering that the tax was made retrospective to a relatively short period of time (two years), the Supreme Court held that there had been no violation of due process. Thus, the harsh and oppressive test puts a fairly high barrier for a challenge to retrospective taxation to succeed.

The judicial approach to retrospective taxation in the United Kingdom, while using different parameters, is on similar lines.[13] While Brexit might result in the use of different terms in the future, the current leading UK cases on the merits of retrospective taxation interpret the language of the European Convention on Human Rights because of the application of the Human Right Act, 1998. A representative example is *Huitson v. HMRC.*[14] The UK Parliament enacted retrospective legislation in order to turn back a tax planning scheme adopted under the UK-Isle of Man Tax Treaty that allowed taxpayers to escape taxation in both countries.

The retrospective tax was challenged as violative of Article 1 of Protocol No. 1 to the Convention, according to which,

> Every natural or legal person is entitled to the peaceful enjoyment of his possessions. No one shall be deprived of his possessions except in the public interest and subject to the conditions provided for by law and by the general principles of international law.
>
> The preceding provisions shall not, however, in any way impair the right of a State to enforce such laws as it deems necessary to control the use of property in accordance with the general interest or to secure the payment of taxes or other contributions or penalties.

Article 1 protects the right to property ('peaceful enjoyment of possessions'), but the protection is not absolute; it is subject to the 'public interest'. Essentially, Article 1 leads to a facts and circumstances test that balances the interests of the taxpayer with the interests of the public in arriving at a determination on an alleged violation of Article 1. In completing such an inquiry, several factors are considered, which are similar in content to those discussed in the *Lohia case*. Some of these factors are mentioned in the following summary by the UK Court of Appeal in *Huitson*:

12. *ibid* 147.
13. For a general overview of the UK legislative approach towards retrospective taxation, see A Seely, Retrospective Taxation, House of Commons Library Briefing Paper, Number 4369, August 27, 2020, available at https://commonslibrary.parliament.uk/research-briefings/sn04369/.
14. [2011] EWCA 893.

> In summary, the crucial points on examination of all the relevant circumstances of this case are that the retrospective amendments were enacted pursuant to a justified fiscal policy that was within the State's area of appreciation and discretionary judgment in economic and social matters. The legislation achieves a fair balance between the interests of the general body of taxpayers and the right of the claimant to enjoyment of his possessions, without imposing an unreasonable economic burden on him. This outcome accords with the reasonable expectations of the taxation of residents in the State on the profits of their trade or profession. The legislation prevents the DTA tax relief provisions from being misused for a purpose different from their originally intended use. There has been no conduct on the part of the State fiscal authorities that has made the retrospective application of the amended legislation to his tax affairs an infringement of his Convention rights.[15]

Notice that the Court of Appeals took a variety of factors into account: the reasonable expectations of taxpayers, the economic burden on the taxpayers, and the intended purpose of the legal provisions in question. Ultimately, the test balances the interests of the taxpayer with the interests of the state in pursuing a reasonable tax policy, keeping in mind that a certain amount of leeway must be provided to the state when it pursues a certain tax policy, including the policy of retrospective taxation. In sum, while the judicial decisions on retrospective taxation in the United Kingdom are based on a right to property, a similar facts and circumstances test is applied as can be discerned from the judicial decisions in the United States and India.

## 5. Concluding Remarks

The retrospective taxation issue in the Vodafone case can be seen from two perspectives: the constitutional prohibitions on unequal or arbitrary treatment and unreasonable restraints on trade and from the perspective of the fair and equitable treatment clause in the India-Netherlands BIT. Ultimately, as seen from the case law discussed above, the tests that judge the merits of retrospective taxation investigate the facts and circumstances of each case and balance the interests of the taxpayer on the one hand and the public exchequer on the other hand.

The balance can tilt one way or the other depending on a number of factors. The retrospective legislation can be impugned as invalid because it targets one particular taxpayer or a class of taxpayers for no rational reason, or that it imposes an unfair economic burden on a taxpayer or a class of taxpayers. Both these arguments are likely to be hard to establish in the courts. The court will usually defer to the government's reasons for imposing a retrospective tax on a certain class of taxpayers.

15. *ibid* 95.

Similarly, the enormity of the economic burden on the taxpayer is by itself unlikely to sway the balancing scales towards the taxpayer. The courts tend to look at a retrospective tax as a legitimate way to raise public finances. [16]

Nevertheless, on balance, this author believes that retrospective taxation in the Vodafone case imposed an unreasonable burden on Vodafone. There are several factors in favour of Vodafone. First, the legislation resulted, through a validating clause, in overturning a verdict regarding a specific taxpayer after the highest court of the land had given a decision in that taxpayer's favour. Second, Vodafone was the buyer of the property, not the seller. Under the ITA, the buyer of a property in certain situations is supposed to withhold the capital gains tax applicable to the seller of the property. Vodafone took the position that there was no tax payable and, therefore, did not withhold any tax. Vodafone's position was vindicated by the Supreme Court decision. By imposing a retrospective tax, which included interest and penalties on Vodafone for non-withholding, the government is trying to hold Vodafone liable for something that even the Supreme Court recognized was not the legal duty of Vodafone. Third, the purpose of the ITA sourcing rules will not be thwarted if the amendments were made prospective in nature. It is not as if international investments will stop flowing post the amendments if the amendments were not made retrospective in nature. On the contrary, it is Vodafone that would be affected by the huge tax bill because of the retrospective amendment.

Finally, there is another important reason that would weigh the scales in favour of Vodafone. There were hardly any reasons provided for the retrospective application of the 2012 amendments. In *Tata Motors Ltd. v. State of Maharashtra*,[17] the Supreme Court struck down a legislation that had been retrospective for a certain period without any accompanying reasons. In the case of the post-Vodafone 2012 amendments, the only reasons proffered were that the amendments were a reaction to 'certain judicial pronouncements' that had 'created doubts about the scope and purpose of Sections 9'.[18] The amendments were offered as a means to 'provide clarificatory retrospective amendment to restate the legislative intent in respect of scope and applicability of section 9 and 195 and also to make other clarificatory amendments for providing certainty in law.'[19]

The reasons provided for the amendment are, in reality, no reasons at all. The 'certain judicial pronouncement' refers to the Supreme Court decision in the Vodafone case. The Supreme Court decision did not create a doubt about the scope

16. See Saul Levmore, 'The Case for Retroactive Taxation', Journal of Legal Studies Vol XXII (June 1993) 265, for an analysis of the advantages of retrospective legislation.
17. MANU/SC/0464/2004.
18. 'Finance Bill, 2012: Provisions Relating to Direct Taxes', p 19, available at https://www.indiabudget.gov.in/budget2012-2013/ub2012-13/mem/mem1.pdf.
19. *ibid.*

and purpose of Section 9; in fact, it helped clarify a dispute about its application between the taxpayer and the government. The amendments could not be reasonably thought of as clarificatory, since there was some uncertainty in the interpretation of Section 9 before the amendment (uncertainty that led to a protracted dispute that went all the way to the Supreme Court), and the amendments are quite a radical overhaul of the notions of property and nexus. Given these elements of the retrospective amendment, the explanation for the amendment was quite misleading and therefore failed to provide a rationale for the amendments. The retrospective amendments were arbitrary in nature, and were, in reality, meant mainly to reinstate the capital gains tax on Vodafone.

When the Indian government decided to amend the India-Mauritius Double Tax Avoidance Agreement (DTAA) to enable India to tax capital gains sourced in India, it did so prospectively from April 1, 2017.[20] Further, a more liberal capital gains regime was put in place for a couple of years following the amendment. The Indian government's approach to the Mauritius-India DTAA was in stark contrast to its approach towards Vodafone, where it imposed a controversial and substantial tax by going back in time.[21] On the whole, the retrospective tax in the *Vodafone* case was an unreasonable exercise of retrospective legislative powers by the Indian state.

20. Protocol Amending the Convention Between the Government of the Republic of India and Government of Mauritius, Article 4 (amending Article 13 of the Convention), available at https://www.incometaxindia.gov.in/Communications/Notification/Notification682016.PDF.

21. The draft report of the Parthsarathi Shome Committee on the retrospective legislative amendments made in response to the Vodafone case stated that retrospective taxation ought to be imposed only in exceptional circumstances to correct obvious statutory mistakes or make genuine clarifications, or to close down highly abusive transactions. A copy of the report is available here: https://itatonline.org/info/download-draft-shome-committee-report-on-vodafone-retrospective-law/.

## REJOINDER

### Parthasarathi Shome

A crucial challenge of tax design is how adversely it may affect business decisions and, therefore, a country's GDP. A concern that emerges strongly from Nigam is that legal constructs around retrospective taxation contradict "common sense" in the framing of tax law. And retrospective taxation can affect business decision-making adversely and severely. Let me explain.

Say a business decides to invest in year *t* after taking into account its risk preferences. If say in *t*+5, after five years of its investment decision and during full-fledged operation, the government declares that the tax law has now been changed but that it will be applied from five years prior to the present day, that is from year *t*. Then the basis of the original investment crumbles. Effectively, the government informs the business investor today in time *t*+5 that the law five years back in time *t* was actually different from what had been written down as the law in time *t*.

Such retrospectivity in taxation renders a business decision to invest, taken in the past, untenable. If unanticipated taxes have to be paid in significant amounts at a time in the future, then the earlier cost, income, and profit calculations are rendered baseless. This leads to what I term as an "impossibility to perform".[22] The impact goes beyond any risk planned or accounted for by the investor. Though he can assess risk based on his "attitude towards risk", a retrospective tax takes the investor into a realm of "uncertainty", about which he possesses little ability to assess. He is thus robbed of a planned approach to business decision-making and management.

Yet certain tax jurisdictions have tended to use this route through the redefined legal interpretation of the law with the objective of capturing revenue already lost. This fundamentally opposes taxpayer rights that should be protected in taxpayer charters. On the other hand, if taxpayers, in particular MNEs, indulge in sustained tax avoidance by taking advantage of loopholes available in different tax statutes worldwide, global authorities can intervene and install detailed reporting requirements and mechanisms for the exchange of information amongst themselves.

MNEs have complained that retrospective legislation leads to scaling back or withdrawal of investments in such jurisdictions. And such withdrawal can be brisk reflecting the high mobility of international capital. What is often missed is that lower investment leads to lower economic growth and, therefore, to lower tax revenue collection. And the deleterious effects on growth could be near-permanent, rather than merely transitory.

22. Government of India. 2012. Expert Committee Report on Retrospective Amendments Relating to Indirect Transfers. New Delhi: Ministry of Finance.

The impact on economic growth should be a compulsory aspect of the training of tax officers, setting aside the usual practice of keeping it outside their area of concern. It is ironic that policymakers express concern about and attempt to measure GDP growth rates constantly. Yet, their tax officials remain oblivious of how their push for certain matters of tax legislation and their implementation are directly in contradiction to economic growth. International taxation does not comprise the daily concern of policymakers who, upon being elected, may suddenly find themselves having to deal with the intricacies of international taxation. They may not possess the wherewithal of pushing strongly, when needed, against their tax officials.

Therefore, if tax law is not designed to protect against significant setback in economic growth, for example, if retrospective taxation is introduced to suit an administration's will, taxpayers are bound to express dissatisfaction eventually. And, if the judiciary is unbiased, the courts are likely to interpret the law in taxpayers' favour. Usually, however, tax laws are prospective and provide protection from both retroactivity (transactions completed) and retrospectivity (transactions in progress) to taxpayers.

These issues have assumed significance, in particular, in the context of India's recent declining GDP experience (see Shome, Chapter 1) to combat which increasing investment, including foreign direct investment (FDI) is crucial. To expect investment—both domestic and foreign—to increase on a large scale while a regime of retrospective application of tax law rages is folly. Unless this policy is reined in through changes in the law, and only prospective application of tax changes is assured, tax will continue to determine GDP, rather than tax being the outcome of GDP and GDP growth.

Several authors in this volume have made efforts to bring the issue of retrospective taxation to the attention of policymakers over the last decade. Their work has been cited in ongoing academic work, court judgments, and international arbitral awards, including in the just published Cairn versus Government of India arbitral award which has cited Baker and Shome exhaustively. They are excerpted in Appendices 1 and 2. That work will continue until the issue of retrospective taxation causing impossibility for businesses to perform is resolved.

# Appendix 1

## References to Philip Baker in *Cairn v. Republic of India* Award

Previous work and roles of the author have been referred to exhaustively in subsequent discussions on retrospective taxation including in the just published Cairns arbitral award document: Philip Baker (in pages 280, 281, 468, 497, 502, 503, 504). These are elaborated below.

### Page 280

This distinction is similar to one proposed by English tax barrister Philip Baker QC, for tax legislation:[23]

> "Retroactive legislation" refers to legislation, which imposes a tax burden, or a higher tax burden, on income that has already been earned, or a gain that has already been realised, or an inheritance that has already been received (etc.). It is concerned with the scenario, therefore, where at the time that income was earned (etc.), there was no tax burden under the law at that time, or a lower tax burden, and the retroactive legislation imposes a burden or a higher one.

This may be contrasted with "retrospective legislation" which imposes a tax burden, or a higher tax burden, on future income (or gains or inheritance [...]) from a transaction which has already been completed.

### Page 281

Notably, neither Party has attempted to define what the terms "retroactive" and "retrospective" mean in Indian law. This is so despite the fact that, in its earlier briefs, the Respondent took issue with the Claimants' use of these terms, and in particular with its reliance on Baker's definition quoted above. In its Rejoinder, the Respondent argued that "the Claimants seek to use the terms 'clarificatory' 'retroactive', [and] 'retrospective' in a vacuum disconnected from Indian constitutional law, as if they had an independent and universal meaning assessment [...]."[24] Yet, the Respondent itself did not attempt to define what these terms mean in Indian constitutional law. It merely noted, as the Claimants already had, that the distinction proposed by Baker was "hardly universal",[25] and argued that the Claimants could not rely on the Finance Minister's or the Shome Committee's characterization of the 2012 Amendment as "retrospective" because "Parliament is endowed with plenary powers of legislation, and it is competent to

23. Philip Baker QC, "Retroactive Tax Legislation", 2012, 6(48) International Taxation 780, CLA-60, p 780.

24. R-Rejoinder, ¶ 502.

25. R-Rejoinder, ¶ 503(c), citing C-SoC, ¶ 332.

legislate with prospective or retrospective effect and such power to legislate retrospectively is upheld by the Courts",[26] and because there is no "undefined customary international law standard of taxation."[27] However, these arguments go to the legitimacy of the retroactivity/retrospectivity, and not to its meaning. And while the Respondent did make submissions on the general meaning of these terms in its Answers to the Tribunal's Questions, it did not do so on the basis of Indian constitutional law.

## Page 467-468

So far as the record of this proceeding shows, to date, there has been no determination as to the constitutionality or not of the 2012 Amendment by any Indian court. Despite this, the Tribunal has examined the caselaw filed in this proceeding (although it has not received any expert opinion on the constitutional question) and has reviewed the general rules and principles that the Indian courts have used to deal with retroactive amendments of the tax laws. As in Indian tax and corporations law, there is considerable English law influence in the general approach to retroactivity. But in one material respect, namely in the application of its Constitution, Indian law appears to afford a further protection against retroactivity to the taxpayer than does English law.[28]

---

26. R-Rejoinder, ¶ 503(a), citing Expert Committee, Draft Report on Retrospective Amendments Relating to Indirect Transfer (2012), Exh. C-56, p 30.
27. R-Rejoinder, ¶ 503(b), citing C-SoC, ¶ 298.
28. The Tribunal has observed that there is some consistency of approach in the legal systems of the two States party to the BIT. Both countries adhere to the doctrine of Parliamentary supremacy, which requires the courts to give effect to Parliament's will. Hence the common law of both countries have developed various interpretative rules to attempt to rein in an apparent excess of retroactive effect. For example, in *L'Office Cherifien des Phosphates v. Yamashita-Shinnion Steamship Co Ltd.* [1994] 1 AC 486 (HL), Lord Mustill formulated the test as being: "whether the consequences of reading the statute with the suggested degree of retrospectivity are so unfair that the words used by Parliament cannot have been intended to means what they might appear to say." (Lord Mustill at p 525, quoted in David Williams in CLA-381, Hans Gribnau, Melvin Pauwels, *Retroactivity of Tax Legislation*, (EATLP International Tax Series, 2013), p 397. In addition, in England and Wales, Parliament itself has, through the *Interpretation Act, 1968*, section 16, set out a series of presumptions to soften the rigour of legislation that repeals prior legislation. See in this respect, Williams at pp. 390-391.

    The Supreme Court of India adverted to the issue of parliamentary supremacy in *Govinddas v. Income Tax Officer*, MANU/SC/0248/1975 : (1976) 1 SCC 906, a case cited with approval in *Vatika Township Private Ltd.*, (2015) 1 SCC 1, Exh. R-26:

    The general rule as stated by Halsbury in Vol. 36 of the Laws of England (3rd Edn.) and reiterated in several decisions of this Court as well as English courts is that all statutes other than those which are merely declaratory or which relate only to matters of procedure or of evidence are prima facie prospectively [sic] and retrospective operation should not be given to a statute so as to affect, alter or destroy an existing right or create a new liability or obligation unless that effect

[Footnote No. 28 contd.]

## Page 497-98

In this connection, the Tribunal found some assistance in Philip Baker QC's short discussion of retroactive tax legislation, in which he discussed the treatment of such legislation by different countries and under international human rights conventions such as Article 1 of the First Protocol to the European Convention on Human Rights ("ECHR").[29]

Noting that retroactivity and retrospectivity in tax legislation "both undermine legitimate expectations where the taxpayer has either anticipated a particular tax outcome for previously earned income, or, in the case of retrospective legislation, anticipates a particular future outcome," Baker accepts that neither is objectionable "where the taxpayer, viewed realistically, had no legitimate expectation of the previous outcome", i.e., "where the avoidance was so abusive that no reasonable taxpayer, properly advised, could have had a legitimate expectation of enjoying the fruits of the avoidance."[30] (Based on what the Tribunal has already found, Baker's test, the "no reasonable taxpayer, properly advised, could have had a legitimate expectation of enjoying the fruits of the avoidance" test, has not been transgressed in the present case such that a basis for permissible retroactive legislation would be met.)

In his concluding comments, Baker made an observation of relevance to the legislative reaction to the Supreme Court's judgment in *Vodafone*:

> Retroactive tax legislation which fails to grandfather final and binding court decisions is a clear breach of human rights norms: it infringes the right to a fair

**[Footnote No. 28 contd.]**

cannot be avoided without doing violence to the language of the enactment. If the enactment is expressed in language which is fairly capable of either interpretation, it ought to be construed as prospective only.

However, unlike the United Kingdom, India has a written constitution that protects certain fundamental freedoms. The courts are thus empowered to strike down legislation if it breaches a citizen's constitutional rights. In this sense, the Indian courts have a broader power to control retroactive legislation than do the English courts. In the United Kingdom, in addition to the Rees Principles employed by Parliament as a "policy base" and the March 2011 "protocol" applicable to retroactive or retrospective tax announcements (see Exh, CLA-60, **Phillip Baker QC**, "Retroactive Tax Legislation" at 781 in this respect), the English courts have employed human rights conventions to which the UK is a party as a check on parliamentary supremacy. But short of the protection that international law affords, as Williams noted, when discussing the "Reasons for lack of judicial limits to retroactivity," the position under English law is simple: "Parliament is sovereign." See David Williams' chapter on the United Kingdom in CLA-381, Hans Gribnau, Melvin Pauwels, *Retroactivity of Tax Legislation*, (EATLP International Tax Series, No. 9, 2013), 389 at 397. In India, by contrast, Parliament is the ultimate interpreter of its own acts, but that power is subject to judicial supervision under the Constitution.

29. Philip Baker QC, "Retroactive Tax Legislation", 6(48) International Taxation 780 (June 2012), CLA-60, p 781.
30. *Id.*

> trial and the right to enjoyment of possessions, or the freedom from arbitrary misappropriation. It is a failure to respect the rule of law, and therefore contrary to the principles of law recognised by all civilised nations...[31]

This statement is of course of greatest relevance to the situation in which the successful litigant, Vodafone, found itself, but Baker's comment has salience for other foreign investors which, like Vodafone, structured their exits from India based on an understanding of the meaning and application of Section 9(1)(i) that the Supreme Court later confirmed. The Tribunal considers that the change to the reach of Section 9(1)(i) after the Supreme Court issued a definitive interpretation of the provision, made retroactive to 1962, not only directly affected Vodafone but also adversely affected other foreign investors such as Cairn which had similarly ordered their affairs in line with the view that the law applicable at the time of their transactions did not reach indirect transfers.

## Page 502

This is the approach towards retroactive taxation under Article 1 of Protocol 1 of the ECHR. The Baker article, to which the Tribunal has previously referred, concludes, after analysing the ECHR's jurisprudence on retroactive taxation, that:

> Such [retroactive tax] legislation is not per se an infringement of the Convention. However, it will be zealously scrutinized to ensure that it can be justified. *The government concerned will need to show why the objective could only be attained by introducing retrospective provisions.*[32]

## Page 503-04

<u>*Combatting abusive practices*</u>: A major justification invoked in respect of retroactive taxation is the State's power to combat tax abuse.[33] In particular, where taxpayers exploit an inadvertent legislative loophole in a manner that is abusive and manifestly contrary to the object and purpose of the tax law, the State may be justified to close such a loophole with a retroactive effect and without breaching its own law or applicable international law. The specific purpose that this retroactivity achieves in such a case is to discourage and prevent a future abusive utilisation of similar loopholes by taxpayers. In other words, the legislator is warning taxpayers that

31. *Id.,* p 784.
32. Philip Baker, "Retrospective tax legislation and the European Convention on Human Rights", (British Tax Review, 2005), RLA-291, p 8 (emphasis added).
33. Philip Baker, "Retrospective tax legislation and the European Convention on Human Rights", (British Tax Review, 2005), RLA-291; Hans Gribnau, Melvin Pauwels, *Retroactivity of Tax Legislation* (EATLP International Tax Series, 2013), CLA-381, see, e.g., for UK – RLA-282, for Germany – RLA-302, S. 3.8.5.2., for Italy - RLA-303, S. 3.11.4.1, for The Netherlands – RLA-304, S. 3.13.2.2.J.W.

actively seeking and exploiting tax loopholes does not pay off, since the State may shut them off with retroactive effect and the taxpayers will not benefit, even temporarily, from their own wrongful conduct. In addition to this specific public purpose, retroactive taxation of abusive transactions is also less intrusive on taxpayers' interests of legal certainty and predictability, since taxpayers that actively engage in abusive practices can hardly have a legitimate interest to benefit from their conduct.[34]

The European Commission of Human Rights expressed similar views when scrutinising the permissibility of the UK's retroactive taxation of transactions whereby solicitors entered into sham partnership agreements with their clients (commodity futures dealers) in order to offset the trading loss against the solicitors' earnings. The Commission held that the retroactive legislation "was enacted to counteract a specific form of tax avoidance", and that "the only way in which this particular form of artificial tax avoidance could be combatted effectively was by making s. 31 retrospective."[35]

*Correcting inadvertent technical errors*: According to the ECtHR, "[t]here is in fact an obvious and compelling public interest to ensure that private entities do not enjoy the benefit of a windfall in a changeover to a new tax- payment regime and do not deny the Exchequer revenue simply on account of inadvertent defects in the enabling legislation".[36]

34. Philip Baker QC, "Retroactive Tax Legislation", 6(48) International Taxation 780 (June 2012), CLA-60, p 781.

35. A, B, C and D v. UK, quoted at Philip Baker, "Retrospective tax legislation and the European Convention on Human Rights", (British Tax Review, 2005), RLA-291.

36. Philip Baker, "Retrospective tax legislation and the European Convention on Human Rights", (British Tax Review, 2005), RLA-291, p 4.

## Appendix 2

## References of Parthasarathi Shome in *Cairn v. Republic of India* Award

As in the case of Baker, Shome's previous work and roles have been referred to in many discussions on retrospective taxation including in the just published Cairns arbitral award document: Parthasarathi Shome (in pages xi, 40, 213, 214, 220, 252, 255, 281, 289, 294, 295, 296, 297, 303, 490 and 500) either directly or through committee or commission chairmanships. These are elaborated below.

### Page xi:

| Shome Committee | Committee led by Dr Parthasarathi Shome to examine the implications of the 2012 Amendment |
|---|---|

### Page 40

On 30 July 2012, the Prime Minister appointed a special tax expert committee (the "Shome Committee") to examine the implications of the 2012 Amendment. The committee was led by Dr. Parthasarathi Shome, an advisor to the Finance Minister. The Shome Committee issued its draft report on 1 October 2012.[37]

In May 2014, an expert group (consisting of Dr Parthasarathi Shome and former government officials) which had been tasked with "address[ing] the thus-far missing elements of best practices in tax administration in a comprehensive manner"[38] 'eleased the "First Report of the Tax Administration Reform Commission" (the "TARC Report"). Amongst many of its observations, the committee indicated a series of "major fault lines in the tax administration", and commented on the 2012 Amendment.[39]

### Page 213 -14

According to the Claimants, the retroactive nature of the 2012 Amendment is confirmed by (i) the history of the ITA 1961, (ii) the Supreme Court's interpretation of Section 9(1)(i) in Vodafone, (iii) statements by the Finance Minister who promoted the 2012 Amendment, (iv) the analysis of special tax committees tasked by the Indian Government to assess the impact of the 2012 Amendment, and (v) the fact that the Government of India felt the need to further

37. Expert Committee, Draft Report on Retrospective Amendments Relating to Indirect Transfer (2012), Exh. C-56.
38. C-SoC, ¶ 235; Tax Administration Reform Commission, First Report of the Tax Administration Reform Commission, *Tax Administration Reform in India: Spirit, Purpose and Empowerment,* May 30, 2014 ("TARC Report"), Exh. C-137, p ii.
39. *Id.*, pp 6, 249.

amend or clarify the 2012 Finance Act because of the Amendment's unanticipated effects.

First, the Claimants emphasise that, for nearly 50 years (from the enactment of the ITA 1961 until 2007, when the ITD launched its "test case" against Vodafone), "no serious suggestion had ever been made that Section 9(1)(i) could be interpreted to tax indirect transfers by non-residents."[40] According to the Claimants, there is no evidence that this was the legislature's original intent, nor was this interpretation ever suggested in the ensuing decades until the *Vodafone* case.[41] The Claimants rely in particular on comments made by the Shome Committee,[42] the legislative history of the ITA 1960,[43] comments made by the 2002 Task Force,[44] and by the amendments proposed by the new direct tax codes that the MoF attempted to introduce in 2009 and 2010 (the DTC 2009 and DTC 2010).

Fourth, according to the Claimants, all three special tax committees appointed by the Indian Government after the 2012 amendment (specifically, the Shome Committee, the TARC Committee, and the Damodaran Committee) acknowledged "without any ambiguity" that the 2012 Amendment did not clarify existing obligations, but rather created new ones and imposed them retroactively.[45]

## Page 219-20

More specifically, the Claimants assert that "the Respondent's actions breached every conceivable strand of the FET standard, any one of which would breach Article 3(2) of the Treaty"[46], as follows:

Stability: Citing the Supreme Court of India, the Claimants submit that "[c]ertainty and stability form the basic foundation of any fiscal system".[47] The Claimants contend that the Respondent breached its obligation of stability "by making an 'overnight change' in Indian tax law that had 'held ground for decades', leaving 'tax officials to rake up settled positions'."[48] Citing the Shome Committee, the Claimants argue that "[t]he language and scope of the amendments led [...] to

40. C-SoC, ¶ 308.
41. *Id.*, ¶¶ 309-311.
42. *Id.*, ¶ 308; C-PHB, ¶ 70, citing Expert Committee, Draft Report on Retrospective Amendments Relating to Indirect Transfer (2012), Exh. C-56, p 33.
43. *d.*, ¶ 310, referring to Legislative Assembly Debate dated 13 March 1947, Exh. C-113, p 1897; Legislative Assembly Debate, April 7, 1947, Exh. C-114, p 3029.
44. *Id.*, ¶ 311, citing Task Force on Direct Taxes, Report of the Task Force on Direct Taxes (December 2002), Exh. C-133, p 56.
45. C-SoC, ¶ 315.
46. *Id.*, ¶ 599.
47. C-Updated Reply, ¶ 599, citing *Vodafone International Holdings B.V. v. Union of India & Anr,* [2012] 6 SCC 613, Exh. C-59, ¶ 91.
48. *Ibid.*, citing TARC Report, Exh. C-137, p 249, V.3.e.

apprehensions about the certainty, predictability and stability of tax laws in India", and that "[t]he legislation with retrospective application in particular obviating an earlier Supreme Court decision on the matter of indirect transfer was not expected."[49]

## Page 252

Third, the Respondent contends that "the Claimants' case boils down to an argument that the 2012 Amendments were bad policy."[50] Indeed, the Claimants rely on the Shome Committee Report and the Damodaran Report, which considered the desirability of retrospective legislation from a policy perspective, and on policy statements of past and present Finance Ministers.[51] However, the Claimants themselves recognise that they cannot challenge India's policy decisions.[52] According to the Respondent, this concession "wholly undermines the Claimants' claims", because "[t]he function of this Tribunal is not to adjudicate the wisdom of policy and its effect on encouraging or discouraging foreign investment", which would be "beyond the Tribunal's authority."[53]

## Page 255

Reasonableness: the Claimants have not pleaded in their pre-hearing submissions that the 2012 Clarification was in any way "unreasonable", and it is not open to the Tribunal to find for the Claimants on that basis. In any event, according to the Respondent, this is a simple requirement – which one can also see at play in domestic administrative law systems – that the measure must bear a "reasonable relationship to some rational policy".[54] When applying this standard, the Tribunal must pay proper respect and deference to the sovereignty of the host State, and not simply substitute its own judgment to that of the elected government of the host State. The Tribunal should thus give no value to the Claimants' heavy reliance on several reports that have criticized the 2012 Amendment on the basis of policy.[55]

---

49. *Ibid.*, citing Expert Committee, Final Report on Retrospective Amendments relating to Indirect Transfer (2012), Exh. C-376, p 4.
50. *Id.*, ¶ 474.
51. *Ibid.*
52. *Id.*, ¶ 475, citing C-Updated Reply, ¶¶ 17, 38-39.
53. *Id.*, ¶ 476.
54. *Saluka Investments BV v. Czech Republic*, UNCITRAL, Partial Award, March 17, 2006, CLA-44, ¶ 460.
55. Expert Committee, Final Report on Retrospective Amendments Relating to Indirect Transfer dated 2012 ("Shome Report"), Exh. C-376; Report of the Committee for Reforming the Regulatory Environment for Doing Business in India submitted September 2, 2013 ("Damodaran Report"), Exh. C-136; TARC Report, Exh. C-137.

## Page 281

Notably, neither Party has attempted to define what the terms "retroactive" and "retrospective" mean in Indian law. This is so despite the fact that, in its earlier briefs, the Respondent took issue with the Claimants' use of these terms, and in particular with its reliance on Baker's definition quoted above. In its Rejoinder, the Respondent argued that "the Claimants seek to use the terms 'clarificatory' 'retroactive', [and] 'retrospective' in a vacuum disconnected from Indian constitutional law, as if they had an independent and universal meaning assessment [...]."[56] Yet, the Respondent itself did not attempt to define what these terms mean in Indian constitutional law. It merely noted, as the Claimants already had, that the distinction proposed by Baker was "hardly universal",[57] and argued that the Claimants could not rely on the Finance Minister's or the Shome Committee's characterization of the 2012 Amendment as "retrospective" because "Parliament is endowed with plenary powers of legislation, and it is competent to legislate with prospective or retrospective effect and such power to legislate retrospectively is upheld by the Courts",[58] and because there is no "undefined customary international law standard of taxation."[59] However, these arguments go to the legitimacy of the retroactivity/retrospectivity, and not to its meaning. And while the Respondent did make submissions on the general meaning of these terms in its Answers to the Tribunal's Questions, it did not do so on the basis of Indian constitutional law.

## Page 289-90

There is no evidence of an intent that the fourth limb of Section 9(1)(i) should bear a meaning other than its natural meaning, either in 1946, 1956 or 1961. To the contrary, the record suggests that indirect transfers by non-residents were not discussed in the relevant parliamentary debates at that time.[60] Nor, as the Shome Committee later concluded, is there evidence of such an intent in the ITA 1961 itself. After noting that "[t]he retrospective amendments carried through Finance Act, 2012 relating to indirect transfer have been specified by the Government as clarificatory in nature and as a restatement of the legislative intent", the Shome Committee "analyse[d] various provisions of the [ITA 1961] to see if there is any indication of such legislative intent in the past."[61] The Committee concluded that the various provisions of the ITA 1961 "clearly show not only the absence of any

56. R-Rejoinder, ¶ 502.
57. R-Rejoinder, ¶ 503(c), citing C-SoC, ¶ 332.
58. R-Rejoinder, ¶ 503(a), citing Expert Committee, Draft Report on Retrospective Amendments Relating to Indirect Transfer (2012), Exh. C-56, p 30.
59. R-Rejoinder, ¶ 503(b), citing C-SoC, ¶ 298.
60. Legislative Assembly Debate, 13 March 1947, Exh. C-113, p 1897; and Legislative Assembly Debate, April 7, 1947, Exh. C-114, p 3029.
61. Shome Committee Report, Exh. C-56, p 30.

evidence proving that these retrospective amendments are clarificatory in nature but also demonstrate lack of any legislative intent of taxation of capital gains arising on account of indirect transfer."[62]

## Page 294-95

The Shome Committee's conclusions are particularly relevant. The Shome Committee, which was led by Dr Parthasarathi Shome (an advisor to the Finance Minister), was tasked, inter alia, with examining "the implications of amendment made to the Income Tax Act, 1961 (the Act) relating to the taxation of non-resident transfer of assets where the underlying asset is in India, particularly in the context of the tax liability of portfolio investors and Foreign Institutional Investors (FIIs)."[63]

The Shome Committee explained that "[r]etrospective amendments" could be of the following types "(i) to correct apparent mistakes/anomalies in the Statute"; "(ii) to remove technical defects, particularly in procedure, which had vitiated the substantive law"; "(iii) to 'protect' the tax base from highly abusive tax planning schemes that have the main purpose of avoiding tax, without economic substance"; and "(iv) to 'expand' the tax base."[64] The Committee went on to say that:

> Retrospective amendments as mentioned at (i) & (ii) are necessary and fair as they do not create any additional burden on the taxpayer. Retrospective amendments at (iii) above may also be justified as any avoidance of tax through exploitation of any loophole in the system means a windfall to a dishonest taxpayer at the cost of general body of the taxpayers. However, retrospective amendment as mentioned at (iv) is against the basic tenet of the law as it affects the certainty of law.[65]

The Committee thus recommended that "retrospective application of tax law should occur in exceptional cases, and exclusively to address types (i), (ii) & (iii) above", and "should be confined to matters that are genuinely of a clarificatory nature, or to 'protect' the tax base by countering highly abusive tax planning schemes, rather than 'expand' the tax base".[66] It is the Tribunal's understanding that this statement is about good policies and best practices and not about the validity of a Statute that would be retroactive, which is a different question. However, the Shome Committee does distinguish between what it would consider to be clarificatory and what would be considered to be in effect changing the reach of an existing taxing Statute.

62. *Id.*, p 33.
63. Shome Committee Report, Exh. C-56, p 12.
64. *Id.*, p 30.
65. *Ibid.*
66. *Ibid.*

## Page 296

The Tax Administration Reform Commission ("TARC"), another expert group chaired by Dr. Shome (which had been mandated post 2012 "to review the application of tax policies and tax laws in the context of global best practices and to recommend measures for reforms required in tax administration to enhance its effectiveness and efficiency"[67]) reached a similar conclusion. The TARC characterized the 2012 Amendment as a "retrospective amendment" introduced to counter a prior interpretation by the judiciary, noting that it had caused an "overnight change" in the interpretation of a provision:

> Retrospective amendments have further undermined the trust between taxpayers and the tax administration. Many seem to feel that it has become the order of the day. Many of the retrospective amendments have been introduced to counter interpretation in favour of the taxpayer upheld earlier by the judiciary. <u>The most famous is the introduction of provisions for taxation of 'indirect transfer' with effect from April 1, 196[2], to overrule a Supreme Court judgement which held that Indian tax authorities did not have territorial jurisdiction to tax offshore transactions, and therefore, the taxpayer was not liable to withhold the taxes. An overnight change in the interpretation of a provision, which earlier held ground for decades,</u> provides scope for tax officials to rake up settled positions. This approach to retrospective amendments has resulted in protracted disputes, apart from having deeply harmful effects on investment sentiment and the macro economy.[68]

## Page 297

The Respondent has argued that these committees were asked to look at issues of policy and were not tasked with assessing the constitutionality or validity of the 2012 Amendment. While this is undisputed, it does not deny their factual conclusion (at least in the case of the Shome Committee and TARC) that the 2012 Amendment was not clarificatory in nature or constituted a change in the content of the law. The Tribunal does not employ these documents for their policy statements or recommendations; it is concerned only with their determinations that the 2012 Amendment effected a change in the law and did so retroactively.

## Page 303

In making this finding, the Tribunal is aware that even the most experienced advisors are not immune from making mistakes and the mere fact that an advisor does not qualify his/her advice is not dispositive of the question. The judgments of

67. TARC Report, Exh. C-137, p ii.
68. *Id.*, p 249 (emphasis added).

courts around the world are replete with examples where taxpayers, even with the advice of leading law and accounting firms, have been found to have run afoul of a country's tax laws. But here, the Tribunal is not considering RSM's advice in a vacuum; as already seen in the Tribunal's discussion of the Shome Committee and the TARC, as well as Explanations 6 and 7, the consideration of RSM's advice forms only a part of a much fuller factual context. The key point is that RSM's advice, terse as it might have been, was consistent with that other evidence, and, as shall be seen below, is consistent with the Tribunal's own view of the meaning of Section 9(1)(i) – a view which the Tribunal shares with no less an authority than the Supreme Court of India.

## Page 490

As the Parties acknowledge, the principle of legal certainty is particularly relevant in the context of retroactive legislation.[69] The Claimants submit that "retroactive legislation that imposes fresh obligations in respect of past events is fundamentally contrary to the very essence and purpose of the rule of law."[70] They add that "[f]undamental to the rule of law is the recognition that citizens should be able to understand the obligations and sanctions that the legal system imposes on them and to rely on clear rules to guide their actions. Retroactive laws that change the legal consequences of past transactions are inimical to this norm because they deny individuals the ability to conform their conduct to the law and to forecast the benefits or penalties associated with their actions."[71] While they acknowledge that not all retroactivity is wrongful, they argue (citing the Shome Committee) that "retrospective application of tax law should occur in exceptional or rarest of rare cases, and with particular objectives".[72] According to the Shome Committee, only the following types of retroactive laws are acceptable: "those that

(1) correct apparent mistakes/anomalies of the statute;

(2) remove technical defects, particularly in procedure, which had vitiated the substantive law;

(3) protect the tax base from highly abusive tax planning schemes that have the main purpose of avoiding tax, without economic substance; and

(4) [are meant to] expand the tax base."[73]

---

69. Melvin Pauwels, "Retroactive and Retrospective Tax Legislation", (2013), ¶ 2.2.4.1, in Hans Gribnau, Melvin Pauwels, *Retroactivity of Tax Legislation* (EATLP International Tax Series, 2013), CLA-381.

70. C-SoC, ¶¶ 294, 325.

71. *Id.*, ¶ 329.

72. *Id.*, ¶ 333, citing Expert Committee, Draft Report on Retrospective Amendments Relating to Indirect Transfer (2012), Exh. C-56, p 30.

73. *Ibid.*

## Page 500

As to the Respondent's argument that retroactivity is legitimate under Indian law, as the Respondent itself recognises, this is only the case if certain constitutional limitations are met. As discussed above, even absent a specific commitment from the State, an investor in India is entitled to trust that, as a general rule, the law will apply prospectively. Even where retroactive legislation is arguably frequent, as the Respondent contends is the case in India, retroactive legislation requires a specific justification. As the Shome Committee recognised, the "retrospective application of tax law should occur in exceptional or rarest of rare cases, and with particular objectives".[74]

74. 2244 Expert Committee, Draft Report on Retrospective Amendments Relating to Indirect Transfer (2012), Exh. C-56, p 30.

CHAPTER 5

# The Vodafone Case—A Plea for Tax Treaty Arbitration

**Hans Mooij**

## 1. Introduction

When the Supreme Court of India released its decision in the *Vodafone* case, back in 2012,[1] it was generally applauded – except by the Indian tax authorities, obviously. I recall at the IFA Congress that year in Boston, many Indian delegates proudly commenting that "at least India had its Supreme Court to preserve the rule of law". I am wondering if the recent arbitral decision in the case before the Permanent Court of Arbitration under the Netherlands/India bilateral investment treaty[2] deserves a similar round of applause. In any case, I personally do not feel much like applauding this time. I am content with the outcome striking down the retroactive taxation as unfair and inadmissible - the Indian Government's attempt to 'repair' the Supreme Court's verdict - no doubt about that. My reservations, rather, are about the arbitral procedure adopted.

## 2. Flaws in Arbitral Procedure and Member Composition

First, next to the names of the arbitrators, only the arbitral award was made public but none of the considerations supporting it. This can only be because either the Indian Government or Vodafone or both, did not want to publish them. It is difficult to perceive what concerns they might possibly have had. The dispute in every detail has been all over the place, for many years, in the course of the subsequent procedures before the Indian courts. According to the arbitral award[3]:

> ...the imposition of ... an asserted liability to tax notwithstanding the Supreme Court Judgement is in breach of the guarantee of the fair and equitable treatment...

1. Decision of January 20, 2012, Civil Appeal No. 733/2012.
2. Decision of September 25, 2020, PCA Case No. 2016-35. There appears a second arbitration pending under the United Kingdom/India bilateral investment treaty, but I am unaware if this still has any purpose.
3. Para. 363, *supra* (3).

There is no word on either the issue of the retroactivity of the tax charge imposed or the liability to tax of indirect transfers under the amended income tax law introduced by the Finance Bill 2012, which under the prior law, was the subject of the Supreme Court case. This makes it difficult to assess what relevance the arbitral decision may have for the future similar disputes in India or elsewhere if it has any.

Further, the composition of the arbitral panel reveals that all three arbitrators were generalist arbitration experts, none of them being a tax expert. As I understand, Messrs. Berman, Fortier, and Oreamuno Blanco are all outstanding professionals in their own domain. But tax issues should be dealt with by tax experts; it is as simple as that. For tax treaty arbitrations, the OECD's multilateral instrument (MLI)[4] requires "expertise or experience in international tax matters" as the sole condition for appointment as arbitrator. Likewise, does the OECD Sample MoU on arbitration.[5]

The United Nations Sample MoU[6] only recommends that the chairperson of an arbitral panel have "familiarity with tax issues", but this is on the assumption that disputing tax authorities in their own good interest select "qualified and suitable persons" as their two appointed arbitrators who, one may expect, are tax specialists just the same. While one can imagine a generalist arbitrator acting as chairperson in order to supervise fair trial and case management,[7] for the majority of arbitrators to have profound tax knowledge and tax experience is indispensable. Otherwise, it is impossible to properly understand and assess the special and often intricate details tax disputes typically have.

## 3. No Difference Between Investment and Tax Treaty Arbitrations

For investment arbitrations, this should not be any different than for tax treaty arbitrations. The Vodafone investment arbitration is not unique in its sort. In fact, the number of investment arbitrations dealing wholly or partly with tax issues has increased substantially over recent years. Nonetheless, very few tax experts feature on the lists of available arbitrators that established arbitration institutes offer to disputing parties.

It is a good question to raise why tax disputes end up in investment arbitrations in the first place. One simple explanation is that, as yet there is only a limited number of tax treaties providing for mandatory arbitration, as per a taxpayer claim, and mostly between developed countries; hardly any with developing countries

4. Multilateral Convention to Implement Tax Treaty Related Measures to Prevent BEPS, Article 20(2)(a).
5. Annex to the Commentary on Article 25 of the OECD Model Income Tax Convention, Article 3(1).
6. Annex to the Commentary on Article 25(5) (alternative B) of the United Nation Model Double Taxation Convention, Article 15 of the Commentary on the Annex.
7. The United Nations Sample MoU, ibidem, refers to: "experience with the types of procedural, evidentiary and logistical issues which are likely to arise in the course of the arbitral proceedings".

where investment disputes are concentrated. Tax treaties generally do allow voluntary arbitration, by mutual agreement between countries' competent authorities, either generally or in an individual case,[8] but this is a route which, in practice, tax authorities appear very reluctant to take.

A belief seems to prevail that the mere reference in this respect in the OECD Commentary is not enough and that it would take explicit authorization by a treaty itself for tax authorities to be able to proceed to voluntary arbitration, which virtually no tax treaty provides for. More fundamental is the limited scope tax treaties usually have as they deal only with international double taxation. Except for some narrowly defined cases of non-discrimination, tax treaties leave countries free in how they shape their taxation on the items of income the treaties allot to them.

It is difficult to see why countries, while surrendering their residents for taxation to other countries should not, at the same time, also demand protection of their taxpayer rights, application of the rule of law, access to proper and effective dispute resolution, fair trial, and, indeed, also 'fair and equitable treatment' like investment treaties.

In the *Vodafone* case, there was no tax treaty protection in place since the alienator of the shares was a company established in the British Virgin Islands, which has itself no tax treaty with India nor, for that matter, an investment treaty. This could be viewed as a case of poor tax planning, or so it may seem. In exploring the option of investment arbitration, Vodafone clearly stepped up its jurisdiction shopping, using avenues of both Netherlands and the United Kingdom investment treaties with India. Investment treaty shopping apparently is less controversial than tax treaty shopping.

In reaction to the Vodafone investment arbitration, the perception is that the Indian Government is now adopting a different policy, aiming to have tax issues altogether excluded from the scope of arbitration under its investment treaties. The question that immediately arises is, what comes in place? Traditionally, India has been opposed to tax treaty arbitration. Is that position now going to change as well? It may be hoped so.

Internationally, it is not unusual for countries to exclude, to some extent, tax measures from the scope of investment arbitration. As a most prominent example, the United States, under its Model Bilateral Investment Treaty,[9] excludes arbitration in those cases where countries' competent authorities mutually agree that a tax measure is too minor to qualify as an appropriation. The United States Model[10] also recognizes, more generally, provisions of tax treaties to take precedence over provisions of investment treaties. In line with the latter, one may well imagine, once tax treaty arbitration has become more customary, that countries agree as a rule to have cases excluded from investment arbitration where tax treaty arbitration is available.

8. Commentary on Article 25 of the OECD Model Income Tax Convention, para. 69.
9. 2012 U.S. Model Bilateral Investment Treaty, Article 21(2).
10. Article 21(4).

The alternative, however, of not having any arbitration available anymore for tax issues would seem a dangerous path to take if that might indeed be the nature of the official position in the future. It would damage the attractiveness for foreign direct investment and cause major foreign investors to consider turning to competitor countries in the region which are more diligent in offering tax certainty by way of mandatory arbitration provisions, under either investment treaties, tax treaties, or private contracts with investors, as the case may be.

## 4. Ramifications of Infructuous Tax Treaty Arbitration

It is interesting to consider why India opposes mandatory tax treaty arbitration. Ordinarily, only those countries oppose arbitration which realize their position is weak and tend to anticipate losing. Mr. Michael Lennard, the Secretary of the United Nations Tax Committee, once called this the 'implied veto right'[11] – blocking an unfavorable treaty outcome by creating a dispute and refusing to cooperate in its resolution. But, in reality, it cannot be viewed as exercising a right, rather, quite the opposite. While the OECD and United Nations Model Tax Conventions, according to their literal reading, only require from tax authorities that they "endeavour … to resolve",[12] and not actually resolve, authorities no doubt are due to, at least, seriously negotiate a possible amicable settlement through a treaty provided mutual agreement procedure (MAP).

Anita Kapur, when she was Chair of India's Central Board of Direct Taxes (CBDT), used to submit that there was no tax treaty dispute which India could not resolve by MAP, and hence, India would never need any tax treaty arbitration. Over the years, India indeed has discovered the means of MAP negotiations. According to recent OECD statistics,[13] India, as of the end of 2019, had almost 1,000 MAP cases pending. The vast majority were on transfer pricing issues and with the United States. Reportedly, India would have managed to conclude large numbers of MAP cases with the United States, and successfully, by retaining the taxing right under the treaty.

This, however, does not necessarily mean India had the better arguments. In one of the cases that India won, that of E-Funds IT Solution,[14] the taxpayer, a US resident company, subsequently turned to the Indian Supreme Court arguing that the MAP outcome—the determination of a taxable permanent establishment in India—was ill-founded, and succeeded in having it overthrown. According to the taxpayer, the US tax authorities, while rejecting the Indian position, had only conceded the case in MAP as a gesture to the company, as a fellow resident, in order

11. Michael Lennard, *Transfer Pricing Arbitration as an Option for Developing Countries*, INTERTAX, Vol. 42 (2014), Issue 3, p179 ff.
12. Article 25(2) of both OECD and United Nations Models.
13. OECD, Mutual Agreement Procedure Statistics for 2019.
14. Decision of October 24, 2017, Civil Appeal No. 6082/2015.

to relieve it from the extremely adverse situation of permanent, unresolved double taxation which otherwise would have resulted.

It is known that some countries indeed apply as a deliberate strategy in MAP negotiations not to concede at all and to simply sit and wait for another country, most typically the taxpayer's resident country, instead to give in. This may be viewed as a 'beggar thy neighbour' stance. Whether India adopted a comparable stance in the *E-Funds* case remains unconfirmed since MAP proceedings are not public and any reports from taxpayers are no more than hearsay. It is for the Indian tax authorities to conclude if they recognize this strategy as theirs. The upshot is the adverse impact on investment and, in turn, growth.

It may be recalled that India's turn towards the MAP resolution was intended to relieve some of the pressure on its overloaded domestic court system. In *E-Funds*, the victory in MAP that India had heavily battled for, only to find it annulled by a subsequent Supreme Court decision, turned out to be Pyrrhic. Not only did India lose its tax claim, it also made dual investments of qualified personnel and costs in two dispute resolution processes—treaty and domestic—unnecessary, as these processes are meant to be alternative instead of cumulative and, in the finally outcome, both in vain.

While an amicable settlement on which tax authorities mutually agree in MAP does not per se bind taxpayers—this is the price authorities have to pay for not admitting or allowing taxpayers as participants in the MAP negotiations—in most other countries, taxpayers ordinarily would not lightly refuse a MAP resolution, since this would mean their double taxation to revive again. In a litigious environment as prevails in India, however, this may be different, and cases like E-Funds may occur more frequently.

## 5. Need for Arbitration

MAP strategies of the beggar-thy-neighbour type clash with the interpretation of treaty good faith the OECD propagates - MAP is not about winning or losing, but about cooperating to resolve. However noble a view, this is naïve of course. In particular, where there are huge budgetary or principled interests in dispute, it is only natural for countries wanting to hold on to their position for as much and as long as they possibly can. Besides, such severe disputes usually do not come dropping out of the blue. They are often carefully prepared, if not planned, with prior commitment from the central authorities in charge of tax treaty policies and MAP. Conceding on a good position purely for the sake of compromising is unnecessary, arguably shortsighted even. But deliberately sticking to a poor position, just to wait and see if the other side is so weak or desperate to make the first move, works equally deleteriously on the other side.

Mandatory tax treaty arbitration clauses are designed precisely to prevent such poor practices and, according to its advocates, above all, those of the 'baseball' type in which arbitrators have the option to only choose either of the two disputing authorities' positions. Some even argue that under the pressure of the mere foresight of otherwise having to go to arbitration, tax authorities would be quick to resolve at the last minute. But I believe mandatory arbitration clauses may just as well work in the opposite direction. Tax authorities feeling theirs is a strong position may be less inclined, and wisely so, to strike a last-minute deal at all cost if they stand a good chance of being confirmed in their right in a subsequent arbitration.

Arbitration is the mechanism allowing a resolution to be reached even if there are issues on which the tax authorities despite their best endeavours have been unable to reach agreement through negotiations. According to the OECD MAP statistics mentioned, of all MAP cases closed in 2019 this was for only 52 percent due to authorities reaching agreement in MAP. The figures for India were mixed, with 86 percent of transfer pricing cases and 16 percent of other cases amicably resolved, but at the enormous cost of an average duration per case of over 5 years – far beyond the universal minimum standard of 2 years of BEPS Action 14,[15]

This comprises convincing evidence that arbitration is indeed needed, either to resolve cases or to cut short otherwise endless MAP negotiations. Taxpayers are not as a rule bound by an arbitral decision, neither by a MAP settlement between tax authorities. But the risk of a taxpayer ever wanting to litigate a case which independent, unbiased, and expert tax arbitrators have already decided, may safely be regarded as next to nil, even perhaps in India.

In its present discomfort with mandatory tax treaty arbitration, India should be bothered less by concerns over either giving up sovereignty, capacity issues or costs of arbitration, as are common among developing countries. First, the sovereignty argument is obviated by the reality that countries concede on their sovereignty by agreeing on tax treaties, not by agreeing to the resolution of issues that arise afterward in their interpretation or application.[16] Losing an arbitration just because of a country's tax authorities' incapacity is unnecessary of course, as there is ample external, independent tax expertise available which they can call on for assistance.

Second, and more importantly perhaps, there is the advantage of having tax experts as arbitrators who can be trusted to recognize the substantial merits of an argument, however poor its presentation may be, just as much as they know how to look through any sleek presentation.

---

15. OECD/G20 BEPS Project, Making Dispute Resolution Mechanisms More Effective, Action 14 – 2015 Final Report, p15/16.
16. Luís Eduardo Schoueri, *Arbitration and Constitutional Issues*, in: Lang and Owens (eds.), *International Arbitration in Tax Matters*, IBFD (2016), p185 ff.

Third, costs of tax treaty arbitration may be far less than that of investment or commercial arbitration, since ordinarily no external legal representation by an arbitration lawyer is anticipated, which in those other arbitrations make the bulk of costs. This is because the disputing tax authorities usually avail of a legal representative of their own, from within their own office or from their country's Foreign Affairs or Justice Department.

If felt needed, countries may in addition agree a trust fund construction to support countries with limited resources with training facilities and finances, like, for instance, those trust funds member countries of the World Trade Organization have organized for arbitrations there.[17]

## 6. Hesitance Towards Arbitration

The predominant reason why tax authorities may be reluctant about going to tax treaty arbitration is that they realize their positions are often daring and risky, and therefore the weaker in an arbitration, and they would be destined to lose more than win on that account. Such a reason, however, may be too embarrassing for them to speak about. Was this the case of India's *Vodafone* or *E-Funds*, and other similar cases may be asked rhetorically.

Perhaps it is better to 'look before you leap'. Tax authorities should not enter any MAP processes in the first place when their tax auditors continue to provide them with flawed favourable arguments. It is for good reason that the OECD Model Income Tax Convention,[18] as a rule, urges tax authorities, when faced with a taxpayer request for a MAP procedure, to first try and achieve a satisfactory solution internally by themselves before deciding to engage in MAP.

## 7. OECD'S Two-Pillar Unified Approach

### 7.1. Unified Approach

Mandatory tax treaty arbitration forms an essential part of the two-pillar 'Unified Approach' the OECD/G20 launched in early 2020 following intense discussions within their Inclusive Framework.[19] In particular, the proposals under Pillar One on the taxation of the digital economy apply innovative and flexible norms to allow for consensus between the many and different views among the Framework members and consequentially provide a large scope for misunderstanding, misapplication, and

17. Hans Mooij, *Arbitration Institutes: An Issue Overlooked*, INTERTAX, Vol. 47 (2019), Issue 8&9, p737 ff.
18. Article 25(2).
19. OECD/G20 Inclusive Framework on BEPS, Statement on the Two-Pillar Approach to Address the Tax Challenges Arising from the Digitalisation of the Economy, January 2020, p18/19.

disputes. This makes arbitration indeed indispensable, next to intensified administrative coordination at audit level, through 'review' and 'determination panels' as outlined by the Pillar One Blueprint of October 2020.[20]

## 7.2. Mandatory Arbitration

More generally, it is anticipated that the Update of BEPS Action 14 will make mandatory arbitration a minimum standard, instead of a mere recommendation as at present. Mandatory tax treaty arbitration is a main feature, too, under the Tax Certainty project of the OECD and International Monetary Fund.[21] Even the China led BRITACOM cooperation, in its attempts to improve tax dispute resolution, should be seriously contemplating mandatory arbitration.[22]

It is no secret that the United States was one of the main drivers behind mandatory tax treaty arbitration under the MLI and now again under both Pillars of the Unified Approach, and that India was and is its main target. Under the Trump administration, despite its general aversion to international cooperation, this has been no different than under the prior Obama administration, and it will undoubtedly be the same again under the new Biden administration. India, in its rejection of tax treaty arbitration, is rapidly becoming isolated and under increasing pressure from other countries. The key question therefore appears to me how much longer anymore India will be able to stick to its position.

## 7.3. Reservations Regarding MLI Clauses

However much the OECD's pushing for mandatory tax treaty arbitration at a global scale is laudable, this is not to say that there are no reservations about the specific arbitration clauses of the MLI[23] and the OECD Model Tax Convention.[24] To begin with, arbitration according to these clauses may only be at the request of a taxpayer. I imagine it must come as an embarrassment to tax authorities if it requires a taxpayer to expose their failure to amicably resolve before they may proceed to arbitration. The United Nations Model Tax Convention[25] offers a better alternative in my view, making arbitration mandatory if one of the tax authorities requests it. A combination of the two approaches, allowing either taxpayer or one, or both, of the tax authorities to request arbitration, would seem best.

20. OECD/G20 Inclusive Framework on BEPS, Report on Pillar One Blueprint, October 12, 2020, p181 ff.
21. OECD/IMF 2019 Progress Report on Tax Certainty.
22. Belt and Road Initiative Tax Administration Cooperation Mechanism, Wuzhen Action Plan (2019-2021).
23. Article 19(1).
24. Article 25(5).
25. Article 25(5) (alternative B).

Secondly, under the MLI and OECD clauses, as well as the United Nations clause, arbitration may only come at the very end, as a 'nuclear option', after two or, in some cases, even three years of unsuccessful MAP negotiations. This despite the fact that some cases are so controversial that any attempt for an amicable settlement would appear deemed to remain fruitless from the very outset, also in the eyes of tax authorities themselves. Furthermore, this 'nuclear' moment may occur only many years after the dispute had arisen in the process of auditing, reflecting that tax authorities usually demand an assessment to be final before engaging in MAP.

### 7.4. Early Initiation of MAP

Some tax authorities allow the early filing of a MAP request, but it may well last a long time before they actually enter into MAP. This delay makes not only taxpayers but often also tax auditors unhappy with MAP, particularly when an auditor's performance rating or salary depends on timely finalization of assessments. It explains why some tax auditors are known to offer taxpayers a 'discount' on an amending assessment as a premium to abstain from requesting MAP – a deplorable practice but no less real.

One solution might be if MAP processes could commence sooner, say when a tax treaty dispute arises. This is relevant where expertise on tax treaty issues is low among tax auditors. Such a solution obviously draws heavily on the tax authorities' capacity, which may also be limited and may, therefore, mean replacing one capacity issue for another.

Alternatively, a preferred solution may be arbitration, as well as the other alternate dispute resolution instruments of mediation and expert technical advice, might be allowed as early as at the audit stage, as soon as it becomes clear, for instance, from discussions in the OECD proposed review and determination panels, that differences in views between tax auditors are fundamental and difficult to bridge. This would give a substantial boost to the effectiveness and wider acceptance of tax treaty arbitration, leading to the appreciation by tax authorities and taxpayers alike.

## 8. Digital Economy Taxation

Discussions on the taxation of the digital economy within the OECD/G20 Inclusive Framework are now extended until mid-2021, to allow more time for reaching an agreement. While the prospects do not look particularly good at this time, it may nonetheless be hoped that this effort will eventually succeed, and an international tax order of some type will be preserved. Despite India's unilateral introduction of an 'equalization levy', a tax on the turnover of digital services in the same vein as France and Italy, India is reported to be supportive of a multilateral tax order over that of countries adopting individual and likely divergent paths. Logically so, since India's economy thrives on globalism; India cannot afford globalism to go astray. Perhaps India should accept tax treaty arbitration as the price to pay for consensus.

Apparently, India is now turning its eye to a recent United Nations alternative for taxing the digital economy, which allows for source taxation on automated digital services at a higher allocation level than the OECD/G20 Blueprint proposals, while not providing for any mandatory arbitration.[26] India may not have been much of a supporter of the United Nations Tax Committee or its work in the past. This sudden adherence may, therefore, suit its present needs. However, the United Nations alternative may turn out to be even more controversial than the OECD/G20 proposals and, by consequence, still more unlikely to win universal acclaim. Besides, the United Nations would do better to embrace instead of rejecting mandatory tax treaty arbitration since, as Carl Shoup, U.S. economist,[27] opined early in the 1980s, developing countries often may lack resources, skills, and economic and political powers to be able to stand up in tax disputes against foreign multinationals or developed countries, and arbitration may be the only means available for them to have such power imbalances repaired by way of an independent, expert and fair judgment of their dispute.

## 9. Concluding Remarks

If the international community fails to reach any common consensus, India's alternative would be to actively pursue bilateral solutions.[28] While India may then continue to reject having mandatory tax treaty arbitration with the rest of the world, with the United States, and perhaps some European or Asian countries with which it has close economic relations, India, in negotiating for the best deal it aspires on digital taxes, may find itself forced to concede arbitration just the same.

26. United Nations Committee of Experts on International Cooperation in Tax Matters, October 11, 2020, E/C.18/2020/CRP.41.
27. Carl S. Shoup, *International Arbitration of Transfer Pricing under Income Taxation*, in: Rugman and Eden (eds.), *Multinationals and Transfer Pricing*, Croom Helm (1985), p291 ff.
28. Mukesh Butani, *Digital taxes, if multilateral fails, look for bilateral solutions*, in: Financial Express, October 21, 2020.

## REJOINDER

**Mukesh Butani**[29]

## 1. Introduction

Hans Mooij makes a case for adoption of tax treaty arbitration by reference to some anomalies in the bilateral investment treaty (BIT) case of Vodafone and faults with other existing dispute resolution mechanisms.

## 2. Mooij's Views

Mooij's views and arguments may be broadly distilled and summarized as follows:

- The cloud of confidentiality and non-public nature of the Award renders it difficult to assess its relevance to "similar disputes" in the future, in "India or elsewhere".
- The arbitral panel whose eminence notwithstanding is not the right "experts" and that tax disputes are to "be dealt with by tax experts".
- It is a foregone conclusion that Vodafone was a case of tax avoidance – "[i]ndirect transfers of assets almost typically do," and investment treaty proceedings led by generalist arbitrators with no tax background, affording protection to cases of tax avoidance, make them inappropriate for resolution of tax issues.
- The appropriate solution is one of mandatory tax treaty arbitration conducted with the help of tax experts.
- India's opposition to mandatory tax treaty arbitration is misplaced, suggesting that "only those countries oppose arbitration which realize their position is weak and are afraid of losing".
- India has a patchy record with the mutual agreement procedure (MAP), with such cases on an average taking 5 years to resolve, which is a "convincing evidence" that tax treaty arbitration is indeed needed.
- India is increasingly isolated in its rejection of tax treaty arbitration, with the dominant trend being in favour of acceptance of the same, expressing serious concerns regarding citing sovereignty.

## 3. Investment Treaty Arbitrations and Tax Matters

The author's primary basis for advocating the adoption of tax treaty arbitration is that the investor-state dispute settlement (ISDS) system is ill-suited for considering tax issues. The key points raised are that the non-publication of awards such as in

29. With inputs from Krishnan S, Advocate.

the Vodafone case makes it difficult to assess the efficacy of the system in addressing tax issues, and the lack of expertise on tax issues among investment tribunal members does not inspire much confidence either.

While it is true that there is a strong case in favor of publication of investment treaty awards, especially those that deal with significant public interest issues, quite often, states (that are parties to such disputes) are reluctant to consent to the publication of such awards, for a host of reasons. For example, the maintenance of confidentiality may be perhaps favored over concerns that different tribunals dealing with such disputes arising out of the same policy measure may be unduly influenced by prior decisions (notwithstanding the lack of precedential value of such awards) in respect of such a measure, especially when such prior decisions are prejudicial to a party's interest.

## 4. Taxation and Investment Treaties

On the more substantial question as to whether taxation is outside the purview of investment treaties, it depends entirely on the language of a given treaty, and there cannot be a blanket view one way or the other. Even in cases involving state actions to tackle instances of "tax avoidance" (which according to the Mooij – Vodafone is an obvious one), investment tribunals are mandated to assess the impact of such tax measures on the substantive treatment standards of the investment treaty in accordance with its language. As Park puts it, "tax-related investment disputes remain qualitatively different from commercial or tax treaty context", in that the "very legitimacy of the tax is put into question".[30]

### 4.1. Vodafone Case

In the case of Vodafone, it must be noted that prior to the commencement of the BIT arbitration, the issue of "tax avoidance" was comprehensively dealt with by the Supreme Court of India in January 2012,[31] where it reconciled its earlier decisions in the case of *McDowell*,[32] rendered in the context of commercial tax and *Azadi Bachao Andolan*[33] being rendered in the context of double taxation avoidance agreement (DTAA) between India and Mauritius. As regards affording legal protection under investment treaties by tribunals with no expertise in tax, I must confess that I have not looked at the composition of the tribunals that have handed out bilateral investment protection agreement (BIPA) awards and hence, will not like to offer comment.

30. William W Park: Arbitrability and Tax, Chapter 10, Arbitrability: International & Comparative Perspectives, para. 12.
31. *Vodafone International Holdings B.V. v. Union of India & Anr*, (2012) 6 SCC 613.
32. *McDowell & Co. Ltd. v. Commercial Tax Officer*, AIR 1986 SC 649.
33. *Union of India v. Azadi Bachao Andolan*, (2004) 10 SCC 1.

If the criticism of investment tribunals dealing with tax-related issues is borne out of a fear of potentially absurd interpretations of a treaty, wherein a tribunal appropriates jurisdiction to itself incorrectly (including say where tax matters are excluded), such a situation can be remedied by the respondent state in most major jurisdictions, by arguing *de novo* on such jurisdictional issues before the jurisdictional challenge court (such as Singapore court in the instance of Vodafone where India has reportedly filed its challenge).

## 4.2. State Autonomy

Much of the issue lies in the fact that states at the time of having negotiated and signed their first set of investment treaties perhaps did not fully comprehend the potential scope of such treaties, and consequently the drafting exercise did not perhaps fully grasp the possibility of even issues such as the sovereign exercise of taxation being dealt with under such treaties (India's express exclusion of tax matters in its 2016 Model BIT[34] is an example of this belated realization). Autonomy over fiscal matters is core to any nation's sovereignty which is the key element that states wish to ring-fence against the dictates of investment treaty claims. In the absence of express exclusions or carve-outs regarding matters concerning tax measures, it is not all that unsurprising that foreign investors expect the host state to accord fair treatment to their investments even when it comes to the imposition of a tax, given the text of a treaty between its home state and the host state.

Taxation measures by host states have frequently been challenged under investment treaties broadly on the basis that such tax measures were imposed in a capricious, arbitrary or discriminatory manner violative of the Fair and Equitable Treatment (FET) clause or that the effect of such tax measures resulted in (non-compensated) expropriation.[35] The outcome of such arbitrations has been varied depending on the language of the relevant treaty, with no discernible trend favouring either party. In some treaties such as the US-Ecuador BIT, the text expressly provides for the challenge of tax measures as violative of the FET standard.[36] Indeed one of the first cases involving a challenge to a tax measure being in breach of FET was under the US-Ecuador BIT. In *Occidental Petroleum v. Ecuador*, the tribunal found that "the tax law was changed without providing any clarity about its meaning and extent and the practice and regulations were also

34. Model Text for the Indian Bilateral Investment Treaty, Article 2.4 (ii): https://dea.gov.in/sites/default/files/ModelTextIndia_BIT_0.pdf (accessed on January 18, 2021).

35. There are over 40 reported cases of investment treaty cases involving challenge to tax measures in which the outcomes of those proceedings are evenly in favour of investors and states.

36. Treaty between the United States of America and the Republic of Ecuador concerning the Encouragement and Reciprocal Protection of Investment, Article X (1) – "With respect to its tax policies, each Party should strive to accord fairness and equity in the treatment of investment of nationals and companies of the other Party."

inconsistent with such changes", and such a change was violative of the FET clause on account of the Ecuador's failure to provide "stability of the legal and business framework" which it considered to be "an essential element of the fair and equitable treatment".[37] There are other instances where the imposition of tax measures has been challenged as expropriator in nature, for example, in *Tza Yap Shum v. Peru,* where under the China-Peru BIT, interim confiscatory measures carried out by Peruvian tax authorities in respect of a tax demand was found to be a case of expropriation.[38]

### 4.3. Carve-out for Tax Measures

In terms of carve-out provisions in investment treaties relating to tax measures, those also vary from treaty to treaty. Chaisse classifies the typology of tax exceptions in investment treaties into seven different categories ranging from a general exclusion to specific and explicit exclusions, including a specific exclusion of the FET standard.[39]

For example, the Hong Kong–New Zealand BIT completely excludes tax matters from its purview, with such matters to be dealt with either domestic law or a tax treaty. Article XII of Ecuador-Canada BIT on the other hand provides for a tax veto carve-out that gives the national tax authorities of the home and host state an opportunity to jointly 'veto' an investor's claim of expropriation in relation to a tax measure. There are treaties that provide for exclusion based on type of taxes, such as, Article 21 of the US-Uruguay BIT, which excludes the application of the treaty to direct taxes. India's 2016 Model BIT's tax carve-out is widely phrased with "any law or measure regarding taxation, including measures taken to enforce taxation obligations" to be excluded from the treaty (however, the additional clarificatory provision within the article on non-justiciability is not entirely clear). In *Cargill v. Mexico,* the tribunal found that tax measures are excluded under the FET standard of the North American Free Trade Agreement (NAFTA) by virtue of its carve-out clause (although in some cases it may lay out the contextual basis for breach of the FET standard by other non-tax measures). The United States-Mexico-Canada Agreement (USMCA), the successor to NAFTA, also contains a tax-veto clause in so far as the agreement between US and Mexico is concerned. In sum, whether one looks at the first-generation investment treaties or the more recent ones with specific

37. Occidental Exploration and Production Company v Republic of Ecuador, LCIA Case UN3467, Final Award, paras. 183-187.
38. *Señor Tza Yap Shum v. The Republic of Peru,* ICSID Case No. ARB/07/6, Award, July 7, 2011.
39. The E-15 Initiative: Strengthening the global trade and investment system for sustainable development, Julien Chaisse, January 2016, Annex 1 – General exclusions, Conflict clauses in favour of tax treaties application, Tax veto to expropriation case, Specific and explicit exclusions: to non-discrimination standards, type of taxes (direct and indirect taxes), to fair and equitable standard and combination of diverse exceptions within exclusion.

carve-outs relating to tax measures, it all comes down to the specific text of each treaty, and even a minor ambiguity could lead to the initiation of investment claims challenging a state's tax measures.

### 4.4. Tax Expertise

In view of the above, even if one considers it to be generally desirable to have tax experts adjudicate such disputes within the framework of tax treaties, such a step may not result in any efficiencies until the existing investment treaties are overhauled (or where 'sunset clauses' remain in treaties that are already terminated) with clearly worded exclusions. If states do shift to the mandatory tax treaty arbitration model, it still does not automatically preclude a potentially aggrieved investor from arbitrating under an investment treaty if the language of such treaty provides for such a possibility. The arduous process of renegotiating existing treaties means that there are no easy answers on this issue in the near term.

## 5. India's Experience with MAP

### 5.1. Long Time Taken

The point on the inappropriateness of the ISDS system to deal with tax matters aside, the author's other basis for advocating the adoption of tax treaty arbitration is due to India's supposedly uninspiring tryst with the MAP procedure, which he observes on an average takes over "5 years" to resolve matters. It is true that the average time was reported to be over 64 months for the period pre-2016.[40] However, for cases since 2016, the average resolution time is around 19 months (which is below India's desired goal of resolution within two years and the global average).[41] In addition, India's commitment to implement minimum standards under OECD's BEPS Action 14 to improve the MAP process coupled with its maturing advance pricing agreement (APA) program holds optimism for the future of MAP. Besides, the average period for MAP resolution process in OECD members states has been steadily rising in the past decade.

### 5.2. Fear of Mandatory Arbitration

Moreover, on the issue of adoption of mandatory and binding arbitration of disputes not resolved by MAP, the then Indian minister at a G-20 finance ministers meeting in 2014, had stated on record that "[t]his not only impinges on

40. OECD Statistics, 2019 - In the MAP Statistics Reporting Framework, a distinction is made between the cases received before or as from January 1, 2016, which is the date as from when the reporting jurisdictions committed to the implementation of the Action 14 minimum standard.
41. OECD Statistics, 2019 https://www.oecd.org/tax/dispute/mutual-agreement-procedure-statistics.htm (last accessed on January 18, 2021); https://www.oecd.org/tax/dispute/2019-map-statistics-india.pdf (last accessed on January 18, 2021); MAP Guidance/2020 - CBDT Circular No. F.No. 500/09/2016-APA-I dated August 7, 2020.

the sovereign rights of developing countries in taxation, but will also limit the ability of the developing countries to apply their domestic laws for taxing non-residents and foreign companies".[42] This issue of sovereignty certainly still appears to be the dominant concern for India's reluctance towards accepting arbitration under MAP.

On the issue of sovereignty, it is suggested that states cede sovereignty by being party to tax treaties (which is also the case in regard to investment treaties) and not by agreeing to an arbitration procedure under such treaties.[43] While this is theoretically true, the fear among some states, including select OECD members that have adopted the 2010 model tax convention, is that by agreeing to mandatory and binding arbitration, they run the risk of adverse findings that will limit their ability to tax non-residents at a time when globalization and digitalization already pose significant challenges in that respect.

## 6. System Design Solution

While certainly there are solutions in terms of system design that can address the concern of states regarding the adoption of mandatory tax treaty arbitration, perhaps the negative experience of some states in the developing world with the investor-state dispute settlement system has made them wary of ceding any ground on what is seen as the last bastion of state sovereignty. For states such as India to be persuaded to change its stance, it would require more than just a theoretical basis and some rhetoric on the importance of foreign investment to do so. As to India's position to not accept mandatory arbitration in its treaties, due to it being a core sovereign function and other related reasons, it is a much-debated issue, with valid arguments on both sides.

This author's own view on the mandatory arbitration standard is that, it is time for India to review its tax treaty policy and selectively look at adopting mandatory arbitration with jurisdictions that are significant long-term investors (and correspondingly negotiate on a bilateral basis to create a tax carve-out/exclusion in the investment treaties with those jurisdictions). This would, in my view, go some way in avoiding instances such as the Vodafone and Cairn arbitration claims.

## 7. Conclusion

The adoption of tax treaty arbitration by India and other states will largely depend on the success of such a mechanism in resolving issues for a broad array of existing adopters, including developing states. The inappropriateness of the ISDS system for

42. https://indianexpress.com/article/business/economy/india-urges-all-nations-to-join-tax-information-pact/ (last accessed on January 18, 2021).
43. "The Vodafone Case – A Plea for Tax Treaty Arbitration", footnote 16 - *Arbitration and Constitutional Issues,* in: Lang and Owens (eds.), International Arbitration in Tax Matters, IBFD (2016), Luís Eduardo Schoueri, p 185 ff.

the resolution of tax disputes or the supposed mixed experience of states under the MAP procedure, all on their own, are not sufficient to persuade states such as India to view tax treaty arbitrations more favorably. In the same breath, India should recognize that it has the third largest MAP cases after the U.S. and Germany, and with the growing complexity coupled with principle-based interpretation, treaty disputes are bound to rise.[44] Hence, a medium to long term approach should guide India to "take the bull by the horn". This will mean an all-out reform on treaty dispute resolution – enhancing the efficacy of its MAP, including the time to resolve, speedy conclusion of APA's, particularly bilateral APA's, revamp of the advance ruling mechanism, and rigor in training & development of tax officials dealing with cross-border tax audits/assessments.

44. https://www.oecd.org/tax/dispute/mutual-agreement-procedure-statistics-2019-per-jurisdiction-all.htm.

## REJOINDER

### Philip Baker (Oral Comments)

Baker stood apart from Mooij on selected issues. Baker said that he had read the Vodafone arbitration award, and he had acted as an expert for Vodafone all the way through the process. He was involved in the case as an expert from before the High Court hearing. Baker commented that:

- It would be erroneous to critique the arbitrators for not having a tax background. The issue was not a tax question before them, but whether it was in breach of the general obligation of fair and equitable treatment, which was guaranteed to all investors. To enable an investor to litigate a matter all the way up to the Supreme Court of the country to win the case and then reverse the law with a retrospective effect would appear to breach that obligation.
- Mooij's view was that arbitrators who came from different backgrounds would be perfectly entitled to reach the conclusion that they did. This was a general issue of trade arbitration law. They were aware of the background; they were presented with a great deal of material, and they had Baker's expert report.[45] At the end of the day, he did not think that, globally, any lawyer would not have come to the same conclusion: to allow an investor to litigate up to India's Supreme Court to win the case, and then reverse the law retrospectively does not respect the rule of law. They would all conclude that it was a breach of fair and equitable treatment.
- He knew that the Indian government was considering challenging the arbitration award.[46] He was a bit nervous that Mooij's comments might be taken into account by the Indian authorities.
- One of the things that Mooij said was that if you had a weak case, then recognize that you had a weak case and give up. Baker agreed and indicated that he felt that it was time that the Indian government asked itself whether it was not doing significant damage to India's position internationally by carrying on fighting what was basically a weak case.
- To recount, India lost before its own Supreme Court in a unanimous judgement. It then lost before three arbitrators who were fully aware of the facts: carrying it on further would be a waste of the Indian taxpayer's money.

---

45. He indicated politely that he did not know if that helped them or not but they did have a full explanation of the background.
46. Subsequent to the conference, the Indian government indicated its intention to do so.

- Baker also commented on Vodafone and tax avoidance that Mooij had brought up. Baker felt that one had to remember that Vodafone was the acquiring company in this case. It had not been involved in establishing any of the structures. And if there had been any issue of tax avoidance, one would not have seen the transaction taking place at the level of the Cayman Island and BVI companies since Vodafone did not establish the structures.
- This transaction could have taken place under the cover of the Mauritius Treaty because there were Mauritian companies involved. The transaction was structured in a particular way for entirely commercial reasons. It could not be suggested that there was a tax avoidance motive behind the structure of the disposal. The Indian Supreme Court's view on this is clearly based on the commercial angle rejecting any argument based on the application of anti-avoidance principles in India.
- In concluding, Baker indicated that he felt an urgency to intervene into the matter, acting to do the right thing to correct any erroneous interpretation of the unpublished arbitral award.

# ADDENDUM

## Hans Mooij

Recent press coverages reveal that the Indian government has decided to undertake action against the Permanent Court of Arbitration (PCA) Vodafone arbitration, this time with the Singapore International Arbitration Centre (SIAC) arbitration court in Singapore. Ordinarily, had India been a party to the New York Arbitration Convention, it could have sought recourse with a local Dutch court, Netherlands having been the place of arbitration, and on the terms of that Convention and applicable Dutch domestic law. But not being such a party, it remains to be seen whether this leaves India with more options to try and have the PCA arbitration nullified or not. This is food for arbitration lawyers of course.

As for the contents of the arbitral decision, without having the full text of the decision available, it remains impossible to form a solid opinion on whether they provide any substantial grounds for nullification. The Indian government and Vodafone should agree to publish after all, if only for academic sake. Tax experts find it hard to digest a tax avoidance scheme gaining legal protection, for there can be little doubt that there was a tax avoidance scheme in play. Indirect transfers of assets almost typically do. That the Indian Supreme Court in its prior decision in the case judged the anti-avoidance provisions of the Indian Income-tax Act, as it stood at the time, ineffective—which the Indian government afterward sought to repair by introducing a GAAR—does not mean that the transfer in itself was not about tax avoidance. These are two different things.[47]

It is further noted that in other countries, tax avoidance is not usually permitted as an excuse for the tax authorities to apply tax laws amended with a retroactive effect of some extent or other. Retroactive legislation in the Indian government comprised the core of the Vodafone dispute.[48] One should be aware that Vodafone is not a tax case but an investment case. Still, it is doubtful that the object and purpose of investment treaties include mechanisms that coveri up for tax avoidance and, if they do, then it is time that this is changed. Perhaps also the all-generalist arbitrators in the Vodafone case were less appreciative of the aspect of tax avoidance, or less sensitive, as they

47. In the so-called 'Danish cases' the EU Court of Justice ordered that tax benefits be denied on grounds of tax avoidance even absent any anti-avoidance rules in either EU or Danish domestic law (CJEU, decisions of February 26, 2019, *Skatteministeriet v. T Danmark and Y Danmark ApS,* Joined Cases C-116/16 and 117/16, and *N Luxembourg 1, X Danmark A/S, C Danmark I and Z Danmark ApS v. Skatteministeriet*, Joined Cases C-115/16, C-118/16, C-119/16 and C-299/16).

48. In my own country The Netherlands for example, retroactive taxation of a transfer beyond the date of a contrary court decision like in *Vodafone* would be unprecedented, but retroactive taxation of gains accrued before such date but realized thereafter has occurred more than once. This is purely unilateral practice.

revealed insensitivity too to the apparent jurisdiction shopping in the case, Vodafone being a UK, and not a Dutch company.

Would it not be that tax simply is too difficult an area to handle for generalist arbitrators? The OECD explains why an increasing number of investment treaties[49] demand prior joint determination by tax authorities whether a tax measure constitutes an expropriation fit to be admitted to arbitration for this main reason, which the OECD regards more important than concerns over retaining tax sovereignty:

> This may reflect the perception that special knowledge must be available to assess issues related to tax … matters which are unlikely to be available to arbitration panels.[50]

Actually, it is probable that tax sovereignty concerns are caused by poor judgments on tax issues by generalist arbitrators. Only occasionally, in major investment arbitrations, have arbitrators dismissed tax issues as 'not arbitrable' or referred them back to disputing parties to resolve among themselves by mutual settlement. This author has himself been in one such arbitration as an expert witness. Generally, however, arbitrators are known not to say 'no' to a case easily. 'Tax disputes should be arbitrated by tax experts' is the main reason why Tribute, a tax organization that I chair, was created. Tax expertise is by now is a standard qualification requirement under all multilateral and bilateral provisions for tax treaty arbitration (including MLI, OECD Sample MoU, and EU Directive). After all, to obtain an expert decision is the very purpose for which parties turn to arbitration.

Rather than attempting, unsuccessfully, to challenge the legal jurisdiction of the arbitrators over tax issues in the absence of any provisions to this effect in the India-Netherlands investment treaty, it would seem more realistic to question the arbitrators' individual ability for tax issues. That said, the Indian government itself selected one of the arbitrators and apparently accepted the other two without objections. Rather than giving up altogether on arbitration in cases involving tax issues, it would be better to be more cautious in selecting arbitrators for such cases.

49. Following the example of the US 2012 Model Bilateral Investment Treaty which I mentioned in my article, the OECD mentions Canada, Colombia and Peru among other countries to have adopted similar policies.

50. Gordon, K. and J. Pohl (2015), "Investment Treaties over Time – Treaty Practice and Interpretation in a Changing World", at p 31, *OECD Working Papers on International Investment*, 2015/02, OECD Publishing.

# IN SEARCH OF INTERNATIONAL CONSENSUS

CHAPTER 6

# Profit Attribution Approaches and Conflicts[1]

**Sumeir Ahuja & Riya Gupta**

## 1. Introduction

Allocation of taxing rights between contracting states necessitates uniform interpretation of tax and treaty law. Varying interpretation is bound to cause tax uncertainty and problems of double taxation or double non-taxation. Although separate entity approach and the arm's length principle form the basis for attribution of profits, discrepancy between domestic regulations may cause significant variations. This problem is accentuated with global economies undergoing a digital transformation at a breakneck speed. Digitalization has paved the way for multinational corporations to operate seamlessly across borders. Traditional tax laws have failed to keep up with changing business models. The emergence of unique digital business models has led to decreasing relevance of physical presence in the market, increasing importance of intangibles and integrated value chains.[2]

This gathered momentum at global and domestic level to bring structural and comprehensive changes to the international tax principles governing digital taxation in particular and profit attribution in general. In this vein, OECD developed Action Plan 1 report during its BEPS project highlighting the challenges posed by unique business models of MNCs leading to undesired outcomes in terms of low or no taxation. While the report discussed the potential solutions for these broader challenges, no adaption of the framework for international taxation were suggested for implementation. With several jurisdictions resorting to unilateral measures, the work at OECD level[3] was intensified to counteract the trend of unilateral actions by

1. This chapter was reviewed by Mukesh Butani.
2. Marcel Olbert and Christrop Spengel, *International Taxation in the Digital Economy: Challenge Accepted?* World Tax Journal, February 2017.
3. OECD has released several interim reports in its endeavor to conceptualize a viable solution to effectively tax the digital economy. This include: **Pillar I Approach** accessible as: Organisation for Economic Cooperation and Development/G20 Based Erosion and Profit Shifting Project,

**[Footnote No. 3 contd.]**

developing a globally coordinated solution.[4] However, achieving consensus might prove difficult as national budgets and the "overall balance of taxing rights" will be affected, besides several issues at technical and administrative level will have to be dealt with. The package of Blueprints released on October 12, 2020, by the OECD has highlighted convergence and divergent views of the Inclusive Framework members and has revised the timeline for reaching a consensus-based solution by mid-2021. The fact that such a framework will have to be agreed upon by 137 countries makes the task even more challenging.[5]

All proposed solutions for taxing the digital economy suggest attribution of profits that go beyond the arm's length principle (ALP). These proposals acknowledge value creation in the market/user jurisdictions and allocate profits in the absence of physical presence of the enterprise. Even though ALP does not address remote taxable presence, it is not wise to completely discount the principle. Hence, it should either be re-examined or applied in tandem with other approaches to arrive at an outcome.

With this background, the present chapter first, delves into the reallocation of taxing rights and discusses nexus-based issues in the context of Indian domestic laws and its tax treaties. With traditional brick and mortar businesses being overhauled by digitalized businesses, this portion of our chapter elaborates upon the wider discourse around whether there is a need to relook at the traditional rules of permanent establishment (PE) due to artificial avoidance challenges of PE, posed by digital advancements and attribution principles. The chapter will discuss the observations of OECD led BEPS Project (under Action Plan 1 and 7) which seeks to address the challenges posed by digitalization of economy combined with its plan to prevent the artificial avoidance of PE status. Second, it elaborates upon the different approaches to profit attribution under the Indian regulations (Rule 10, Section 9(1)(i), explanations thereto and 92 of ITA) and treaty framework (Article 5 & 7) by focusing on the tenets of allocation rules. Highlighting different approaches

---

**[Footnote No. 3 contd.]**

Addressing the Tax Challenges of the Digitalisation of the Economy – Policy Note, (January 23, 2019). **Pillar II Approach** accessible as: Organisation for Economic Cooperation and Development, Public Consultation Document – Global Anti-base Erosion Proposal ("GLoBE") Pillar II (8 November 2019-2 December 2019). **Unified Approach under Pillar I** accessible as: Organisation for Economic Cooperation and Development, Public consultation document Secretariat Proposal for a "Unified Approach" under Pillar One, (October 9, 2019 –November 12, 2019).

4. OECD/G20 Inclusive Framework, *Programme of Work to Develop a Consensus Solution to the Tax Challenges Arising from the Digitalisation of the Economy*, p. 7, paras. 11-13 (OECD 2019), available at www.oecd.org/tax/beps/programme-of-work-to-develop-a-consensus-solution-to-the-tax-challenges-arising-from-the-digitalisation-of-the-economy.pdf.

5. Steffen Postler, "*OECD/International- The OECD' Work on Profit Allocation and Nexus Rules for a Digitalized Economy – A Potential Improvement for the International Tax Framework?*" Bulletin for International Taxation, 2020 (Volume 74), No. 2.

by the OECD and UN, it explains the apportionment methodology. It goes on to discuss proposals that have been presented to tax the digital business models and are being debated to find a consensus-based solution at international level.

## 2. Dissecting the 'Permanent Establishment' Test

### 2.1. Framework of Permanent Establishment under OECD and UN Model Convention

The basic rules of a PE are found in Article 5 of OECD and UN Model Convention ('MC'). The concept of a PE can be either seen as an enabling or a restrictive one.[6] In cases wherein the foreign enterprise has a PE in the source country, it gets the right to tax its cross-border business on net basis. However, if the PE is not established, the source country does not have the right to tax such business income of the enterprise – in this sense it can be a restrictive concept. In essence, PE amounts to a virtual projection of the foreign enterprise of one country into the soil of another country.[7]

In order to analyse India's policy perspective, observations and judicial discourse on the concept (and types) of PE, it is important to understand holistically Article 5 as envisaged under OECD and UN Model Convention. Article 5(1) of the OECD MC defines PE to mean a fixed place of business through which the business of an enterprise is wholly or partly carried on. Article 5(2) provides an inclusive list of establishments constituting a PE - it includes a branch, office, factory, workshop, etc. However, the list is non-exhaustive and can cover other types of establishments too. Article 5(3) is a specific section to include a building site/construction/ installation project within the ambit of a PE if it is in existence for more than 12 months. Article 5(4) excludes certain kinds of "preparatory and auxiliary activities" to not be covered within the scope of a PE – includes the use of facilities solely for the purpose of storage, display or delivery, maintenance of stocks of goods or merchandise for the purposes of processing by other entity, etc. Lastly, Article 5(5) is an Agency PE wherein a PE is deemed to be established in cases wherein a person acts on behalf of an enterprise or habitually concludes contracts/plays a principal role leading to conclusion of contracts (in source country) in the name of foreign enterprise.

While the UN MC is substantially like OECD MC on the definition of a PE (with few variations), the difference between the two conventions is that the OECD

---

6. D.P. Sen Gupta, Chapter 16: India in New Trends in the Definition of Permanent Establishment, (G. Maisto, IBFD).
7. *Commissioner of Income Tax, AP v. Vishakhapatnam Port Trust*, (1983) 14 ITR 146 (Supreme Court).

model does not recognize a service PE.[8] According to UN MC, a service PE is constituted in cases where services are furnished through an employee or other personnel continuously (in same or connected projects) for more than 183 days in any 12-month period.

In terms of India's position on the concept of a PE, a few of India's old treaties with Egypt and Greece are on the lines of the 1962 draft OECD Model. However, all the recent treaties tend to expand the ambit of a PE and corollary are closer to the prevalent UN model.[9] Article 5(1) of OECD and UN MC are worded similarly, and all of Indian tax treaties except with Bulgaria[10] follow the same language. The difference in language is evident (in India's tax treaties) in terms of Article 5(2), (3), (4) and (5).

In terms of Article 5(2) of the Model Conventions, Indian tax treaties include other items such as 'warehouse in relation to a person providing storage facility for others', 'farm, plantation or other place where agriculture, forestry, plantation or related activities are carried on', or 'premises used as a sales outlet or for receiving or soliciting orders' in the list of illustrations.[11] In the context of Article 5(3) with regard to building sites, installation projects, and construction sites being considered as a PE, most of the Indian tax treaties follow the UN MC with variation in the time threshold.[12] The Indian tax treaties also follow the UN model in terms of inclusion of the provision of a service PE[13] and an insurance PE[14]. Indian tax treaties

8. The OECD Model Convention has specifically excluded services PE on account of various policy and administrative considerations. Determining service PE could increase compliance and administrative burden as rules are specifically designed basis time spent by the personnel in the source state. However often, enterprise would run into the risk of constituting a PE in unexpecting circumstances where they would be unable to determine in advance as to how long personnel would stay in a particular country. Another issue pertains to attribution of profits owing lack of fixed place of business (OECD Commentary 2017).
9. *Supra* note 19.
10. The treaty with Bulgaria has added "separately or together with other persons".
11. Treaties with Armenia, Belarus, Brazil, China, Jordan, Morocco, Namibia, Philippines, Qatar, Romania, Russia, South Africa and Ukraine include installation or structure used for the purpose of exploration of mineral resources, either separately or in conjunction with Article 5(2)(f) of the model Conventions.
12. Art. 5(3)(a) of the UN MC provides a time- period of more than 6 months for a building site, construction, assembly or installation project or any supervisory activities in connection therewith to constitute PE. Treaties with Iceland, Luxembourg, Namibia and Saudi Arabia broadly follow Art. 5(3) of the UN MC with few variations in terms of time threshold.
13. Art. 5(3)(b) of the UN Model envisages service PE rule providing for 6-months' time- period. Most Indian treaties such as USA, UK, Singapore, Luxembourg, Canada, etc. contain such clause with varied time-period in the range of 3-9 months. Treaties with Canada, China, Singapore, Switzerland, UK and USA do not contain the expression 'same or connected projects' in Art. 5(3)(b).
14. Insurance PE has been stipulated under Article 5(6) of UN Model. See Art. 5(6) of India - Zambia Income Tax Treaty (2018); Art. 5(6) of Finland - India Income Tax Treaty (2010); Art. 5(6) of India - Malaysia Income Tax Treaty (2012).

also omit exclusion of "use of facilities for the purpose of delivery of goods belonging to the enterprise" as contained in the OECD MC (Article 5(4)(a)).[15]

Before delving into the nuances of the kinds of PEs, it is pertinent to highlight that OECD led BEPS Project as launched by OECD released several BEPS Action reports, which addressed measures to counteract double non-taxation, end treaty abuses, and ensure that profits are taxed at the place of their value creation. To this end, "Multilateral Convention to Implement Tax Treaty Related Measures to Prevent Base Erosion and Profit Shifting" (MLI) was released and has been presently signed by almost 94 developed and developing countries, including India. MLI, which is effective in India since October 1, 2019[16] seeks to modify almost 93 (as Covered Tax Agreements) of India treaties to implement tax treaty-related measures as suggested in BEPS Action Reports. In the context of a PE, Article 12-15 of the MLI provides for measures contemplated under BEPS Action 7 to curb artificial avoidance of PE through commissionaire arrangements, specific activity exemptions (as stipulated under 5(4)); and splitting of contracts.

The subsequent paragraphs will elaborate upon the three main kinds of PE as recognized by Indian tax treaties – (a) Fixed place of business PE (b) Agency PE, and (c) Service PE. While discussing each of these types, the paragraphs will also highlight India's policy stance/observations, judicial discourse on the ambit of such PE, and the impact of MLI provisions (pertaining to PE) on India's tax treaties.

### *2.1.1. Fixed place of business PE*

A fixed place business PE is constituted in fulfilment of following requirements:

- There must be a fixed place.
- Business of an enterprise should be carried on wholly or partly through such fixed place.
- The business/activities of such enterprise should not fall within "preparatory and auxiliary activities" under Article 5(4) of OECD Model.

A 'place of business' includes any premise, facility, machinery, etc. used by the foreign company to conduct its business in India.[17] Consequently, a moving vehicle or a ship cannot constitute a PE (unless the operation of ship is restricted to a

15. Treaties such as Turkey and Singapore contain the term "Occasional delivery" under the list of exclusions for PE.
16. India signed MLI on June 7, 2017. On June 25, 2019, India deposited its instrument of ratification to OECD, Paris along with its terms of CTAs, Reservations, Options and Notifications under the MLI, as a result of which MLI will enter into force for India on 01st October 2019 and its provisions will have effect on India's DTAAs from FY 2020-21 onwards. See: https://pib.gov.in/PressReleasePage.aspx?PRID=1576728#:~:text=On%2025th%20June%2C%202019%2C%20India,and%20its%20provisions%20will%20have.
17. OECD Model Commentary 2017 on Article 5.

particular area that has commercial and geographic coherence). Further, in order to attract the taxing statute, there has to be some activity performed on a regular basis through the place of business.[18] It has been held that even automated equipment used for carrying on the core business of a foreign enterprise without human intervention may result in a PE.[19],[20] It is pertinent to highlight that India has not accepted the OECD position, which stipulates that a PE is not constituted if the enterprise merely sets up machines and then leases the machines to other enterprises.[21]

*'At the disposal' test*

Even though the 'at the disposal' test does not find mention in tax treaties, the Indian judiciary has often relied on this test to determine the existence of a fixed place PE. The Supreme Court has observed that "for ascertaining whether there is a fixed place or not, a permanent establishment must have three characteristics: stability, productivity, and dependence". Further, the fixed place of business must be a location *at the disposal* of the enterprise through which business is carried on.[22] Basis this test, the Delhi ITAT has held that a related company's office,[23] office of the agents,[24] and occasional use of place[25] do not constitute a place at the disposal of an enterprise, thereby not making them a fixed place PE.

In this context, India has not accepted the OECD commentary in relation to the 'right-to-use test,' – which stipulates that in cases where an enterprise does not have a right to be present at a location and does not use the location itself, the location cannot be considered to be at the disposal of the enterprise (through which business is conducted). In the *E-Funds* case, interpreting the word 'through', Delhi High Court has observed that the word 'through' must be interpreted and read in the manner that the foreign enterprise should have the right to use the location in the second state. Similarly, in *Rolls Royce* Case, the Court observed that Article 5(1) does not refer that the premises should belong to the enterprise, but it should be able to use the same, and it is an identified and distinct location on which he exercises the control, then only it will constitute a PE within Article 5(1).[26]

---

18. Though there can be some interruption of operation – OECD Commentary on Article 5.
19. IN: ITAT Delhi, *Amandeus Global Travel Distribution SA v. DCIT* (2007), ITA Nos. 2143-45/Del/2000.
20. Even automated equipment such as server can also create PE AAR, *MasterCard Asia Pacific Pte. Ltd.*, (2018), AAR No. 1573 of 2014.
21. OECD Commentary on Article 5 (Paragraph 41).
22. *Formula One World Championship Ltd. v. Commissioner of Income Tax, International Taxation-3, Delhi and Ors*, (2017) 394.
23. *Motorola Inc v. DCIT,* 95 ITD SB 259.
24. IN: SC, October 24, 2017, *E-funds IT Solution Inc. v. Asst. DIT*, Civil Appeal No. 6802 of 2015.
25. IN: ITAT, May 21, 2010, *Airlines Rotables UK v. Joint Director of Income Tax.*
26. *Rolls Royce Plc v. DDIT* (122 TTJ 359) (Delhi ITAT).

*'Permanence or fixity' requirement*

There must be certain degree of permanence or a link between the place of business and a definite geographical area of location to constitute a "fixed place of business". However, India's observations to the OECD commentary suggest that the Indian Revenue tends to assert more on source country taxing rights. For instance, India has not agreed with the OECD position,[27] which stipulates that satellite footprint in the space of the source country cannot be treated as a

PE. Similarly, India has not agreed to the OECD position,[28] which does not treat undersea cables and pipelines lying in the territorial jurisdiction of a source country as the PE of an enterprise. In a case where a taxpayer rendered services to the Oil and Natural Gas Corporation of India through its vessels, the AAR ruled that the vessels in high seas pass all three tests of constituting a fixed place PE - permanence, fixed place (which are the vessels in the high seas in a definite and composite geographical area) and 'at the disposal' test.[29]

In terms of timeline, India's DTAAs do not specify any time threshold relating to the presence of a foreign company in the country for it to constitute a PE.[30] Indian judiciary, having realised this, has been of the opinion that based on the business activities of foreign companies in India, their presence in the country should be for a 'reasonable period of time' for them to constitute a fixed place PE.[31] Recently, the Supreme Court has held that a foreign company can constitute a PE even if its activities in India are undertaken only for three days. The decision is premised on the reasoning that if a foreign enterprise conducts business in India for a limited number of days during which it has complete control over and access to it, it is sufficient for it to constitute a PE in India.[32]

### *2.1.2. Agency PE*

Article 5(5) defines constitution of Agency PE on satisfaction of following conditions:

- There needs to be a person acting on behalf of an enterprise;
- Such person much undertake activities on behalf of the enterprise, including habitually concluding the contract or playing the principal role in leading to its conclusion; and

27. Para 27 of OECD Commentary to Article 5.
28. Paragraph 64 of the OECD Commentary to Article 5.
29. *Seabird Exploration FZ LLC* (AAR NO. 1295 of 2012).
30. Both OECD and UN commentary recognize that is a foreign company maintains a fixed place of business in another country for a period of more than 6 months, it is likely to constitute fixed place PE.
31. *Visakhapatnam Port Trust* (AP HC) (1985); *Subsea Offshore Ltd.* (Mum ITAT) (1998); *Fugro Engineers BV* (Delhi ITAT) (2008).
32. *Formula One World Championship Ltd. v. Commissioner of Income Tax, International Taxation-3, Delhi and Ors,* (2017) 394.

- Activities undertaken by such person should not fall under "preparatory and auxiliary activities" under Article 5(4).

*Person acting on behalf of enterprise*

A person in a contracting state acts on behalf of an enterprise when legally enforceable rights and obligations are created between the enterprise (on behalf of which the person is acting) and the third party with which such contract is concluded. However, an agency PE would not be constituted in cases wherein an enterprise carries on business dealings through an independent agent. The determination of whether a person acting as an agent is independent is largely dependent upon the extent of the obligation, which the person has vis-a-vis the enterprise. Some of the determinative factors would be (a) whether the agent is subject to detailed instructions or comprehensive control of enterprise - in this regard, contractors have been recognized as independent agents as they are independent of any control or interference and are only bound to produce specified results.[33] (b) whether the entrepreneurial risk has to be borne by the person or by the enterprise the person represents (c) whether the agent has undertaken to conduct activities of the principal in its ordinary course of business.[34] (d) whether his activities are wholly or almost wholly on behalf of the foreign enterprise[35]

*Person must undertake activities on behalf of enterprise, including habitually concluding the contract or playing the principal role in leading to the conclusion of contract*

The term 'habitually exercises' has been held to mean a systematic course of conduct on the part of the agent. However, it has been held that in order to constitute a dependent agent PE, it is necessary that the agent should have habitually and actually exercised such authority and merely having authority does not constitute a PE.[36] [37]Further, the phrase "or playing the principal role in leading to the conclusion of contract" is aimed at situations where the conclusion of a contract directly results from the actuals that the person performs in a contracting state, even though under relevant law, the contract is not concluded by that person in the state. Where a person is soliciting and receiving orders that are sent directly to a warehouse

33. In re: ABC (2005) 193 CTR 328 (AAR).
34. OECD Commentary on Article 5(5).
35. *Western Union Financial Services Inc. v. ADIT*, ITA No. 4889/Delhi/04.
36. IN: *B4U International Holdings Ltd. v. DDIT*, ITAT Mumbai May 28, 2012, the tribunal noted that the agent was an independent contractor as it did not have authority to conclude contracts. It also had no authority to fix the rate or to accept an advertisement. It can merely forward the advertisement and the taxpayer had the right to reject; In *Western Union Financial Services Inc. v. ADIT* the tribunal opined that the fact that agent concluded in India the commitment of the taxpayer made abroad cannot be considered as an authority to conclude contracts.
37. IN: ITAT Mumbai: September 7, 2010, *Salil Serventilal Shah* (2010), ITA 3229/Mum/2009.

from which goods belonging to the enterprise are delivered, and the enterprise routinely approves such transactions – these transactions will be considered as a person who is habitually playing the principal role in the conclusion of contracts.[38]

### *2.1.3. Service PE*

As noted above, India has taken a divergent approach from the OECD in terms of service PE and has followed the UN MC, on the same. Under Article 5(3)(b) of the UN MC a service PE is constituted in cases where employees or personnel engaged by the enterprise furnishes services, including consultancy service within a contracting state for more than 183 days in any 12-month period. Additionally, India also added the provision for taxing fees for technical services in 1976,[39] which includes services in the nature of managerial, technical, or consultancy. India's desire to thrust services PE is also evident when Supreme Court ruled that for Section 9(1)(vii)[40] of the Income-tax Act, 1961, to be applicable, services should be utilized and rendered in India. This led to the retrospective amendment of the law and a new Explanation was added to clarify the legislative intent that for purposes of this section, the income of a non-resident will be deemed to accrue or arise in India if it is utilised in India and that services need not be rendered in India.

In respect of outsourcing arrangements, the Delhi High Court has clarified that even if the core activities of the foreign enterprise are outsourced to an Indian affiliate under a sub-contract arrangement, with the Indian affiliate bearing the limited risk, it should not create a PE for the foreign enterprise. It also confirmed that the visits by personnel of the foreign enterprise for stewardship activities or secondment of personnel who work under the direction and control of the Indian affiliate should not result in a service PE.[41] The ruling is in variance with the Supreme Court decision in Morgan Stanley[42] case wherein it was held that secondment of personnel by Morgan Stanley US to Morgan Stanley India resulted in a service PE of Morgan Stanley US since the personnel had a lien on their employment with Morgan Stanley US, even if they were working under the control and supervision of the Indian entity. Following the Supreme Court ruling, the Delhi High Court has observed that so long as there is a lien on employment with the foreign employer and the right of termination of the seconded employee vest with

38. OECD Commentary on Article 5, 38[89].
39. The source rule for taxation of "royalty" / "FTS" was introduced vide Circular No. 202 dated May 7, 1976.
40. Section 9(1)(vii) deals with "fees for technical services".
41. *DIT v. e-funds IT Solution and Ors*, (2014) 42 taxmann.com 50 (Delhi High Court).
42. *DIT (International Taxation) Mumbai and Ors v. Morgan Stanley and co. Inc. and Ors*, (2007) 7 SCC 1.

the foreign employer, a "service PE" is constituted.[43] The issue[44] around the secondment of employees remains tricky, considering that in most cases, foreign expatriates prefer to retain their employment with the foreign parent for the purpose of continuing their social security contributions.[45]

## 2.2. Nexus for Income Taxation under Indian Income-tax Act, 1961 and Indian Tax Treaties

Internationally, jurisdictions have recognized two basic principles for allocation of taxation rights *i.e.,* residence-based taxation and source-based taxation. Broadly put, state of source is the *situs* where a certain income originates while the state of residence is the state where the person earning such income has its residence. Most jurisdictions, including India tax their residents based on the global income applying residence-based taxation rules and tax non-residents on their income sourced in that country applying source-based taxation rules.[46]

To curb jurisdictional and economic double taxation, most often, the domestic laws of countries prescribe the threshold for taxing business profits of a foreign enterprise carrying on business within their taxable territory. Under the Indian domestic law,[47] while the global income of a resident is taxable, the taxability of income of a non-resident is limited to income that *arises or accrues in India, or is*

43. *DDIT v. Tekmark Global Solutions LLC,* (2010) 131 TTJ 173; *Centrica India Offshore Pvt ltd v. CIT,* (2014) 44 taxmann.com 300 (Delhi High Court).

44. Under the OECD Model, such an arrangement could only create a PE for the seconding company if the employee is not the "economic employee" of the secondee company. The concept of the "economic employer" is used to determine whether a non-resident enterprise is providing services via its employee to a customer in the host state or whether the worker in question has, in reality, become a de facto employee of the host state customer. The concept of "economic employer" is addressed in the Commentary on Article 15 and also in the Commentary on Article 5. See: para. 39 of the 2012 Discussion Draft. See also: paras. 8.12 to 8.28.

45. In contrary to OECD positions, in *Centrica India Offshore Private Ltd v. CIT* AAR No. 856 of 2010 it was decided that a PE arose in India where foreign affiliates seconded managerial staff to the Indian affiliate, even though the seconded employees worked under the direction of the Indian company and the seconding companies were not responsible for the work performed by the secondees. Because the salaries are normally reimbursed in full by the Indian companies to the non-resident employers, little Indian tax arises in connection with this type of PE. However, where the reimbursement of the salary cost to the overseas employer is characterized by India as technical service fees, then WHT is normally in point. It has been noted that under a secondment whereby the Indian affiliate becomes the economic employer, the only Indian taxes due are employment taxes See: *M/s IDS Software Solutions (India) Private Limited v. Income Tax Officer (International Taxation Bangalore* (ITA No. 87/Bang/08) and *Verizon Data Services India (P.) Ltd v. DDIT,* (2011) AAR No. 865 of 2010.

46. Mukesh Butani and Parul Jain, *Permanent Establishment Concept – The Indian Concept,* Asia Pacific Tax Bulletin, July/August 2014.

47. Section 5 of ITA. The resident status is provided in section 6 of ITA.

*deemed to accrue or arise in India, or is received or is deemed to be received in India.*[48] Section 5(2) of the Income-tax Act, 1961 (ITA) explains the scope of 'total income', a term which has been defined in Section 2(45) of the ITA. Income is said to be received when it actually reaches the assessee's hands; but short of receipt, when the right to receive the income becomes vested in the assessee, it is said to accrue or arise.[49] The words 'deemed to accrue' have only relation to what has been so made to accrue under the provisions of the Act; whereas it is not in reality so, but by the force of the statute, it is treated to be so.[50]

Section 9 of the ITA encapsulates income that is deemed to accrue or arise in India by way of 'Business Connection Test' ('BC').[51] The ITA however, did not specifically define the phrase 'Business Connection' until 2004. The BC connection rule has been a feature under the tax code dating to the 1922 Act, and given India's rich jurisprudence, it has been a constant subject of interpretation by India's tax tribunal and courts, including the Supreme Court. Besides constant amendment to the BC test over the years, the focus of the lawmakers has resulted in the proliferation of foreign direct investment and the consequential surge in cross-border transactions. In the following paras, we have listed changes in the law as regards expansive profit attribution principles.

From AY 2004-05, Explanation 2[52] was added to provide an inclusive definition of BC. Later, Explanation 2(a) was amended *vide* Finance Act 2018 to widen the scope of business connection test[53] with an aim to curb commissionaire arrangements (aligning itself with BEPS Action Plan 7). The amended Explanation 2 includes within the scope of BC – any person acting on behalf of a non-resident who habitually exercises in India an authority to conclude contracts or habitually plays the principal role leading to the conclusion of contracts; habitually maintains stocks of goods in India;[54] habitually secures orders[55] wholly or mainly for the non-resident.[56]

48. A. Datar (Ed.), *Kanga and Palkhivala's The Law and Practice of Income Tax*, 332 (2014); V. Gupta, Comprehensive Guide to Direct Taxes, 87 (2014); *CIT CEPT v. Bhogilal Laherchand*, [1954] 25 ITR 50 (SC).
49. *Seth Madan Lal Modi v. CIT*, [2003] 126.
50. *CIT v. Jai Prakash Om Prakash Co. Ltd.*, [1961] 41 ITR 781 (Punj.).
51. Section 9(1)(i) of ITA.
52. Inserted by the Finance Act 2003, w.e.f. 1.4.2004.
53. The amendment provided for a wider ''Dependent Agency Test' than that provided before the amendment. Explanation 2(a) prior to amendment read as: "has and habitually exercises in India, an authority to conclude contracts on behalf of the non-resident, unless his activities are limited to the purchase of goods or merchandise for the non-resident;".
54. Explanation 2(b) to 9(1)(i) of ITA.
55. In *Rolls Royce plc. v. Dy. DIT*, [2008] 19 SOT 42 (Delhi) it was observed that the phrase "secure orders" does not require that the resident must have the authority to conclude orders on behalf of the non-resident. The same phrase, when used in the India-UK DTAA, has been interpreted to cover situations where the agent "has no authority to negotiate and enter into contracts for and on behalf of appellant.
56. Explanation 2(c) to 9(1)(i) of ITA.

In essence, BC is a source rule formed on the premise that if a non-resident has sufficient (economic) nexus with India, so as to postulate a *real and intimate* relation[57] between an activity carried on outside India and a business activity undertaken in India, and the relation between the two contributes to the earning of income by the non-resident such income is attributable to BC thereby taxable in India.[58] For business connection test to be satisfied, courts have observed that there must also be an *element of continuity*[59] between the non-resident taxpayer doing business with a person in India[60] [61]; some part of business operations *must be performed in India,* [62]and the transaction should not be on a *casual and isolated* basis.[63]

The scope of BC has been expanded by addition of 'Significant Economic Test' ('SEP') *vide* Explanation 2A to Section 9(1)(i) of ITA.[64] The amendment aligns itself with measures suggested under BEPS Action Plan 1 Report and has been defined to cover:

- Any transaction with respect to goods or services (including downloading of data) in India exceeding a prescribed amount of aggregate revenue.

---

57. *CIT v. Hindustan Shipyard Ltd.*, 1975 Indlaw AP 33; *GVK v. ITO*, 1997 Indlaw AP 162. "common thread of mutual interest must run through the fabric of the trading activities carried on outside and inside the taxable territory".
58. *CIT v. R.D. Aggrawal & Co*, (1994) 56 ITA 20 (SC). The Court distinguished this case from the earlier case of *Abdullabhai Abdul Kadar v. CIT*, [1952] 22 ITR 241 (Bom.), where the agents, in a similar fact situation, were entrusted with the authority to accept orders on behalf of the non-residents. It was emphasized that the fact that the non-residents were not obliged to accept the orders canvassed by the assesses and therefore found that there was no real and intimate connection in the present case.
59. *Sutron Corpn. v. DIT*, [2003] 268 ITR 156 (AAR) - "It must be shown that there exists as "a course of dealing and continuity of relationship and not a mere isolated or stray nexus between the business of the non-resident outside India and the activity in India."
60. Th*e commissioner of Income Tax v. Fried Kupp Industries*, (Tax case Nos. 357 to 360 of 1976 dated 2 May 1980).
61. Recently the ITAT has also stressed upon the concept of 'virtual and intangible connection' in a matter concerning withholding tax on the amount to be paid for a celebrity appearance at a promotional event (by the assessee). The Court noted that: "*Today,* ***virtual and intangible business connections*** *are perhaps far more critical, important and commonplace than the conventional brick and mortar business connections half a century ago, and, therefore,* ***to disregard these business connections as a real and intimate business connection*** *leading to earning of income by the non-residents, only because Hon'ble Courts, while delivering judgments several decades ago, could not visualize the same and hedge their observations about such possibilities, will certainly be travesty of justice.*" See: *Volkswagen Finance Pvt. Ltd. v. Income Tax Officer, International Taxation Ward,* 2020 SCC Online ITAT 132.
62. *The Commissioner of Income Tax v. Assam Consolidated Tea Estates Ltd.* (IT Reference NO. 343 of 1975).
63. *Anglo French Textile Co. Ltd. v. The Commissioner of Income Tax*, (Civil Appeal No. 12 of 1952 dated December 22, 1952). Further the term business has been defined to mean 'profession' or 'vocation' in *Barendra Prosad Ray v. ITO*, (Civil Appeal No. 1038 of 1973 dated April 7, 1981).
64. Inserted by the Finance Act, 2018, w.e.f.1-4-2019.

- The continuous soliciting of business or interacting with users through digital means in India.

Though the SEP provision was expected to be made effective from April 1, 2018, its implementation was deferred to April 1, 2021 by the Finance Act of 2020. The deferment was owing to several reasons including non-finalization of nexus attribution principles, absence of its efficacy to apply to treaty countries, absence of amendment to PE rules and in anticipation of OECD consensus approach.

The transaction or activities shall constitute SEP in India whether the agreement for such transactions is entered into India or the non-resident has a resident or place of business in India or renders services in India. Analysis of SEP provision under ITA suggests that it adopts both (a) revenue-based test, (b) user-based test, and (c) it applies to all forms of nexus – digital and non-digital forms of business. In contrast to what has been suggested under BEPS Report 2015, both tests have been provided under the ITA as alternatives – suggesting that satisfaction of each of the tests would lead to the constitution of SEP in India. Therefore, it is clear the SEP test as adopted in India is wider than that recommended by BEPS.[65]

For now, the discussion is largely academic, considering the Finance Bill, 2020 has deferred the enforcement of the said SEP provision up to April 1, 2022.[66] The deferral is in light of much awaited global consensus on the subject of digital taxation. It is important to point out that the SEP test, which will technically be applicable (to non-treaty countries), goes beyond the nexus rules that are being envisaged under the OECD Unified Approach. It widens the reach of the BC test and suggests India's policy stance.

Besides the deferral, the SEP provision was further amended[67] to categorically lists down certain income that will be attributable to the operations carried out in India. The said amendment as applicable from April 1, 2021 includes income from[68]:

- Advertisement which targets a customer who resides in India or a customer who accesses the advertisement through IP address located in India;
- Sale of data collected from a person who resides in India or from a person who uses IP address located in India; and
- Sale of goods and services using data collected from a person who resides in India or who uses IP address located in India.

65. ASSOCHAM and BMR Legal Report, "Equalisation Levy 2.0: India's Digital Service Tax in the making", June 7, 2020.
66. Finance Bill 2020, Provisions relating to Direct taxes available at: https://www.indiabudget.gov.in/doc/memo.pdf.
67. Explanation 3A to Section 9, ITA.
68. *Supra* note 24.

It is pertinent to highlight that such expansion of SEP provision under ITA converges with Equalization Levy 2020.[69] This has significant implications as once the SEP provisions become effective, it may render the application of Equalization Levy 2020 redundant. Hence, it is imperative that the government clarifies that EL 2020 is a temporary measure till the time SEP law comes into force.

While the application of BC is relevant from the perspective of the application of Section 9 of ITA, the concept of PE becomes relevant for assessing the business profits/income of a non-resident under DTAA.[70] The word 'Permanent Establishment' postulates the existence of a substantial element of an enduring or permanent nature of a foreign enterprise in another country, which can be attributed to a fixed place of business in that contracting state. According to the concept of PE,[71] the profits of a contracting state are taxable in the other state only if the enterprise constitutes a PE in the latter state to the extent of profits attributable to such a PE. It has been established that the concept of BC under the ITA is wider than the concept of PE under DTAAs, hence if a non-resident has a PE in India, the business connection in India stands established.[72] The application of the concept of PE becomes relevant in cases whereby a foreign enterprise (carrying business activities in India) is a resident of a country with which India has a DTAA, in such cases business income of such an enterprise would be taxable in accordance with the DTAA. Such determination has two elements: (a) determination of BC or a PE under Article 5 of DTAA, and Rule 10 read with Chapter X for determination of income between related parties under arm's length principle. However, for enterprises residing in a country with which India does not have a DTAA such enterprises would be taxable in accordance with BC test under the ITA. The following sections will elaborate upon the nuances of PE test under India's DTAAs.

## 2.3. PE and Multilateral Instrument

### *2.3.1. Article 12: Artificial avoidance of PE through commissionaire arrangements*

A 'commissionaire arrangement' encapsulates an arrangement through which a person sells products in a state in its own name but on behalf of a foreign

69. Equalization Levy 2020 has been introduced *vide* Finance Act 2020. It expands the scope of Equalization levy provisions as introduced vide Finance Act 2016. The Equalization Levy 2020 as stipulated under Section 165A is a 2% levy on non-resident or a person who owns or manages a digital electronic facility for online sale of goods or provision of services or both. The tax is paid on consideration for e-commerce supplies or services.

70. *Ishikawajima Harima Heavy Industries Ltd v. DIT Mumbai*, AIR 2007 SC 929.

71. Article 7 of OECD Model Convention on Income and on Capital 2017 and UN Model Double Tax Convention between Developed and Developing Countries 2017 (hereinafter referred as: OECD and UN Model Convention)

72. *Formula One World Championship Ltd. v. Commissioner of Income Tax, International Taxation-3, Delhi and Ors*, (2017) 394 ITR 80 (Supreme Court).

enterprise,[73] the actual owner of the products. As highlighted in BEPS Action 7 Report,[74] through such arrangements, a foreign enterprise is able to sell its products in a contracting state without having a PE to which such sales would ordinarily be attributed for tax purposes, primarily for this reason the person that concludes the sales does not own the products it sells, hence, can only be taxed on the remuneration that it receives for its services (commission). Another BEPS strategy that is employed to avoid the application of Article 5(5) involves scenarios wherein contracts, which are substantially negotiated in a contracting state are not concluded in that state. This is because if the contracts are finalised/authorised abroad, or where the person habitually exercises an authority to conclude contracts – it would constitute an 'independent agent' thereby falling within the exception of Article 5(6)[75] of the OECD MC. Such tactics prevent the establishment of a PE and eradicate the taxable base of the state wherein sales or negotiations took place.

To this end, Action Plan 7 suggests certain amendments to the wordings of Article 5(5) and 5(6) of OECD MC,[76] which have been embodied in Article 12 of MLI. Article 12(1) provides that where a person acting on behalf of the enterprise habitually concludes contracts or habitually plays the principal role leading to the conclusion of contracts[77] that are routinely concluded without material modification by the principal, then the enterprise will be deemed to have a PE. The caveat to the application of para (1) is that such activities should not be preparatory or auxiliary in nature. The provision aims to curb commissionaire arrangements. Further, Article 12(2) provides that an independent agent in his ordinary course of business is not covered unless such a person acts exclusively or almost exclusively for one or more entities to which he is closely related (Refer to discussion in Article 15).

*Apropos* India, it has not made any reservations to Article 12 of MLI.[78] However, applying Article 12 to a particular CTA of India is subject to its other treaty partner not exercising its right of reservation to Article 12 and having notified the same. For instance, Singapore, Sweden, and UK have exercised their right to reservation for the entirety of Article 12, hence the changes stipulated under the MLI will not amend agency PE definition under such DTAA. Interestingly, even though India has not

73. OECD/G20 Base Erosion and Profit Shifting Project, "Preventing the Artificial Avoidance of Permanent Establishment Status" Action 7: 2015 final report. Accessible at: https://www.oecd-ilibrary.org/docserver/9789264241220-en.pdf?expires=1603954694&id=id&accname=guest&checksum= ED0AEB9E756BE1FBACD0F798554A629F

74. *Ibid.*

75. Even though such independent agent is closely related to the foreign enterprise on behalf of which it is acting.

76. Such amendments have been suggested to Article 5(5) and 5(6) of OECD Model Convention 2014.

77. The contracts are either (i) in the name of the enterprise (ii) for the transfer of ownership or the right to use property belonging to the enterprise; or(iii) for providing services by the enterprise.

78. See: http://www.oecd.org/tax/treaties/beps-mli-position-india-instrument-deposit.pdf.

made any reservation on this Article, it has stated its position on Article 5(4) of OECD Model (2017) to the effect that it reserves the right to omit the word 'routinely' in its treaties. Further, recently notified treaties of India with Kenya[79] and Hong Kong[80] do not incorporate MLI recommended provisions under Article 12.

Further, as noted in the preceding section, the Indian government has aligned the domestic law regarding agency related Business Connection in line with the treaty definition *via* Finance Act, 2018.[81] Post amendment, the mere purchase for exception does not constitute BC. Further, in contrast to MLI the phrase 'routine conclusion of contracts without material modification by the enterprise' has not been adopted in the domestic law. This also explains India's reservation on the word 'routinely' under Article 5(4) (of OECD 2017) despite fully adopting MLI provision.

### *2.3.2. Article 13: Artificial avoidance of PE through specific activity exemptions*

Article 13 of MLI deals with artificial avoidance of PE through specific activity exemption under Article 5(4) of PE. As per Article 5(4) of OECD MC a PE is deemed not to exist where a place of business is used solely for the activities as stipulated in the said article. However, as noted in BEPS Action 7 Report,[82] at the time of introduction of Article 5(4), the activity so exempted were generally considered to be of preparatory and auxiliary in nature. In recent years with the economy witnessing vast digitalization, there has been a monumental change in the way businesses are conducted – activities previously considered to be of preparatory or auxiliary in nature may nowadays correspond to core business activities. In order to ensure that profits derived from core activities performed in a country can be taxed in that country, BEPS Action 7 Report suggests modifications to Article 5(4), which are encapsulated under Article 13.

Article 13 provides parties to MLI two set of options: Option A replaces the treaty provision to the extent that (i) all activities currently included (whether or not they are preparatory or auxiliary in nature); (ii) any other activity not already mentioned in the treaty; and (iii) a combination of activities in (i) and (ii) to fall within the specific activity exemption provision only if all such activities (or the overall activity of a fixed place business from a combination of activities) are of preparatory or auxiliary in nature. Hence, Option A does not change the original list of activities stipulated under Article 5(4) but introduces a qualification to avail specific activity exemption to establish a fixed place PE.

---

79. Notified on February 19, 2018. Further under MLI there is a notification mismatch as both the countries have not identified a similar provision. Article 12(2) would apply with respect of Article 5(7).
80. Hong Kong has concluded its treaty with India on March 19, 2018 and notified on November 30, 2018. Hong Kong is not part of India's CTA so Article 12 of MLI will not be applicable.
81. Explanation 2(a) to 9(1)(i) amendment *vide* Finance Act, 2018.
82. *Supra* note 66, Page 9.

Option B was brought in to address the concerns of certain states which felt that activities referred under sub-paragraphs (a) to (d) of Article 5(4) are intrinsically preparatory or auxiliary in nature and hence in order to ensure greater certainty for both taxpayers and administration, Article 5(4) should not be subjected to any qualification. Further, the policymakers argued that most of the BEPS concerns originate from the fragmentation of activities between closely related parties and hence, most of these concerns would be addressed by the inclusion of an anti-fragmentation rule as provided under Article 13(4). Basis this rationale, Option B allows the countries to continue with the existing conditions mentioned therein.

Additionally, an anti-fragmentation rule is stipulated under Article 13(4), which applies to both options. As per the said provision, specific activity exemption will not be applicable in cases where the enterprise or its closely related enterprise carries on business at the same place or another place in the same contracting jurisdiction. The proviso further clarifies that for non-applicability of specific activity exemption as stipulated under Article 13(4) it has to be ensured that the combined activities by the non-resident and closely related non-resident enterprises result in cohesive business operation such that the overall activities performed in the source state are not merely preparatory or auxiliary in nature.

India has chosen Option A and has not reserved against paragraph 4. Thus, India's CTAs will be amended to the extent its treaty partner has opted for Option A.[83] It is expected that such a choice would be able to tackle recurring issues wherein taxpayers have successfully claimed that an Indian subsidiary having a fixed place only provided preparatory or auxiliary activities (under treaty) to the enterprise that directly supplied relevant goods or services to Indian customers.[84]

### *2.3.3. Article 14: Splitting up of contracts*

Article 14 of MLI stipulates in cases wherein an enterprise's project is carried on for more than 30 days, and connected activities are carried on at the same project (in respect of a building site, construction project etc.) by related entities at different times for a period exceeding 30 days, in such a case the different periods of time will be aggregated for calculating the overall time limit. The provision also includes 'supervisory activities' and 'consultancy services' undertaken in connection with specified activities, including contraction or installation at building sites for determination of a construction PE. The word 'supervisory' and 'consultancy' are

83. India-Sweden DTAA to remain unchanged as Sweden as reserved the application of Article 13. Netherlands has notified Option A. France and Singapore have chosen Option B with no reservation on Article 4 – hence India's treaty with France and Singapore will be modified to the extent of changes suggested under Article 13(4).
84. D.P. Sen Gupta, Chapter 16: India in New Trends in the Definition of Permanent Establishment, (G. Maisto, IBFD).

not included in Article 5 of the OECD MC but have been provided as options in the OECD Commentary.[85]

Article 14 has been implemented to redress the abuse of Article 5(3) of the OECD MC, which stated that building sites or construction shall constitute a PE only if such projects lasted beyond 12 months.[86] It was noticed that time threshold of 12 months had led to several cases of abuse – enterprises (mainly contractors or subcontractors working on a continental shelf) divided their contracts up into several parts, each covering a period less than 12 months and attributed to a different entity, however, owned by the same group. BEPS Action 7 Report noted that even though such kinds of misuse caused by splitting of contracts can be addressed by the Principal Purpose Test under Article 7, it provided an alternative provision (in the form of Article 14) for those countries specifically looking to address the issue.[87]

None of India's existing treaties provides for a similar provision pertaining to the splitting of contracts (as provided under Article 14). Even the most recently notified treaties with Kenya and Hong Kong does not incorporate the newly proposed anti-fragmentation rule as proposed by MLI. Hence, India has not stated its reservation to Article 14 of MLI. Consequently, Article 14 will be applicable to all of India's CTAs to the extent its treaty partner has not made a reservation. The new provision will majorly impact work contracts and the formation of service PEs in India. Thus, foreign enterprises will have to revisit their business models as it would be difficult to fragment operations considering Article 14 and anti-abuse provisions (PPT) under MLI.

### *2.3.4. Article 15: Definition of a Person Closely Related to an enterprise*

The discussion in the preceding paragraphs on measures to address artificial avoidance of PE primarily relies on the phrase 'closely related enterprise'. Hence, it has been separately defined in Article 15. The phrase has been defined to mean that enterprises are closely related if one has control over the other or if both are under common control. In any case, direct or indirect beneficial ownership of more than 50% of the beneficial interest will mean that the enterprises are closely related.

India has not exercised its right to reservation with respect to Article 15, and consequently, all its CTAs stand modified to include this provision. Interestingly, India has expressed its position on Article 5(6) of the OECD Model 2017 to reserve

85. Para 50, OECD Model Commentary on Article 5 (2017).

86. Several Countries have incorporated this provision with varying threshold. India follows UN MC - Art. 5(3)(a) of the UN MC provides a time- period of more than 6 months for a building site, construction, assembly or installation project or any supervisory activities in connection therewith to constitute PE. Treaties with Iceland, Luxembourg, Namibia and Saudi Arabia broadly follow Art. 5(3) of the UN MC with few variations in terms of time threshold.

87. BEPS Action Plan 7 Report Page 11.

its right to include the words 'to which it is closely related' to all its treaties. This is because India believes that control can be exercised even if enterprises are not closely related.

## 2.4. Permanent Establishment in the Context of Digitalization of Economy

### *2.4.1. Taxation of e-commerce transactions*

The proliferation of technology into our day-to-day lives has enabled the conduct of *business without boundaries*, allowing remote conduct of trade and commerce seamlessly at a global level, defying time and distance, unencumbered by infrastructural and technical issues. With traditional brick and mortar business being overhauled by digitalized businesses, the wider discourse is that whether the rules of PE as discussed above needs to be revamped to cope up with the challenges posed by such unique digital advancements.

The traditional concepts of PE have often led foreign enterprises fragment their business activities across several jurisdictions so as to avoid constituting a PE in those jurisdictions, thereby minimizing their taxes. The OECD led BEPS Project (Action Plan 1 and 7) seeks to address the challenges posed by the digitalization of economy and its plan to prevent the artificial avoidance of PE status.

In this regard, BEPS Action Plan 1 recognizes that tax on foreign entities could be imposed *via* the virtual PE mechanism. However, it has been emphasized that such implementation should be through bilateral negotiation with treaty partners.[88] However, in the absence of any amendments to include the virtual PE, internationally, within the scope of PE, mere existence of a website cannot create a PE owing to the fact there may not be a 'place of business' merely by hosting a website on a particular server situated at a particular location. In this regard, India tax authorities have adopted a unilateral position to contend that websites could, in certain circumstances, constitute a PE and have expressed their reservation to the OECD commentary pertaining to PE exposure owing to (a) website hosted on a third-party server which are not leased or otherwise available at the enterprise's disposal and (b) leased automated equipment which is not operated and maintained by the lessor enterprise post-setup.[89]

In relation to revenue earned through advertisement (by search engines such as Google and Yahoo), the Kolkata ITAT has upheld the OECD's position (as stated in the commentary) and noted that a virtual PE can be constituted only when the business of a non-resident is carried through a website hosted on a server in India and where the non-resident has the server at his disposal. However, if a server is not located

88. *Supra* note 1, Page 148.
89. Automated equipment such as server can also create PE as observed in *MasterCard Asia Pacific Pte. Ltd.* (2018), AAR No. 1573 of 2014.

in India, a virtual PE cannot arise by virtue of a website itself.[90] A similar position has also been upheld in the Yahoo case, observing that the payment made by the assessee (a subsidiary of Yahoo Inc., USA) to Yahoo Holdings (Hong Kong) Ltd. ('YHHL') for upholding and display of banner advertisement of the Department of Tourism of India were in the nature of business profits. It was noted that the rendering of the said services did not constitute a PE in India as there was no direct use by the assessee either of the portal or of the server owned by YHHL (outside India).[91]

In this regard, a contrary position has been observed by the Bangalore ITAT in the case of Google[92] on the issue of taxability of payments made by Google India Private Limited in favour of Google Ireland Limited for the purchase of AdWords space (for resale to Indian advertisers as per distribution agreement entered between the parties). Apart from the distribution agreement, Google India had also entered into a service agreement for the provision of IT and ITeS services to Google Ireland.[93] Relying on the Rights Florists case, Google India had contended that the payments for the purchase of such AdWords space should be characterised as business income in Google Ireland's hands. (in the absence of a PE of Google Ireland in India). However, the tribunal distinguished Google's case from earlier rulings,[94] to observe that in the instant case Google India had been given access to the trademarks, brand features, derivate works, confidential information, and other intellectual property of Google Ireland for the discharge of its functions under both agreements. On this basis, the tribunal held that the payment being made was for the use of these intangibles and therefore, should be considered in the nature of royalty and not business income.[95]

---

90. *ITO v. Rights Florists Limited*, ITA No. 1336/Kol/2011.

91. *Yahoo India (P.) Ltd. v. Deputy Commissioner of Income Tax, Range 7(3), Mumbai*, (2011) 140 TTJ 95 (Mumbai) It was noted by the Court that the banner hosting services did not involve use or right to use by the assessee any industrial, commercial or scientific equipment and no such use was granted by YHHL. Further, there was nothing to show any positive act of utilization or employment of the portal owned by YHHL.

92. *Google India (P.) Ltd. v. Joint Director if Income Tax (International Taxation), Range -1, Bengaluru*, (2018) 194 TTJ 385 (Bangalore).

93. For which Google India was being remunerated at cost plus 17.5% basis for the IT services and 15.5% basis for the ITeS.

94. Historically, the Indian courts have consistently held that advertising revenue and payments made under distribution arrangements are in the nature of business income. See: *ITO v. Right Florist*, (2013) 25 ITR (T.) 639; *Pinstrom Technology Ltd., v. ITO* (2012) 54 SOT 78 (Mum. Trib.) and *Yahoo India Pvt. Ltd., v. CIT* 140 TTJ 195 (Mum.Trib.); *Set India Pvt. Ltd.*, ITA No.4372/Mum/2004; *Taj TV Ltd.*, in ITA No. 4678/Mum/2007.

95. While drawing this conclusion the Bangalore tribunal relied on *CIT v. Synopsis International Ltd.*, [2013] 212 Taxman 454 (Karnataka) wherein the Karnataka High Court had held that while there was no transfer of exclusive right of copyright there was a transfer of certain rights which the owner of a copyright possesses, and any consideration paid for use or for the right to use confidential information would amount to royalty income.

In the context of computer server resulting in the constitution of a PE, the Indian judiciary have digressed form the traditional principles of fixed place PE. It has held that non-resident companies providing computerized reservation services (CRS) and engaged in providing real-time access to airline fares and enabling booking are liable to be taxed in India, even though the server was placed outside India. The reasoning is premised on the fact that since part of the CRS was located in the premise of the subscribers where the computer is placed, such premise constitutes a fixed place of business for the non-resident.[96] In the light of the rulings, one can conclude that the establishment of a fixed PE or a dependant agent PE would depend on the infrastructure facilities extended to Indian counterparts and the nature of the scope of operations carried out by the Indian counterpart.

### *2.4.2. BEPS challenges in the context of digital economy*

The OCED's Task Force on digital economy in the Action 1 Final Report has produced an elaborate study on the technological foundations and characteristics of the digital economy.[97] It has regarded the development of Information and Communication Technology ('ICT') as the enabling factor for the digitalization of business in several areas. In addition, the OECD has observed that major players in the digital economy rely on diverse ways of creating, using, and generating revenue with online content, as well as collecting and analysing data. Such diverse ways/ developments include concepts of Internet of Things, virtual currencies, cloud computing, 3D printing,[98] which not only influence the unique nature of digital models but have also created BEPS opportunities in particular relevance to the digital economy.

The four areas of BEPS opportunities[99] as identified by BEPS include (a) eliminating or reducing tax in the market country (b) reducing tax in the resident country, in particular, if valuable (intangible) assets are transferred to an affiliate of low tax regimes (c) avoidance of withholding taxes and (d) elimination or reduction of tax in the intermediate country through the use of specific contractual payments and imposition of holding companies.

The adoption of tax planning strategies that exploit gaps and mismatches in tax rules to artificially shift profits to low or no-tax jurisdictions is further exacerbated in the digital era owing to multi-sided business models with features of reliance on user

---

96. *Galilieo International and Maruthi Info and Tech Centre v. DCIT*, (2007) 114TTJ 289 (ITAT Delhi). A similar approach was also adopted in the case of *Amandeus Global Travel Distribution SA. v. DCIT and DDIT*, (2007) 113 TTJ 767 (ITAT Delhi).
97. OECD/G-20, Addressing the tax challenges of the Digital Economy, Action 1-2015 Final Report (October5, 2015), available at https://www.oecd.org/ctp/addressing-the-tax-challenges-of-the-digital-economy-action-1-2015-final-report-9789264241046-en.htm.
98. *Id.*, At 42-48.
99. *Supra* note 1.

data, mobility, volatility, which enable them to create value without any physical presence. Few examples of such digital business models based on their core business activities are: provision of goods or services digitally in exchange for one-time payment (E.g., Coursera, Amazon), subscription-based models (E.g., Netflix, Amazon Prime Video), participative network platforms (E.g., social networking sites, online gaming websites), and E-commerce marketplace (E.g., Amazon, MakeMyTrip).[100]

Such digital business models with their unparalleled reliance on intangible assets, massive user data, capture value from externalities generated by free products. With these arise difficulties in determining the jurisdictions which create the value and, consequently, to profit attribution as there are no international precedents/ benchmark for taxing such models. There are also issues pertaining to the misalignment of reported revenue with the share of users and digital buyers.[101] Even where such digital service players reportedly carry out significant economic activity in the source country, the margins reported by the players are lower than those reported for global parent company. Consequently, the taxable profits are also a small fraction of their worldwide operations.[102]

In response to these broader challenges OECD in its 2015 report,[103] recommended three possible options:

- A **new nexus**-based approach in the form of SEP test, which would create a taxable presence in the country based on factors that provide evidences of a purposeful and sustained interaction with the economy.
- A **withholding tax** on payments made by residents (and local PEs) on digital goods and services from non-resident providers.
- An **Equalization Levy** to remove the disparity between domestic and foreign suppliers engaged in the similar business. The levy would target those businesses which establish a sustained interaction with users or customers of a specified country via an online presence.

However, OECD did not specifically recommend any one option as internationally agreed standard because such options required further deliberation/work.

100. Vidhi Centre for Legal Policy and BMR Legal Report, *"Removing the Roadblocks in Taxing Businesses Income in the Digital Era: Building Global Consensus for an Equitable Solution"* June 2020.

101. Suranjali Tandon, *Tax Challenges Arising from Digitalization, Asia-Pacific Tax Bulletin*, 2018 (Volume 24), No. 6, November 27, 2018.

102. *Supra* note 10; See also: ProwessIQ database, Centre for Monitoring Indian Economy; Based on GAAP accounting: https://abc.xyz/investor/news/earnings/2016/Q4_alphabet_earnings/; https://investor.fb.com/investor-news/press-release-details/2017/Facebook-Reports-Fourth-Quarter-and-Full-Year-2016-Results/default.aspx.

103. *Supra* note 1.

# 3. Attribution of Profit

## 3.1. Profit Attribution – Various Approaches

Article 7 of the Model Tax Convention (OECD & UN) provides guidance on the allocation of profits to the PE. Under Article 7(1) of the OECD MC, a host state may tax profits of an enterprise (resident in the other contracting state) only to the extent attributable to the PE. The UN MC is broader in scope and includes profits from the sale of goods and other business activities in the host state, even if they are not attributable to the PE but similar to the business carried on by the PE.[104] Similarly, there are other points of friction between the OECD and UN MC as the latter allows allocation of profits based on apportionment methodology[105] while the former permits allocation based only on transfer pricing principles and the arm's length approach using the FAR analysis (functions performed, assets used, and risks assumed). There is not much guidance available as to what can be exclusively covered within the ambit of the term 'profits' in relation to Article 7. There appears to be two distinct sets of profit attribution approaches divided between ideologies shared by developing/emerging (housed under the UN MC) and developed countries (housed under the OECD MC).

India's approach is based on the interpretation of Article 7 of the UN MC, which until 2010 was aligned to the OECD MC. The difference being that India disagrees with 2010 Authorized OECD Approach (AOA)[106] and interprets the UN Model, particularly Article 7(4) for customary approach, which in a way (as India's believes) overrides Article 7(2), which approves separate entity approach and aligned to AOA.

For attribution of profits to PE there are certain principles that are followed. These principles are known approaches to determine profits of PE and have been discussed at length under this section of the chapter.

### *3.1.1. OECD MC*

Since the 1930s, the profits are being attributed to a PE on the assumptive basis of "separate enterprise" concept and the application of arm's length principle, as incorporated in Article 7(2) of the OECD MC.[107]

In 2006,[108] the OECD Working Party 6 identified two distinct interpretations of Article 7(1) and 7(3) of the OECD MC, i.e., the "relevant business activity"

104. Article 7(1) of the 2017 UN Model Convention.

105. Article 7(4) of the 2017 UN Model Convention.

106. 1.1, Position of non-member countries. India has reserved the right to use the Article 7 that was included in the OECD MC before the 2010 update.

107. P. Baker & R.S. Collier, The attribution of profits to permanent establishments: General Report, in IFA Cahiers de droit fiscal international, The attribution of profits to permanent establishments, Vol. 91b (Amersfoort: Sdu Fiscale en Financiële Uitgevers, 2006), pp 22-67.

108. OECD, Report on the Attribution of Profits to Permanent Establishments (December 2006), p 23.

approach and the "functionally separate entity approach". After considering the merits of both approaches, the OECD member countries consented to adopt the latter approach as the Authorized OECD Approach (AOA) being the preferrable interpretation to Article 7(1).[109] The interpretations that finally led to AOA are discussed below –

*(i) "Relevant Business Activity" Approach or Single Enterprise Approach*

Article 7(1) of the 1963 OECD MC read, "*profits of the enterprise* may be taxed in the other State but only so much of them as is attributable to that permanent establishment". This interpretation necessitated that the business activity, in which the PE had some participation, should make profit for the PE to be taxed in the host state.

Under this approach, the profits/losses of the enterprise as a whole would be considered from that business activity. This would impose a limit on the profits that can be attributed to the PE, especially when the relevant business activity includes operations by other entities of the enterprise and those operations result in a loss. The loss would decrease the overall profit of the enterprise from that business activity (carried on by the PE) and reduce the profit attributable to the PE.

As an illustration, an enterprise, engaged in the business of manufacturing electronic equipment undertakes aggressive marketing of products worldwide. Its PE in India performs only distribution function. Due to high research and development and marketing expenditure, there is a loss incurred by the enterprise. Now if the "relevant business activity approach" is followed, profit/losses from all activities pertaining to a certain product line, i.e., research and development, manufacturing and distributing, etc., will be considered. In such a condition, it is not possible to attribute profit to the PE for performing only the distribution activity. Losses incurred for the product line by other segments performing connected activities will also be attributed to the PE. This may not be in accordance with the comparability analysis of uncontrolled transactions undertaken by independent distributors. In case the distribution activities were outsourced to an independent distributor, such distributor will have to be remunerated as per the arrangement in free market conditions irrespective of any losses incurred by the enterprise as whole.

*(ii) Functionally Separate Entity Approach*

Unlike the "relevant business activity" approach, this approach has a close consonance with Article 7(2) of the 1963 OECD MC and reads as "attributed to the permanent establishment the profits which it might be expected to make if it were a *distinct and separate enterprise* … dealing wholly independently with the enterprise". Similarly, under this approach, the profits to be attributed to the PE are

109. *Id.* Pg. 27, Para 78.

those profits that the PE would have earned at arm's length were it a "separate and independent" enterprise performing the same or similar activities under the same or similar conditions, determined by applying the arm's length principle.

Under this approach, the profits attributable to the PE are not limited by the profits/losses of the enterprise. So, even if the enterprise is making a loss on a global level, the PE may still be attributed profit as if it was a separate, distinct entity. There may also be situations where the enterprise as a whole makes a profit, but no profits may be attributed to the PE due to a loss at the level of the PE. This approach focuses on the arm's length approach using the FAR analysis to determine the profits attributable to the PE in the host state.

As an illustration, an enterprise engaged in the business of manufacturing electronic equipment undertakes aggressive marketing of products worldwide. Its PE in India performs only distribution function. Due to high research and development and marketing expenditure, there is a loss incurred by the enterprise. Now, if the "functionally separate entity approach" is considered, the PE will be treated as a separate, distinct entity carrying on distribution activity for the enterprise. Losses incurred for the product line by other segments performing connected activities will not affect the attribution of profit to the PE. This is in accordance with the comparability analysis of uncontrolled transactions undertaken by independent distributors. The PE will be remunerated as if the distribution activities were outsourced to an independent distributor as per the arrangement in free-market conditions irrespective of any losses incurred by the enterprise as a whole.

*(iii) Authorized OECD Approach (AOA)*[110]

The authorized OECD approach does not give any specific mechanism for profit attribution but only sets a limit on the amount of attributable profit that may be taxed in the host country of the PE. Therefore, the profits to be attributed to a PE are the profits that the PE would have earned at arm's length if it were a separate and independent enterprise performing the same or similar activities under the same or similar conditions taking into account the FAR analysis. This is in accordance with the fundamental rationale behind the PE concept, which is to allow, within certain limits, the taxation of non-resident enterprises in respect of their activities in the host jurisdiction. In addition, the authorized OECD approach is not designed to cause any hindrances to the application of any domestic law, which is aimed at preventing abuse of tax losses or tax credits by shifting the location of assets or risks.[111]

The interpretation of Article 7(2) under the authorized OECD approach is to be undertaken in steps. First, a functional and factual analysis, conducted in accordance

110. 2010 Report on The Attribution of Profits to Permanent Establishments. Available at: https://www.oecd.org/ctp/transfer-pricing/45689524.pdf.

111. Para 9 of *ibid*.

with the guidance found in the TP Guidelines. It requires a hypothesis to treat the PE and the remainder of the enterprise (or a segment or segments thereof) as if they were associated enterprises, each undertaking functions, owning and/or using assets, assuming risks, entering into dealings with each other, and transactions with other related and unrelated enterprises. Under the first step, a functional and factual analysis must identify the economically significant activities and responsibilities undertaken by the PE. This analysis should consider the PE's activities and responsibilities in the context of the activities and responsibilities undertaken by the enterprise as a whole.[112]

Under the second step, the remuneration of any dealings between the hypothesized enterprises is determined with TP tools by taking into consideration the functions performed, assets used, and risk assumed by the hypothesised enterprises. The result of these two steps will be to allow the calculation of the profits (or losses) of the PE from all its activities, including transactions with other unrelated enterprises, transactions with related enterprises, and dealings with other parts of the enterprise.[113]

A hypothetical situation is considered while determining attribution of profits to a PE, as if it were a legally distinct and separate enterprise performing the same or similar functions under the same or similar conditions and dealing wholly independently with the enterprise of which it is a PE. Here, we must understand that the hypothesis by which a PE is treated as a functionally distinct and separate enterprise is a mere fiction necessary for purposes of determining the business profits under Article 7. The authorized OECD approach should not be viewed as implying that the PE must be treated as a separate enterprise entering into dealings with the rest of the enterprise of which it is a part for purposes of any other provisions of the Convention.

In case of *DIT (Int taxation) v. Morgan Stanley and Co. Inc.*,[114] the Apex court held that for profit attribution, no generalization was possible. There is a need to depend upon functional and factual analysis and the data placed by taxpayer to be examined in each case. It also held that in the context of a service PE that payments of ALP extinguish any further attribution of profits to head quarter if arm's length analysis is exhaustive of functions, assets and risks. In this case, no further attribution was done beyond the ALP calculated.

### *3.1.2. UN MC Principle of Force of Attraction*

UN MC contains a limited force of attraction rule, which allows the host state to tax not only the profits attributable to the PE, but other profits of the enterprise derived in that state to the extent allowed under Article 7(1). It reads as:

112. Para 10 of *ibid.*
113. *Ibid.*
114. (2007) 292 ITR 416 (SC).

"(b) sales in that other State of goods or merchandise of the same or similar kind as those sold through that permanent establishment; or

(c) other business activities carried on in that other State of the same or similar kind as those effected through that permanent establishment."

It is noted that the force of attraction rule is limited to business profits covered by Article 7 and does not extend to the income covered by other treaty provisions. Those in favour of such a rule argue that neither sales through independent commission agents nor purchasing activities would become taxable to the principal under that rule. Some members from developed countries pointed out that the force of attraction rule had been found unsatisfactory and abandoned in recent tax treaties concluded by them because of the undesirability of taxing income from an activity that was totally unrelated to the establishment and that was in itself not extensive enough to constitute a permanent establishment.[115]

Some of Indian tax treaties that contain the force of attraction rule are New Zealand, Belgium, Canada, Denmark, Italy, Poland, Portuguese Republic, Spain, Germany, etc.[116]

The Mumbai Tribunal in the case of *DCIT v. Roxon OY*[117] held, "It is also important to appreciate that although India-Finland tax treaty provides for the force of attraction clause, such clause is restrictive in nature as the words same and similar have been used in clause (b) of Article 7(1). Accordingly, not all the profits of the assessee-company from its business connection in India would be taxable in India, but only so much of profits as having an economic nexus with the PE in India, would be taxable in India. This economic nexus should be in relation to sale of goods or merchandise of same or similar nature as sold or effected through the PE. This condition, in our considered opinion, is not satisfied in the case before us."

### *3.1.3. Apportionment of profits*

The theory of apportionment is based on the idea of providing fair and proper division of global profits. It does not attempt to determine the market price for inter-company transactions. It is an alternative to the arm's length principle.

Global formulary apportionment would allocate the global profits of an MNE group on a consolidated basis among the associated enterprises in different countries on the basis of a predetermined and mechanistic formula. There would be three essential components to applying global formulary apportionment: determining the unit to be taxed, i.e., determining the subsidiaries and branches of an MNE group that should comprise the global taxable entity, accurately determining the global

115. Pg. 215 – Para 6 of Commentary on Article 7(1) of the 2017 UN Model Convention.

116. https://www.taxsutra.com/experts/column?sid=1201.

117. [2007] 106 ITD 489 (Mum).

profits, and establishing the formula to be used to allocate the global profits of the unit. The formula would most likely be based on some combination of costs, assets, payroll, and sales.[118]

Article 7 contained in the 1963-2008 version of OECD MC allowed apportionment as a customary method (a departure from the arm's length principle). Article 7(4) of the UN MC 2017 reads, "In so far as it has been customary in a Contracting State to determine the profits to be attributed to a permanent establishment on the basis of an apportionment of the total profits of the enterprise to its various parts, nothing in paragraph 2 shall preclude that Contracting State from determining the profits to be taxed by such an apportionment as may be customary; the method of apportionment adopted shall, however, be such that the result shall be in accordance with the principles contained in this Article"

India follows Article 7(4) of the UN Convention, which authorizes attribution of profits to a PE on a country's customary approach; for India it is Rule 10 of Income-tax Rules, 1962. It allows leeway to use "customary" methods in allocation if required such as the "sixth method" for TP, which several jurisdictions in Latin America embraced. India notified the sixth methodology by bringing changes in the Finance Act, 2012. The commentary on Article 7(4) of the UN MC reads as "each country concerned would have to be given the right to compute the profits according to the provisions of its own laws."[119]

In *CIT v. Hyundai Heavy Industries Co Ltd.*[120] the Apex court held that revenue and costs attributable to the installation activities of a PE in India must be determined based on generally accepted principles of accountancy. In this case, the PE did not maintain books of accounts; and the foreign enterprise itself pleaded during the assessment that Section 44BB (deemed profit legislation) of the IT Act read with CBDT Instruction 1767 should be applied while determining the profits of the PE. Therefore, the court held that the profit attributable to installation, commissioning activities etc. carried out by the PE in India was held to be 10% of the gross receipts on account of such activities in India (based on Section 44BB).

## 3.2. Indian Position on Profit Attribution

### *3.2.1. Rule 10 under Income Tax Rules, 1962*

Where a non-resident has a business connection in India, the next step is to compute the taxable income for which the non-resident has a responsibility to maintain such books of account to compute the income. However, an unbridled empowerment is available to the tax administration to apply Rule 10 (akin to global

118. Para 1.17 of OECD Transfer Pricing Guidelines, 2017.
119. Pg. 236 – Para 19 of Commentary on Article 7(4) of the 2017 UN Model Convention.
120. (2007) 291 ITR 482 (SC).

formulary approach) if the tax inspector is of the opinion that actual income from such business connection 'cannot be definitely ascertained'. In our view, in situations when the tax administration exercises power to apply formulary approach under Rule 10 for the computation of income from business connection, arm's length standard set under Section 92 of the Income-tax Act cannot be ignored, even in an unrelated party situation. This view was affirmed by the Delhi High Court when it recalled its own order in the context of determining profit attribution of a dependent agent in the context of India-UK treaty.[121]

The apportionment of profits under any one of the three prescribed methods should be on a rational basis considering the facts and circumstances of each case at hand.[122] [123] It is clear from the wording of this rule that before invoking Rule 10, the assessing officer must demonstrate that the income of the non-resident accruing or arising from any business connection in India cannot be ascertained from accounts or from material available on record. If the assessing officer fails to give such reasons, he cannot straightaway apply Rule 10 and reject the income computed by the assessee.[124]

Rule 10(i) signifies the test of reasonableness, thereby leaving the scope to apply the arm's length principle. However, Rule 10(ii) restricts the assessing officer to from following a purely mathematical approach. The powers given to the assessing officer under Rule 10(iii) are very wide and allows the assessing officer a lot of subjectivity while making the assessment and the courts have held that the assessment should not be arbitrary.[125]

Once the assessment has been made by the assessing officer, and he has taken into account all the relevant facts and circumstances and come to a fair estimate, the courts cannot interfere with the assessment. Even if the apportionment was based on guesswork, the courts might not interfere if the assessee had not placed proper material before the income tax authorities, which would have facilitated the making of a more definite and certain apportionment.[126] It is clear from established jurisprudence that Rule 10 allows broad discretion to the tax authority without any clear or specific guidance leading to ad hoc determination.

### *3.2.2. Section 92 of the Income-tax Act, 1961*

Chapter X of the Income-tax Act relates to "Special provisions relating to avoidance of tax" and is applicable where there is an income from an international transaction that needs to be computed at arm's length price. For the application of Section 92 there must be:

121. Rev. Pet. No.658 of 2011 in ITA No.1278 of 2010.
122. *Hukumchand Mills Ltd. v. CIT*, [1968] 70 ITR 450 (Bom.).
123. *Nortel Networks India International Case*, TS – 355 / TII – 71 (Del ITAT).
124. *Hyundai Rotem Co. v. Asstt. DIT, (International Taxation)*, [2012] 53 SOT 142 (URO).
125. *Annamalais Timber Trust & Co. v. CIT*, [1961] 41 ITR 781 (Mad.).
126. *Blue Star Engg. Co. (Bombay) (P.) Ltd. v. CIT*, [1969] 73 ITR 283 (Bom.).

(a) An international transaction (as explained under Section 92B)

(b) Between associated enterprises – related parties (as explained under Section 92A)

(c) For the computation of arm's length price (as explained under Section 92C)

In case there is a difference between the transfer price reached by the assessee and the arm's length price reached by the tax authority under guidance from the statute, adjustments can be made by the tax department to arrive at an appropriate transfer price. As per Section 92(3), the provisions of Section 92 will apply only if such adjustment is increasing the income to be taxed in India.

The expression 'international transaction' has been defined in an inclusive manner, and it includes every kind of transaction having at least one non-resident and having a bearing on the profits, which includes revenue and capital transactions.[127] [128] If there is no possibility of shifting profits outside India then those transactions will not fall within the purview of transfer pricing regulations.[129]

The definition of 'associated enterprise' under Section 92A is inclusive and includes any relationship between the enterprises, which may result in the manipulation of prices of their transactions.[130]

Section 92C lists the methods for determining the 'arm's length price', the most appropriate method being specific to the facts and circumstances of each case.[131]

## 3.3. CBDT Committee Proposal for Amendment of Rules for Profit Attribution to Permanent Establishment

To bring greater clarity and predictability, the Central Board of Direct Taxes (CBDT) formed a committee to examine the existing scheme of profit attribution to a PE under Article 7 of the DTAAs and recommend changes to Rule 10 of the Income Tax Rules. The committee released the proposal for public consultation on April 18, 2019. The proposal first discussed the applicable regulations in the context of taxation of non-residents, specifically, with respect to the DTAAs and Rule 10, which were causing concerns over excessive taxation due to its uncertainty and ad hoc basis for determining profits attributable to a PE. Further, concerns were expressed on the attribution of profits generated from digital businesses and the need to address the importance of user participation in emerging economies.

127. *Perstorp Chemicals India (P.) Ltd. v. ITO*, ITA No. 6078 and 7160/Mum/2011.

128. *Siro Clinpharm Pvt. Ltd. v. DCIT* (ITAT Mumbai), [2016] 177 TTJ 609.

129. *IJM (India) Infrastructure Ltd. v. Asstt. CIT*, [2014] 147 ITD 437 (Hyd. – Trib.).

130. *Morgan Stanley and Company Inc. v. DIT*, (2007) 7 SCC 1.

131. *GE Energy Parts Inc. v. ADIT*, ITA No. 671/Del/2011 [TP analysis is accepted to the extent that it remunerates Functions, Assets and Risks (FAR)], Further, in the same case, Rule 10(iii) was accepted as FAR analysis was not enough to enough to attribute profits.

It was pointed out by the committee that three versions of Article 7 (UN, pre-2010 OECD & 2010 OECD) in the Model conventions had different standards for the attribution of profit to the PE. The pre-2010 version having a lot of similarities with the UN version, which in addition also has the 'force of attraction'[132] rule and 'limitation of deductible expenses'. However, both versions allow the application of the apportionment method by the source state if it is in accordance with the domestic laws. The 2010 OECD version introduced FAR analysis under the AOA approach by doing away with the apportionment method. The committee believed, as sales in the market jurisdiction is not a consideration under the FAR analysis, the 2010 OECD version of Article 7 is purely a supply- side approach.[133] It was observed that India had expressed its disagreement with the 2010 OECD version of Article 7 by not only reserving its right not to include it in its tax treaties, but also rejecting the AOA approach.[134] As the FAR analysis did not take into account the demand-side factors of the sales revenue and attributed profits based only on functions, assets and risks (regarding the PE as a distinct and separate entity), none of the Indian treaties have incorporated it.

Accordingly, the committee concluded that both demand and supply of goods were integral contributors to business profits and a mixed approach that accounts for both these factors should be used to attribute profits.[135] As the market jurisdictions maintain markets that enable their residents to pay for the goods and services, leading to sales, their contribution is essential, and profits should be allocated based on this economic justification.

The committee recommended fractional apportionment as it takes into account only those profits that have been derived from India and then apportioning them based on certain factors. It was of the view that fractional apportionment could form the uniform method under Rule 10, bringing clarity and objectivity to the attribution of profits. To note that Rule 10 comes into play only in cases where books of accounts are not maintained by the PE, which could be arguably on an arm's length basis.

Listing the merits of this approach, the committee said that fractional apportionment takes into account both demand and supply-side factors, uses a three-factor formula to allocate profits (one-third to sales and two-third to supply), has a long precedence in international practice and was recently proposed by the European Union. The three-factor formula of sales, manpower and assets is in vogue in the US in relation to state taxation. It is relatively simple and does not require extensive country by country information, thus avoiding disputes and litigation.

---

132. Any income such as other business profits, dividends, interest and royalties arising from the source State become taxable even if it is not attributable to the permanent establishment.

133. Para 45 of the proposal.

134. Position of Non-member countries, Materials on International, TP & EU Tax Law- Volume A, selected and edited by Kees van Raad, Seventeenth Edition, Pg – 295.

135. Para 59 of the proposal.

To apply this method, in practice, the following steps were recommended by the committee:

1. By determining the profits in relations to the India operations. In case the MNE is incurring a global loss or the operational profit margin is lower than 2%, profits derived from India will be taken at 2% of the turnover derived from India.
2. By apportioning the profits from Indian operations of an Enterprise based on three factors of sales (33%) and manpower and assets (together 67%).
3. By deducting any profits from India operations of the enterprise, any profits that may have already been taxed in India, whether in the hands of the non-resident enterprise or its associated enterprise in India.

After discussing the role of user participation (in digital businesses) and their significant contribution to the profits of the enterprise, the committee concluded that where applicable, it should also be considered for profit attribution as the fourth factor for apportionment in addition to the other three factors. The business models were divided into three categories depending on the intensity of user participation (low, medium and high). The low and medium user participation was assigned a weight of 10%, and the high user participation was assigned a weight of 20%. It was also decided that to accommodate this fourth factor, a downward adjustment would have to be made to the weight assigned to the other two supply- side factors, namely employees and assets. A complex formula was finalized by the committee.

Profits attributable to operations in India =

**'*Profits derived from India*[136]' × [SI/3 × ST + (NI/6 × NT) + (WI/6 × WT) + (AI/3 × AT)][137]**

Profits attributable to operations in India in cases of low and medium user intensity business models=

**'*Profits derived from India*' × [0.3 × SI/ST + (0.15 × NI/NT) +(0.15 × WI/WT) + (0.3 × AI/3xAT)] + 0.1]**

136. Profits derived from India = Revenue derived from India x Global operational profit margin.
137. SI = sales revenue derived by Indian operations from sales in India,
ST = total sales revenue derived by Indian operations from sales in India and outside India,
NI =number of employees employed with respect to Indian operations and located in India,
NT = total number of employees employed with respect to Indian operations and located in India and outside India,
WI= wages paid to employees employed with respect to Indian operations and located in India,
WT = total wages paid to employees employed with respect to Indian operations and located in India and outside India,
AI = assets deployed for Indian operations and located in India,
AT = total assets deployed for Indian operations and located in India and outside India.

In case of digital models with high user intensity, the users should be assigned a weight of 20%, while the share of assets and employees be reduced to 25% each after keeping the weight of sales as 30%, as under:

Profits attributable to operations in India in cases of high user intensity business models =

***'Profits derived from India'* × [0.3 × SI/ST + (0.125 × NI/NT) + (0.125 × WI/WT) + (0.25 AI/3 × AT)] + 0.2]**

The committee recommended the changes to Rule 10 to incorporate such fractional apportionment method.

Several considerations arise from this proposal:

- It is supposed to address profit attribution to non-residents in all forms of businesses, but the proposal provides no clarity on its application in the context of treaties. The whole rationale of this proposal is to reduce the arbitrariness in the allocation of profits (from formulary to fractional apportionment). However, the same has not been achieved and may increase cases of Mutual Agreement Procedure due to double taxation.
- As Rule 10 is applied only in specific situations (when the accounts of the PE are not available or the amount of profits attributable to the PE is incapable of determination in the view of the Indian tax authority or the ascertaining thereof by that tax authority presents exceptional difficulties); this restricts the scope of the proposal.
- The proposal disregards established arm's length transfer pricing principles as tax is being proposed based on revenue and non-profitability criteria. The proposal has introduced taxation without considering whether that activity in India is resulting in profit and assumes that the global operating profit margin is commensurate with the functions and risks of the Indian PE, which may not be the case. It taxes income in India even in situations of global loss.
- Four allocation factors have been used in the proposal and each factor has been assigned a weight. No justification or reasoning has been provided as to the assignment of ad hoc weights. Even in the case of digital businesses where different weights have been assigned based on user intensity, no objective criteria have been given to classify them.
- Going with the proposal means different approaches will have to be used to attribute profits to a PE and a subsidiary. In the case of a PE, the formulary approach will be followed and the arm's length approach in the case of a subsidiary. This sounds illogical as enterprises will be incentivized to adopt the form of business presence that will reduce their tax liability.

- To arrive at the global operational profit margin, country-wise information will be required which may not be available.

# 4. Taxation of the Digital Economy

## 4.1. OECD Proposal

Intending to deliver a consensus-based solution by mid-2021, the Programme of Work (PoW) adopted by the Inclusive Framework on BEPS had released Pillar 1 & 2 under the Unified Approach. Pillar 1 proposal deals with nexus rules and profit allocation by proposing 'user participation', 'marketing intangible,' and 'significant economic presence' as three independent considerations, which go beyond the arm's length principle. It applies to consumer-facing businesses and automated digital services. The Unified Approach is a two-tier profit allocation mechanism, proposes to retain profit allocation (between taxing jurisdictions) based on arm's length principle in cases where it is working as intended; a formula-based solution is introduced for cases where it has failed to allocate appropriate profits particularly on digital business models. New nexus rules have been proposed, which are based on sales and user participation, without physical presence. It allocates taxing rights to emerging economies, where the users of highly digitalised business models are located.

The proposal introduced two profit allocation mechanisms:

- Amount A – a share of deemed residual profit allocated to market jurisdictions using a formulaic approach, i.e., the new taxing right.
- Amount B – a fixed remuneration for baseline marketing and distribution functions that take place in the market jurisdiction (ALP approach).

The new profit allocation rules go beyond the arm's length principle and the limitations imposed on taxation due to absence of physical presence. They work in tandem with the existing scheme of rules to allocate profits in market jurisdictions in a way, which avoids double taxation and improves tax certainty. Three thresholds have been put in place to avoid unnecessary compliance burden on a taxpayer[138]:

1. Gross revenue
2. Aggregate in-scope revenue
3. De minimums amount

138. OECD (2020), Statement by the OECD/G20 Inclusive Framework on BEPS on the Two-Pillar Approach to Address the Tax Challenges Arising from the Digitalisation of the Economy – January 2020, OECD/G20 Inclusive Framework on BEPS, OECD, Paris. www.oecd.org/tax/beps/statement-by-the-oecd-g20-inclusive-framework-on-beps-january-2020.pdf.

Negotiations have been proposed for having lower threshold limits for emerging economies and small markets. Segmented accounting has been suggested to capture the in-scope revenue and profits. Digital differentiation has been weighted in different business lines to account for degrees of digitization. Arm's length approach has been suggested for computing the fixed returns under Amount B.

Pillar 2 proposes various intertwined mechanisms to ensure minimum taxation at a global level. In trying to address BEPS challenges *via* a web of interlocking rules, the Pillar 2 proposal has envisaged rules which are very similar to the global intangible low tax income (GILTI) and base erosion and anti-abuse tax (BEAT) in the United States. It addresses the risks from structures that allows MNEs to shift profit to jurisdictions where they are subject to no or very low taxation.

The four components of the Pillar 2 proposal are:

1. Income inclusion rule – that would tax income of a foreign branch or a controlled entity if it were taxed at an effective tax rate below a minimum rate.
2. Undertaxed payments rule – that denies deduction in source jurisdiction if that payment (to a related party) is not taxed at or above a minimum rate.
3. Switch-over-rule – would allow the residence jurisdictions to switch from an exemption to credit method when profits attributable to a PE or income derived from an immovable property is taxed below the minimum rate.
4. Subject to tax rule – would complement the untaxed payments rule and subject such payments to source taxation and its eligibility for treaty benefits when it is taxed below the minimum rate.

This proposal has a very wide scope, and it is not restricted to digital business models. It proposes substantial changes to the international tax rules.

The package of Blueprints[139] released by the OECD on October 12, 2020, has highlighted the convergent and divergent views of the Inclusive Framework members. Broadly these documents focus on three parameters (policy, technicality & administration) to develop a consensus-based solution to tax the digital economy. These two Blueprints have identified the political and technical differences that need to be bridged to take this project to the next level towards a consensus-based solution.

Specific considerations for this proposal:

- Pillar 1 seeks to give away taxing rights of ultimate parent companies countries and hence, a consensus will need to be arrived at to maintain the balance between residence, source, and market jurisdictions failing which, chaos shall prevail.

139. https://www.oecd.org/tax/beps/oecd-g20-inclusive-framework-on-beps-invites-public-input-on-the-reports-on-pillar-one-and-pillar-two-blueprints.htm.

- To effectively apply Pillar 2, all the rules will have to be applied in a consistent and coherent manner across jurisdictions. To calculate the effective tax rate in different jurisdictions coupled with timing differences may be challenging.
- Encourage a dialogue with technology giants in market jurisdictions to understand their business model, avenues of revenue, ALP by correlating to CbCR like horizontal monitoring process, outside of the audit function.
- This proposal gives India nexus-based taxing rights, though not simple to implement and may retain transfer pricing complexities. Solidarity towards the Inclusive Framework may improve India's image as an attractive destination for business.
- The tax debate is not exclusive to tax considerations alone, it encompasses a wide range of policy frameworks. Data localization measures being undertaken by the government, which carries the implication of local data storage in India by the technology giants.

## 4.2. UN Proposal

On August 6, 2020, the UN Tax Committee released a proposed new article in the UN Model Double Taxation Convention between Developed and Developing Countries on "income from automated digital services". This article grants taxing rights to the treaty country where customers of a treaty-partner automated digital services provider are located. Article 12B(1) reads as, "Income from automated digital services arising in a contracting state and paid to a resident of the other contracting state may be taxed in that other state". The proposed new Article 12B requires foreign providers of automated digital services to pay income tax at source by means of either

(i) a withholding on gross income (whose rate is to be agreed upon by the parties to the treaty), or

(ii) on qualified profits from automated digital services pursuant to an apportionment formula.

Under the proposal, the foreign automated digital services provider is allowed to choose whether to assess the tax on a gross basis or on qualified profits.

Article 12B does not require any threshold, such as a permanent establishment, fixed base, or minimum period of presence in a contracting state as a condition for the taxation of income from automated digital services.[140]

A service is regarded as automated when the user is able to make use of the service because of equipment and systems being in place, which allow the user to obtain the

140. Para 8 of Commentary on the paragraphs of Article 12B.

service automatically, as opposed to requiring a bespoke interaction with the supplier to provide the service. In determining whether a service requires minimal human involvement, the test only looks to the supplier of service, without regard to any human involvement on the side of the user[141].

The following services are considered to be automated digital services: (i) online advertising services; (ii) online intermediation platform services; (iii) social media services; (iv) digital content services; (v) cloud computing services; (vi) sale or other alienation of user data; (vi) standardized online teaching services.[142]

Income from automated digital services does not include: (i) customized services provided by professionals; (ii) customized online teaching services; (iii) services providing access to the Internet or to an electronic network; (iv) online sale of goods and services other than automated digital services; (v) broadcasted services including simultaneous internet transmission; and (vi) composite digital services embedded within a physical good irrespective of network connectivity.[143]

*Hypothesis to demonstrate the difference between Article 12B(2) v. Article 12B(3)*

*Assumptions:*

- Let us suppose that company X (resident of Germany) provides automated digital services in India. As services are provided over internet, no PE is formed.
- X receives a gross annual revenue of INR 100 as beneficial owner from providing the automated digital services in India.
- X has a global profitability ratio (total annual profits divided by the total annual revenue) of 1/5.
- Article 12B under India-Germany DTAA is identical to the proposal, with a 2% (mutually negotiated) withholding rate under Article 12B (2)
- Domestic tax rate in India is 25%.

*Solution:*

Stream of Income – Income of INR 100 received by X for providing automated digital services in India.

As X is a German resident, Germany may tax X according to its domestic law.

As India is a source jurisdiction, Article 12B gives an option to X (beneficial owner of the income) to be taxed in the source jurisdiction under Article 12B(2) or under Article 12B(3).

141. Para 31 of Commentary on the paragraphs of Article 12B.
142. Para 34 of Commentary on the paragraphs of Article 12B.
143. Para 36 of Commentary on the paragraphs of Article 12B.

1. Taxation under Article 12B(2)

   As the India-Germany DTAA provides for a 2% withholding rate (agreed between India and Germany) and the gross annual revenue received by X from India as a beneficial owner for providing automated digital services is INR 100, India may tax X's gross annual revenue at the rate of 2%. Indian may derive a tax revenue of INR 2 [100@2%].

2. Taxation under Article 12B(3)

   If X chooses to be taxed under this article, it will have to compute the qualified profits which will be taxed at the domestic tax rate of India.

   Qualified profits (QP) = 30% of (Gross annual revenue from India* Profitability ratio of X)

In the present case:

- Gross annual revenue is INR 100 from the automated digital services in India.
- X has a global profitability ratio (total annual profits divided by the total annual revenue) of 1/5.

So,

QP = 30% of (100 * 1/5), QP = 30% of 20; QP = 6.

As the domestic tax rate in India is 25%, INR 6 (qualified profit) may be taxed at the rate of 25%.

India may derive a tax revenue of INR 1.5 [6@25%].

*Conclusion:*

As X may pay a tax of INR 2 under 12B(2) and a tax of INR 1.5 under 12B(3), X will choose the latter option.

## 5. Concluding Remarks

Profit attribution to PEs is a highly fact intensive exercise and for the traditionally understood forms of PEs, should be based on well-established arm's length principles. However, the debate on the attribution of profits seems to have assumed renewed thrust in the age of digitalization of business. The traditional ALP, which has undergone various revisions in the past two decades does not seem to have delivered a solution. This included the 2017 revision to the OECD TP guidance, which elaborately dealt with value creation and the subsequent guidance with regard to HTVI. One reason for this is perhaps that while ALP analysis factors functions performed, assets employed and risks assumed, it does not factor variables, which cannot be attributed to the parties, e.g., existence of a market itself.

The taxing right sought by market jurisdictions seems to be independent of such a FAR analysis, as taxability is sought owing to customers provided by the market jurisdiction and not due to activities of the taxpayer in the market jurisdiction. Market jurisdictions are seeking taxability based not only on account of presence of the business, but also on account of the business' customers in their jurisdictions. While the former (presence of business) has been around as a concept for decades and profit attribution for the same remains highly debatable between tax officers, taxpayers, and even competent authorities; the latter (taxability owing to customer base) is a very new phenomenon, and it will be interesting to see how consensus/debate around the same unfolds. The current thinking of a formulary apportionment with an underlying base of thresholds computed using the arm's length principles is fraught with its own challenges, however, it cannot be denied that in an increasingly global and digitized world, taxation based on traditionally understood concepts of 'presence' have become outdated, and hence, both permanent establishments and consequent attribution of profits need to be viewed through a different lens. Even more undeniable is the need to provide some level of certainty to taxpayers, and thus an Inclusive Framework such as the OECD/G20 BEPS project with over 135 countries agreeing to one common taxing framework for new ways of business (which obliviate the need for traditional definitions of presence), seems to be the most pragmatic way forward.

# REJOINDER

## P. V. Srinivasan

## 1. Introduction

The concept of permanent establishment (PE) in international fiscal law originated at a time when production factors were relatively permanent, labour mobility was limited, and fixed capital featured in business enterprises, both at the national as well as international level. International transportation was the only significant mobile international industry, which was governed by special international treaties and later incorporated as special provisions in tax treaties. Today, the century-old treaty concept of PE emphasizing permanence and physically located sites is proving inadequate for taxation of modern mobile international enterprises based on mobile production factors allowing them to perform economically significant operations in a short duration and technology and tele-communication allowing them flexible location. The proportion of intellectual capital and the use of intangibles in the value creation chain has increased manifold. In this context, the chapter by Ahuja and Gupta provides a comprehensive coverage of the associated issues and conflicts.

## 2. International Positions—US and OECD

The US approach to PE is through the application of three tests *viz.* asset test, agency test, and activities test. The UN approach includes an additional "rendition of service test". The "activities test" embraces factors such as continuity of activity and active conduct of business but excludes such business activities performed through a fixed place of business, which do not constitute a PE. The agency test covers a PE based on agency and relationship, including subsidiaries and associated entities. Much of the discussion on PE through Articles 12, 14, and 15 of MLI[144] is to prevent abuse in the application of these tests and must, therefore, be construed as anti-avoidance measures aimed at plugging widespread misuse. Regarding the application of the agency test, the MLI could have made it even simpler by making any agent a PE, removing the requirement of dependent status. Such a PE would require compensation of arm's length price, which is the case of an agent of independent status.

The fixed place of business, being the essential nexus condition, is covered by the "asset test", which includes place of business, its permanence, and location. Article 13 of MLI alone is novel as it narrows down the scope of exclusions covered by "activities, which are generally considered to be preparatory and auxiliary in nature".

144. Action 15 of the OCED / G20 Base Erosion and Profit Shifting Project.

The OECD Commentary on "right of use" attached to a place of business is only a reiteration of the tax treaty condition in Article 5 that the business of the enterprise, whether wholly or partly, must be performed "through a place of business". The historical "fixed place of business" is the objective side of a PE, which meets "presence" and "permanence" criteria in a visible way. It is evident that digitalization has paved the way for multinational corporations to operate seamlessly across borders.

Only a subjective presence could be applied when business models have so progressed, and it requires a new co-operation between developed and developing countries. The subjective presence of a PE must be such that it establishes the business connection between the enterprise and the place of business in the source country. The place of business need not be visible, but it must be permanent. A global consensus is sought to be achieved by equating a "fixed place of business" to a "discernible place of business" and this context provides the legally discernible factors for taxation purposes. User participation, significant economic presence, market intangibles are proposed proxies to determine a legally discernible place of business. Nevertheless, the business activity must be performed "through the place of business", which would allow the enterprise a "right of use".

## 3. Can Prevailing Practice Work in the Future

In the past, too, there has never been a clear economic principle on allocating profits when more than one jurisdiction claims taxing rights. Customarily, it was possible to apply the arm's length principle (ALP) for allocating profits by treating PE, which is legally integrated to the foreign headquartered enterprise, as a separate enterprise under international fiscal laws.

The separate enterprise principle cannot be fairly adopted when the business activity is integrated or inter-related. Further, a multinational enterprise (MNE) can be organised as several corporations incorporated in different countries. The current practice amongst nations for determining profits of each member corporation and attributing it to its PE in source countries is unlikely to work when substantial profits are derived through the exploitation of intangibles. In such cases, there is a need to take a global view of business profits. Countries must agree on a common system for taxing business profits based on combined reporting, disregarding the legal form of organization. A combined reporting by itself does not suggest formulary apportionment of profits, but it is a practical necessity.

The ALP under transfer pricing (TP) regulations is complex, litigation prone, and difficult to administer. In any event, the profits-based methods in TP allocate profits by formula and do not accurately determine the ALP as in transaction-based methods. Countries tend to agree on a formulary apportionment of profits based on salient features such as simplicity, consistency, and fairness. The mathematical three-factor formula, based on sales, wages, and property, is simple for the apportionment of global profits. The wages factor may be split into two sub-parts to include number of employees and wages to remove any skewness on account of wage disparities and the effect of foreign exchange translations.

A formulary apportionment of profits is a lot simpler as income gets allocated based on factors that are easily identifiable to a geographical location. The sourcing rules endeavour to achieve the opposite and a far more difficult result i.e., assign a geographical location to income. It must be remembered that sharing of river water passing through several countries, which touches upon livelihood of innumerable stakeholders, is far more complex.

## 4. Moving Away from ALP

If a PE were to be regarded as a separate enterprise as envisaged in Article 7(2) and the Authorized OECD Approach, the profit attributable to a PE would include even profits derived by the PE from sources outside the PE country. In contrast, in formulary apportionment, the profit attribution would be restricted to factors within the geographical location. This aligns well with the attribution of profits to the "business connection" under the domestic tax law, which restricts the attribution only to so much of income as is attributable to transactions or activities within the country.

Non-application of ALP for profit attribution to a PE has another benefit. The determination of arm's length price applying TP regulations can become academic. Making secondary adjustments would also become academic.

There can be only one tax assessment irrespective of the number of PEs existing in a country in a tax year. While user participation, significant digital presence, market intangibles [invisible factors] are sufficient for the determination of a discernible place of business, they stand on a separate footing from physically located PEs and agency PEs. It cannot be the case that profit attribution to physically located PEs and agency PEs must adhere to the arm's length principle, while profit attribution to invisible factors will be based on formulary apportionment. It may lead to double taxation of profits in the source country itself. There will also be a proliferation of litigation if invisible factors are absent and in which case, alone, profit attribution must be determined applying the arm's length principle.

The term "business" is not defined in the tax treaty. The tax treaty will fall back on the definition of the term in "domestic tax law". In the Indian Income tax, "business" includes any trade, commerce or manufacture or adventure or concern in the nature of trade, commerce or manufacture. Most domestic tax laws define "business" similarly. There can be an argument that the presence of users in a country alone is not sufficient to constitute a business.

## 5. UN Proposal and Emerging Economies

The domestic tax laws must treat any income as business income and have the necessary rules for taxing only the net income. Interest, royalty, fees for technical services, capital gains, etc. derived by a business entity are also its business income. Emerging economies must give up on gross income basis of taxation, whether as a withholding tax or as an equalization levy.

The UN proposal[145] on income from automated digital services is well thought out, keeping in mind that business enterprises prefer simplicity and do not mind paying some additional tax to avoid prolonged litigation. The foreign providers of automated digital services may elect to pay income tax at source either as a withholding tax on gross income or on qualified profits pursuant to an apportionment formula. While the well-known criticism against gross income taxation would apply, its adverse impact can be significantly diluted by prescribing a low rate of tax withholding.

## 6. Conclusion

Any formulary apportionment of profits using combined reporting may provide a simple answer for profit apportionment to the PE country. However, it is equally important to allow a foreign tax credit. Article 23 requires the resident country to give relief for foreign taxes. The "resident" used in Article 23 is a stand-alone corporation and not the MNE as a whole, headquartered in the resident country. It is easy to visualise the chaos, which mismatch can lead to. Obviously, there should be another mechanism to apportion the group profits of MNE to individual entities. Undertaking an exercise of combined reporting for profit attribution and subsequently disaggregating the profits for allowing foreign tax credit is certainly not a merry-go-round game that business enterprises would be happy to play. It has serious tax consequences. Countries may be forced to adopt consolidated tax reporting for promoting business competitiveness.

145. UN Tax Committee proposal of August 6, 2020.

CHAPTER 7

# OECD'S PILLAR ONE AND PILLAR TWO—AN OVERVIEW

**Hitesh D. Gajaria, Jitesh Golani & Radhika Karadkar**

## 1. Introduction

Taxation of e-commerce businesses and the digital economy has been debated for well over a decade now. The OECD began working in 2005[1] but gained momentum after releasing the Final Report on Action 1 - Addressing the Tax Challenges of the Digital Economy.[2] In March 2018, the OECD released an interim report[3] as a follow up to the Action 1 report.

In January 2019, OECD's policy notes[4] emphasized on two central pillars. The first focussed on challenges relating to the digital economy, allocation of tax rights, and the second addressed the remaining concerns of base erosion and profit shifting (BEPS). In late 2019 the OECD released its proposals on Unified Approach on Pillar One[5] and a consultation document on Pillar Two[6] with an intent to arrive at a consensus by the end of 2020.

In the meantime, in 2015, some countries took unilateral measures to levy taxes on the digital economy companies. These took various forms and names, such as digital sales tax, equalization levy, significant economic presence, etc. Such uncoordinated unilateral measures result in an increased uncertain tax environment with possibly unintended tax and compliance burdens on taxpayers.

---

1. OECD, E-Commerce: Transfer Pricing and Business Profits Taxation, No. 10, OECD Tax Policy Studies (OECD Publishing, 2005).
2. https://www.oecd.org/tax/beps/addressing-the-tax-challenges-of-the-digital-economy-action-1-2015-final-report-9789264241046-en.htm.
3. https://www.oecd.org/tax/beps/tax-challenges-arising-from-digitalisation-interim-report-9789264293083-en.htm.
4. https://www.oecd.org/tax/beps/policy-note-beps-inclusive-framework-addressing-tax-challenges-digitalisation.pdf.
5. http://www.oecd.org/tax/beps/public-consultation-document-secretariat-proposal-unified-approach-pillar-one.pdf.
6. https://www.oecd.org/tax/beps/public-consultation-document-global-anti-base-erosion-proposal-pillar-two.pdf.pdf.

In October 2020 OECD released Blueprints containing draft proposals from an Inclusive Framework of more than 125 countries on Pillar One[7] and Two,[8] with an intent to reach global consensus in mid- 2021.

It is important to understand and prepare for these far-reaching rules, that operate very differently from the existing entity focused Arm's Length Price based international tax regime.

## 2. The Pillar One Framework

### 2.1. Key Elements of the Pillar One structure are Grouped into Three Parts:

(a) Amount A: a new taxing right for market jurisdictions over a share of residual profit calculated at a multi-national enterprise ('MNE') group (or segment) level.

(b) Amount B: a fixed return for certain baseline marketing and distribution activities taking place physically in a market jurisdiction.

(c) Processes to improve tax certainty through effective dispute prevention and resolution mechanisms.

### 2.2. Pillar One Blueprint Recognizes 11 Building Blocks ('BB') at the Foundation of Proposed New Tax Structure:

**Table 1. Pillar One Framework**

| Amount A | Amount B | Tax certainty |
|---|---|---|
| 1. Scope<br>2. Nexus<br>3. Revenue sourcing<br>4. Tax base determination<br>5. Profit allocation<br>6. Elimination of double taxation | 7. Scope<br>8. Quantum | 9. Dispute prevention and resolution for Amount A<br>10. Dispute prevention and resolution beyond Amount A |
| 11. Implementation and administration | | |

*Source:* Authors

7. https://www.oecd.org/tax/beps/tax-challenges-arising-from-digitalisation-report-on-pillar-one-blueprint-beba0634-en.htm.
8. https://www.oecd.org/tax/beps/tax-challenges-arising-from-digitalisation-report-on-pillar-two-blueprint-abb4c3d1-en.htm.

## 3. Amount A (Pillar One)

Existing international tax rules generally attach a taxing right to profits derived from a physical presence in a jurisdiction. However, given globalization and the digitalization of the economy, businesses can participate in an active and sustained manner in the economic life of a market jurisdiction with or without the benefit of local physical operations. Accordingly, the allocation of taxing rights and taxable profits can no longer be exclusively circumscribed by reference to physical presence.

Amount A seeks to address this problem by creating a new taxing right for market/ source jurisdictions by allocating a portion of non-routine/residual profits of the MNE Group. This is achieved through multiple thresholds and steps, as discussed below in each BB.

### 3.1. Scope (1st BB)

For the applicability of Amount, A (i.e., the new taxing right), an MNE group should satisfy two tests viz., an activity test and a threshold test. Conversely, MNE groups not satisfying either test would be out-of-scope for Amount A purposes.

*Activity test*

It was generally believed that Pillar One or more specifically Amount A would focus just on automated digital businesses (since it was a fall-out of the BEPS Action Plan 1 on tax challenges of the digital economy).

However, the Pillar One Blueprint clearly spells out that the scope of Amount A extends not only to 'automated digital services', but also to 'consumer facing businesses.' The rationale behind inclusion of consumer facing businesses was consistent with the objective of the OECD to cover those businesses which can have a sustained and significant interaction with consumers of a market jurisdiction without a corresponding level of physical presence.

Definitions of covered businesses are:

(A) *Automated digital services ('ADS')*

- Considering the ever-evolving nature of ADS, Pillar One Blueprint defines ADS through a positive list, a negative list, and a general definition. Practically, there would be three steps to check if a business would be covered by ADS.
- The 1st step would be to check if the business falls within the positive list, and if it does, it would satisfy the activity test. The positive list covers: online advertising services, sale or other alienation of user data, online search engines, social media platforms, online intermediation platforms, digital content services,

online gaming, standardized online teaching services, and cloud computing services.

- If a business does not fit within the positive list, the 2nd step would be to verify if it falls within the negative list and if it does, the activity test is not satisfied. The negative list covers customized professional services, customized online teaching services, online sale of goods and services that are not themselves ADS, revenue from the sale of a physical good, even if it has "Internet of Things" connectivity, and services providing access to the Internet or another electronic network.
- Ultimately, if a business also does not fit within the negative list, the 3rd step would be to check if the business falls within the ambit of the 'general definition'. If a business does not fit within the general definition, it would be out-of-scope. The general definition is built on two elements:
    - (a) automated, i.e., once the system is set up, the provision of service to a particular user requires minimal human involvement on the part of the service provider; and
    - (b) digital, i.e., provided over the Internet or an electronic network.

(B) *Definition of consumer-facing businesses ('CFB')*

- Pillar One Blueprint defines CFB as a business that:
    - (a) supplies goods or services, directly or indirectly, that are of a type commonly sold to consumers; and/or
    - (b) licenses or otherwise exploits an intangible property that is connected to the supply of such goods or services.
- The term 'sold to' includes a sale, lease, license, rent or delivery, whether directly or indirectly (e.g., through a broker, agent, intermediary or representative). Consequently, the sale of goods by an MNE group through an in-country distributor would also be covered by the definition of CFB. An MNE would be regarded as being a CFB if it is the owner of the consumer product/service and holder of the rights to the connected intangible property (including franchisors and licensors). This is the MNE whose "face" is apparent to the consumer.
- The Pillar One Blueprint also discusses the application of the above definition to peculiar cases such as pharmaceuticals, franchising, licensing, dual use goods/services, and dual use intermediate products and components.

- Further, certain businesses have been excluded such as natural resources, financial services, construction, sale and leasing of residential property, and international airline, and shipping businesses. Further work is being undertaken to decide if 'fintech' business should be included in the 'financial services' exemption.

***Threshold test***

Pillar One Blueprint requires MNE groups doing ADS/CFB to fulfil two threshold tests to bring them within its scope. These are:

(a) Global consolidated revenue threshold: To be applied at the MNE group level, it relies on its consolidated financial statements ('CFS'). These can either be the published CFS or separate CFS prepared specifically for Amount A purposes (refer $4^{th}$ BB for further discussion*)*. An Economic Impact Assessment[9] indicates using the current Euro 750 million threshold currently being used for Country-by-Country reporting and expects 2,300 MNE groups to be covered.

(b) Foreign in-scope revenue threshold: Proposes including only those MNE groups that have foreign in-scope revenue exceeding a threshold, which is yet to be agreed.

## 3.2. Nexus ($2^{nd}$ BB)

Pillar One framework introduces a new nexus test, which does away with the mandatory requirement of physical presence in the market/source jurisdiction. Different tests are prescribed for ADS and CFB.

Market revenue threshold is the first nexus test, i.e., an MNE group can be said to have nexus with a market jurisdiction if it has in-scope revenues exceeding a threshold in that jurisdiction. It's possible to consider an additional duration test, which may require satisfaction of the market revenue threshold over a period of more than one year.

To identify revenues connected to a market jurisdiction, new and detailed revenue sourcing rules are proposed. Revenues could be attributed to the jurisdiction of the user/viewer rather than the jurisdiction of the buyer of services (refer to the $3^{rd}$ BB for further discussion).

As ADS businesses can establish significant and sustained interaction with a market jurisdiction without any physical presence, the market revenue threshold alone can be used. However, for CFB, it's not appropriate to determine nexus solely

9. Tax Challenges Arising from Digitalisation – Economic Impact Assessment published by the OECD on October 12, 2020. https://www.oecd.org/tax/beps/tax-challenges-arising-from-digitalisation-economic-impact-assessment-0e3cc2d4-en.htm.

based on market revenues since they are less able to participate remotely. For CFB, the satisfaction of additional/'plus' factors is also necessary to determine if the MNE group *(with in-scope CFB)* has significant and sustained interaction with the jurisdiction.

One such additional/plus factor could be the physical presence of the MNE in the market jurisdiction through a subsidiary/permanent establishment ('PE'). Work is being undertaken to determine if it is necessary to establish a link between in-scope revenues and activities undertaken by the subsidiary/PE in the market jurisdiction.

However, the satisfaction of such additional/plus factors would not be necessary, if in-scope revenues of the MNE group from a market jurisdiction exceed a higher level of threshold. Here it will be deemed that the MNE group has interaction/ engagement with the market jurisdiction ('deemed engagement').

Simply put, for CFB, an MNE group can have nexus to a particular market jurisdiction when:

(a) market revenue threshold is met + there is an existence of additional/plus factors; or

(b) market revenue threshold is met + deemed engagement through higher revenues.

Pillar One Blueprint proposes separate thresholds for ADS and CFB to be kept the same for all countries irrespective of the size of their gross domestic product ('GDP'). A proposal to determine if separate smaller thresholds could be introduced for some countries is under consideration.

## 3.3. Revenue Sourcing Rules (3rd BB)

Under current international tax principles, revenues are typically considered to be sourced from the location of the payer or where the services/activities are performed or consumed. This has proven difficult in the current highly digitalized environment and hence, needed new rules for sourcing revenues for Amount A purposes.

Pillar One Blueprint proposes detailed and precise revenue sourcing rules for various streams of income covered by Amount A.

For ADS businesses *(specifically those covered by the positive list)*, revenue from online advertising, sale, or other alienation of user data, digital content services, and cloud computing services can be considered to be the prevalent revenue streams. Further, revenues from CFB can be categorized into revenues from consumer- facing goods/services and revenues from franchising goods/services or from licensing intangibles related to goods/services.

The manner of application of the rules is as under:

- The MNE group first would have to identify the relevant revenue streams.
- For each revenue stream, there is a defined revenue sourcing principle (as described in the table below).
- For each revenue sourcing principle, there is a set of indicators in a predetermined hierarchy.

An MNE will apply the indicator that appears first unless that information is unavailable or unreliable as noted within each rule. An MNE Group is expected to maintain documentation.

Revenue sourcing principles under Pillar One Blueprint are:

**Table 2. Revenue Sourcing Principles For ADS**

| Revenue From | Revenue Sourcing Principle |
|---|---|
| **Online advertising services/sale or other alienation of user data** | |
| *Based on real time location of viewer / user* | Real time location of the viewer/user |
| *NOT based on real time location of viewer/user* | Jurisdiction of ordinary residence of viewer/user |
| **Online intermediation platform services:** | |
| *Tangible goods* | 50:50 split between jurisdiction of the ordinary residence of the purchaser & seller |
| *Tangible services* | 50:50 between jurisdiction of real-time location of purchaser & jurisdiction where service is performed |
| *Intangible goods/services* | 50:50 between jurisdiction of real-time location of purchaser & jurisdiction of seller |
| **Digital content services** | Jurisdiction of ordinary residence of the purchaser |
| **Cloud computing services:** | |
| *Individual purchaser* | Location of purchaser |
| *Business customer* | Location where business uses the service |

*Source:* Authors

**Table 3. Revenue Sourcing Principles for CFB**

| Revenue From | Revenue Sourcing Principle |
|---|---|
| Consumer-facing goods | Place of final delivery of the goods |
| Consumer-facing services | Place of enjoyment/use of the service |
| Franchising goods/services or licensing intangibles attached to goods/ services | Place of final delivery of the goods or place of enjoyment/use of the services |

*Source:* Authors

Pillar One Blueprint provides hierarchical indicators for each revenue sourcing principle.

For example,[10] if the identified revenue stream is 'revenue from online advertising services based on real-time location of the viewer', the revenue sourcing principle would be 'real time location of the viewer' and the hierarchy of indicators would be as under:

- The jurisdiction of the geolocation of the device of the viewer at the time of display; or if unavailable or unreliable.
- The jurisdiction of the IP address of the device of the viewer at the time of display; or if unavailable or unreliable.
- Other available information that can be used to determine the jurisdiction of the real-time location of the viewer.

### 3.4. Tax Base Determinations (4th BB)

To identify eligible Consolidated Financial Statements ('CFS'), Pillar One Blueprint guides:

- CFS prepared as per IFRS and eligible[11] GAAPs[12] are acceptable for Amount A purposes.
- CFS prepared as per any other GAAPs are also acceptable provided their use does not lead to material distortions.
- For MNEs whose ultimate parent entity do not prepare any CFS, they would be obligated to prepare CFS solely for Amount A purposes.

After determination of the CFS, the next step is computation of the 'consolidated profit before tax'. For this purpose, the starting point would be the 'consolidated profit after tax' as per the identified CFS, subject to a few book-to-tax adjustments

10. Para 238 and 239 of the Pillar 1 Blueprint.
11. Eligible GAAPs include GAAPs of Australia, Canada, China, Hong Kong, India, Japan, Singapore, South Korea, and the United States.
12. GAAP – Generally accepted accounting principles.

*(e.g., disallowance of expenses typically not allowable for public policy purposes such as fines, penalty, bribery, etc.; dividend income and gains/losses arising in connection with shares recognized under equity method).* Inter-GAAP adjustments are not proposed.

Considering that the consolidated profit before tax could also include profits attributable to out-of-scope activities, it is essential to identify profits solely attributable to in-scope activities (i.e., CFB and ADS). To achieve this, the Pillar One Blueprint offers the stepwise approach as given below:

(a) Segregate of consolidated revenues to identify revenues attributable to in-scope businesses.

(b) Segregate profit either using a revenue allocation key *(especially for MNE groups below a particular threshold)* or rely on published segmented results or prepare separate segmented accounts *(if not already prepared).*

Pillar One Blueprint proposes allowing MNE Groups to carry forward in-regime losses *(at the MNE Group level or segmented level as the case may be)* while leaving open the question on allowing carry forward and set-off of pre-regime losses.

Pillar One Blueprint also discusses the concept of 'profit shortfalls', which are given treatment akin to losses. Profit shortfalls arise when an MNE group earns profits below the routine profitability threshold. The intent of profit shortfalls is to maintain equilibrium between businesses earning regular profits viz-à-viz those earning irregular profits *(typically startups).*

### 3.5. Profit Allocation (5th BB)

Amount A seeks to allocate a portion of the non-routine profits of MNE groups to market jurisdictions through a formulaic approach. This process involves the following three steps:

**Step 1 - Identification of non-routine profits**: Specify routine profitability percentages, above which all profits would be considered as non-routine profits. The threshold would be based on a simplified convention *(a PBT to revenue ratio).*

**Step 2 - Applying reallocation percentage**: Considering that non-routine profits generated by the MNE group arise on account of a variety of functions, which are not only related to the market jurisdiction(s), Pillar One Blueprint proposes the allocation of only a portion of the non-routine profits to market jurisdictions. The allocable amount is determined by applying a reallocation percentage to the total non-routine profits. The reallocation percentages would be prescribed upfront and could be separate for each activity *(i.e., for ADS and CFB).*

**Step 3 - Profit allocation to market/source jurisdictions**: The last step is allocation of Amount A to eligible market jurisdictions that satisfy the nexus test based on a revenue allocation key.

Pillar One Blueprint notes that where MNE groups already have a taxable presence in the market jurisdiction, there could be a possible overlap with the income already offered to tax viz-à-viz Amount A. In order to tackle this issue of double counting, the Pillar One Blueprint proposes a marketing and distribution profits safe harbour that would compare the following two amounts:

(a) Profits already allocated to market jurisdiction as per existing profit allocation rules ('existing marketing and distribution profits'); *compared with*

(b) Safe harbour return comprised of the following elements:

  (i) Amount A, as computed under Amount A formula; and

  (ii) Fixed return for in-country routine marketing and distribution activities, which include an industry and regional uplift (to be prescribed).

Where the profits already allocated to the market jurisdiction exceed the safe harbour return, there would be no further allocation of Amount A.

### 3.6. Elimination of Double Taxation (6th BB)

Elimination of double taxation arising due to Amount A is perhaps the most controversial aspect of the entire Pillar One framework. This step involves identification of the entity/entities that would pay Amount A to the market jurisdiction(s) and consequently, lead to the determination of the country, which should alleviate the double taxation *(i.e., jurisdiction in which each entity is a resident)*.

The identification of paying entities is a somewhat complicated process involving following steps:

- **Step 1**: Identify the entities within an MNE group that perform activities that make a material and sustained contribution to the group's ability to generate overall residual profits. This would be done through a FAR[13] analysis of the entities concerned.
- **Step 2**: Apply profitability test to ensure that entities identified have the capacity to bear the Amount A tax liability. This would ensure that entities earning routine/low profits or incurring losses are not identified as paying entities.
- **Step 3**: Allocate, in the order of priority, amount A tax liability to the entities that have a connection with the market(s) where amount A is allocated.
- **Step 4**: Allocate, on a pro-rata basis, where no sufficiently strong connection(s) is (or are) found or where those with a market connection lack the necessary amount of profit.

13. Functions performed, assets owned, and risks assumed analysis.

As an alternative to the above, Pillar One Blueprint also proposes a simplified two-step approach which would involve the following steps:

- **Step 1**: application of a profitability test to identify entities within the group that earn non-routine profits; and
- **Step 2**: if more than one entity is identified, allocate Amount A tax among such entities in the ratio of their non-routine profits.

With regards to the method for elimination of double taxation, Pillar One Blueprint proposes either exemption or credit method. For the latter method, there is no clarity if there will be a uniform global tax credit mechanism.

## 4. Amount B (Pillar One)

Amount B seeks to standardize the remuneration of related party distributors that perform baseline marketing and distribution activities in the market jurisdiction. This simplifies the administration of transfer pricing rules for tax administrations, reduces compliance costs for taxpayers and minimizes tax litigation.

### 4.1. Scope (7th BB)

Pillar One Blueprint proposes to define in-scope 'marketing and distribution activities' by reference to a positive list of typical functions performed, assets owned, and risks assumed by a routine distributor. At the same time, it also proposes a negative list of such factors that are not typically performed by a routine distributor.

Currently, the definition of 'baseline marketing and distribution activities' is narrower –e.g., it does not cover commissionaires or sales agents. Further work is being undertaken if the scope can be broadened to include similar activities, including determination of fixed return for such additional activities.

Baseline marketing and distribution functions[14] include:

- Importation of products for resale within the market and customs clearance, including charge of freight, insurance, and customs costs.
- Purchase of goods for resale within the market; development and execution of sales budgets and plans within the market, within the MNE group's guidelines, and under its oversight, and/or subject to the MNE group's approval.
- Development and maintenance of local customer relationships within the market.
- Determination or negotiation of pricing and other contract terms with third party customers, within the MNE group's pricing guidelines or price lists,

14. Para 668 of the Pillar 1 Blueprint.

and under its oversight or approval where necessary (e.g., to adapt based on market demand, competition and currency, or to allow certain discounts);

- Processing of orders and contracts with customers; inventory: monitoring and routine management of inventory (e.g., on the books or by means of joint systems or by receiving regular updates from an entity providing storage and logistics services).
- Management of logistics, warehousing and transportation of products to customers (which includes situations when these are outsourced to another entity).
- General administration functions, e.g., sales invoicing, processing, and collection of payments, accounts, and financial and tax reporting obligations.
- Routine input into demand planning activities undertaken by the MNE group; and marketing activities:
    - (a) pre-sale services: provision of product information to prospective customers (e.g., product demonstrations);
    - (b) execution of global marketing plans in local jurisdictions with no further material adaptation (advertising campaign, trade shows).
    - (c) translation of marketing, advertising material, and business website to local language;
    - (d) market research for planning and marketing purposes, e.g., provision of input to foreign related party on trends, customers, consumers, demands, local input; and
    - (e) routine after-sales services,: including processing complaints, and providing non-technical support.

Qualitative assessment would also be further supported by some quantitative indicators, e.g., where a distributor exceeds certain financial thresholds or metrics *(e.g., its marketing expenses exceed a fixed proportion of total costs),* indicating that the entity is performing more than just 'baseline' activities and thus, not covered by Amount B.

## 4.2. Quantum (8th BB)

Transaction Net Margin Method ('TNMM') is stated to be the most appropriate transfer pricing method associated with the adequate remuneration for the baseline marketing and distribution activities performed by distribution entities in-scope of Amount B.

A fixed return would be assigned through a 'return on sales' profit level indicator. The return could vary across geographies and industries, which would require preparation of separate benchmarking sets for each of the regions and industries.

Pillar One Blueprint also provides that a MNE group could challenge the fixed return by providing evidence of another transfer pricing method that would be most appropriate under the given circumstances *(for e.g., availability of a reliable CUP)*.

Further, the application of Amount B would be prospective i.e., it would not supersede MAP settlements or advance pricing agreements entered into force before the implementation of Amount B.

## 5. Tax Certainty (Pillar One)

In addition to creating new nexus and profit allocation rules, Pillar One Blueprint also recommends innovative tax dispute prevention and resolution mechanisms.

### 5.1. Dispute Prevention and Resolution for Amount A (9th BB)

Pillar One Blueprint recognizes that it would be impractical *(if not impossible)* to allow all affected tax jurisdictions to assess and audit an MNE's calculation and allocation of Amount A.

The Amount A mechanism would work through a self-assessment system wherein MNE groups *(through an Amount A coordinating entity)* would be required to submit self-assessment return/documentation package, which would then be assessed by the lead tax administration ('LTA') and all affected tax administrations ('ATA') through an exchange of information framework. The LTA and ATA would be free to audit such return and propose adjustments. Pillar One Blueprint notes that a mandatory dispute resolution mechanism would need to be developed.

As a dispute prevention measure, MNE groups can opt for an early tax certainty process wherein the matter can be referred to a review panel. During this period, the ATA shall not commence any audit activity. There could be multiple outcomes of such tax certainty process, discussed hereunder:

- The review panel arrives at a conclusion and the same is accepted by remaining ATAs *(that are not on the panel)* – MNE group receives binding tax certainty across all Inclusive Framework members;
- The review panel arrives at a conclusion and the same is not acceptable to the remaining ATAs *(that are not on the panel)* – matter referred to determination panel.
- The review panel fails to arrive at a conclusion – matter referred to a determination panel.

When an MNE group withdraws its request for tax certainty after a review panel recommendation has been agreed by all ATAs or after a determination panel has completed its review, it is being contemplated if tax administrations should still be bound by panel conclusions.

### 5.2. Dispute Prevention and Resolution beyond Amount A (10th BB)

Pillar One Blueprint recognizes that any disputes related to application of Amount B would also be subject to mandatory dispute resolution, the mechanics of which are being developed.

Further, in order to resolve transfer pricing disputes that may arise on account of adjustments made which are unrelated to Amount A, Pillar One Blueprint also has an over-arching proposition. It states that a mandatory binding dispute resolution will be available as a backstop to existing dispute resolution tools for all disputes regarding transfer pricing and permanent establishment issues for MNE groups that are within the scope of Amount A.

## 6. Implementation (Pillar One)

The implementation of Pillar One will require action across the following three different dimensions:

(i) Changes in domestic tax laws of Inclusive Framework members.

(ii) Public international law (possibly through a new multilateral instrument).

(iii) Guidance to supplement (i) or (ii) or both.

Further, the consensus-based agreement under Pillar One shall also include a commitment from Inclusive Framework members to implement the agreement and to remove any unilateral measures/actions taken so far.

## 7. The Pillar Two Framework

The objective of Pillar Two is to provide a solid basis for a systematic solution to address the additional BEPS challenges and to specify a set of rules that would afford jurisdictions a right to "tax back".[15] Such right to tax back will be available where other jurisdictions have not exercised their primary taxing rights, or the payment is subject to an otherwise low level of effective taxation.

Pillar Two proposes a set of rules to levy a top-up tax on MNE groups where their overall effective tax rate is below an agreed minimum rate. At a policy level, these rules are aimed at minimizing harmful tax competition between countries by creating a potential disincentive for countries to adopt low or nil effective tax rates.

The rules attempt to ensure that large internationally operating businesses pay a minimum level of tax regardless of where they are headquartered or the jurisdictions in which they operate. A number of interlocking rules are proposed that seek to:

---

15. https://www.oecd.org/tax/beps/tax-challenges-arising-from-digitalisation-report-on-pillar-two-blueprint-abb4c3d1-en.htm.

(a) ensure minimum taxation while avoiding double taxation or taxation where there is no economic profit;

(b) cope with different tax system designs by jurisdictions as well as different operating models by businesses;

(c) ensure transparency and level playing field;

(d) minimize administrative and compliance costs.

While the rules are complex and detailed, and many important aspects, including the all-important question of the global minimum tax rate, are yet to be settled. It is expected that the global minimum tax rate will be somewhere between 10%-15%.

To achieve the above objective, the Pillar Two has proposed four new rules:

(a) Income Inclusion Rule ('IIR')

(b) Undertaxed Payments Rule ('UTPR')

(c) Subject to Tax Rule ('STTR')

(d) Switch- Over Rule ('SOR')

Pillar Two comprises of a two-pronged approach to achieve minimum level of taxation, i.e., Income Inclusion and Tax on Base Eroding Payments. The IIR and UTPR are the two re-enforcing rules of Pillar Two for achieving the global minimum tax and are together known as the GloBE rules. The IIR is supported by two treaty-based rules: the STTR and the SOR.

## 8. Scope of Globe

Pillar Two Blueprint discusses rules for determining whether a taxpayer is within the scope of the GloBE rules. It defines the in-scope groups and entities and provides a list of excluded entities. It specifies rules on consolidated group revenue threshold for the application of GloBE rules.

### 8.1. In-Scope Groups

GloBE rules will generally apply to MNEs and their constituent entities, which are subject to the country-by-country reporting ('CbCR') regulations, particularly, groups of entities including permanent establishments ('PE') that are required to prepare consolidated financial statements for financial reporting purposes and have annual revenue of more than €750 million.

However, certain ultimate parent entities ('UPEs') that typically benefit from exclusion or an exemption from tax under the laws of the jurisdiction where they are incorporated are excluded (discussed further in point 0).

The definition of a constituent entity includes entities that would be excluded from consolidated financial statements based on size or materiality. The Blueprint treats a PE as a separate constituent entity, provided it has separate financial statements. The Blueprint notes that the separate treatment of a PE ensures comparable treatment of foreign subsidiaries and PEs under the GloBE.

Further, the GloBE rules provide guidelines for the determination of an acceptable accounting standard in order to ensure consistency in determining the MNEs that are in scope.

### 8.2. Excluded Entities

Some entities at the top of the ownership chain are specifically excluded from the application of the GloBE rules. These entities have a particular purpose or status under the laws of the jurisdiction in which they are created and are generally exempt from domestic income tax to preserve a specific policy outcome.

The Blueprint provides for a list of excluded entities with specific definitions for each category.[16] Certain investment and pension funds, governmental entities such as sovereign wealth funds, and international and non-profit bodies, which are typically exempted under the applicable domestic tax law, are excluded. The exclusion is specific to the entity itself and generally does not extend to entities owned by it that are not themselves on the list.

Further consideration will be given to cases in which the exclusion arguably should still apply in respect of a constituent entity that is not otherwise the ultimate UPE, such as certain life insurance and pension structures that are consolidated within an MNE Group and whose income is not beneficially owned by the MNE Group.

Accordingly, for the entities that are subject to a tax transparency regime, their income is excluded from the GloBE rules. The exclusion for UPEs subject to a tax neutrality regime appears to be intended to cover S corporations (fiscally transparent entities) and certain types of cooperatives.

The definitions of excluded entities include wholly-owned entities, but the criteria for wholly-owned entities vary slightly depending on the category. In general, wholly-owned entities must not carry on a trade or business in order to qualify for the exclusion. The Blueprint says that a business that earns all or substantially all of its income from dividends, interest, and capital gains would not be a commercial trade or business. The Blueprint does not discuss entities that derive income from rents or share trading activity, which are important revenue streams for many investment entities.

The Blueprint specifies that further work will be required on whether and to what extent the GloBE rules should apply to the international shipping sector.

16. Para 71-75 of the Pillar 2 Blueprint.

### 8.3. Consolidated Revenue Threshold

GloBE rules are intended to apply to MNEs that have a consolidated revenue of above €750 million or equivalent in the immediately preceding financial year. This creates synergy with current CbCR rules and excludes small businesses.

## 9. Calculating the Effective Tax Rate ('ETR')

### 9.1. GloBE ETR

To apply the GloBE rules, an MNE Group must determine its ETR. The GloBE ETR is calculated on a jurisdictional basis, this requires both income and taxes to be assigned across those jurisdictions where an MNE operates. The calculation is the amount of 'covered taxes' divided by the amount of income as determined under the GloBE rules [ETR for a jurisdiction = adjusted covered taxes/adjusted GloBE income].

The jurisdictional ETR requires the income and taxes to be allocated between jurisdictions, generally by identifying the jurisdiction where the income was earned and associating the covered taxes with that location.

The Inclusive Framework's intent is to create a globally uniform tax base to facilitate the determination of whether a constituent entity's income is low-taxed. The creation of a global tax base is a fundamental departure from existing international tax practice and is a key innovation.

A tax is a compulsory, unrequited payment to government. Specifically, covered taxes are defined to mean any tax on an entity's income or profits (including a tax on distributed profits), and include any taxes imposed in lieu of a generally applicable income tax. It also includes taxes assessed on an alternative basis levied at the state or local government level, corporate equity taxes, and taxes paid under controlled foreign corporations (CFC). Covered taxes also include taxes on retained earnings and corporate equity.

The list of non-covered taxes includes digital services taxes, and other taxes that are not based on income.

The Blueprint covers the rules and explanations relating to the calculation of the ETR, and top-up tax under the GloBE rules.

### 9.2. Fundamental Aspects of the Top-Up Tax

A key feature of Pillar Two is the top-up tax at the UPE level. The IIR applies to determine the ETR on a jurisdictional basis. The top-up tax in the UPE jurisdiction will apply if the ETR of a constituent entity in a jurisdiction is less than the rate to be determined. As stated above, the ETR is the amount of covered taxes divided by the amount of income in the jurisdiction determined under special GloBE rules.

The top-up tax is the difference between the ETR in a jurisdiction and the agreed minimum rate and is determined without reference to any other attributes of the UPE.

Top-up tax for an entity = adjusted GloBE income of the entity x (GloBE minimum ETR – actual ETR)

## 9.3. Allocation of Income and Taxes

The income of PEs and constituent entities with a residence tax jurisdiction is assigned to the PE location or entity residence. The income of flow-through entities with no tax residence (stateless entities) is assigned to their owner if that owner's jurisdiction treats it as transparent or assigned to a "stateless" category otherwise.

## 9.4. Tax Base

The initial steps for calculating the ETR are the financial accounts of each constituent entity prepared in accordance with the financial accounting standard used by the parent of the MNE in its consolidated financial statements. To these financial accounts, a limited number of adjustments are then made, i.e., to add or eliminate specified items in order to arrive at the GloBE tax base or any modifications to be made to address timing difference.

- Entity-level financial information that is used in preparing the parent's consolidated financial accounts can be used, even if such financial information is not prepared strictly in accordance with the parent's financial accounting standard where (a) it is reasonable to do so, (b) the information is reliable, and (c) the use of such information does not result in permanent material differences from the accounting standard of the parent.
- Special rules for the treatment of a series of situations will require entities subject to the GloBE to keep a separate set of books. Adjustments to the financial accounting rules *inter-alia* include intercompany items, dividends and dispositions of stock, stock-based compensation, covered taxes, and adjustments for Pillar One outcomes.
- Adjustments to the GloBE tax base are based on the materiality and commonality of the items and are generally made to address permanent differences or avoid duplication. The GloBE tax base eliminates items such as intra-group dividends and investments accounted for on the equity method, as well as gain or loss realized in connection with a nontaxable reorganization or restructuring.

## 9.5. Accelerated Depreciation and Immediate Expensing

Adjustments will also be made for deductions related to immediate expensing and accelerated depreciation to preserve the benefits intended by domestic tax rules, by either modifying the carry-forward approach for the deferred tax or using the local tax depreciation rules to reduce the GloBE tax base.

## 10. Carry Forwards and Carve-Outs

Two adjustments that may be made to the top-up tax calculation for a particular jurisdiction:

- *The carry-forward adjustment*: This allows an MNE to carry forward losses or excess taxes paid in prior periods to subsequent periods to ease out the volatility arising out of local laws or timing differences. The carry-forward adjustment ensures that the Pillar Two does not result in the imposition of additional tax where low ETR is simply a result of timing differences in respect of the recognition of income or imposition of taxes.
- *The formulaic substance-based carveout*: This is intended to exclude a fixed return for substantive activities within a jurisdiction from the scope of the GloBE rules. The GloBE rules reduce the taxable income base for a jurisdiction by an amount equal to a percentage of payroll and a percentage of tangible assets located within the jurisdiction. This exclusion, in particular, may be relevant for groups, which, in response to the BEPS Project and other local tax rules, have invested in building substance in subsidiaries in low tax countries. Depending on how this carve-out is finally structured, the impact of the Pillar Two proposals could potentially be mitigated for such groups.

The GloBE rules are impacted by the local losses and excess local taxes or IIR liability that is owed.

- Losses are defined as the excess of expenses over income included in the GloBE tax base of the jurisdiction. Local losses, i.e., losses in a jurisdiction, can be carried forward for an unlimited period and be allowed as a deduction in the subsequent year, thereby reducing the GloBE tax base in that year or increasing the loss carry-forward arising in that year.
- Excess taxes paid in a local jurisdiction create either an IIR tax credit or a local tax carry-forward or both. Excess taxes mean the amount of local tax in excess of the minimum tax rate threshold and will be limited in duration when being used to create an IIR credit or to increase the covered tax expense.

One of the recommendations made to the OECD as part of the Pillar Two work was that benefits arising from incentive regimes that pass the review of harmful tax practices as per BEPS Action 5 should be excluded from Pillar Two levies. The OECD however, seems to have gone in a different direction by instead providing for some substance-based exclusions. If this remains intact in the final versions, many incentive regimes, including those that are structured in line with the Action 5 recommendations, may be at risk.

## 11. Simplification Options

The Blueprint suggests several potential simplification measures but has not yet decided which measures to adopt in the final design of the GloBE rules. Simplification options considered:

(a) *Country-by-country reporting (CbCR) ETR safe harbor:*

MNE groups that prepare their CbCR report based on their parent company's consolidated financial statements would not be required to perform a separate GloBE ETR calculation for a jurisdiction in which the ETR calculated on the basis of the CbCR report, with certain number of adjustments, is above a specified threshold.

(b) *De minimis profit exclusion:*

Exclude jurisdictions from the GloBE rules that have less than a specified percentage of the MNE's pre-tax profit.

(c) *Permitting a single jurisdictional ETR calculation to cover multiple years:*

MNE would not be required to compute the ETR of a particular jurisdiction for a specified period of years where the ETR of that jurisdiction exceeded a specified threshold rate (in the base year).

(d) *Tax administrative guidance to identify low-risk jurisdictions:*

Establish a process for tax administrations to work along with stakeholders to identify jurisdictions where the tax base does not materially depart from the GloBE tax base, and the tax rate is sufficiently high, thus presuming that an MNE's ETR would exceed the agreed minimum rate.

## 12. Income Inclusion Rule ('IIR') and Switch-Over Rule ('SOR')

The IIR applies at the level of the parent jurisdiction and levies top-up tax on the low-taxed income of foreign constituent entities, which are directly or indirectly controlled by the parent. The SOR allows a jurisdiction to override the exemption method in certain cases. The SOR rule allows the application of the IIR to certain branch structures when the tax treaty otherwise exempts the earnings of the branch. The rule is being explored to ensure that a parent entity's jurisdiction of residence would be permitted to apply its domestic law IIR to tax the profits attributable to a PE of the parent, even where a tax treaty would otherwise exempt those profits.

### 12.1. Income Inclusion Rule ('IIR')

The Income Inclusion Rule triggers inclusion at the shareholder level when the income of a controlled foreign entity is taxed below the effective minimum tax rate. The shareholder would be subject to a top-up tax in respect of the proportionate share of income of the low-taxed entity so as to bring its ETR up to the agreed minimum.

While determining IIR, instead of jurisdictional ETR, adopting a global ETR may potentially serve the purpose of rationalising group level tax rate and not result in unnecessary tax and compliance burden.

Where multiple IIRs could apply to the same income of a constituent entity, a coordination rule (the 'top-down approach') gives priority to the jurisdiction of the constituent entity that is closest to the top of the ownership chain in the MNE group, beginning with the UPE. An exception to the top-down approach applies in the case of 'split ownership' structures in which a significant portion (e.g., 10% or more) of the equity interests in a constituent entity are held by persons that are not part of the MNE group.

To simplify, under the top-down approach you give priority to IIR application to higher-tier entities within the group, in many cases, this will be the MNE parent itself. This ultimate parent entity will pay the top-up tax to their home tax authority, although in some instances, it might drop down to a lower-tier intermediate parent in the group, and IIR would be applied at that level.

From an outbound perspective, for large Indian headquartered IT/ITeS groups in particular, the IIR could lead to increased taxation in India. For instance, if such groups have significant profits in subsidiaries in low tax jurisdictions, the IIR could be relevant for them.

## 13. Undertaxed Payments Rule ('UTPR')

The rule applies when a constituent entity is not already subject to an IIR, i.e., it is intended to serve as a backstop for IIR. Accordingly, the rule might only apply in limited circumstances.

The UTPR would allocate the top-up tax with respect to a low-taxed entity to other members of the group, based on deductible payments made by those other group members. The UTPR is also intended to reduce incentives for tax driven inversion and to address base-erosion through deductible intra-group payments.

The top-up tax amount is allocated among constituent entities that are subject to the UTPR based on a two-step allocation method[17]:

- For UTPR taxpayer that make deductible payments to the low-tax entity, the top-up tax is allocated as under:

  *Payments made by the UTPR taxpayer to the low-tax entity/All intragroup payments from UTPR taxpayer to the low-tax entity*

- For any remaining unallocated top-up tax, the remainder is allocated among UTPR taxpayers that have net intragroup expenditure as under:

17. Para 685-687 of the Pillar 2 Blueprint.

*Net intragroup expenditure of the UTPR taxpayer/ total related party expenditure of all UTPR taxpayers*

The sum of the top-up tax allocated under the UTPR among constituent entities will not exceed the total amount of the top-up tax. The Blueprint provides multiple formulas for enforcing a cap on amounts allocated under the UTPR to achieve this result.

The UTPR has been compared to the U.S. BEAT, but the UTPR differs from the BEAT in fundamental ways. Perhaps most importantly, the application of the BEAT does not depend on the tax treatment of the recipient of deductible payments made by a U.S. taxpayer, while the UTPR is applied only to allocate an amount of top-up tax with respect to a constituent entity that has an ETR below the minimum agreed rate.

## 14. Special Rules for Associates, Joint Ventures and Orphan Entities

A separate rule covers associates and joint ventures, and another covers orphan entities. The first rule applies a simplified IIR to the income of an MNE attributable to ownership interests in entities or arrangements that are reported under the equity method. The second rule extends the application of the UTPR to orphan entities or arrangements that could otherwise be used to extract profit from the MNE, which can be viewed as giving rise to issues relating to base erosion and shifting of profits.

## 15. The Subject to Tax Rule ('STTR')

This rule denies treaty benefits for certain deductible intragroup payments that are subject to no or low rates of nominal taxation in the recipient jurisdiction. The STTR helps source countries protect their tax base.

The STTR would be designed as a treaty-based rule that will apply to payments between connected persons. The excluded entities list is in line with those under IIR/ UTPR. The trigger rate for STTR is not yet fixed, though it seems that it will be around 7% or 8%.

The STTR applies to a certain set of payments, which raise concerns relating to base stripping for, e.g., interest, royalty, insurance premium, rent for movable property, guarantees, brokerage, financing, rentals, agency, intermediation, marketing, procurement fees, etc.

The STTR considers various materiality thresholds based on total amount of covered payments, size or revenue of the MNE, a ratio of covered payments made to connected persons in other jurisdictions.

STTR is a little bit different in comparison to IIR and UTPR. The IIR and UTPR are triggered based on ETR, but STTR applies when payment is subject to a tax rate below the minimum, in the payee jurisdiction. STTR applies based on the adjusted nominal tax rate in payee jurisdiction, arrived at after considering preferential tax regimes in that jurisdiction. For example, if the payment has been made to a connected party in another jurisdiction, and such connected party is benefiting from the offshore source regime, this will be taken into account in determining whether the adjusted nominal rate is beneath the trigger rate for STTR.

The STTR will be applied either through a withholding tax or an ex-post annualized charge, a matter still under discussion.

Like many source-based countries, primarily, the STTR (on payments that are made to a recipient jurisdiction having a lower tax rate), amongst the other rules, will likely have significant revenue implications for India.

The Blueprint currently contemplates that the STTR would apply only to certain deductible intra-group payments. However, consideration is being given to certain gains, including transactions between entities that are not connected. If capital gains are sought to be covered by the STTR, it could possibly affect grandfathering benefits under India's treaties, since in such cases capital gains are not brought to tax in the country of residence.

Considering that the STTR applies prior to the GloBE rules, treatment of GILTI [discussed in paragraph 00] as a qualifying IIR will not preclude the STTR from applying to constituent entities of U.S.-parented groups.

## 16. Illustration on the Interlocking Rules

**Figure 1. Functioning of the Interlocking Rules**

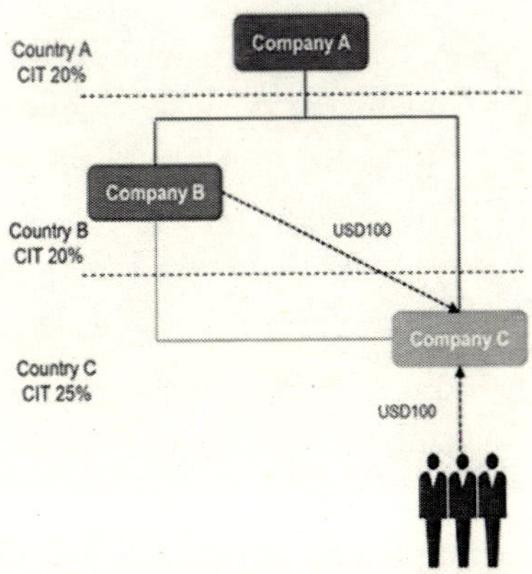


**Assumptions:**

— STTR trigger rate 7.5%; Global min tax rate 12%

— Company C local statutory rate 25%, but special regime reduces tax to 20% of normal rate (i.e. 5%). All third party income tax exempt

— Company B ETR 20%

**Rules application:**

| Step 1: Apply STTR | |
|---|---|
| Company C special regime tax rate | 5%<7.5% |
| WHT under STTR | 2.5%*100=2.5 |
| Step 2: Apply IIR (assuming Country A introduces IIR) | |
| Company B ETR | 20%>12%, No need to include in IIR |
| Company C ETR | (5+2.5) / (100+100) =3.75%<12% |
| Company C top-up tax | 200* (12%-3.75%) =16.5 |
| Step 3: Apply UTPR (assuming Country A does not apply IIR and Country B introduces UTPR) | |
| Company C top-up tax | 16.5 |
| Company B denied deduction under UTPR | 16.5/20%=82.5 |

*Source:* OECD, Pillar Two Blueprint.[18]

18. OECD. 2020. *Tax Challenges Arising from Digitalisation – Report on Pillar Two Blueprint: Inclusive Framework on BEPS*, OECD/G20 BEPS Project, Paris. https://doi.org/10.1787/abb4c3d1-en., (last accessed on January 17, 2021).

Here is a simple example[19] illustrating how all the interlocking rules function together There is an MNE group with Company A, Company B, and Company C, all in moderately highly taxed jurisdictions. However, Company C is subject to a special low tax rate of 5% on the income received from Company B [say USD 100]. The income received from other parties is tax-exempt, so it is a low-taxed company overall.

The first rule that will be looked at is the STTR. The STTR would take into account the fact that Company C paid 5% tax under the special regime on the payment from Company B. The STTR trigger rate is 7.5%, the difference between tax under the special regime and the trigger rate for STTR is 2.5. That is 2.5 percent of USD 100, which is USD 2.5. That is the STTR tax paid by Company B to the Country B tax authorities.

The next step will be to apply IIR at the level of Company A. The Company C ETR calculation takes into account both, taxes paid by Company C to the Country C tax authority and STTR tax. The ETR for Company C is 3.75% [(5+2.5)/(100+100)], which is lower than the global minimum tax of 12% (assumed). Accordingly, there will be a top-up tax of 16.5 USD [200* (12%-3.75%)], which needs to be paid by Company A to the Country A tax authorities.

If the IIR does not apply because Country A has not adopted the IIR, then go to Company B, which will apply the UTPR. UTPR works as if Country B, by denying the deduction will collect USD 16.5 dollars. Accordingly, the local tax rate of Country B is 20%,so gross the USD 16.5 of top-up tax to USD 82.5;. this is the amount of tax deduction denied by Company B to pay the UTPR tax.

This is under the basic first UTPR rule; there is also a backup second UTPR rule. If Company B did not make a direct payment to Company C, the rules would identify net related payment entities within the group, regardless of whether they pay anything to Company C. Then allocate the UTPR tax to these companies, and they deny tax deductions. This is how the UTPR forms an effective backup to the IIR.

## 17. Implementation and Rule Coordination

The Blueprint discusses issues on implementation, including the treaty compatibility of the GloBE and other Pillar Two rules with existing tax treaty obligations, mechanisms to promote effective coordination, and address potential disputes that may arise from the application of the rules.

The Blueprint envisages the possible development of model legislation, treaty language and guidance, a multilateral review process, and a potential multilateral convention, which could also include new provisions on dispute prevention and resolution.

19. Refer Chapter 10- Example 10.2.1A and 10.2.1B of Pillar 2 Blueprint.

As regards the rule coordination, the STTR applies before IIR/UTPR. The additional tax from STTR will be taken into consideration while determining the ETR in the income for the purpose of IIR/UTPR. Between IIR and UTPR, the IIR would take priority, and UTPR will serve as the backstop. The IIR and UTPR will be enacted under a particular jurisdiction's domestic law and are expected not to violate the existing tax treaties, whereas the STTR and SOR will be enacted through amendments to tax treaties.

## 18. Global Intangible Low-Taxed Income ('GILTI') Co-existence

The Blueprint recognizes that an agreement on the co-existence of the GILTI and the GloBE rules will be essential to ensure political agreement on Pillar Two. The shared purpose of the GILTI and GloBE regime, the fact that GILTI formed a fundamental part in supporting the momentum behind the GloBE regime, and the challenges posed in changing GILTI given its relatively recent enactment as part of major U.S. tax reform, all suggest that to ensure this co-existence, GILTI should be treated as a qualifying IIR.

Having said which, even if GILTI is treated as a compliant IIR, some technical issues will remain to be addressed. Further, as discussed above, questions around GILTI co-existence with Pillar Two, i.e., how the UTPR applies to US multinationals and the potential need for adjustments to the GILTI and BEAT rules, also remain.

## 19. Concluding Remarks

Pillar Two is expected to generate about 42-70 USD billion additional revenues globally, which is approximately 90% of the expected additional revenue from both the Pillars,[20] The Pillar Two proposals could go a long way in eliminating the tax rate competition. The proposals are innovative, and by giving the right to other countries to tax income, which is not taxed in a particular country, the proposals will likely push several low-tax countries to revisit their tax rates and incentive regimes. It is possible that many countries with low taxes may choose to increase their tax rates up to the level of the OECD Minimum Tax or the STTR threshold rate to avoid having these revenues getting taxed by other countries.

As discussed, Pillar Two proposals are expected to generate significant revenues but the important thing to note is that these do not necessarily mean that countries like India with medium-to-high tax rates will automatically benefit from large tax inflows.

20. https://www.oecd.org/tax/beps/tax-challenges-arising-from-digitalisation-economic-impact-assessment-0e3cc2d4-en.htm.

The proposals are complex, and involve placing significant compliance burdens on taxpayers, and administrative burdens on the department and the courts. Critical consideration must be given to ascertain whether the burdens on the compliance and administrative framework would be disproportionate in comparison to the expected revenue impact on India.

The process of implementation will be the most critical aspect. The rules proposed in Pillar Two are highly sophisticated and differ from how Indian laws are customarily structured. Accordingly, it is important to ensure that these rules are incorporated in domestic law in a manner that can provide clarity and leave the minimal need for interpretation. Detailed guidance is expected from the OECD in relation to these rules. It would be essential to formally incorporate such guidance into the Indian law by way of circulars/notifications, etc., so that there is a certainty on its binding effect. A sufficient time frame is also necessary to consider the compatibility of the new rules with the existing domestic law and treaty provisions. In addition to adequate time for implementation, policymakers should also give due regard to ensure capacity building and training for the tax administration to ensure that these rules are implemented effectively.

# REJOINDER

Parthasarathi Shome

## 1. Introduction

The chapter by Gajaria et al. on the OECD's Pillar One and Pillar Two proposals with respect to digital economy taxation is a meticulous deconstruction of these proposals and their actual implications for tax contributions. To recount, the backdrop of the OECD's proposals was the G20's direction to suggest cross-country taxing rights for digital economy taxation. Pillar One and Two are the vehicles that emerged from the OECD's effort.

## 2. OECD Recommendations

Pillar One focussed on the (1) allocation of taxing rights among countries, and seeks to undertake a coherent and concurrent review of (2) the profit allocation and nexus rules. Pillar Two recommended a minimum tax on the digital economy to be introduced by all jurisdictions. There was more agreement on Pillar Two than on Pillar One, reflecting the US being more at ease with Pillar Two's minimum tax recommendation that it itself employs.

In January 2020, the OECD's Inclusive Framework (IF), comprising 135 countries reiterated its commitment to the two-Pillar approach. It developed a note entitled, "Outline of the Architecture of a Unified Approach on Pillar One". An updated Programme of Work identified 11 building blocks for further work towards a solution. A progress note on Pillar Two was also agreed. An IF meeting occurred in October 2020 towards the agreement of a package. Yet subsequently, a statement was issued indicating that the work was being set aside. This clearly indicates the underlying lack of consensus on the issue. The crux of the final position rested on the US essentially disagreeing with its MNEs being taxed in source jurisdictions and insisting that tax revenue should accrue to the US where digital companies are headquartered.

However, the reality is that recent business models such as cyberspace (digital economy) and outsourcing allow non-residents (NR) to have a significant presence in countries without a taxable permanent establishment (PE) there.[21] The US essentially does not want such NRs to be taxed through any tax on digital economy activity where the taxable nexus is based on the site of the server. A tax based on the

21. Parthasarathi Shome (edited). 2020. *International Taxation in the Digital Era*, with a Foreword by Professor Judith Freedman, Oxford University, ITRAF, Oakbridge, Gurugram.

source of such income generated within its jurisdiction, which is often the emerging economy, has been unacceptable to the US.

In the absence of a multilateral consensus, countries have begun to take unilateral measures designed to generate revenue on a source basis to tax the digital economy. India's Equalization Levy could be perceived as an aspect of source-based taxation, that is, where turnover is generated. Perhaps the source principle should assume permanence in international tax rules: it is rational; both emerging and advanced economies other than the US have been progressing towards accepting the ramifications of the source principle.

There has been criticism about how much revenue source countries could obtain even if the source principle was followed. This reflects the calculation of revenue accruals based on tranches that would basically ensure that residence jurisdictions would continue to receive a significant portion of the revenue. Essentially, (1) the first allowable Amount (A) is too small, while (2) the subsequent amount (B)is truncated by prevailing limits and arbitration that are likely to favour residence countries. Gajaria et al. have explained the calculations in some detail (see their Sections 3 and 4).[22] Tax experts have expressed views that given the various checks and balances of thresholds, and the mandatory acceptance of any arbitration that may come about, the likely revenue outcomes would not be ample.[23]

Pillar Two was based on the US Tax Cuts and Jobs Act (TCJA) and implements as a modified version of the US Global Intangible Low-taxed Income (GILTI) and Base Erosion and Anti-abuse Tax (BEAT) that is a minimum tax on both outbound investment and inbound investment. Under Pillar Two, there should be a minimum residence tax if the source country does not tax, such as in GILTI, and a minimum source tax if the residence country does not tax (a modified version of BEAT). The minimum tax rates under Pillar Two were low and were subject to limits. So, revenue would not be significant.

A final question remains: e-commerce being mobile, where do 'mind and management' really reside (the principle behind residence-based taxation). It remains difficult to pin down, particularly in the digital economy context.

22. The original Pillar One (Oct. 9, 2019) set up three taxing rights for the market economies: amounts A, B, and C. The Blueprint for Pillar One drops Amount C. Hence now there are only Amounts A and B. See DeSouza, Glenn. 2020. 'Blueprint on Pillar One—What's New and Important', Bloomberg Tax, November 3. https://news.bloombergtax.com/transfer-pricing/blueprint-on-pillar-one-whats-new-and-important, (last accessed on March 4, 2021).

23. Rueven Avi-Yonah. 2020. Lecture, "Global Tax Talks 2020", Universidad Torcuato Di Tella (UTDT), Buenos Aires, August 26.
https://www.youtube.com/watch?v=FmNqrFXoT5U&list=PLmZkgXYrGwgjLtF0z62Thp1_My9OZyqU9&index=1, (last accessed on January 6, 2021).

## 3. UN Recommendations

The OECD was not the only player in the game of digital economy taxation. The UN made its own proposal. In August 2020, the UN proposed an optional UN model tax treaty provision for granting additional taxing rights to countries where an automated digital services provider's customers are located.[24] The tax base would include payments for services provided on the internet or an electronic network requiring minimal human involvement from the service provider. Thus, the tax base would include the sale, and other alienation of user data.

Activities covered would include online advertising services, online intermediation platform services, social media services, digital content services, cloud computing services, and standardized online teaching services. Drawn up by an ad hoc drafting group, the UN differs from the OECD's Inclusive Framework's unified approach to Pillar One, though both the OECD and the UN have, as their objective, the granting of greater taxing rights to source countries. The UN cites two routes for source countries to tax cross-border payments for automated digital services: (1) a 'gross-based tax' at a rate agreed upon by the two treaty parties; and (2) a net income-based tax using an apportionment formula; however, it also highlights problems with route (1).

The UN net income formula apportions 30 percent of net income from automated digital services to countries where sales revenues arise. This is broader than the OECD because it does not have the size, profitability, or local revenue thresholds that are in OECD's Pillar One. It is also more straightforward to determine taxable income in the source country without any thresholds.

## 4. Equalization Levy: Cross-country Experience

Pursuant to BEPS Action Plan I that laid the foundation for digital economy taxation, a Task Force for Digital Economy (TFDE) identified one alternative to tax the digital economy. It was the Equalization Levy (EL), a unilateral interim measure that a country could take to tax the digital economy. The levy could be limited to those businesses that engaged in transactions through a digital platform.

In 2018, EU proposed a 3 percent digital service tax on gross revenue from activities where users played a major role in creating value. It was to be levied on a list of selected digital activities. Several countries started implementing unilateral measure. Italy introduced a new web tax and unilaterally amended the definition of PE to tax the digital economy (PVE). The UK introduced the concept of diverted

24. Julie Martin. 2020. 'UN committee proposes new model treaty provision altering taxation of automated digital services,' MNE Tax, August 6. https://mnetax.com/un-committee-proposes-new-model-treaty-provision-altering-taxation-of-automated-digital-services-39609, (last accessed on January 6, 2021).

profit tax to tax diverted profit that arises in a company in an accounting period. France, India, Italy and Turkey have done so too. France's tax base is narrow. India's is potentially wider.

## 5. India's Equalization Levy

### 5.1. 2016 Version

A government appointed committee constituted in 1999 submitted a report in 2001. It examined e-commerce transactions under existing taxation laws. It looked into the issue of characterizing the income arising from digital transactions and advocated a broader interpretation of the term's 'royalty' and 'fee for technical services'.

A government committee was constituted in 2016 to examine taxation of the digital economy. The committee analyzed alternatives proposed by the OECD. It concluded that the option of introducing the concept of significant economic presence (SEP) or levying withholding tax would require amending tax treaties. Hence, the most viable option would be to impose an equalization levy. The committee acknowledged that since the technology was changing rapidly, business models would continue to evolve, and the list of taxed services would need to be reviewed and modified from time to time.

India introduced an EL through Finance Act, 2016. It provided for the imposition of a 6 percent levy on the amount received by a non-resident taxpayer not having a PE in India for providing specified services. Its objective is to equalize the tax burden on a NR providing digital services and operating in the Indian market, and their domestic competitors.

Initially, a services list had not been notified by the government; hence, the scope of the levy was limited only to advertisement services. It was applied to specified services, "online advertisement, any provision for digital advertising space or any other facility, or service for the purpose of online advertisement, and includes any other services as notified by Central Government". Other business models such as subscription-based or marketplace models were not covered.[25]

### 5.2. 2020 Version

Finance Act 2020 extended the EL's scope to e-commerce companies, lowered the rate to 2%, and shifted the burden of paying the levy from resident companies paying for services onto e-commerce operators themselves. It was implemented from

25. Vinti Agarwal and Alok P. Kumar. 2020. "Challenges in the Design of Digital Taxation in India", in P. Shome edited, *International taxation in the Digital Era*, OakBridge, Gurugram.

April 1, 2020. The scope now encompasses services intended for Indian residents and persons availing such services using an Indian Internet Protocol (IP) address.

The widely worded provision should technically cover online transactions ranging from hotel bookings and software purchases to even buying certain components from overseas. It is applicable to considerations received or receivable by NR e-commerce operators, and so might have a substantial impact on the business models of e-commerce giants such as Walmart-owned Flipkart, Amazon and Club Factory.[26]

### 5.3. Unclear Elements

Several unclear elements have been pointed out by analysts. The EL coverage could extend to a transaction with no relation whatsoever with India. For instance, a person present in India ordering some goods from Amazon to be delivered to and paid for by a relative residing in the United States would be covered within its all-embracing scope. This is contrary to the design considerations for ELs suggested by the OECD in 2015, which limited its application to NRs with a SEP in the country.

Many internet users resort to a Virtual Private Network ('VPN') for a secure connection or to dodge geographic restrictions on websites, and this is a challenge to tackle. A literal interpretation of the provision might cover within its ambit a foreign internet user using an Indian IP address on a VPN. Thus, levying the EL based upon the use of Indian IP will compel e-commerce operators to go to great lengths to ensure that they have sufficient means and infrastructure to identify and distinguish IP addresses.

The term "consideration received or receivable" used in the Act has created a dubious situation for the e-commerce operators. There seems to be not much clarity on whether the EL will be levied on the gross amount received by the operator from the customer or on the fee charged by the operator for its facilitation services. This difference is significant in revenue terms and in the generation of market distortions. This depends on how the payment mechanism works: Some operators retain commission from the gross amount received from the customer before sending the balance to the seller. In other models, the entire gross amount is sent to the seller and the operator receives commission thereafter. They will imply a significant difference in the tax base.

If the former, the seller would get subjected to EL in the hands of e-commerce operators on the gross amount received--because the EL's wording can be misinterpreted to infer that the entire amount paid by the customer (and at first

26. Dibya Prakash Behera and Hrishav Kumar. 2020. Equalization Levy on Non-Resident E-commerce Players: India's Ace in the Hole or a Stumbling Block for Foreign Players?, International Centre for Tax and Development, (ICTD), August 4. https://www.ictd.ac/blog/equalization-levy-non-resident-ecommerce-india-block-foreign-players/, (last accessed on January 6, 2021).

received by the e-commerce operator) is subject to EL and not just the commission that the e-commerce operator earns from such transaction.[27]

### 5.4. Problem of Double Taxation

One of the primary critiques of the unilateral measures being adopted by countries to tax the digital economy has consistently been that it leads to double taxation. The EL imposed in India is no different. First, it results in double taxation as per domestic laws due to its coverage in the GST base (though the EL may be viewed as an income tax). Second, the EL may result in international double taxation if the state of residence does not provide any credit of the EL paid in the source country under their domestic laws.

Currently, there are no provisions under any of the tax treaties entered into by different countries with India that bind the state of residence to provide for any relief with respect to the EL paid. Of course, there is no expressed or even implied bar to impose a tax that results in double taxation. Tax statutes cannot be invalidated merely on the basis of the argument that the levy results in double taxation. However, though legally there is no bar on taxing the same subject twice, it is not desirable if economic growth is not to be jeopardised by double taxation.[28]

Even though the EL is imposed with a sound objective, in its current form, it may be burdened with too many questions of compatibility with international taxation. Other emerging economies may emulate India and endeavour to include the digital tax within their taxation framework, though this may not be the best to introduce an EL in its prevailing forms. Several tax experts in India are currently analysing the problem to recommend possible ways to tax the digital economy in more meaningful ways.[29]

## 6. US Reaction to Equalization Levy

The US view the EL and other prevailing digital economy taxes as ring-fencing the digital economy. In 2019, the Office of the US Trade Representative (USTR) initiated an investigation into a 3 percent digital services tax (DST) adopted by France on revenue generated from providing certain digital services to or targeted at, persons in France. On completion, the USTR concluded that the DST was unreasonable, unfair and discriminatory towards US commerce. French DST was

27. Behera and Kumar (2020), op. cit.
28. Agarwal and Kumar (2020), op. cit.
29. Vinti Agarwal, Vidushi Gupta, Mukesh Butani, and Sumeir Ahuja. 2020. Removing Roadblocks in Taxing Business Income in the Digital Era: Building Global Consensus for an Equitable Solution, Vidhi Centre for Legal policy and BMR Legal Advocates, June. https://vidhilegalpolicy.in/wp-content/uploads/2020/06/20200620_-Digital-Economy-report-VIDHI-and-BMR.pdf, (last accessed on January 6, 2021).

applied to revenue rather than to income, hence, inconsistent with accepted principles of international tax policy. Further, it was retroactive and extraterritorial in the application. It was held to discriminate against US companies. Accordingly, the US set a deadline of January 6, 2021, to impose a 25% tariff on French cosmetics, handbags, and other imports valued at $1.3 billion approximately, though actual collection is not reported to have begun.

Indian officials had expressed the view that India's EL as having a wide base in contrast to that of France. Hence it could not be viewed as discriminatory towards US companies. As events unfolded, however, it was reported on January 7, 2021,[30] were that the USTR found that India, Italy and Turkey discriminated against US tech firms such as Amazon.com, Apple, Facebook, and Google, elaborating that the taxes were "unreasonable" because they were "inconsistent with principles of international taxation, including due to its application to revenue rather than income, extraterritorial application, and failure to provide tax certainty."

## 7. Conclusion

The rapidly emerging developments in the unilateral actions on the digital economy taxation and widely targeted US reaction against them could be the harbinger for retaliatory tariffs though they were not immediately specified. Nevertheless, these countries must reflect on the intense need for tax revenue in the pandemic environment. Can they easily abandon a revenue base just because the international taxation community is slow in finding a solution for its appropriate taxation? They need to weigh their revenue needs against the increased post-tariff product prices at market entry and the associated decrease in the international competitiveness of domestic firms on whom the burden of US tariffs would fall.

Any equilibrium in the form of multilaterally agreed taxation of the digital economy is yet to be achieved and, instead, an increasingly fractured structure of digital taxes and commodity counter-tariffs seems to be here to stay for the foreseeable future.

30. David Lawder. 2021. "USTR slams India, Italy, Turkey on digital taxes but holds off on tariffs", *Reuters*, Washington, January 7. https://www.reuters.com/article/usa-trade-digital-tax/update-1-ustr-slams-india-italy-turkey-on-digital-taxes-but-holds-off-on-tariffs-idUSL1N2JH34Z, (last accessed on January 7, 2021).

CHAPTER 8

# Source and Nexus of Income

H. Padamchand Khincha, Neha Khincha & Priya Kothari

## 1. Introduction

'Source' is a generative force. In the context of an income, it has historically been a place, person, thing or act. The locale of one or any of these formed the clinching factor to fasten tax. As time elapsed, the visible locale of the source got a little feeble. The smog of the virtual world started overpowering the tangible sources. Source is now often a shadow whose presence is becoming increasingly aerial. The challenge of viewing the source in this form is the new norm. Concomitantly, disruptive change has unsettled the norms of nexus. The privity and connect of the nexus are more digital, transmittal or virtual than physical. The thresholds of nexus are undergoing an unforeseen low. This transition (nay transformation) entailing interlacing and evolution of source and nexus theorems are sought to be captured in this chapter.

This chapter is broadly bisected into two segments. The first segment deals with the concept of 'source'. The second focuses on 'nexus'. In the first segment, this chapter opens up with the connotation of the phrase 'source of income', along with its role and setting in the context of Indian domestic laws. Some of the Indian judicial verdicts on this matter have been discussed to bolster the conceptual understanding. Internationally, 'source of income' has established its primacy right from the period of League of Nations spanning over various tax treaties. As a closing portion, the chapter throws light on the exclusive residence and source-based taxation. The second segment deals with the doctrine of nexus. Key principles from the Indian judiciary on the territoriality and the evolution of nexus have been captured. With the dawn of the digital world, there was a massive surge in base erosion and profit shifting (BEPS) practices and mechanisms. A snapshot of the Organization for Economic Co-operation and Development (OECD) initiative to counter BEPS and its Indian adaptation has been dealt with to provide a picture of the prevailing tax environment.

## 2. Source

### 2.1. "Source" and "Source of Income"

The term "source" means a point of origin or procurement,[1] the place where something begins, where it springs into being.[2] A source of a river, for example, would be the place from where it originates.

Income tax is a tax on 'income'. 'Income' in its ordinary sense connotes a return from a source. For an income to be taxable, it should be established to have originated from a 'source'. If a source is not identifiable, the amount cannot be taxed. Money found on the road may not be taxable in the absence of a source.

The Indian Income-tax Act, 1961 ("Act") uses the term "source" not just in the context of income but also for deduction, and collection of tax, etc. Some instances where the term 'source' is used in the Act are:

(a) Section 2(11) defining "previous year" envisages a different previous year in respect of **each source** of income.

(b) Section 5, which is concerned with the scope of income declares that the total income of a person includes all incomes, **from whatever source derived.**

(c) Section 9(1)(i) uses **source of income in India** as one of the criteria for deeming incomes to accrue or arise in India.

(d) The residuary head for classifying income chargeable to tax under Section 14 is "Income from **other sources.**"

(e) Section 70 permits set off of loss from **one source** against income **from another source** under the same head of income.

Source is an abstract concept. The term is easy to perceive but difficult to pigeonhole in text form with certainty. Courts have said "source is what a common man understands as source".[3] Anchors or proxies such as (i) carrying on an activity; (ii) physical rendition of service; (iii) a property or its location; and (iv) a person, are used to identify source of income.

The Advanced Law Lexicon, 3rd Edition, 2005, relies on the judgement pronounced by *Rhodesia Metals Ltd v. Commr of Taxes*[4] to define "source". In this case, the Privy Council approved the passage quoted by Mr Justice de Villiers from Mr Ingram's work on Income-tax:

1. https://www.merriam-webster.com/dictionary/source.
2. https://www.definitions.net/definition/source.
3. *Rhodesia metals Ltd v. Commr of Taxes*, (1941) 9 ITR (Supp) 45, 52 (PC).
4. (1941) 9 ITR (Supp) 45, 52 (PC).

> "Source means not a legal concept but which a practical man would regard as a real source of income; the ascertaining of the actual source is a practical hard matter of fact."

## 2.2. What is Source of Income?

Section 5 of the Act, which outlines the scope of income, provides for including incomes "from whatever source derived". Irrespective of the type or nature of source, income therefrom would be a part of scope of total income. The Privy Council in *Shaw Wallace's* case,[5] stated that "income connotes a periodical monetary return, coming in with regularity or expected regularity, from definite sources". This definition outlines the various attributes of income, one of it being that income should arise from a definite source. For an item to be taxed as income, its source has to be proved.

In its natural sense, source is a genus from which the income generates as specie. Any natural income has a source. The statute may also constitute a source., e.g. – Gift from non-relatives. In the case of gifts, which essentially are capital receipts, the statute itself constitutes the source.

The expression "source of income" is neither defined in the Act nor is adequate official guidance available on its meaning. In the absence of a statutory definition, one may have to refer to a) common understanding or b) judicial exposition of the said term. The Advanced Law Lexicon, 3rd Edition, 2005, defines the term relying on an extract from the case of Courtney Terrell[6] "the source of income must be considered in its proximate rather than in its ultimate significance."

This means the source of income is to be considered by its closest or immediate factors rather than the larger context. For example,– a company earns agricultural income and pays dividend to its shareholders. The dividend cannot be treated as agricultural income in the hands of the shareholders, as the proximate cause of income in the hands of the recipient of the dividend is shareholding and not the agricultural land.

The Allahabad High Court in the case of *Seth Shiv Prasad v. Commissioner of Income-Tax*[7] elaborated on what could be considered as "source of income" -

> "A source of income, therefore, may be described as the spring or fount from which a clearly defined channel of income flows. It is that which by its nature and incidents constitutes a distinct and separate origin of income, capable of consideration as such in isolation from other sources of income, and which by the manner of dealing adopted by the assessee can be treated so."

5. 6 ITC 178.
6. AIR 1934 Pat 178 (SB) Courtney Terrell.
7. (1971) 1972 84 ITR 15 (All).

Source is an originating cause. "Source" should be a thing having some width in point of duration and some content in point of quality. If the "source" of income vanishes the moment it is born or is abstract in quality, it can hardly be labelled as such.[8]

A source of income is different from an income. A source may exist without an income, but a natural income does not exist without a source. The source of income is not, in the context of the discussion, a legal concept. It is something that a practical man would regard as a source. Unless the source of income is established, a particular receipt may not be taxed at all. Receipts for refraining from doing a particular act; receipts as inducement from a prospective employer are some instances where it had been held to be not taxable, primarily because it was not possible to pinpoint a source. By legislative amendments, such receipts are now taxable. Section 68 and 69 family considers income having accrued to the assessee on the satisfaction of the conditions stipulated therein without the revenue having to prove the source. The underlying assumption for such a consequence is that the assessee is unwilling to disclose the source of which he is fully aware of.

## 2.3. Source and Head of Income

In the case of *Kusumben D. Mahadevia v. Commissioner of Income-Tax,*[9] it was held,

> "It thus appears that in the Act, the expression "source" and the expression "heads of income" are used in one and the same sense and it means property, movable or immovable, belonging to an assessee or the activity of an assessee that yields or brings income to him, within the meaning of the Act. Further illuminating and guiding are sage words of Apex court in 61 ITR 428 holding that "Whether an income falls under one head or another has to be decided according to the common notions of practical men for the Act does not provide any guidance in the matter."

Section 14 of the Act outlines the various heads of income into which the income to be taxed is classified. The residuary head is "Income from other sources". The Act is so structured that income from a source and the head of income to which it belongs is identified. The computation mechanism is then applied to each such source of income. The classification of income into various heads assumes significance as the computation mechanism under these heads of income is not uniform.

Under one head, there may be more than one source of income. For example, under the head "Income from House Property" each property is a source of income. In some cases, income from one source might fall under different heads of income.

8. *Sampath Iyengar's Law of Income Tax,* 10th Edition, Volume 1, p. 630.
9. (1961) 47 ITR 214 (Bom HC).

For example, Banking may constitute one source of income. Income from banking business may be taxed as property income or business income or income from other sources depending on the nature of income.

There have been attempts recently to fine tune the concept of "source wise" computation. This has been done through the incorporation of "activity wise" computation, e.g., Section 10A provides for computation of deduction, undertaking-wise. Section 80-1A/80-1B also provide for a similar computation. Till recently, it was accepted that if there is an interlacing of funds, unity of control and management, interdependence, all activities would constitute a single source, warranting a single computation of income from all activities so covered. The undertaking-wise computation marks a departure from this settled and accepted principle.

## 2.4. "Source" under Section 5 and Section 9 of the Act

Income arising from a particular source would have to fall within the scope of the charging provisions, particularly Section 5. By virtue of its attribute, of being a charging section, Section 5 could also operate as an exemption section. This is for the reason that if a receipt of income falls outside Section 5, it may not be charged to tax, despite fulfilling the characteristics of income and being derived from some source.

Section 5 of the Act deals with the scope of total income. It states,

> "5. (1) Subject to the provisions of this Act, the total income of any previous year of a person who is a resident includes all income **from whatever source derived** (emphasis supplied) which—
>
> (a) is received or is deemed to be received in India in such year by or on behalf of such person; or
>
> (b) accrues or arises or is deemed to accrue or arise to him in India during such year; or
>
> (c) accrues or arises to him outside India during such year.
>
> (2) Subject to the provisions of this Act, the total income of any previous year of a person who is a non-resident includes all income **from whatever source derived** (emphasis supplied) which—
>
> (a) is received or is deemed to be received in India in such year by or on behalf of such person; or
>
> (b) accrues or arises or is deemed to accrue or arise to him in India during such year."

Under Section 5, incomes received or accruing from **whatever source** is liable for inclusion in the total income. The prefix of 'whatever' to the term "source" is to make the type of source irrelevant. In order that the income is referable to Section 5, such income is to be identified with a source, whatever such source is. While source is *sine qua non* the same could be of any type. Section 5 dispenses with the type of source by mentioning 'whatever'. However, there is no such apparent dispensation in respect of place of source as there is no mention of word 'wherever'.

Section 5 provides that residents are taxed on their income sourced to India and in some cases, even outside India. Non-residents are taxed on India sourced income only viz i) income received in India, ii) deemed to be received in India, iii) income accrued in India, and iv) deemed to be accrued in India.

Section 9 outlines what incomes are deemed to accrue or arise in India. It enacts a fiction for a range of incomes, from interest and dividend to salary and royalty to 'accrue or arise' in India for tax purposes. These incomes, do not accrue or arise in India *per se.* By employing a legal fiction, the legislature has drawn them into the tax net on the basis of their linkage with India. Section 9 does not alter the entity with respect to whom the income arises, but rather uses the legal fiction to shift only the situs of accrual of income.

The relevant portion of Section 9 of the Act pertaining to the aspect of 'source' is as below:

> "Income deemed to accrue or arise in India.
>
> 9. (1) The following incomes shall be deemed to accrue or arise in India:—
>
> (i) all income accruing or arising, whether directly or indirectly, through or from any business connection in India, or through or from any property in India, or through or from **any asset or source of income in India**, (emphasis supplied) or through the transfer of a capital asset situate in India.
>
> (v) income by way of interest payable by—
>
> (b) a person who is a resident, except where the interest is payable in respect of any debt incurred, or moneys borrowed and used, for the purposes of a business or profession carried on by such person outside India or for the purposes of making or earning **any income from any source outside India**; (emphasis supplied)
>
> (vi) income by way of royalty payable by—
>
> (b) a person who is a resident, except where the royalty is payable in respect of any right, property or information used or services utilised for the purposes of a business or profession carried on by such person outside India or for the purposes of making or earning any income **from any source outside India;** (emphasis supplied) or

(c) a person who is a non-resident, where the royalty is payable in respect of any right, property or information used or services utilised for the purposes of a business or profession carried on by such person in India or for the purposes of making or earning any income **from any source in India** (emphasis supplied)

(vii) income by way of fees for technical services payable by—

(b) a person who is a resident, except where the fees are payable in respect of services utilised in a business or profession carried on by such person outside India or for the purposes of making or earning any income **from any source outside India;** (emphasis supplied) or

(c) a person who is a non-resident, where the fees are payable in respect of services utilised in a business or profession carried on by such person in India or for the purposes of making or earning any **income from any source in India** (emphasis supplied)"

Section 9(1)(i) deems the accrual or arisal in India on the basis of various criteria. Source of income is one such criterion. If the source of income is in India, the relevant income is deemed to accrue or arise in India. This statement recognizes that the place of accrual and place of source need not be the same.

In *CIT v. Pgnatale*[10] the Gujarat High Court, while interpreting Section 9(1)(ii) of the Act, linked the source to where the liability to pay "salaries" arose. It was held that the requirement of "earned in India" is not met if the liability to pay "salaries" arises outside India even if the services are rendered in India. Though the judgment was interpreting the words phrase "earned in India", it militated against the well-known tax principle that the source of income in the nature of "salaries" is the physical rendering of service in a jurisdiction. This prompted the insertion of the Explanation under Section 9(1)(ii) by the Finance Act, 1983 with retrospective effect from April 1, 1979 to provide that remuneration relatable to services rendered in India accrues or arises in India.

The physical rendition of service in India as a source is not the invariable rule. Under Section 9(1)(iii), the salaries payable to government servants for services rendered outside India is charged to tax in India, irrespective of the place where such services are rendered. The place of exercise of employment is ignored in such cases.

Section 9, in its original form, applied *inter alia* to business connections, transfer of assets, income from property, or from an asset, or a source of income in India. Vide the Finance Act, 1976, the deeming fiction was expanded through the

10. 124 ITR 391.

insertion of clauses (v), (vi), (vii) dealing with interest, royalty, and fees for technical services, respectively. These three additions substantially modified the character of Section 9. The liability of non-residents was hitherto based on substantive territorial nexus. Post 1976, the section created liability for a non-resident, even if the contract from which the income arose was performed entirely outside India, the only basis for attracting liability being the fact that the payment was made by a resident of India or that these items were attributable to a business or a source of income in India.

In the case of *Performing Rights Society Ltd v. CIT,*[11] the Supreme Court dealt with a case where the appellant, a company incorporated under the English Companies Act, had granted permission to All India Radio (AIR) to broadcast western music of composers, authors, and publishers of copyright musical work and received fees for the music broadcast by AIR. The appellants made out a case that the mere "source" of income being in India is not sufficient in order to fix the liability under Section 9(1)(i) of the Act. Based on facts such as the contract having been entered into in England; the Society not carrying on any business in India in so far as the receipt of such fees is concerned; and also, payments having been made in England by AIR, the appellants argued that the fee it earned is not an income accruing or arising, directly or indirectly, through or from any asset or source of income in India. The Supreme Court concluded that the source of income was the broadcasting of western music by AIR. That being so, it was held that the royalties which the Society received from AIR should be deemed to accrue or arise in India within the meaning of Section 9(1)(i) of the Act.

In *Kusumben D. Mahadevia v. Commissioner of Income-Tax*[12] the Bombay High Court stated that it is not possible to hold that income from or profits of a source would necessarily accrue or arise at the place where the source is located, a principle earlier approved by the Supreme Court in *CIT v. Ahmedbhai Umarbhai.*[13] Thus, it was possible to contend that the source of dividend may be the shares, but the situs of shares itself would not determine the place of accrual of the dividend income. In this context, it is understandable that Section 9(1)(iv) of the Act provides that dividend paid by an Indian company outside India is deemed to accrue or arise in India.

In *CIT v. Aktiengesellschaft Kuhnle Kopp and Kausch*[14] it was held that royalty payable to a foreign company on export sales would not be taxable in India for the reason that the source for royalty was the sales outside India. The Madras High Court placed reliance on the **activity test**. The activity was carried on outside India, and accordingly, payments for such services were held not chargeable to tax in India.

11. (1977) 106 ITR 11.
12. (1961) 47 ITR 214 (Bom HC).
13. (1950) 18 ITR 272.
14. [2003] 262 ITR 513 (Mad).

The concept of activity constituting a source of income was affirmed by the Supreme Court in the *PILCOM v. CIT (SC)*[15] case. The Supreme Court held that income referable to world cup cricket matches played outside India was not taxable in India for non-resident sports associations, as the source (being the cricket matches) was not in India.

As noted earlier, the Finance Act, 1976 made significant changes by inserting clauses deeming interest, royalties, and fees for technical services as accruing or arising in India under particular circumstances. These provisions enabled the taxation of specified income of non-residents in India even though the source of the income for the non-residents remained outside India. It gave rise to questions on limitations on Parliamentary powers viz whether the Parliament can legislate only for the territory of India. The Supreme Court in *GVK Industries v. ITO*[16] held that the Parliament had the power to make laws with respect to extra-territorial aspects or causes that had an impact or nexus with India. A far-reaching law was laid, even though the question before the Supreme Court in the said case was more to do with the scope of "fees for technical services".

As per Section 9(1)(vii), income by way of fees for technical services is deemed to accrue or arise in India. Explanation 2 to Section 9(1)(vii) defines the expression 'fees for technical services'.

Rendering of managerial, technical, or consultancy services (including the provision of services of technical or other personnel), for a consideration is regarded as 'fees for technical services' (FTS). If technical services are utilized (i) in a business or profession carried on by a resident outside India; or (ii) for the purposes of making or earning any income from any source outside India, then the payment, even though covered under the definition of FTS would be outside the scope of Section 9(1)(vii).

The conjunction between these two exceptions is 'or'; indicating them to be 'alternate' exceptions. The former deals with the fee payable 'in respect of' technical services 'utilized' in 'business carried on outside India' and the latter deals with the fee payable 'for the purpose of' making or earning any income from any 'source' outside India.

The second exception to Section 9(1)(vii) states that if the payment is for the purposes of making or earning any income from any source outside India, then the payment, even though covered under the definition of "FTS" would be outside the scope of Section 9(1)(vii). The second exception to Section 9(1)(vii) is triggered if the purpose or intent of the payment is earning income from a source outside India. The 'purpose' or 'intent' is reckoned from the contracts or documents executed by the parties and the surrounding circumstances.

15. TS-219-SC-2020.
16. 332 ITR 130.

The source of income has to be outside India for the exception to Section 9(1)(vii) to apply. The Delhi High Court in *DIT v. Lufthansa Cargo India*[17] held that "the place of business activity constitutes the source of income". Applying the dictum laid down in the Lufthansa case, the source of income for non-residents would be the business activity which they carry on outside India. Under such circumstances, the payment received by the non-residents would not constitute income arising from a source in India.

The law outlined above, in the context of fees for technical services would similarly apply for interest under Section 9(1)(v) and royalty under Section 9(1)(vi) of the Act.

## 2.5. "Source" Under Various Other Provisions of the Act

Section 14 is the classification section. It specifies the various heads under which income is chargeable to tax. The Act is so structured such that income from a source is identified. The income is classified into specific heads depending upon the source from which it arises. Section 14 reads as under:

> "Heads of income.
>
> Save as otherwise provided by this Act, all income shall, for the purposes of charge of income-tax and computation of total income, be classified under the following heads of income:
>
> A.—Salaries.
>
> B.— [***]
>
> C.—Income from house property.
>
> D.—Profits and gains of business or profession.
>
> E.—Capital gains.
>
> F.—Income from other sources"

The residuary head in the above is "Income from other sources". The words "other sources" used in the residuary head is indicative that the first four heads of income also comprise of and represent "sources of income".

Section 56 reads as under:

> Income from other sources
>
> (1) Income of every kind which is not to be excluded from the total income under this Act shall be chargeable to income-tax under the head "Income from other sources", if it is not chargeable to income-tax under any of the heads specified in Section 14, items A to E.

17. (2015) 375 ITR 85.

Section 70 deals with set off, or carry forward and set off of losses. As per the section, loss from one source is set off against income from another source under the same head of income. Section 70 reads as under:

> "(1) Save as otherwise provided in this Act, where the net result for any assessment year in respect of any source falling under any head of income, other than "Capital gains", is a loss, the assessee shall be entitled to have the amount of such loss set off against his income from any other source under the same head."

Certain features of Section 56 emerge from the juxtaposition of its language with the language of the charging sections of the various heads outlined in Section 14. Charging sections are as under:

Section 15 – for the head "Salaries"

Section 22 – for the head "Income from House Property"

Section 28 – for the head "Profits and Gains from business or profession

Section 45 – for the head "Capital Gains"

Under all these heads, the computation of income is source wise. Further, if the income falls under one head or source or income, it cannot fall under any other head or source of income and will be taxed only under that head where it falls.

The Hon'ble Apex Court in 1957 in the case of *United Commercial Bank Ltd. v. Commissioner of Income Tax, West Bengal*[18] held,

> "the heads of income provided for in the Sections of the Income Tax Act, 1922 are mutually exclusive and where any item of income falls specifically under one head, it has to be charged under that head and no other. In other words, income derived from different sources falling under a specific head has to be computed for the purposes of taxation in the manner provided by the appropriate section and no other".

The Supreme Court in *East India Housing and Land Development Trust Ltd. v. Commissioner of Income Tax, West Bengal*[19] held,

> "if the income from a source falls within a specific head, the fact that it may indirectly be covered by another head will not make the income taxable under the latter head. Therefore, if the income is included under any one of the heads, it cannot be brought to tax under the residuary provisions of Section 56..."

18. (1957) 32 ITR 688.
19. (1961) 42 ITR 49.

In the case of *Nalinikant Ambalal Mody v. CIT*[20] (SC), the issue raised was whether the income from business or profession can be taxed under the head "Income from business or profession" after the assessee has ceased to carry on his business or profession. If such income is not taxable under the head "Income from business or profession", then can it be taxed under the residuary head "Income from other sources"?

The Supreme Court held that receipts in the present case were the outstanding dues of professional work done and, therefore, would fall under the head "Profits and gains of business, profession or vocation". Further, the Court held that the said receipts were not taxable under the said head as the said receipts were taxed on cash basis, and in the year of receipt, no profession at all had been carried on by the assessee. The Court held that heads of income are mutually exclusive, and if the receipts are governed under one head, they cannot be brought under any other head. The idea of having separate heads of income was to have separate computation mechanisms for different types of income depending upon the nature of income.

More recently this has been succinctly explained by Apex court in the case of *Raj Dadarkar & Associates v. ACIT*[21] holding that,

> "Before dealing with the respective contentions, we may state, in a summary form, scheme of the Act about the computation of the total income. Section 4 of the Act is the charging Section as per which the total income of an assessee, subject to statutory exemptions, is chargeable to tax. Section 14 of the Act enumerates five heads of income for the purpose of charge of income tax and computation of total income. These are: Salaries, Income from house property, Profits and gains of business or profession, Capital gains and Income from other sources. A particular income, therefore, has to be classified in one of the aforesaid heads. It is on that basis rules for computing income and permissible deductions which are contained in different provisions of the Act for each of the aforesaid heads, are to be applied. It is also to be borne in mind that income tax is only One Tax which is levied on the sum total of the income classified and chargeable under the various heads. It is not a collection of distinct taxes levied separately on each head of the income."

The principle that may be inferred from these cases is that the five heads or sources apply when the source of income is existing/identified like there exists a business, or a capital asset, or a house property, or an employment, etc. If the source is inchoate or the income remains anonymous in nature, Sections 68 to 69D (dealing with unexplained income in form of cash credit, investment, money, expense, etc) may be applied.

20. (1966) 61 ITR 428 (SC).
21. [2017] 394 ITR 592.

## 2.6. Source of Income versus Source of Monies

The tax policy in India has turned a full circle with regard to taxation of non-residents, i.e., from source-based taxation to taxation based on the payer from whom the monies are received. This process started in a limited way in 1976, when deeming rules were created for taxing income from interest, royalty, and fees for technical services. This process is now witnessing a quantum leap with the introduction of the concept of significant economic presence (SEP). Under SEP, the number of users in India or payments beyond the threshold that would be prescribed will create a tax exposure for the non-resident payee. A "source of income" in India was for a long time the cause of a deemed accrual of income in India. This is now moving to a payer in India, triggering such deeming fiction.

The Supreme Court in *GVK Industries Ltd v. ITO*[22] observed that a payer may be regarded as the source of income. The relevant observations of the Supreme Court read as follows:

> "On a studied scrutiny of the said clause, it becomes clear that it lays down the principle what is basically known as the 'source rule', that is, income of the recipient to be charged or chargeable in the country where the source of payment is located, to clarify, where the payer is located. The clause further mandates and requires that the services should be utilized in India."

The decision of the Karnataka High Court in *Vodafone South Ltd v. DDIT*[23] held that the payer is the source of income.

An argument in favour of the activity test prevailing over the payer test could also be made. Under this argument, the source of income is the activity carried on by the non-resident payee. The origin of income is not the payer or customer. The payer is the source of money or monies and not the source of income. This analogy is supported by the decision of the Delhi High Court in *DIT v. Lufthansa Cargo India.*[24] The Delhi High Court in this case, after taking note of the decision in *GVK case* (*supra*), rejected the contention that the payer is the source of income. It held that the business activity constitutes the source of income. The AAR in *International Hotel Licensing Co*[25] held that a payer cannot be regarded as a source of income. The Delhi High Court in *CIT v. Havells India Ltd*[26] held that a customer/payer cannot be considered as the source of income though he is the source of the monies received.

22. 371 ITR 453.
23. [2015] 44 ITR(T) 330 (Bang).
24. ITA 95/2005.
25. In re (2007) 288 ITR 0534 (AAR).
26. (2013) 352 ITR 376.

The Supreme Court itself in *GVK* case, after delineating that a payer could be a source of income, also gave prominence to the place of economic or business activity or place of transaction for determining the source of income. This is evident from the following observations of the Supreme Court:

> "Having stated about the "source rule", it is necessary to appropriately appreciate how the concept has developed…
>
> The two principles, namely, "Situs of residence" and "Situs of source of income" have witnessed divergence and difference in the field of international taxation. The principle "Residence State Taxation" gives primacy to the country of the residency of the assessee. This principle postulates taxation of world-wide income and worldwide capital in the country of residence of the natural or juridical person. The "Source State Taxation" rule confers primacy to right to tax to a particular income or transaction to the State/nation where the source of the said income is located. The second rule, as is understood, is transaction specific. To elaborate, the source State seeks to tax the transaction or capital within its territory even when the income benefits belongs to a non-residence person, that is, a person resident in another country. The aforesaid principle sometimes is given a different name, that is, the territorial principle …
>
> The two principles that we have mentioned hereinabove, are also applied in domestic law in various countries. The source rule is in consonance with the nexus theory and does not fall foul of the said doctrine on the ground of extra-territorial operation. The doctrine of source rule has been explained as a country where the income or wealth is physically or economically produced. [See League of Nations, Report on Double Taxation by Bruins, Einaudi, Saligman and Sir Josiah Stan (1923)]. Appreciated on the aforesaid principle, it would apply where business activity is wholly or partly performed is a source State, as a logical corollary, the State concept would also justifiably include the country where the commercial need for the product originated, that is, for example, where the consultancy is utilized.
>
> From the aforesaid, it is quite vivid that the concept of income source is multifaceted and has the potentiality to take different forms [See *Klaus Vogel, World-wide v. Source Taxation of Income* - Review and Revision of Arguments (1988)]…"

Though the Supreme Court began with equating the payer to the source of income, it went on to finally conclude that the place of source of income would depend upon the place where the activity/transaction is carried out.

What is discernible in the path of tax law growth is the attempt to increasingly move away from the source concept to a payer-based exposure to tax. Apart from the concept of SEP, the introduction of Equalization Levy is a further manifestation of this journey.

## 2.7. "Source" under International Law

In the early 1920s, with the increase in global trade, the League of Nations took up the task of studying the issue of global double taxation affecting businesses. Formulating general principles, which would become the basis of an international tax framework, and which would be capable of preventing double taxation was one of the foremost objectives of that study. The outcome of the study conducted by the League of Nations was the concept of "economic allegiance". That became the basis for designing an international tax framework. Economic allegiance is based on factors aimed at measuring the existence and extent of the economic relationships between a particular state and the income or person to be taxed. The study also identified four factors comprising economic allegiance, namely (i) origin of wealth or income, (ii) situs of wealth or income, (iii) enforcement of the rights to wealth or income, and (iv) place of residence or domicile of the person entitled to dispose of the wealth or income.

The study concluded that in general, the greatest weight should be given to "the origin of the wealth (i.e., source) and the residence or domicile of the owner who consumes the wealth (i.e., residence)". The League of Nations advocated that tax jurisdiction should generally be allocated between the state of source and the state of residence depending on the nature of the income in question.

While the general principle for the basic framework for international taxation was formulated as allocation between countries of source and residence, the mode of resolution of the conflict of double taxation was not. There existed no challenges in simple situations where all factors of economic allegiance coincided and were in one jurisdiction. The jurisdiction to tax would remain exclusively with the state where the elements of economic allegiance were located. In more complex situations in which conflicts between the relevant factors of economic allegiance arise, jurisdiction to tax would be shared between different states on the basis of the relative economic ties with the taxpayer and the income. The above theoretical background enunciated in the 1923 Report of the League of Nations has remained intact and is generally considered as the "intellectual base" for all the future models, including the modern bilateral tax treaties.

The international tax framework developed around a vast network of bilateral tax treaties following the "classification and assignment of sources" method, in which different types of income are subject to different distributive rules. Most of the tax treaties follow distributive rules for taxation of income, which entail a preliminary step, whereby the income subject to conflicting claims is first classified into one of the categories of income defined by the treaty. Where an item of income falls under more than one category of income, double tax treaties resolve the conflict through ordering rules. Once the income is characterised for treaty purposes, the treaty provides distributive rules that generally either grant one contracting state the exclusive right to exercise domestic taxing rights or grant one contracting state priority to exercise its domestic taxing right while reserving a residual taxing right for the other contracting state.

The choice between (or a combination of) source or residence-based taxation alternatives has a number of macroeconomic ramifications apart from the mere avoidance of international juridical double taxation. This choice may be influenced by the state of a country's economic development, the need for foreign investments and capital inflows, its international economic ties, the state of its tax administrative and enforcement machinery, and such other factors. The challenge in making this choice, based on a State's long-term economic policy, is evident when one considers some of the pros and cons of choosing an exclusive residence based or source-based taxation regime.

## 2.8. Tax Treaties

Tax treaties represent an important aspect of the international tax rules of many countries.

Over 3,000 bilateral income tax treaties are currently in effect. The overwhelming majority of these treaties are based on the United Nations Model Convention or the OECD Model. The main difference between the two model Conventions is that the UN Model Convention imposes fewer restrictions on the taxing rights of the source country; source countries, therefore, have greater taxing rights under it compared to the OECD Model Convention. For example, unlike Article 12 (Royalties) of the OECD Model Convention, Article 12 of the United Nations Model Convention does not prevent the source country from imposing a tax on royalties paid by a resident of the source country to a resident of the other country.

The objective of a tax treaty, broadly stated, is to facilitate cross-border trade and investment by eliminating the tax impediments to these cross-border flows. This broad objective is supplemented by several more specific, operational objectives like elimination of double taxation.

The relationship between tax treaties and domestic tax legislation is a complex one in many countries. The basic principle is that the treaty should prevail in the event of a conflict between the provisions of domestic law and a treaty. In general, tax treaties apply to all income and capital taxes imposed by the contracting States.

Tax treaties do not impose a tax. Tax is imposed by domestic law. Tax treaties limit the taxes otherwise imposed by a State. In effect, tax treaties are primarily relieving in nature. Many of the provisions of tax treaties do not operate independently of domestic law.

## 2.9. Exclusive Residence-Based Tax System

Applying source-based tax principles (including the PE concept) in an electronic commerce setting poses the question of whether these difficulties can be overcome by adopting an exclusive residence-based tax system. Under such a system, source countries would not have jurisdiction to tax e-commerce transactions. Income therefrom would be taxed exclusively in the countries where the enterprises conducting the business are considered to be resident. While such an approach may, at first glance, appear to be too arbitrary and one-sided in favour of residence countries, it could also be that, unless electronic commerce transactions are taxed in the country where the enterprises engaging in the transactions are resident, the transactions may escape taxation altogether. Residence-based tax rules are generally easy to apply. There is a relatively higher degree of certainty with respect to the trigger point for the tax liability. It is simpler to determine the state of residence of an individual or a corporation than to conclude on the source or situs of a specific income stream. For instance, one does not have to determine whether a host of servers spread across the world and used in a complex e-commerce transaction constitutes a PE in a particular contracting state.

Under a residence-based tax regime, the state of residence of the enterprise owning and operating the servers would exercise the right to tax any income from such a transaction. A state may lay down certain bright line tests for determination of residence in terms of number of days' presence, place of control or management, etc. In case of conflict of residence rules between two states, the relevant tax treaty may provide some sort of an objective 'tie breaker' test to determine the state of residence.

The US Treasury has been a prominent advocate of residence-based taxation and at different times, indicated its preference for such a system. In 1996, and relevantly in the context of electronic commerce, the US Treasury hinted at the possible ascendancy of residence-based taxation in the face of emerging technologies; by stating as follows:

> "The growth of new communications technologies and electronic commerce will likely require that principles of residence-based taxation assume even greater importance. In the world of cyberspace, it is often difficult, if not impossible, to apply traditional source concepts to link an item of income with a specific geographical location. Therefore, source-based taxation could lose its rationale and be rendered obsolete by electronic commerce. By contrast, almost all taxpayers are resident somewhere."

The above is not unheard of. There is a long history of shipping profits being exempt from source-country taxation and a more recent history of air navigation profits being similarly exempt.

While there are advantages to an exclusive residence-based system, the disadvantages of such a system are many. They include the absence of a universally accepted robust residence definition, the risk of capital flight, the potential unfairness to countries that are net importers of goods and services sold electronically. Most countries would be unwilling to support this. The required international consensus is unlikely to be obtained to enable the successful implementation of such a system.

## 2.10. Exclusive Source-Based Tax System

The logic behind source-based taxation is that states have a right to tax all income that is generated within their territory. A source or territorial-based taxation system, therefore, seeks to compensate the source country for its contribution to the sustenance of the economic activity.

Source-based taxation is also supported by the principle of economic allegiance, which originated in the League of Nations era and was considered a guiding principle for determining the taxing rights of the State of source and residence. There have also been views that the source State should receive a larger share of the taxing rights since there is greater economic allegiance with the State of source, which also was more capable of enforcing these rights at the point of origin.

The obvious limitation of source-based taxation is the difficulty in applying conventional source-based rules in modern day transactions involving intangibles and a fleeting presence in the territory of the source State. Unless there is some sort of consensus among States regarding the structure and exact threshold for taxation, and the scope for conflicting interpretations is reduced, source-based taxation may in several cases, lead to double taxation in terms of a general policy. The present reality is an admixture of residence as also source-based taxation. The exact contours of this combination are bilaterally agreed upon during the course of treaty negotiation.

India has been aggressive in asserting as well as expanding its source-based taxation rights. This is quite typical of capital importing countries. India has also been increasingly 'dynamic' while enforcing its source tax rules, especially in the context of electronic commerce and cross-border movement of intangibles. Both, treaty as well as domestic law practice suggest that India is poised to push forward its reliance on source-based taxation and defend itself against any sort of potential erosion of tax base.

Source whether traceable to physical or intrinsic events, occurrences or location or jurisdiction, will continue to remain elusive, allowing interference through treaty negotiations or judicial interpretation. The question on the source, though important, is answered in not many judicial pronouncements in a span of over 100 years. With technological evolutions on the rise and performances of activities from different and distinct jurisdictions, source of taxation is bound to undergo a thorough overhaul. One has to wait and see how far traditional theories get retained, buried, and blurred.

In view of its inherent characteristics, the discussion on "source" and its evolution can never come to a full close. The categories of sources of income can never be fully exhausted. The multiplicity of forms, which "source" may assume, is beyond enumeration. The increasing variants to any particular type of transaction and the consequent complexities thereto, have helped unfurl many new facets and dimensions of the source. Nations across the world are increasing their role in public welfare. The need for resources is on the rise. What is in evidence is the crunch of such resources for many a nation. This has compelled governments to be increasingly wary of protecting their tax base; while being innovative about how additional resources could be raised. The novelty in the measures adopted has been at the cost of violation of the hitherto settled principles. This is accompanied by a trend to rely more on transaction-based taxation, than on income-based taxation. In this process to justify the right to levy tax, States are toying with the idea of innovating new "source" rules.

## 3. Nexus

Section 1 of the Income-tax Act, 1961 deals with short title, extent, and commencement. Sub-section (2) of the section states that the Act extends to the whole of India. This implies that the income sought to be charged to tax must be connected to the territory of India. There has to be a nexus between the subject matter of tax and the territory of India. Such a nexus, could be founded upon residence, or business operation, or source of income in India. The existence of such nexus is the cornerstone of taxation. Once nexus with a particular territory is established the subject may be exposed to a tax in such territory.

The term 'Nexus' signifies a link or a connection; a series of connections linking two or more things; or *an important connection between the parts of a system or a group of things.*[27] Nexus is defined as "Bond of connection; (the cash nexus consisting in money payments) (Oxford Dic.). Bond link or connection. Physical connection with the taxing state where the customer is located (Cyber Law)"[28]

The term 'Territorial nexus' was explained[29] as follows:

> "**Territorial Nexus.** The standing invitations in respect of the prize competition, the filling up of the forms and the payment of money take place within the State of Bombay. The tax is on gambling although collected from

27. https://dictionary.cambridge.org/dictionary/english/nexus.
28. Advanced Law Lexicon, 3rd Edition 2005, Book 3, Page 3192.
29. Advanced Law Lexicon, 3rd Edition 2005, Book 4, Page 4660.

the promoters. All these constitute sufficient territorial nexus which entitles the State of Bombay to impose a tax on the gambling that takes place within its boundaries and the law cannot be struck down on the ground of extra territoriality. *State of Bombay v. R.M.D. Chamarbangwala*, AIR 1957 SC 699, 711. [Constitution of India, Art. 245]"

In tax law, nexus is the relationship between a taxing jurisdiction, such as a state, and a business or a stream of income. It is the connection (and may represent diverse points of contact) between the income of a taxpayer and a taxing jurisdiction that is constitutionally and statutorily sufficient for any jurisdiction to impose a tax. A nexus must exist before a taxing authority can impose a tax on an enterprise. This requires that there be a link of more than an ephemeral nature between the jurisdiction and the business. In *Ishikawajima's case,*[30] the Supreme Court held that the first precondition for the imposition of income tax by the Indian tax authorities is the existence of a sufficient territorial nexus with India.

### 3.1. Territorial Nexus

As per the doctrine of territorial nexus, laws made by a particular state legislature are applicable in that particular state and not outside the territorial boundary of that state, except in scenarios where there is shown a sufficient nexus between that state and the object. This signifies that the object to which the law is applied need not be physically located within the territorial boundaries, but what is necessary is that it should have a sufficient territorial connection. The person, event, or activity sought to be taxed must have territorial nexus with the state seeking to tax. This nexus or connection must be real and not illusory. The liability sought to be imposed must be pertinent to that connection. As long as the nexus is real, the enormity of the tax burden sought to be imposed is irrelevant.

Territorial nexus is dealt with in Article 245 of the Constitution of India. If Article 245 is attracted, the legislative power of the Parliament is complete, and the courts of India would have to give effect to all the laws without any limitation or qualification. Article 245 is as follows:

"245. Extent of laws made by Parliament and by the Legislatures of States

(1) Subject to the provisions of this Constitution, Parliament may make laws for the whole or any part of the territory of India, and the Legislature of a State may make laws for the whole or any part of the State

(2) No law made by Parliament shall be deemed to be invalid on the ground that it would have extra territorial operation."

30. *Ishikawajima-harima Heavy Industries Ltd. v. Director of Income-Tax*, [2007] 288 ITR 0408.

An Act is said to have an extra-territorial operation if it seeks to regulate, punish or directly deal with any act done beyond its territorial limits or seeks to impose a liability on property situated outside its jurisdiction or on a person resident outside India.[31]

In the context of the power of the Parliament to legislate for India, the Apex Court in *GVK Industries Ltd. v. Income-tax Officer*[32] observed:

> "In granting to the Parliament the powers to legislate 'for' India and, consequently, also with respect to extra-territorial aspects or causes, the framers of our Constitution certainly intended that there be limits as to the manner in which, and the extent to which, the organs of the State, including the Parliament, may take cognizance of the extra-territorial aspects or causes, and exert the State powers (which are the powers of the collective) on such aspects or causes. …
>
> Thus, the Parliament is constitutionally restricted from enacting legislation with respect to extra-territorial aspects or causes that do not have, nor are expected to have any direct or indirect, tangible or intangible impact(s) on or effect(s) in or consequences for: (a) the territory of India, or for any part of India; or (b) the interests of, welfare of, well being of, or security of inhabitants of India and the Indians..."

The Supreme Court in another case[33] held:

> "But unless nexus exists Parliament will have no competence to make the law. Article 245(1) empowers Parliament to enact law for the whole or any part of the territory of India. The provocation for the law must be found within India itself. Such a law may have extra-territorial operation in order to subserve the object, and that object must be related to something in India. It is inconceivable that a law should be made by Parliament in India which has no relationship with anything in India."

The above observations indicate that as long as the law enacted by the Parliament has a nexus with India,[34] even if such laws involve an extra-territorial operation, the laws so enacted cannot be said to be constitutionally invalid. It is only when the '*laws enacted by the Parliament with respect to extra territorial aspects or causes that have no nexus with India*' that such laws 'would be *ultra vires*'.[35]

---

31. *Wallace Bros & Co Ltd v. CIT*, (1945) 13 ITR 39 (FC) affirmed in (1948) 16 ITR 240 (PC).
32. (2011) 4 SCC 36 : [2011] 197 Taxman 337 (SC).
33. *Electronics Corporation of India Ltd. v. Commissioner of Income Tax & Anr* (SC) judgement dated 02/05/1989.
34. Article 1(3) of the Constitution of India specifies what comprises the territory of India.
35. *Metro & Metro, Agra v. Assessee*, I.T.A. No.: 393/Agra/2012.

This "doctrine of nexus" had earlier been endorsed by the Supreme Court in *State of Bombay v. R.M.D. Chamarbangwala.*[36] The Supreme Court observed that the principle of territorial nexus is well established and the rules governing it are beyond dispute.

In the case of *Tata Iron & Steel Co. Ltd., v. State of Bihar,*[37] the following two basic elements to prove the territorial nexus were given:

(a) the connection must be real and not illusory; and

(b) the liability sought to be imposed must be pertinent to that connection.

The court emphasised that there should be a nexus or a connection between the object and the territory.

The supremacy of the doctrine of territorial nexus for the determination of tax jurisdiction of income was further vindicated in the case of *Hoechst Pharmaceuticals Ltd. v. State of Bihar.*[38]

What is an acceptable nexus is a subjective question? Professor Michael Lang[39] says that "in International law practice, there are no significant limits on the tax sovereignty of states. In designing the domestic personal tax law, the national legislator can even tax situations when, for example, only a "genuine link" exists. It is only when neither the person nor the transaction has any connection with the taxing state that tax cannot be levied".

The aspect of nexus or connection may be understood with an example in everyday commerce, like the sale of goods. In respect of a sale of goods, it is possible that all ingredients of a single transaction of the sale may not be located in a single state. Instead, the ingredients of the sale may be located in more than one state. A sale of goods has several ingredients, like, contract, location of goods to be sold, payment of a price, or promise of payment of a price, place of delivery of goods, place where the sale takes place, etc. The territorial nexus theory provides that in case of levy of a tax on a sale of goods, it is not necessary that all ingredients of the sale should be located within the same state. The state can levy a tax on a sale of goods even if it has a slight or some real connection with the sale. For imposing a tax on a sale of goods, what is essential, is that there should be a completed sale and the state have some real territorial nexus with the sale. In such a case, unless there is a prohibition on tax levying powers of the states, all such states, in which at least one ingredient of sale is located, shall be competent for imposing a tax on the said sale. This will result in a levy of tax on a single transaction of sale by more than one state.

36. AIR 1957 SC 699,711.

37. (1958) 9 STC 267,286-287 (SC).

38. 154 ITR 64.

39. In book titled 'Introduction to the Law of Double Taxation Conventions', Michael Lang, Linde Publication, Page 441.

It is discernible from the above, that a tax may be levied on a transaction even where only a part of the operations, which may give rise to an income being generated in a territory. Income that arises out of the said transaction would have to be apportioned to the territories involved. It may not be correct to contend that the entire income "accrues or arises" in each of the jurisdiction.

The issue of territorial nexus was examined in *A.H. Wadia.*[40] The case related to the liability of the Gwalior Durbar to be assessed to income-tax in respect of interest received at Gwalior. The Gwalior Durbar who carried on money lending business in British India through an agent, advanced to a company incorporated in British India with headquarters in Bombay, a loan of Rs. 50 lakhs. The loan was advanced at Gwalior, the interest was payable at Gwalior, and the debentures provided as security were also deposited there. The Durbar received the interest on the loan at Gwalior.

As per Section 42 of the Government Trading Taxation Act,[41] all incomes, profits or gains were deemed to be income accruing or arising within British India if the same arose directly or indirectly in a case, *inter alia*, when arising from any money lent at interest and brought into British India. The interest on the loan of fifty lakh rupees was assessed under this statutory provision. It was held by the majority of the Judges of the Federal Court that the interest on the loan was properly assessable to income-tax under Section 42(4) of the erstwhile Income-tax Act, 1922 and further that the statutory provision as enacted under Section 42(4) was not *ultra vires* of the Indian Legislature on the ground that it was extra-territorial in operation. The taxability was determined by the fact that the company, which borrowed the money from Gwalior Durbar had utilized it for the purposes of its business in British India.

In the case of *Carborandum Co. v. CIT,*[42] it was held that, in respect of a person who is not a resident in the taxable territories, income arising from a business carried on in India, wholly or in part, is liable to a tax. It was pointed out that a business connection must be established before any such income of a non-resident is made liable to a tax under that provision. Once a business connection is in place, income attributable to such business connection is deemed to accrue or arise in India.

In the case of *Sriram Bearings*[43] there was a technical collaboration agreement with a Japanese company. The agreement, though a composite one, was in two parts – under the first part, the Japanese company agreed to sell to the respondent (Indian company), its trade secrets, that is to say, the entire know-how relating to the manufacturing technique, etc. It also included advice relating to a plant layout and installation and the use of patent rights. The other part of the agreement was related

40. 17 ITR 63 (1948).
41. The Government Trading Taxation Act, 1926 (Act 3 of 1926).
42. 108 ITR 335.
43. 224 ITR 724.

to the rendering of technical assistance and training of personnel by the Japanese company. The Apex Court observed that the agreement was in two parts, and though the same were interdependent the consideration for the sale of trade secrets and consideration of technical assistance was separately provided for and mentioned under separate sections. The consideration for the sale of trade secrets could be said to have been not earned in India since the said sale was effected to in Japan, i.e., outside the Indian territory and, hence, was not taxable in India.

A nexus for tax purposes has historically required that a business have a physical presence in that state, but the advent of the internet has driven states to examine online businesses more closely for ascertaining territorial nexus. In the decision of *S. Dakota v. Wayfair Inc,*[44] it was held that older ways of determining tax nexus were artificial and anachronistic. The Court indicated that states have a right to require online sellers to charge and collect sales tax from all online buyers, not just those who are physically located in that state.

### 3.2. Digital Economy

Digital activities are generating significant and ever-growing value. Taxation of income from international digital transactions has been a perplexing issue. At the centre of the debate is whether international income tax rules, developed in a "brick-and-mortar" economic environment more than a century ago, remain fit for the purpose of the modern global economy. The fundamental elements of the global tax system, which determined where taxes should be paid ("nexus" rules based on physical presence) and what portion of profits should be taxed ("profit allocation" rules based on the arm's length principle), have served their purpose well. They have enshrined tax certainty and helped to eliminate double taxation, stimulating global trade.

Today, however, three important phenomena facilitated by digitalization – scale without mass, reliance on intangible assets, and the centrality of data[45] – pose serious challenges to elements of the foundations of the global tax system.

A large amount of internet transactions can be carried out in a source state without having any significant physical presence there. A website can be launched from anywhere and made available to users anywhere in the world. There is no central point, or physical location, for such transactions. It may not thus fall within any country's jurisdiction for taxation purposes. This opens up two possibilities: double taxation or non-taxation, both of which are avoidable.

---

44. 585 US _ (2018) *South Dakota v. Wayfair, Inc.* Oyez, www.oyez.org/cases/2017/17-494. (last accessed on October 12, 2020).
45. OECD (2018), "Tax and digitalisation", OECD Going Digital Policy Note, OECD, Paris, www.oecd.org/going-digital/topics/tax.

A tax nexus needs to be established before a person is liable for taxation in a given jurisdiction. However, establishing such a nexus is challenging in a regime where businesses provide services digitally, having a commercial presence but minimal or no physical presence [and hence, no permanent establishment]. A nexus may, therefore, not be established or be of negligible extent. A company may base the bulk of its value creation in a country (of choice) with an advantageous tax system, and claim that its activities in other countries are negligible, even if it generates a significant amount of profits there. This is becoming possible due to the advances in business techniques aided by developments in technology.

What compounds the problem is that, under current tax rules, it is difficult to determine the value created by intangible assets such as algorithms, which can be easily shifted, and to assess the role of users in value creation. Profits from data analysis increase with the amount of information accumulated (from growing the number of users). It however, is often difficult to quantify the monetisation of data and tax it properly.

In the area of direct taxation, the main policy challenges raised by the digital economy are recognized in the BEPS Action Plan 1[46] under the following three broad categories:

- *"**Nexus:** The continual increase in the potential of digital technologies and the reduced need in many cases for extensive physical presence in order to carry on business, combined with the increasing role of network effects generated by customer interactions, can raise questions as to whether the current rules to determine nexus with a jurisdiction for tax purposes are appropriate.*
- ***Data:** The growth in sophistication of information technologies has permitted companies in the digital economy to gather and use information across borders to an unprecedented degree. This raises the issues of how to attribute value created from the generation of data through digital products and services, and of how to characterise for tax purposes a person or entity's supply of data in a transaction, for example, as a free supply of a good, as a barter transaction, or some other way.*
- ***Characterisation:** The development of new digital products or means of delivering services creates uncertainties in relation to the proper characterisation of payments made in the context of new business models, particularly in relation to cloud computing.*

  *249. These challenges raise questions as to whether the current international tax framework continues to be appropriate. to deal with the changes brought about by the digital economy and the business models that it makes possible, and also*

46. OECD (2015), Addressing the Tax Challenges of the Digital Economy, Action 1 - 2015 Final Report, OECD/G20 BEPS, OECD Publishing, Paris. http://dx.doi.org/10.1787/9789264241046-en.

*relate to the allocation of taxing rights between source and residence jurisdictions. These challenges also raise questions regarding the paradigm used to determine where economic activities are carried out and value is created for tax purposes, which is based on an analysis of the functions performed, assets used, and risks assumed."*

Services could be digitally delivered cross border at the click of a mouse. Such services are not grounded in a specific territory. Tax rules meanwhile, are based on a precise territorial link, which in digital services is either absent or is transient. Having sensed the benefit of digital business, governments have been attracting such endeavours through incentives of various sorts. The tax system not keeping pace with increased business in a changing paradigm leaves a possibility of significant digital revenues remaining uncaptured by the tax system. Digital enterprises offer services and conclude contracts with citizens in a given country. While they benefit from the facilities such as infrastructure and connectivity of the given country, they avoid being regarded as being present for tax purposes.

The current rules are based on the physical presence of taxpayers and assets. There is a general agreement that they are not suited to a digital economy characterised by the reliance on intangible assets and ubiquitous services whose location is often hard to determine. New business models created by digitalization are inevitably putting pressure on the international tax system. International bodies are currently working on how to adapt tax rules to digital reality.

### 3.3. OECD Initiative to Address Tax Challenges of Digital Economy

There is a widespread but not yet universal view that the international tax system needs reform in order to address the digitalization of the global economy. The OECD acknowledged that the digital economy is the new economy itself, and it would be difficult to treat it separately from rest of the economy. The OECD and the G20 nations constituted the BEPS project to target tax strategies aimed at artificially shifting profits to low or no-tax locations. Action Plan 1 "Addressing the Tax Challenges of the Digital Economy" of this project deals with the tax aspects of the digital economy.

For direct taxes, the Action 1 Report observed that while digitalization could exacerbate BEPS issues, it also raises a series of broader tax challenges, which it identified as "nexus, data and characterization". Certain challenges, however, were acknowledged as going beyond BEPS. These were described as chiefly relating to the question of how taxing rights on income generated from cross-border activities in the digital age should be allocated among jurisdictions. A number of potential options to address these concerns were discussed, but none were ultimately recommended. Instead, the Action 1 Report called for continued work in this area, notably by monitoring developments in respect of digitalization, with a further report to be delivered by 2020.[47]

The Committee set up by the OECD under Action Plan 1 of BEPS recommended a new nexus based on SEP. The Committee also recommended that an enterprise should be considered to have a significant economic presence on the basis of factors that have purposeful and sustained interaction with the economy by the aid of technology and other automated tools. It further recommended that revenue factor may be used in combination with the aforesaid factors to determine SEP.

Under the SEP proposal, a taxable presence in a jurisdiction would arise when a non-resident enterprise has a significant economic presence on the basis of factors that evidence a purposeful and sustained interaction with the jurisdiction via digital technology and other automated means. SEP is seen by many as the creation of a new nexus for taxing profits realised by non-resident digital enterprises. This was confirmed by the OECD Public Consultation document,[48] which stressed that in order to create the nexus between the foreign entity and the revenues generated in the relevant country, the digital and economic means in isolation, will not be sufficient. These should be considered alongside other factors such as the existence of a user base or billing and collection in local currency; the responsibility for the final delivery of goods to customers; or the provision by the enterprise of other support services, such as after-sales service or repairs and maintenance.

One or more of the above factors may be considered relevant for constituting the kind of purposeful and sustained interaction with a jurisdiction via digital technology and other automated means.

The Cover Statement by the Inclusive Framework on the Reports on the Blueprints of Pillar One and Pillar Two[49] reiterates the belief of OECD in reaching a multilateral, consensus-based solution to the tax challenges arising from the digitalization of the economy, and other tax deliverables. Paragraph 3 of the statement is as follows:

> "A consensus-based solution comprised of two pillars (Pillar One focused on nexus and profit allocation whereas Pillar Two is focused on a global minimum tax intended to address remaining BEPS issues) can not only play an important role to ensure fairness and equity in our tax systems and fortify the

47. OECD (2019), Programme of Work to Develop a Consensus Solution to the Tax Challenges Arising from the Digitalisation of the Economy, OECD/G20 Inclusive Framework on BEPS, OECD, Paris, www.oecd.org/tax/beps/programme-of-work-to-develop-aconsensus-solution-to-the-tax-challenges-arising-from-the-digitalisation-of-the-economy.htm.
48. Addressing the tax challenges of the digitalisation of the economy – public consultation document, February 13 – March 6, 2019, The "significant economic presence" proposal.
49. As approved by the Inclusive Framework at its meeting on October 8-9, 2020.

international tax framework in the face of new and changing business models; it can also help put government finances back on a sustainable footing. ..."

The report on Pillar One Blueprint[50] reflects a focus on new nexus and profit allocation rules so that, in an increasingly digital age, the allocation of taxing rights with respect to business profits is no longer exclusively circumscribed by reference to physical presence. The report on Pillar Two Blueprint[51] reflects an approach that is focused on the remaining BEPS challenges and proposes a systematic solution so that all internationally operating businesses pay a minimum level of tax.

The OECD, through these reports, agrees to swiftly address the remaining issues with a view to bringing the process to a successful conclusion by mid-2021 and to resolve technical issues, develop model draft legislation, guidelines, and international rules, and processes as necessary to enable jurisdictions to implement a consensus-based solution.

### 3.4. India Initiative

With the advancement in information and communication technology in the last few decades, new business models operating remotely through digital mediums have emerged. The Government has been alive to this issue and has taken many initiatives in this regard. The Central Board of Direct Taxes (CBDT)[52] stated that "the existing nexus rule based on physical presence no longer holds good for taxation of business profits in the source country. As a result, the rights of the source country to tax business profits that are derived from its economy are unfairly and unreasonably eroded."

Taking a cue from OECD BEPS Action 1 (Tax Challenges Arising from Digitalization), India introduced the concept of SEP into its domestic tax law. India has been one of the forerunners in advocating the concept of taxing digital businesses. Right from being the first country to implement an equalization levy, to introducing the concept of 'SEP', India has led the way in implementing recommendations under the BEPS Action Plan 1. The equalization levy paired with the significant economic presence test represents one of the more coordinated efforts to tax digital business models.

---

50. OECD (2020), Tax Challenges Arising from Digitalisation – Report on Pillar One Blueprint: Inclusive Framework on BEPS, OECD/G20 BEPS, OECD Publishing, Paris, https://doi.org/10.1787/beba0634-en.
51. OECD (2020), Tax Challenges Arising from Digitalisation – Report on Pillar Two Blueprint: Inclusive Framework on BEPS, OECD/G20 BEPS, OECD Publishing, Paris, https://doi.org/10.1787/abb4c3d1-en.
52. F. No. 370142/11/2018-TPL, issued by the Government of India, Ministry of Finance, Department of Revenue, CBDT, dated the July 13, 2018. Subject: Framing of Income-tax rules relating to Significant Economic Presence as per Section 9(1)(i) of the Income-tax Act, 1961, Comments and suggestions reg.

Section 9(1)(i) of the Income-tax Act, 1961 was amended to bring in the concept of "Significant Economic Presence" for establishing "business connection" in the case of non-resident in India. The legislation specifies when a foreign enterprise is considered to have an SEP and, therefore, a business connection in India. This expands the scope of taxation under domestic law. Digital transactions or activities could give rise to an SEP (and, hence, be taxable in India), regardless of whether the non-resident has a place of residence or place of business in India or renders services in India.

While introducing the concept of significant economic presence, the explanatory notes to the provisions of the Finance Act, 2018[53] stated as follows:

> **"Business connection" to include "Significant Economic presence"**
>
> "The oranges upon the trees in California are not acquired wealth until they are picked, not even at that stage until they are packed, and not even at that stage until they are transported to the place where demand exists and until they are put where the consumer can use them. These stages, upto the point where wealth reached fruition, may be shared in by different territorial authorities." (excerpts from a report on double taxation submitted to League of Nations in early 1920s)
>
> 6.1 Taxation of business profits on the basis of economic allegiance has always been the underlying basis of existing international taxation rules. Economists gave primacy to the economic allegiance rather than physical location and made it clear that physical presence was important only to the extent it represented the economic location. ..."

The taxing rights sought to be imposed through significant economic presence affirms the dawn of new nexus rules. The law has moved beyond the physical parameters considered essential for establishing a permanent establishment in the country. With the changes in factors driving economies, economic presence is becoming the yardstick of being subjected to tax. Explanation 2A to Section 9(1)(i)[54] declares that the significant economic presence of a non-resident in India shall constitute "business connection" in India. Significant economic presence for this purpose shall mean –

> "(a) transaction in respect of any goods, services or property carried out by a non-resident with any person in India including provision of download of data or software in India, if the aggregate of payments arising from such transaction or transactions during the previous year exceeds such amount as may be prescribed; or

53. Circular No. 8/2018 dated 26.12.2018, F. No. 370142/07/2018-TPL issued by Government of India, Ministry of Finance, Department of Revenue, (CBDT).
54. As amended by Finance Act, 2020.

(b) systematic and continuous soliciting of business activities or engaging in interaction with such number of users in India, as may be prescribed..."

In attributing the income as covered by significant economic presence, the following shall also be reckoned[55]:

- Advertisements targeting resident customers or customers accessing the advertisements through internal protocol address located in India.
- Sale of data collected from residents or person who use internal protocol address located in India (Data such as cookies, search history, preferences etc.).
- Sale of goods or services using data collected from residents or person who uses internal protocol address located in India.

Since the discussions on addressing the tax challenges of digitalization remain ongoing as part of the G20/OECD BEPS project, and a further report is not expected until December 2020, the implementation of the SEP provisions is deferred.

The introduction of the SEP concept into the domestic law and the changes brought about thereon even before the law becoming effective has not been free from criticism. Explaining the implication of above, the commentary in Kanga & Palkhivala's[56] states as follows:

> "Clause (a) to the Explanation does not suggest that the transactions should be through 'digital means' although the intention of inserting the Explanation 2A was to include digital transactions within the scope of "business connection". This seems to be a case of faulty drafting. By the Finance Act, 2020, wherein Explanation 2A is substituted, the words 'in India through digital means' in cl. (b) are deleted. This omission makes the Explanation 2A even more evasive, as to whether it will apply only to digital transactions. It is hoped that the CBDT clarifies that Explanation 2A applies only to digital transactions. It is submitted that traditional business transactions should be covered by Explanation 2 and digital transactions by Explanation 2A. It is important to note that while the definition of "business connection" in Explanation 2 is inclusive, that of "significant economic presence" in Explanation 2A is exhaustive."

Under the new regime, the attempt is to redefine the level of contact necessary to expose a taxpayer to existing domestic tax obligations. States have taken an aggressive approach in expanding traditional notions of nexus. They are continually pushing the legislative and regulatory boundaries to bring increased activities as

55. As per Explanation 3A to Section 9(1)(i).
56. Kanga & Palkhivala's, *The Law and Practice of Income Tax*, Eleventh Edition, Volume I, Chapter II, Basis of Charge, Section 9, Significant Economic Presence, Page 390.

satisfying nexus within their borders. World over, States continue to move forward towards taxing enterprises based on economic nexus.

## 4. Concluding Remarks

The seeds of the present are often found in the past. Cyclical movements are natural. The journey of physical presence becoming economical is only a return to the origin. The discussion on situs, both physical and economic, was present much before modern tax systems evolved. The Financial Committee of the League of Nations, which was entrusted with the study of double taxation, decided in September 1921 to ask certain economists to prepare a report on the matter. After an exchange of views by correspondence, the experts met in Geneva in March 1923 and drew up the report, which was submitted to the Financial Committee. Relevant extract of the part dealing with 'origin or situs' is as follows:

> "In the case of income taxes, we properly speak of the principle of origin and refer to the origin of the income or the place where the earnings are created. In the case of property taxes, however, we should more properly speak of economic location — the place where the property is economically to be found, i.e., the place where are to be found the successive instalments of earnings which are capitalised into the fund of wealth that we call capital or, more popularly, property. The true economic location is to be distinguished from the physical location, usually termed situs. Frequently, of course, these coincide. But in the case of many classes of wealth the temporary situs may be quite distinct from the true economic location. A vessel plying between two ports may at a given time be in a dry dock remote from both; a bond or mortgage on a piece of real estate may be kept in a deposit box distinct from the location of the land or from the home of the owner. **Physical situs is one thing; origin or economic location is quite another thing: they do not necessarily coincide. Physical situs is of importance in economic allegiance only to the extent that it reinforces economic location".**[57]

The said observations made almost a century ago seem prophetic. Series of developments in recent times indicate that the laws find themselves back where they started. Things are coming to a full circle as States failed to appreciate the relevance of economic situs and focused on physical presence.

> "If history repeats itself, and the unexpected always happens, how incapable must man be of learning from experience." – George Bernard Shaw

57. Report on Double Taxation submitted to the Financial Committee — Economic and Financial Commission Report by the Experts on Double Taxation —Document E.F.S.73. F.19 (April 5, 1923) —Volume 4 Section 1: League of Nations; page 25.

# REJOINDER

K. R. Sekar[58]

## 1. Introduction

Governments, the world over, exercise the right to impose tax on income when the 'source' of that income arises from the country itself. Many countries worldwide preferred the concept of 'source'-based taxation', which was considered relevant when business was conducted through physical presence. Few countries, however, followed the residence-based taxation model.

With digitization bringing about a transformational shift in the way business is conducted, taxation experts across the globe are examining whether source-based taxation is relevant in the current scenario or a new order of taxation is required.

In this chapter, Khincha et al. analyses the concepts of 'source' and 'nexus' and state why the source-based principle is no longer effective for taxation of the new digital business model. They further explain why the economic nexus should be considered as the criterion to tax income from digital business. Their chapter not only presents an alternative view on taxation but also explains the concept of market access or customer base as explained by some of the judicial precedents. It also highlights the limitations of the newly delineated market nexus principle that seeks to reallocate global profits.

## 2. Source Based Taxation

### 2.1. Concept

The term 'source' has not been defined per se under the Income-tax Act (ITA) except for the principles or basis of source-based taxation explained in Section 9 of the ITA, 1961. The 'source' of the income must be considered in its proximate rather than its ultimate significance.[59] The concept of source is not a legal concept, but what an individual would regard as the real source of income.

Source-based taxation always refers to any activity carried out in one jurisdiction or holding property in one jurisdiction, whether movable or immovable, by a taxpayer that yields income to the taxpayer.[60] The rationale behind the principle of source-based taxation is that the country has the right to tax income for carrying on activity in the respective country or due to the *situs* of property located in that

58. The views expressed herein are the views of the author and not of any other individual or institution.

59. Courtney Terral C.J. AIR 1934 (Pat) 178-Source-Advanced Law Lexicon by P. Ramanatha Aiyar.

60. *Kusimben D. Mahadevia v. CIT*, (47 ITR 214) (Bom).

country. Through this principle of 'source', in addition to activity or property, the countries started considering the utilization of services or payer of services as a part of source-based principle.

Countries thus sought to tax any income arising or generating from the country through (i) performance of activity, (ii) movable or immovable property, and (iii) utilization of services or knowledge or intangibles. Given the aforesaid principles of source-based taxation, countries started taxing business profits of non-residents or capital gains of non-residents and imposing withholding tax (WHT) on other payments, as a physical presence was not relevant to carry out activities generating revenues. Therefore, the principle of source-based taxation was levied not just on business profits or capital gains but expanded to all categories of income like interest, dividends, and fees for technical or professional services, and royalty.

Revenue authorities (Income Tax department) in India follow the same principle and seek to tax non-residents on the above basis. Though the Indian ITA follows source-based taxation, the Act also provides that no income shall be deemed to accrue or arise in India if the activity is confined to purchase of goods from India. In other words, the provisions of the Act do not consider the activity of purchasing goods from India as a revenue-generating activity warranting the application of the source principle.

### 2.2. Double Taxation Avoidance Agreements (DTAAs)

The imposition of source or residence-based taxation by various countries led to the conclusion of DTAAs by setting up the following principles:

- Creating a legal fiction called 'permanent establishment' (PE) with its scope narrower than the concept of business connection under domestic tax laws and with the exemption for preparatory and auxiliary services like purchasing of goods and processing of information.
- Limiting the rate of WHT on services to a rate lower than the one levied under domestic tax laws.
- Allowing the relief of double taxation in the home country so that income is not doubly taxed in both jurisdictions.

## 3. Is Economic Nexus Essential?

Under Indian tax laws, source-based taxation was considered applicable only for activities carried out in India. In the *Formula One World Championship* ruling, the Supreme Court (SC) observed that Formula One has a business presence in India even though the activity was confined to only three days annually. The Court concluded that since the championship is for a period of five years, it leads to the 'permanency' test, which is not based merely on the number of days the championship is held in India but on whether the recurring nature of the event leads to stability and economic activity, resulting in the business being carried on.

In the *Hyundai Heavy Industries Co Ltd*[61] case, the SC held that payments towards offshore activities would not be taxable in India in the absence of an economic nexus of such payments with India. Similarly, in *Ishikawajima Harima Heavy Industries Ltd v. DIT*, the SC held that the concept of territorial nexus is fundamental in determining the taxability of any income in India and that income from offshore services would not be taxable in India merely because the activities are rendered in relation to an Indian turnkey project.

More recently, the SC in *Samsung Industries Ltd* took the view that even if the foreign company has a project office in India, it does not constitute a PE in India as the project office's activity is only preparatory and auxiliary services. The SC observed that "when it comes to 'fixed place' permanent establishments under the double taxation avoidance treaties, the condition precedent for applicability of Article 5(1) of the double taxation treaty and the ascertainment of a 'permanent establishment' is that it should be an establishment 'through which the business of an enterprise' is wholly or partly carried on. Further, the profits of the foreign enterprise are taxable only where the said enterprise carries on its core business through a permanent establishment. What is equally clear is that the maintenance of a fixed place of business, which is of a preparatory or auxiliary character in the trade or business of the enterprise would not be considered to be a permanent establishment under Article 5. Also, it is only so much of the profits of the enterprise that may be taxed in the other State as is attributable to that permanent establishment".

In the *Vodafone* case, the SC observed that the 'source' in relation to an income had been construed to be where the transaction of sale takes place and not where the item of value, which was the subject of the transaction, was acquired or derived from. Substantial territorial nexus between the income and the territory which seeks to tax that income is of prime importance to levy a tax.

The judicial principle arising out of source-based taxation is that economic nexus and territorial nexus must be established between the activity and the payments sought to be taxed. The courts have observed that India has a right to tax only if the business is carried on in India, i.e., the revenue-generating activity should take place in India.

## 4. Source versus Nexus Based Taxation

The source-based taxation was relevant in the traditional form of business, i.e., carrying on business through the form of a fixed place or through a permanent establishment. In the digital era, however, the way business is conducted has

61. *CIT v. Hyundai Heavy Industries Limited.*

undergone a significant change as most of the business is operated through digital and technological means. Going forward, the concept of physical presence or PE, which is the foundation for taxation of business profits will become redundant. Therefore, market-based countries seek to tax revenue on the basis of 'nexus' principle.

This dimension should also take into account the theory of taxation of income in the country of origin, put forward by Kemmeren who says, "The principle of origin justifies allocation of tax jurisdiction on income to a state if the income has been created within the territory of that state, i.e., the cause of the income is within the territory of that state. The origin of income is where the intellectual element — Hongler-Pistone – Blueprints for a new PE nexus page 18 — (among the assets) is to be found. This intellectual element is provided by the activities of individual human beings. Only individuals can create income and things in themselves cannot."[62]

India also adopted the nexus-based principle by amending the provisions of the Act and including 'significant economic presence' in the definition of PE. The nexus-principle brings income which otherwise would not have been taxable in India due to deemed provisions.

It is interesting to note that the nexus theory considered relevant for taxation of the digital economy extends beyond the realm of economic and territorial nexus to encompass a new nexus principle that is market or user based. Thus, the concept of a PE based on physical presence has changed following the introduction of the 'digital PE' concept due to the sheer number of users. Under normal circumstances, a foreign company's income through sale of goods is taxable in India only if it has a PE in India either by itself or through agents. Conducting business through digital or technological means involves no physical presence, a foreign company, however, is considered to have a PE in India if that company has significant users in India. In addition, this concept calls for reallocation of profits amongst various countries. Based on the said principle, the Organisation for Economic Co-operation and Development (OECD) has recommended Pillar One and Pillar Two approach for taxation of the digital economy based on the nexus principle, which leads to reallocation of profits.

Taxation on the basis of nexus theory, i.e., market nexus, is alien to the fundamental concept of taxation and poses multiple challenges both at the conceptual and implementation levels. Some challenges at the conceptual level are:

- The mere presence of 'users' and the absence of any activity in India presents a significant anomaly in the concept of taxation. Does a change in

62. Working Paper 20 by IBFD Blueprints of New PE Nexus to Tax Business Income in the era of Digital Economy.

the business model from physical to digital warrant a shift in the basis of taxation?

- The new 'nexus' principle seeks to factor in both the supply side and demand side.
- The fundamental issue that needs to be addressed is whether considering the 'demand' side is an appropriate basis for the taxation of business profits. as the basic principles of attribution is generally understood on the basis of economic activity and not the demand factor.
- The absence of economic activity under the 'nexus' principle, but the mere presence of users triggering a revenue in the sourcing country warranting reallocation of profits is beyond the basic principle of taxation of profits.
- Real economic activity is absent under the 'nexus' principle, but do digital transactions, resulting in revenue generation for the source country, warrant reallocation of profits? Isn't this contrary to the basic principle of taxation of profits?
- The source-based taxation seeks to tax only the income, but the Pillar One & Pillar Two approach, which is reflective of the new 'nexus' theory, seeks to tax market value in the form of attribution of profits which is inappropriate.
- The new 'nexus' theory based on the demand factor in a particular market or customers is not the right method to tax income arising out of digital business, as the basis for determining tax could depend on multiple factors and vary from country to country.
- Allocating profits to a user country, based on the number of users in that country availing the products/services, could pose significant challenges as the attribution of profits under DTAAs is normally on the basis of a 'separate entity approach' and not by the 'allocation approach'.
- The disagreements in determining and accepting the arm's length price by various jurisdictions have led to several disputes and resulted in the huge backlog of mutual agreement procedure cases, pending resolution by the competent authorities of countries. Hence, reallocation of profits on the basis of the new Pillar One and Pillar Two approach could pose more challenges, resulting in disputes.

## 5. Conclusion

In this chapter, Khincha et al. explain the concept of nexus-based taxation and the rationale for change from source-based taxation. This rejoinder is an attempt to modify their views, and explains some limitations. It also raises a question on the implementation of the new nexus principle in view of multiple conflicts both in terms of concept and implementation.

While it is imperative for emerging economies to tax the revenue arising from their respective jurisdictions, the source principle has been largely rendered ineffectual in the new digital business model. The moot point is whether the nexus principle and reallocation of profits based on the OECD's new Pillar One & Pillar Two approach are appropriate because they are likely to pose more challenges at both conceptual and implementation levels due to the overzealous approach of the tax authorities in various countries.

The findings of the recent United States Trade Representative (USTR) report, following investigations into India's equalization levy (EL), stated that India's EL is unilateral and hence actionable under Section 301 of USTR. Furthermore, it is also held that the nexus principle of international taxation conflicts with the Ottawa principles of taxation that focus on neutrality, efficiency, certainty and simplicity, effectiveness, fairness, and flexibility on taxation.

Countries, therefore, need to find an alternative framework to achieve the objective of taxation of the digital economy in a more simple and transparent manner in line with Ottawa principles of taxation.

CHAPTER 9

# CRYPTOCURRENCIES—INCOME TAX IMPLICATIONS

**Alok Prasanna Kumar & K. R. Sekar**

## 1. Introduction

The taxation of cryptocurrencies[1] is a challenge as the business model and regulations surrounding cryptocurrencies is a new area and still evolving. The use of cryptocurrencies as legal tender and the legality is a matter of great debate. Jurisdictions around the world are grappling with the emergence of this new technology - should its use be permitted, what are the harms of its use, and how to regulate its use to minimize potential harms are some of the raging issues to address.

The use of cryptocurrencies is a contentious issue, with its legality being a mystery to the public. Cryptocurrencies are a form of digital currency and are not considered to be legal tenders under applicable laws. However, they can function as a medium of exchange akin to money. The lack of a traditional government or bank-backed system to regulate their use makes cryptocurrencies the target of several concerns - there are fears of them being used as a conduit for black money or anonymously funding terrorism. Despite the odds, however, cryptocurrencies have gained popularity worldwide and the cryptocurrency market in India has also been slowly gathering momentum.

The last year saw some major developments in the regulation of cryptocurrencies in India, which are worth noting, and which might have a significant impact on their future tax treatment. In this article, we propose to look at how cryptocurrencies may be regulated and taxed in India. The first part of the article will give the context to recent developments, specifically the Reserve Bank of India's (RBI's) attempts to ban cryptocurrencies and the Supreme Court's judgment in striking down such bans on the grounds of proportionality and non-application of mind. We will also discuss the proposed Banning of Cryptocurrency & Regulation of Official Digital Currency

1. This article analyses the Income-tax implication of cryptocurrency such as Bitcoins and not Indirect tax implications of transactions related to such cryptocurrency.

Bill, 2019, which has not yet been introduced in the Indian Parliament, and whether it offers a suitable way forward in the matter.

Following this, the chapter will consider several questions in relation to the direct taxation of cryptocurrencies. First, what is the nature of cryptocurrency. Second, does cryptocurrency come within the definition of goods or services. Third, whether the developer of cryptocurrency could fall within the definition of a "manufacturer". Fourth, what is the implication of treating cryptocurrency as a "self-generated asset". Fifth, what are the implications of treating cryptocurrency as a capital asset or "stock in trade" for the purposes of income tax.

## 2. Institutional Responses to Cryptocurrency

### 2.1. Ban by the Reserve Bank of India

The RBI issued a "Statement on Developmental and Regulatory Policies" on April 5, 2018, paragraph 13 of which directed the entities regulated by RBI to not deal with or provide services to any individual or business entities dealing with or settling virtual currencies (VCs), and to exit the relationship, if they already have one, with such individuals/business entities, dealing with or settling VCs.[2]

Following the said statement, RBI also issued a circular dated April 6, 2018, titled "Prohibition on dealing in Virtual Currencies (VCs)" in exercise of the powers conferred by Section 35A read with Section 36(1)(a) and Section 56 of the Banking Regulation Act, 1949, and Section 45JA and 45L of the Reserve Bank of India Act, 1934 (hereinafter 'RBI Act, 1934') and Section 10(2) read with Section 18 of the Payment and Settlement Systems Act, 2007, directing the entities regulated by RBI not to deal in virtual currencies nor to provide services for facilitating any person or entity in dealing with or settling virtual currencies, and to exit the relationship with such persons or entities, if they were already providing such services to them.[3]

The said statement and circular were challenged before the Supreme Court of India (SC) by a range of entities in *Internet and Mobile Association of India v. Reserve Bank of India.*[4] In its judgment delivered on March 4, 2020, the Supreme Court concluded that the circular and the press statement were both legally invalid. A three-judge bench of the SC held the circular to be a disproportionate regulatory action in a decision that suggests cryptocurrencies should be subject to considered

---

2. See https://www.rbi.org.in/Scripts/BS_PressReleaseDisplay.aspx?prid=50176#:~:text=This%20Statement%20sets%20out%20various,credit%3B%20deepen%20digital%20payments%3B%20augment.
3. See https://rbidocs.rbi.org.in/rdocs/notification/PDFs/NOTI15465B741A10B0E45E896C62A9C83AB938F.PDF.
4. (2020) 10 SCC 274.

regulation and not blanket prohibition, under Indian law. Further, the bench was also of the view that the RBI had not "applied its mind" satisfactorily to the issue at hand before coming to the conclusion that cryptocurrency transactions ought to be banned entirely in India.[5] However, the Court did conclude that the regulation of cryptocurrencies would fall within the purview of the RBI in accordance with the Banking Regulation Act and the RBI Act.[6]

The following arguments were raised against the validity of the circular by the entities that were affected by it:

- The RBI has no jurisdiction to act in this manner, as a cryptocurrency is neither a 'currency' nor a 'payment system', which are regulated by the RBI. Merely because cryptocurrencies can be used in a manner akin to money does not change the essential legal characteristic of cryptocurrencies, which resemble tradable digital goods or commodities more than they resemble a form of currency and are thus outside the RBI's usual scope of regulation.
- The circular amounted to an arbitrary, unfair, and unconstitutional restriction on a legitimate business activity. In the absence of a 'legislative' ban on cryptocurrencies that declares them res extra commercium, the use of, and trade in, cryptocurrencies is a legitimate business activity.
- The circular effectively placed a complete ban on the use of cryptocurrencies, and such a ban was unreasonable, disproportionate, and based on an erroneous understanding that it was impossible to regulate cryptocurrencies.

In its response to the contentions raised by the petitioners, the RBI responded as follows:

- Cryptocurrencies were capable of being used for illegal purposes (on account of the digital anonymity that blockchain technology affords).
- Widespread use of cryptocurrencies would fundamentally undermine India's credit system and monetary stability.
- The RBI had the right to regulate banking activity (which is what the circular pertained to) as it saw fit.
- In any case, the RBI has the authority to make broad-based decisions on the economic policy of the country, and the SC has traditionally shown deference to RBI's authority.

---

5. *IAMAI v. Union of India* paras 163-169.
6. *IAMAI v. Union of India* para 138.

## 2.2. The Supreme Court

### *2.2.1. Supreme Court Ruling*

The SC ruled that while cryptocurrencies do not constitute legal tender (either in India or in any other jurisdiction that the SC had analysed), they can function as either a medium of exchange, a unit of account, or a store of value (or some combination thereof). The RBI has the statutory authority to notify certain instruments as currencies, and (as the SC observed) it has not chosen to exercise this power with respect to cryptocurrencies. In fact, the RBI has specifically argued in the past that cryptocurrencies do not fall under the statutory definition of 'currency'. Nonetheless, the SC concluded that the way cryptocurrencies are often used in India — as consideration for goods or services provided, or as a facilitator of payment between parties — constitutes an activity that falls within the RBI's regulatory purview.

Having concluded that the RBI did indeed have the power to regulate cryptocurrencies in India, the SC proceeded to evaluate the circular on its merits. While the SC rejected the argument that there had been no application of mind in the RBI's directives and that it did not find the circular to be a colourable exercise of power, the SC did ultimately conclude that the circular was a disproportionate regulatory measure.

The SC noted that the RBI is primarily responsible for the financial institutions that it is required to regulate and that it had argued about the potential harms that cryptocurrencies could cause to those institutions. However, the SC held that the RBI had failed to actually demonstrate the damage that the use of cryptocurrencies had caused to such regulated entities — given that the RBI had not identified any specific adverse impacts of cryptocurrencies on banking and financial institutions in India and had specifically argued (both in previous regulatory guidance and during the course of arguments in the present case) that cryptocurrencies were not actually banned under Indian law.

In prohibiting regulated entities from dealing with a sector that was not subject to a statutory ban, and which had not demonstrably harmed such regulated entities, the RBI was held to have acted disproportionately, and the circular was set aside.

### *2.2.2. Impact of Supreme Court Ruling*

The judgment might have provided temporary relief; due to lack of regulations to regulate cryptocurrencies or virtual currencies, the financial institutions and the banking sector may not be favourably inclined towards investing in them. At this juncture, uncertainty prevails about the future of the cryptocurrency industry in India.

The wide-scale use of cryptocurrencies also seems to be questionable, as the "Banning of Cryptocurrency and Regulation of Official Digital Currency Bill 2019" has been proposed with the aim to ban all private cryptocurrencies. The bill is yet to be brought to the Indian Parliament and receive approval. The bill also proposes the creation of a 'digital rupee'. We need to wait for the final bill and need to examine the implications.

The SC judgment was welcomed as it not only gave partial relief to those dealing in cryptocurrencies but also defined the RBI's powers in this context. The SC noticed the policy flip-flops of the government on the matter of regulation of cryptocurrencies as one reason to show that the use cannot be per se harmful to lead to their prohibition by the RBI.[7]

## 2.3. Legislative Action--Banning of Cryptocurrency & Regulation of Official Digital Currency Bill, 2019 ("the 2019 Bill")

The 2019 Bill is not the first effort at regulating/banning cryptocurrencies in India. The history of cryptocurrency regulation through law is discussed quite comprehensively by the Supreme Court in *IAMAI v. Union of India*,[8] but the first attempt at legal regulation would be the Crypto Token and Crypto asset (Regulation and Banning) Bill, 2018. This was contained in the initial report of the Inter-Ministerial Committee in April 2018, though the fate of this bill is unknown at present. The Inter-Ministerial Committee itself was constituted by the Government of India in November 2017 and consisted of the Secretary (Department of Economic Affairs) and comprising the Secretary, Ministry of Electronic and Information Technology, Chairman, SEBI and Deputy Governor, RBI. Its mandate was to propose the specific actions to be taken in relation to "virtual currencies".

It is important to note however, that this 2018 Bill did not entirely ban the use of cryptocurrencies. The 2018 Bill allows the sale and purchase of digital crypto assets at recognized exchanges and that the registry of all holdings and transactions on the recognized exchanges are to be maintained at recognized depositories.

However, the Inter-Ministerial Committee seems to have changed its mind in February 2019 when it submitted its final report where it recommended the imposition of a total ban on private cryptocurrencies. It proposed to do this through the 2019 Bill, which contained a provision that effectively bans the mining, generation, holding, selling, dealing in, issuing, transferring, disposing of, or using cryptocurrency in India.[9] It further prohibits the use of cryptocurrencies as legal tender, a medium of exchange, a store of value, or a unit of account. Clause 7 lists

7. *IAMAI v. Union of India*, paras 219- 224.
8. paras 4 - 42.
9. Clause 3 of the 2019 Bill.

out specific instances where it cannot be used as a way of illustrating the general prohibition contained under Clause 6.

Somewhat strangely, not all prohibitions result in a criminal offence, but the use of only specific types of cryptocurrency and related transactions in cryptocurrency will invite criminal sanction. While buying, selling, or storing cryptocurrency will not be an offence, using it as a basis of credit will be criminalized. While its use as legal tender or a currency is not criminalized, its acquisition for use as a medium of exchange will attract criminal prosecution.[10]

However, it must be pointed out that while the Bill prohibits cryptocurrencies, it also allows the central government to approve the "digital rupee" as legal tender. It also allows the government to recognize an official foreign digital currency as "foreign currency" in India under the Foreign Exchange Management Act (FEMA).[11]

As it stands, the regulation for cryptocurrency stands in a legal vacuum. The RBI's attempts to regulate the same came to a naught in the Supreme Court for having been disproportionate and without thought, and the 2019 Bill remains a draft for discussion. While cryptocurrencies have not been banned, they are also not subject to any regulations now, even though the Supreme Court has affirmed the power of the RBI to make regulations in this respect even under the existing laws, namely the RBI Act and the Banking Regulation Act.

In its present form, the 2019 Bill will also create more problems than it solves. If implemented wholesale, it would criminalize many activities carried on online that are presently illegal. Implementation difficulties apart, all that it will do is push the market for cryptocurrencies underground, making it even more difficult for the government to regulate it in a manner to minimize harm. If the government manages to drive cryptocurrency transactions underground, it may find it difficult to "put the genie back in the bottle" even if, in the future, it finds that it might need to regulate cryptocurrencies or suitably tax them for the purposes of raising revenue.

## 2.4. Cryptocurrency Characteristics

The taxation of cryptocurrencies depends on their nature and use. Before we analyse the tax issues of cryptocurrencies, let us look at how cryptocurrencies work and the tax treatment depends on how they are used,

### *2.4.1. A Mining Process*

Cryptocurrencies are generated by a "mining" process. This process involves the use of computer hardware and software and may be illustrated with the use of the process by which one cryptocurrency, namely "Bitcoin," is "mined". Once the

10. Clause 8 of the Bill.
11. Clause 4 of the Bill.

hardware is in place, the user can join a 'Bitcoin Mining Pool'.[12] It consists of several people working together to validate 'blocks.' A block is a record of recent transactions carried out using bitcoins. Miners, upon clearing a block, are 'paid' in bitcoins by the bitcoin network for their services. All Bitcoin transactions are marked in a public register called the Blockchain. This is a process by which individuals are rewarded for their efforts by the network. The miners are processing transactions and securing the network using specialized hardware and are collecting new cryptocurrencies in exchange.[13] Bitcoin miners, spread across the globe, drive the cryptocurrency digital currency system. The miners are nothing but a network of computers. The process of mining is a capital-intensive activity as it requires expensive hardware, software, and huge and uninterrupted power.

#### *2.4.2. Cryptocurrency Exchange*

Not everyone can be a Bitcoin miner due to the cost and complexity involved. Hence somebody can buy Bitcoin from Bitcoin exchanges. The Bitcoins so purchased can be stored in digital form and used in exchange for real currency. There are various Bitcoin exchanges like Wazir X, Zebopay, Coinbase, etc. As of January 16, 2021, the value of 1 Bitcoin is equal to Rs 26,66,729.36.[14]

#### *2.4.3. Consideration for Sale of Goods and Services*

Even without the conversion of Bitcoins, they can be used as a currency to buy goods and services from businesses that accept them. Bitcoins use for e-commerce transactions havetaken off primarily because of the ease and speed with which they take place. Bitcoins reduce the number of intermediaries involved in the financial aspect of a transaction as the nature of the technology itself verifies and carries out all the functions that payment intermediaries do in the context of other e-commerce transactions.

### 2.5. Tax Treatment of Cryptocurrency

Indian Taxation law has not yet dealt with the taxation of cryptocurrencies as they are still not recognized as legal tender. But it is important to understand the taxation issues on cryptocurrencies as they are dependent on how cryptocurrencies are used.

The following are the broad classification of issues that need to be addressed in the context of the taxation of cryptocurrencies:

- Is cryptocurrency goods or a service?
- Can the developer of cryptocurrency be considered a manufacturer?

12. Industry Perspective on Bitcoins A report by PHD Chamber of Commerce and Industry.
13. https://cryptocurrency.org/en/faq#economy.
14. https://freebitco.in/site/cryptocurrency/bitcoin/converter/btc-to-inr/.

- Can cryptocurrency be considered a self-generated asset?
- Can cryptocurrency be considered a capital asset in the hands of the developer?
- How do we determine the cost of acquisition of cryptocurrency?
- What is the tax treatment of the income of a trader who trades in cryptocurrency?
- How do we value cryptocurrency if businesses are holding it as inventory?
- Can cryptocurrency be considered as a valid medium of exchange in the absence of legal approval?
- What will be the position of a seller who accepts cryptocurrency in consideration for the sale of goods and services?

### *2.5.1. Is cryptocurrency goods or services?*

The term "goods" is defined in various ways under various legislation. Let us look at the definition under various regulations:[15]

- Goods include all materials, articles and commodities (Constitution of India Article 366(120).
- Goods mean every kind of movable property other than actionable claims and money; includes stock and shares, growing crops, grass and things attached to or forming part of the land, which are agreed to be severed before the sale or under the contract of sale. (Section 2 of Sale of Goods Act)
- Goods mean every kind of movable property other than actionable claims, money, and securities. (Section 2(d) of Forwards Contract Regulation Act, 1952)
- To become goods an article must be something, which can ordinarily come to the market to be bought and sold. *Union of India v. Delhi Cloth Mills.*[16]
- The RBI Act does not specifically define currency, but it does define foreign currency to have the same meaning as in Foreign Exchange Regulation Act, 1973, which has since been replaced by FEMA.
- Currency' has been defined under FEMA to include, 'all currency notes, postal notes, postal orders, money orders, cheques, drafts, travellers' cheques, letters of credit, bills of exchange and promissory notes, credit cards or such other similar instruments, as may be notified by the Reserve Bank'. FEMA defines 'foreign currency' as any currency other than Indian

15. Source: Advanced Law Lexicon by P. Ramanatha Aiyar p 2013 (2005).
16. AIR 1963 SC 791, 795.

currency. Definition of 'Indian Currency' under FEMA states that Indian currency is the currency which is expressed or drawn in Indian Rupees.

- The term currency notes are specifically defined in Section 2(i) of FEMA to mean and include cash in the form of coins and bank notes.

The question that needs to be examined is whether cryptocurrency can come under the definition of the term "currency". The term currency has been defined to include various instruments and the question is whether cryptocurrencies can be considered as similar instruments. By applying the rule of "ejusdem generis"[17] one can argue that cryptocurrencies should be considered as similar instruments. However, the definition provides that the same should be notified by RBI and cryptocurrencies are yet to be notified by RBI. Also, it is relevant to note the principle of '*expressum facit cessare tacitum*' on this issue. Under this principle if any things are stated expressly then what is not expressed is not included. The courts do often consider this principle and if this principle is applied then cryptocurrency is not covered by the definition of currency.

- The Supreme Court in *Tata Consultancy Services v. State of Andhra Pradesh*[18] stated that, "computer software is intellectual property, whether it is conveyed in diskettes, floppy, magnetic tapes or CD ROMs, whether canned (Shrink-wrapped) or uncanned (customized), whether it comes as part of computer or independently, whether it is branded or unbranded, tangible or intangible; is a commodity capable of being transmitted, transferred, delivered, stored, processed, etc. and therefore as a 'good' liable To sale tax."
- Cryptocurrencies are generated by hardware, software etc. By applying the definition of SC, cryptocurrencies could potentially be considered as goods.
- But one of the important features of the definition of goods under the Sale of Goods Act is that it is capable of being bought or sold.
- Though cryptocurrencies do not have a formal or recognized exchange, yet they can be traded through exchanges, which are operating through technology or the internet.
- It may also be noted that shares prior to the allotment are not covered by the definition of goods. (*R. D. Goyal v. Reliance Industries Limited*[19]) However, allotted shares in a company are "goods".[20]
- If "cryptocurrency" cannot be considered as money due to the above proposition, it can be covered by the definition of goods.

17. See *Rajasthan SEB v. Mohan Lal*, [1967] 3 SCR 377.
18. (2005) 1 SCC 308.
19. (2002) 1 SCC 81, Para 39.
20. 28 Bom LR 777.

### *2.5.2. Can a developer of cryptocurrency be considered as manufacturer?*

Definition under Income-tax Act

The term 'manufacture' has been defined in Section 2(29BA) of the Act as follows:

- "manufacture", with its grammatical variations, means a change in a non-living physical object or article or thing, —
- ***resulting in transformation of the object or article or thing into a new and distinct object or article or thing having a different name, character and use;*** or
- bringing into existence of a new and distinct object or article or thing with a different chemical composition or integral structure.

The definition under SEZ Act, 2005[21] is specified as: "manufacture" means to make, produce, fabricate, assemble, process or bring into existence, by hand or by machine, a new product having a distinctive name, character or use and shall include processes such as refrigeration, cutting, polishing, blending, repair, remaking, re-engineering and includes agriculture, aquaculture, animal husbandry, floriculture, horticulture, pisciculture, poultry, sericulture, viticulture and mining."

In the context of the lower rate of taxation under Section 115BAB of the Income-tax Act, the section specifically excludes the development of computer software in any form or in media developed through software and stored in digital media. However, it is interesting to note that the Bangalore Tribunal in the context of *M/S Manhattan Associates India Development Center P Limited v. DCIT* took a position that the development of software is akin to manufacturing and also considered it as an industrial undertaking.

Applying the above rationale, there is a debate whether the development of cryptocurrency can be considered as manufacture. Since it is goods as per the Supreme Court judgment in TCS Limited and applying the rationale of the Bangalore Tribunal, it may be considered as manufacturing but for the exclusion under the provisions of Section 115BAB. The counter to the provisions of Section 115BAB is that cryptocurrency is an end product itself and not a computer software though it must have been developed through computer software.

### *2.5.3. Implication of cryptocurrency being considered as self-generated asset*

The concept of self-generated asset is very much relevant for a cryptocurrency developer. If cryptocurrencies are acquired in a cryptocurrency exchange the cost of acquisition is known. But if the cryptocurrency is developed by a developer the issue of how to measure the cost arises. The cost of developing or acquiring the

21. Section 2(r) of SEZ Act.

cryptocurrency is very important whether we consider cryptocurrency as capital asset or stock in trade. As explained in earlier paragraphs, cryptocurrency is developed by a miner through self-generation by developers.

Section 55 of Income-tax Act 1961, which deals with the cost of acquisition of self-generated assets does not include cryptocurrencies. In those cases of assets falling under Section 55, the cost of acquisition shall be the price paid for the acquisition, and in any other case it shall be NIL. One view is that in the absence of any prescription of the cost of acquisition for self-generated asset and *cryptocurrency being a self -generated asset*, applying the principle laid down by the Supreme Court in *BC Srinivasa Shetty case*,[22] no capital gains arise on the transfer of cryptocurrency if it is considered as a capital asset.

However, the acceptance of this proposition has another challenge. The developers need to capitalize the salary paid and other cost incurred in the books as the same is considered as an intangible asset. Hence if cryptocurrency is considered as an intangible asset, the cost of acquisition of the asset shall be the cost incurred in developing the asset.

Though both the above arguments are possible, it is important to amend the cost of acquisition under Income-tax Act by amending the provisions for crypto currencies.

### *2.5.4. Tax implications of a cryptocurrency as a capital asset or stock in trade*

The treatment of cryptocurrency as a capital asset or stock in trade is dependent on the holding by the owner. Normally, it can be considered that for a developer cryptocurrency is a capital asset, and for a trader or a businessman who deals with cryptocurrency should be considered as inventory. In the case of a capital asset, the cost of acquisition of cryptocurrency can be determined in the manner explained in earlier para, i.e., the amount spent for developing the asset. If the cryptocurrency is exchanged for real currency by the developer, the same is considered as transfer under Section 2(47) as the definition of transfer includes exchange, and hence, the excess of consideration received shall be taxable as capital gains

Further, the value of cryptocurrency is always measured by the market value and the exchange of cryptocurrency, either by the developer or at the exchange, is measured by fair value on the date of the transaction. Hence, the underlying Indian currency for cryptocurrency will be the basis for measurement of consideration for exchange of cryptocurrency.

Also, the issue that need to be addressed is if cryptocurrency is held as inventory then how to record value of cryptocurrency under the tax laws. It is a fundamental principle that inventory is to be valued at cost price or market value, whichever is

22. 128 ITR 294.

lower. Hence, if the fair market value (FMV) of the cryptocurrency as at the last date of the financial year or on the date of valuation is more than the cost of acquisition, the cryptocurrency will be valued at FMV.

Cryptocurrency, so received as a consideration for the sale of goods or services will be considered as income. Till cryptocurrency is recognized as a currency, the exchange of cryptocurrency as a consideration for the sale of goods or services will be considered as an exchange transaction, and the same will be considered as income from 'profits and gains from business'.

Though the above is based on general principles, it is important for the Government of India to codify the rules for taxation of cryptocurrencies for the following reasons:

- Cryptocurrencies, compared to other assets, have an exchange and derive value based on the demand and supply of cryptocurrencies.
- The exchange for cryptocurrencies is only on an informal basis or informal exchange organized through a network.
- Cryptocurrencies are developed through hardware and software; hence, the tax treatment for the developer of cryptocurrency is important. The value of cryptocurrency or the cost of development of cryptocurrency cannot be a simpliciter model on the basis of Section 55 of the Income-tax Act.
- There is a possibility of trading or dealing in cryptocurrencies without actual delivery of cryptocurrencies. The revenue authorities should not consider it as a speculation income and give tax treatment accordingly.
- Further, whether the fluctuation in the value of cryptocurrencies can be considered as notional and should be brought to tax if positive or allowed as loss if it is negative.

In this context, it is important to note the developments in other countries.

The US Government has issued a notice stating that virtual currency be treated as 'property' for US federal tax purposes. The UK Government has released a guidance paper, which provides an overview of the tax treatment for transactions involving cryptocurrencies, specifically bitcoins. It discusses the issue of characterizing income arising from such transactions and provides when such income would be considered as business income or capital gains or other categories. The South African Government's stance reveals that it considers cryptocurrencies as assets of an intangible nature. Other countries are also likely to share their views on how to treat and tax cryptocurrency.

In this context, it is worthwhile to discuss the first judicial decision of the Israeli District Court, pronounced on May 19, 2019, on the taxation of cryptocurrency transactions by individuals. The taxpayer considered the profit as currency fluctuation other than in the course of a business, which is exempt from tax in Israel. The court ruled that cryptocurrency is neither a currency nor a foreign currency, but rather it falls within the definition of an asset in accordance with the circular issued by the Israeli Government on the matter. The District Court, therefore, ruled that profits generated from the sale of cryptocurrency should be subject to capital gains tax.

## 3. Concluding Remarks

As the technology improved and the confidence in the safety of cryptocurrency increased, there has been an increase in the volume of trading in cryptocurrency.[23] This necessarily means that as they are increasingly used, there is a need to regulate their use so that there are no harms caused to users directly or through their misuse for tax evasion and illegal activities. Cryptocurrencies, therefore, need to be regulated in accordance with law by the appropriate agency, which in India's case, would be the RBI. The 2019 Bill is, however, a step in the wrong direction and will only result in increased harms to users and even greater misuse of cryptocurrency for illegal activities by pushing it underground. Rather, a fresh legislative and policy framework is needed to regulate cryptocurrencies, along with the creation of a central bank- backed digital currency, which in India's case would be a "digital rupee".

Along with the regulation, there is a potential to tax cryptocurrencies, and therefore, create a source of revenue for the government and to prevent ruinous speculation in the value of such cryptocurrencies. There is, at present, no clarity on how cryptocurrencies ought to be regulated, and to this end, the government should come out with guidelines on the taxation of cryptocurrencies. In this context it is important to note the observations of Honourable Finance Minister, in his Budget speech while presenting the budget for 2018.

> The Government does not consider crypto-currencies legal tender or coin and will take all measures to eliminate use of these crypto assets in financing illegitimate activities or as part of the payment system. The Government will explore use of blockchain technology proactively for ushering in digital economy. Further, the Central Bank also has chosen to reinforce its earlier message to "users, holders and traders of Virtual Currencies ("VCs") including bitcoins regarding the potential economic, financial, operational, legal, customer protection and security related risks associated in dealing with such VCs." Therefore, considering that cryptocurrency transactions are gradually

23. See https://www.livemint.com/news/india/indians-are-spending-millions-daily-on-cryptocurrency-trading-11606906191740.html.

> picking up in India, while, laws regulating them are significantly absent, we are hopeful that the government will come up with a notification soon to dispel the ambiguity around the legality of bitcoins, their taxability and disclosure requirement of bitcoins.[24]

One hopes that the government moves quickly to dispel the confusion and fill the vacuum with a well thought-out regulation that not only ensures that no harms arise out of cryptocurrency use but also that it provides a sound basis for the taxation of the same.

24. See https://www.indiabudget.gov.in/budget2018-2019/ub2018-19/bs/bs.pdf para 112.

# REJOINDER

**Rohit Roy**

## 1. Introduction

The chapter by Sekar and Prasanna Kumar on the income tax implications on cryptocurrencies is premised on a challenge to a Reserve Bank of India (RBI) circular effectively banning cryptocurrencies and the consequent Supreme Court (SC) judgment in *Internet and Mobile Association of India v. Reserve Bank of India.*

The RBI circular directed entities, which were regulated by the RBI, to not deal with or provide services to any individual or business entities dealing with or settling virtual currencies. The circular and the consequent press statement were both challenged by stakeholder entities on the grounds of legal invalidity and disproportionate regulatory action. These entities argued that any regulation off cryptocurrencies should be subject to nuanced considerations instead of a blanket prohibition.

The very jurisdiction of the RBI when regulating cryptocurrencies was also brought into question. The entities argued that a cryptocurrency was neither a currency nor a payment system and therefore not subject to RBI regulation. They further elaborated, that while it was possible to use cryptocurrencies in a way similar to that of legal tender, this would not change the 'essential legal characteristic of cryptocurrencies' which, as such, resembled digital goods or commodities. In the perspective of the entities, therefore, the circular did seem to be arbitrary, unfair, and unconstitutional in its restriction of a legitimate business activity. The absence of any legislative ban on cryptocurrencies perpetuated their claim of a lack of RBI jurisdiction. The legislative legitimacy (or rather the lack of illegitimacy) would allow for the trading of cryptocurrencies, and their characteristics would keep them outside the purview of the RBI.

This particular line of argument is a familiar confusion arising out of characterisation in the digital economy. Coincidentally, in the 4th ITRAF volume, titled *International Taxation in the Digital Era*, 2020, Prasanna Kumar and Agarwal listed and analysed the characterization of income as one of three essential elements of the digital economy. In the same chapter, the authors were made familiar with, and question the merit of, the seeming arbitrariness of RBI policy decisions.[25]

25. Alok Prasanna Kumar and Vinti Agarwal, 'Challenges in the Design of Digital Taxation in India' in Shome P (ed), *International Taxation in the Digital Era* (OakBridge 2020).

## 2. RBI Policy Making Techniques

The RBI's counterarguments centred around the safety concerns associated with cryptocurrencies. Their contention was that cryptocurrencies can be used for illegal purposes and could also undermine India's credit system and monetary stability. As such, the RBI asserted their jurisdiction in regulating cryptocurrencies by contending that they fall within the realm of banking activity.

The argument whether cryptocurrencies are a banking activity that is currently subject to deliberations and the chapter by Sekar and Prasanna Kumar go into this aspect. However, considering that the RBI believes in the validity of its jurisdiction, one would expect that they (as a specialized regulatory authority) would consider the merits of a legitimate business activity and regulate around it. Such a legislative attitude would go a long way in striking a balance between commercial advantage and national security. Otherwise, a reasonable contention against such commercial hindrances is that a specialised authority is not necessary for handing out blanket bans.

This sentiment is, in fact, demonstrated by the authors to be reflected in the Crypto-Token and Crypto-Asset (Regulation and Banning) Bill, 2018. The Bill propounded a high level of control, rather than a ban, on cryptocurrencies. Since then, however, the legislature has reconsidered its position on the banning of cryptocurrencies and has footed the Banning of Cryptocurrency and Regulation of Official Digital Currency Bill, 2019, in parliament, in a rallying affirmative of the RBI way of thinking. The bill effectively proposes bans to the mining, generation, holding, selling, dealing in, issuing, transferring, disposing of or using cryptocurrency in India. The looming 2019 Bill notwithstanding, the authors pursue their analysis, commensurate to the current situation.

The original RBI circular, while unfortunate, is not particularly surprising. Such forms of lazy policymaking are habitually encountered in the decisions of Indian regulatory agencies. Instead of a nuanced policy based on assessing the pros and cons of the subject area, the general trend has often been unmitigated blanket bans. In *Internet and Mobile Association of India v. Reserve Bank of India*, the SC in fact, is chagrined by this very trend and rebukes the RBI for not having "applied its mind".

While the overturning of the ban on cryptocurrencies may be welcome, the authors point out that this has also created a regulatory vacuum surrounding cryptocurrencies. Currently, cryptocurrencies are not subject to any regulations. Even though the SC has asserted the power of the RBI to regulate cryptocurrencies under the RBI Act and the Banking Regulation Act, post Internet and Mobile Association of India, such regulation is yet to be enacted.

## 3. The Categorization of Cryptocurrencies for Taxation Purposes

The Internet and Mobile Association of India Judgment also reveals to us that certain fundamental queries have to be made and certain fundamental concepts remain to be comprehensively understood. After laying the premise, the authors of the chapter, therefore, embark on such an exercise. The reader is provided with a succinct overview of the technological aspects of digital currencies. A similar exercise may also be found in the previously mentioned ITRAF 4th volume, on the chapter on Blockchains and the potential associations with modern taxation. Ironically, the very technological underpinning (and the lack of understanding of it) that often perpetuates authorities to ignore the benefits for a blank ban or, at times, unfathomable indifference, is the very thing that this chapter in the previous volume is portraying as a potential solution to the complications of modern taxation.[26]

One such query the authors pertinently make about cryptocurrencies is whether they can be categorized as either goods or services. To that end, the authors embark on a lengthy discussion on the statutory and legislative definitions available with regards to goods and services. More importantly, the authors question whether cryptocurrencies can be definitively included under the definition of "currency".

The authors initially look towards the RBI Act to ascertain whether cryptocurrency can be categorized as goods/services. Cryptocurrencies do not, seemingly, fall under any of the available categories explicitly mentioned, either in the Constitution, the Sale of Goods Act, or the Forwards Contract Regulation Act. However, the pointed segregation of money, from the definition of goods, necessitates an enquiry into whether cryptocurrencies can be categorised as 'currency'. The RBI Act points towards the Foreign Exchange Management Act (FEMA), which provides a range of instruments that can be considered as currency. Importantly, FEMA signs of the definition with the words "such other similar instruments as notified by the RBI". The authors, therefore, wonder, at this juncture, if cryptocurrencies can be included under the purview of "similar instruments" (their argument for *ejusdem generis*). They acknowledge, however, that this argument is perhaps rendered moot by the ancillary requirement of the notification by the RBI, and the fact that there has been no such notification.

Interestingly, the authors note the courts' inclination towards adhering to the principle of '*expressum facit cessare tacitum*'. The fact that cryptocurrencies do not fall into the list of actual instruments, which are considered currency under FEMA, it seems more likely that cryptocurrency may perhaps not be considered yet as a currency under Indian laws. Unless the RBI says otherwise, cryptocurrencies simply do not have the legal sanction to be considered currency.

26. Shikha Mehra and Rohit Roy, 'Challenges in the Design of Digital Taxation in India', in Shome P (ed), *International Taxation in the Digital Era* (OakBridge 2020).

Moreover, case law such as *Tata Consultancy Services v. State of Andhra Pradesh*, reveals that Indian courts tend to see computer software as intellectual property. It appears to be a "commodity capable of being transmitted, transferred, delivered, stored, [and] processed", and therefore, goods liable to tax. Such strict associations between software and the idea of goods may become (or may already be) subject to review to the notions of younger and more attuned generations. However, in the current definitional environment, the dependency of cryptocurrencies on hardware and software places them within such notions of association to goods, and therefore, pushing towards defining them as goods.

This is exacerbated by the characteristics of cryptocurrencies to be able to be sold and bought. Under the Sale of Goods Act one of the important features of goods is to be able to do exactly that. While in India, the authors remind us, there still does not exist cryptocurrency exchanges, the fact that there are such exchanges elsewhere highlights the fact that they can be exchanged in such a manner. There is indeed an intuitive inclination towards looking at cryptocurrencies as tender. However, the authors demonstrate that positing available Indian laws and definitions onto the characteristics of cryptocurrencies, excludes them (at least currently) from being defined as legal tender. Thus, the legal inclination in India would be towards corralling cryptocurrencies into the definition of goods.

Establishing this brings the authors to a very interesting juncture. If cryptocurrencies are to be considered goods, are the developers of cryptocurrencies, therefore, manufacturers by extension? More specifically, would the development of cryptocurrency as a software fall under the purview of manufacturing? By the admission of the authors, deliberations on this matter are not conclusive. The Income-tax Act (ITA) and the Special Economic Zones (SEZ) Act define the term manufacture in a way that is favourable towards including the development of cryptocurrencies. However, when establishing lower taxes on income of new manufacturing companies, the ITA specifically excludes the 'business of the development of computer software'. While this might not exclude cryptocurrencies from the general definition of the word 'manufacture', it certainly goes some way in revealing a legislative intent to do so. However, the tax tribunals, in cases such as *M/S Manhattan Associates India Development Centre Pvt. Limited v. DCIT*, have taken contrary positions and stated that development of software is akin to manufacturing.

## 4. Conclusion

Given the uncertainties concerning the assignment of cryptocurrencies as goods, the authors give us a fresh perspective on the deliberations – viewing cryptocurrencies as self-generated assets. They assert that the fundamental factor is the mode or method of acquisition of the cryptocurrency and the determination of the cost of such acquisition. Ascertaining the cost of the currency is necessary for taxation purposes as it would determine whether the instrument is considered a capital asset or stock.

This is relatively more complicated when the acquirer is the person who mined the cryptocurrency as the instrument may fall under the purview of a self-generated asset. Observing the wording of Section 55 of the ITA and the principle laid down by the SC in *Commissioner of Income Tax, Bangalore v. BC Srinivasa Shetty*, the authors determine that there is the possibility of no capital gains arising out of a mined cryptocurrency when considered as a capital asset in the hands of the original miner.

The authors, however, also note that, for the purposes of accounting, salary paid and cost incurred for mining the cryptocurrency could be construed as a cost of acquisition of the asset, and therefore, reveal a cost incurred in developing the asset. Subsequently, if the mined cryptocurrency is sold, it would fall within the definition of 'transfer' under the ITA and the difference in consideration would be easily determined as capital gain and taxed accordingly.

If the cryptocurrency is not in the hands of the primary miner/developer, then the assumption is that the article has been purchased. In such cases, the cost of acquisition is easily determinable by the procedure mandated by the statute. This is revealed to be the market value of the asset – and is determined by the 'fair value' of the cryptocurrency on the date of the transaction. The authors, therefore, determine that the underlying Indian currency from which the fair value is drawn would be the consideration on which taxation is calculated.

If the cryptocurrency in question is not at exchange, but rather seen as part of the inventory of the owner, a similar determination of the valuation of the cryptocurrency is provided for. To that extent, if the fair market value is more than the cost of acquisition, the cryptocurrency will be valued at that fair market value. While the authors based these deliberations on various statute and general principles, they do rightly question that the codification of rules relating to the taxation of cryptocurrencies is extremely important for the future. As demonstrated by them this is already underway in other jurisdictions.

# ADMINISTRATIVE INNOVATION

# CHAPTER 10

# TAXPAYERS' CHARTER

K. R. Girish[1]

## 1. Introduction

Tax levied directly on income earned or indirectly on sale of goods and provision of services are major sources of revenue for any government to provide services or facilities to the public. Developing policies to raise tax revenues has, hence, always been crucial. An effective tax system creates a better economic situation in a country, whereas one not properly controlled could create a disaster.

Tax administration team is entrusted with this vital task of effective collection and utilization of tax revenue. The importance of good tax administration has been emphasized by Organisation for Economic Co-operation and Development (OECD), which is an intergovernmental economic organization, founded in 1961 to stimulate economic progress and world trade. The OECD in its report[2] has provided some guidelines for good tax administration, which includes applying the law in a fair and transparent manner, communicating to the taxpayer their rights and obligations, deliver quality information and addressing inquiries, request, and appeals from taxpayers, protecting the confidentiality of the taxpayer information, and developing a good relationship with the taxpayers, etc.

A recommended administration is not just a one-way process to affix responsibility on the tax administration team. There are also certain basic obligations to be followed by the taxpayer to make the effort effective. The tax administration team is, therefore, required to encourage the taxpayers to fulfill tax obligations in a timely manner, provide the taxpayers necessary services facilitating them to discharge their liability, encourage them to voluntarily register under the tax laws, provide the taxpayers with tutorials to educate them on relevant tax laws, and their compliance requirements, etc.

The responsibility of having an effective tax system has seen follow-up challenges as well. The taxpayer fears levy of excessive tax or double taxation on their income, whereas the tax administration dreads tax planning and tax evasion. This situation

1. Veena Ramachandran, CA and Principal Consultant worked with the author on this chapter.
2. OECD, Principles of Good Tax Administration (Practice Note GAP001, 2001) - (https://www.oecd.org/tax/administration/1907918.pdf).

poses the requirement for a well-informed and thoughtful tax administration procedure to be in place.

Given this background, let us understand some of the common issues/challenges faced by the tax administration/tax authorities and the taxpayers in complying with the tax policies.

## 1.1. Challenges Faced by the Tax Administration

### *1.1.1. Inadequate training in understanding complex tax procedures*

If the tax authorities (the team competent to impose, assess or enforce any liability to tax) are not well educated and trained adequately on complex taxation laws, it could result in unreasonable adjustments to the income disclosed by the taxpayer. This could consume abundant time in litigation on one hand while giving rise to wasteful litigation costs on the other, both for the tax authorities and the taxpayer.

### *1.1.2. Loss of tax revenue*

Complex tax laws could provide opportunities for taxpayers to adopt multiple tax positions, interpretations, tax planning, etc., resulting in tax leakage.

### *1.1.3. Prolonged litigation*

Non-availability of trained resources among tax authorities who could handle litigation may result in excessive unresolved litigation.

### *1.1.4. Piling up of queries/ requests made by the taxpayers*

Several reasons could contribute to stacking up of pending cases of audit/ litigation before the tax authorities such as, non-cooperation by the taxpayers, shortage of resources, lack of trained tax authorities, lack of a strict timeline for the completion of pending cases, etc.

### *1.1.5. Administrative costs*

This mainly includes costs of running and maintaining the tax system such as cost of maintaining the website, cost of handling the litigations, office expenses and costs relating to the formulation and implementation of tax policies, cost of running and maintaining tax administration team, salaries to staffs, pensions to the retired ones, office expenses including the facilities provided to the team at work.

## 1.2. Challenges Faced by the Taxpayers

### *1.2.1. Understanding complex tax provisions*

Lack of awareness/ understanding of complex tax procedures itself could be one of the major contributors to non-compliances in India. Further, to protect the tax base, tax authorities take unilateral measures and amend tax provisions frequently to make it more complex. Also, retrospective amendments to tax laws make it all the more complex, which is an India-specific problem.

*1.2.2. Compliance cost*

Complying with the tax provisions gives rise to consequential operating costs for the taxpayer. First, cost is the tax itself. Second, the cost incurred in adhering to the tax provisions, which includes hiring a tax expert or a competent team, in-house, depending on the level of compliance, consulting/ professional charges, or salaries paid to the consultant or the in-house tax expert or team.

Adhering to complex tax procedures leaves no option to the taxpayers, but depending on consultants/ tax experts for categorizing the income, determining the tax liability therein, disclosing the income in the appropriate form as part of compliance, etc. Certain countries also mandate certification of accounts by eligible tax experts.

With the increase in compliance burden, these costs could be high and significant, sometimes even more than the tax cost.

*1.2.3. Fear of double taxation*

As regards the domestic and international transactions, most governments have taken initiatives to curb double taxation in the hands of taxpayers. However, these provisions do not provide protection in all scenarios. The resultant fear of double taxation is one of the major causes for vehement tax planning by the taxpayers.

*1.2.4. Aggressive taxation measures*

Aggressive tax audit measures adopted by the tax authorities have created a perception in the taxpayers of most countries that tax authorities are not approachable and would never look at a fair tax position.

Delay in the receipt of refunds, vexatious disputes in tax matters, indecisive timelines, etc., are some more contributors to the lack of legal certainty in several countries. This, to a great extent discourages taxpayers from voluntary compliance with tax laws.

Challenges not restricted to the above, have resulted in disparity in the wavelength of the taxpayers and tax authorities. Authoritative position of the tax authorities over taxpayers, the presumption of dishonest taxpayer resulting in niggling assessments for any unintentional error or procedural lapse committed by the taxpayer, etc. results in the negative attitude of the taxpayers towards the voluntary compliance.

Even more, abiding by the tax policies does not come for free. Costs are incurred at both ends – by the tax administration team and by the taxpayer. When both are aware of the responsibilities and the relevant procedures, consequent cost i.e., the administrative cost for the government and the compliance cost for the taxpayer can be minimized.

Under this scenario, having procedures acceptable to both ends became a necessity rather than an option for a healthy tax environment. Measures had to be adopted to encourage taxpayers for voluntary compliance. This led to the introduction of taxpayers' charter in several countries.

A good tax system requires support of the taxpayers. This is hard to achieve unless there is a balance between taxpayers' rights and obligations.

Initiatives taken by governments to overcome this fear or gap between the taxpayer and tax administration is 'taxpayers' charter'. Taxpayers' charter intends to build community confidence. It helps to establish a respectful and trusting relationship between the taxpayer and the tax authorities.

The OECD stated that "The ways by which revenue authorities interact with taxpayers and employees, impact public perception of the tax system and the degree of voluntary compliance. Taxpayers who are aware of their rights and expect, and in fact receive, a fair and efficient treatment are more willing to comply[3]".

Taxpayers' charter aims at improving mutual trust and cooperation between the taxpayer and the tax authorities through the protection of taxpayers' rights and by imposing certain obligations on the taxpayer, which helps in better administration of the tax system.

The same way citizens are expected to pay the legitimate tax they owe to the country, the tax office is also expected to be transparent with the taxpayers. Commitment to build a positive relationship with every taxpayer, will help to implement a non-discriminatory taxpayers' charter.

This chapter provides thoughts on how the tax authorities should perform good practice as set in the taxpayers' charter. Furthermore, the chapter suggests future work on how adherence to the charter contributes to conditions that many regard as fundamental to good governance.

## 2. Evolution of Taxpayers' Charter

Post-World War II, the UN General Assembly adopted the Universal Declaration of Human Rights in 1948. The document expressed the principle that everyone is entitled to peaceful enjoyment of their own possessions, of which they cannot be deprived except by the rule of law. There is no explicit mention that this document is legitimate for the countries to levy taxes.

For many years after that, taxpayers' rights were not given as much importance as human rights. Taxpayers' rights are closely related to human rights. Human rights subsume taxpayer rights. Therefore, developments in human rights also substantially affect taxpayers' rights.

3. OECD, Principles of Good Tax Administration (Practice Note GAP001, 2001), p 3. 9 - (https://www.oecd.org/tax/administration/1907918.pdf).

Almost forty years later, countries started realizing the need for co-operation between the taxpayer and the tax administration. Governments began to consider more targeted charters to cover the rights of taxpayers.

With a focus on the importance of tax policies, the OECD had suggested that, tax authorities issue a taxpayers' charter consisting of basic taxpayers' rights and obligations.

In 1990, the OECD's Committee of Fiscal Affairs Working Party published a document entitled "Taxpayers' rights and obligations – A survey of the legal situation in OECD countries". The results of the survey conducted by OECD was published, which showed that although taxpayers' charter was not in place in many of the member countries, some of the basic rights were provided to the taxpayers in the legislature, such as the opportunity of being heard, right to appeal, right to be informed, assisted, and heard, right to pay no more than the correct amount of tax, right to certainty, right to privacy, etc.

The results of the survey also revealed that there were certain obligations entrusted to taxpayers. A set of behavioral norms expected of taxpayers by governments such as, the obligation to be honest, provide accurate information, keep proper records, obligation to pay taxes on time, etc. After this report, some countries began to publish bills of taxpayers' rights.

These expected behaviors were believed to be fundamental to the successful operation of taxation systems. Without this balance of taxpayers' rights and obligations, taxation systems could not function effectively and efficiently.

Further, the International Bureau of Fiscal Documentation (IBFD) in its report[4] "Towards Greater Fairness in Taxation: A Model Taxpayer Charter", has provided model rights and obligations based on the provisions, which were derived from a survey of taxpayer rights and responsibilities in 41 countries, collectively representing over 80 percent of world GDP.

The report has spelled out guiding principles of a taxpayers' charter on rights and responsibilities from which more specific provisions can be largely defined:

**Table 1. Taxpayers' Rights and Responsibilities**

| Taxpayers' Rights | Taxpayers' Responsibilities |
|---|---|
| Integrity and equality | Be truthful |
| Certainty | Provide information |
| Efficiency and effectiveness | Be co-operative |

4. Towards greater fairness in taxation -A Model Taxpayer Charter by Michael Cadesky, Ian Hayes, David Russell (https://www.ibfd.org/sites/ibfd.org/files/content/pdf/16_001_Towards_Greater_Fairness_in_Taxation_final_web.pdf).

| Taxpayers' Rights | Taxpayers' Responsibilities |
|---|---|
| Appeal and the right to dispute resolution | Make payment |
| Appropriate assistance | Comply with the law |
| Confidentiality and privacy | Maintain records |
| Pay correct amount of tax | Take due care |
| Representation | Retain responsibility for advisors |
| Proportionality | Show courtesy |
| Honesty | Comply cross border |

*Source:* Refer footnote 64.

Many countries around the world as mentioned above, have elaborated these basic rights and obligations in the taxpayers' charter they drafted. Even countries without a taxpayers' charter attach equal importance to taxpayers' rights.

Some countries developed customised charter, for example USA introduced Taxpayer Bill of Rights initially in 1996, which later was revised in 1998 and Taxpayer Bill of Rights 3 was introduced.

As on date, several countries around the world have successfully introduced taxpayers' charter. The United Kingdom was the first to adopt a taxpayers' charter, in 1986. A number of countries have subsequently adopted taxpayers' charters in the past three decades - Canada (Declaration of Taxpayers' Rights–1985), France (Taxpayer Charter– 1987), New Zealand (Statement of Principles–1986), England (Taxpayer Charter– 1986), the USA (Taxpayer Bill of Rights–1988), Turkey in 2006, Australia, Italy, Ireland, South Africa, Philippines, Russia, Spain, Uganda, etc.[5]

Broadly, taxpayers' charter has been introduced by countries in any of the following approaches[6]:

- Administrative, which focuses on protecting and enhancing quality of regular interaction between the taxpayer and the tax administration team.
- Legislative charter protects the taxpayer from breach of legal rights in relation to the applicable tax laws.
- A combination of legislated rights and administrative charter where there is a legal framework to protect rights and effective compliance.

5. An empirical analysis of taxpayers' fairness preferences from Canada's Taxpayer Bill of rights by Jonathan Farrar (https://pdfs.semanticscholar.org/443b/7701b18b6b76cd12cebd745a1e1cc7f6c65a.pdf).
6. The taxpayers charter -A case study in tax administration by Simon James, Kristina Murphy, Monika Reinhart (https://www.researchgate.net/publication/29811451_The_Taxpayers'_Charter_a_case_study_in_tax_administration).

Countries like Belgium, Brazil, Chile, Italy, USA, Kenya, and Mexico are some of the countries which have taxpayers' charter as part of their statute. Most of the countries have taxpayers' charter that is administrative in nature. Countries like Australia, Canada, Qatar, Hongkong, New Zealand, Ireland are some of the counties which have taxpayers' charter as administrative guidelines but do not have protection of the statute. Many countries have taxpayers' rights and obligations in judicial precedents or any other legislation, but not in a comprehensive document.

## 3. Contents of Taxpayers' Charter

Taxpayers' charter aims at encouraging mutual trust and respect between the tax administration and the taxpayer. It is a two-way initiative where the government intends to serve the taxpayer in a fair and efficient manner, at the same time it must be firm with those who try to avoid their obligations.

Mostly, taxpayers' charter drafted by each country includes two sets of rules, one set on taxpayer rights, which elaborates on what a taxpayer can expect from the tax authorities, and the second set being taxpayer obligations, which discusses what is expected from a taxpayer.

Taxpayers' rights can be explained as the rights given to taxpayers in the legal relationship between the state and the taxpayer in the taxation process.[7]

Assigning responsibilities and obligations to each role is a practice set by most democratic societies. Taxpayers and tax authorities are no exception to this. Precisely, for this reason, most of the countries have laid down legislations governing taxpayers' rights and obligations.

In many countries, taxpayers' rights and obligations are provided in various places of the legislation but not in a separate comprehensive document. Taxpayers' charter is a comprehensive document where taxpayers' rights and obligations are listed in a single place.

Considering the diversity of the environment, it is difficult to have blanket rights and obligations, which are applicable globally. Although basic rights and obligations could be identified, each country needs to fine-tune the same based on their environment.

Below, we have listed rights and obligations, which are generally found in the taxpayers' charter of different countries selected for comparison such as USA, UK, Canada, Qatar, Australia, Hongkong, New Mexico, Kenya, Ireland, and New Zealand.

7. A comparative analysis of taxpayer rights in Turkey and the USA (https://pdfs.semanticscholar.org/d64c/e1b473726e644489300dcd3909e464f8d3dd.pdf).

## 3.1. Rights Provided by Most Countries in their Taxpayers' Charter

- **Right to be treated as honest**

  The tax authorities should accept the information given by the taxpayer as complete and accurate unless they have the reason to believe otherwise.

- **Right to privacy and confidentiality**

  Information regarding the taxpayer, such as personal and financial information, etc., should be kept confidential and should not be shared with others except as required by law.

- **Right to be represented by any other person**

  Taxpayers can authorize anyone to represent them in front of the tax authorities on their behalf. However, he will still be responsible for discharging any liability under the Act.

- **Paying only the tax due under the law**

  Taxpayers have the right to pay only the amount of tax legally due, including interest and penalties. Further, the tax authorities have to apply all tax payments properly.

- **Right to be treated fairly and reasonably**

  Taxpayers should be treated with courtesy and consideration by the tax authorities.

- **Right to be treated in a professional manner**

  The tax authorities should act within the powers conferred by law and should deal with the taxpayers in a professional way.

- **Right to appeal**

  If taxpayers are not satisfied with the service of tax authorities, they have the right to submit a complaint to the tax authorities or to the ombudsman. If the taxpayer disagrees with the amount of their tax assessment, they have the right to objection and appeal.

- **Right to consistency and equity**

  Tax authorities should apply the law consistently so that everyone pays the right amount of tax. Tax authorities should take the circumstance of the taxpayer into consideration as far as the law allows.

- **Right to question the authorities**

  Taxpayers have the right to question the information, advice, and services provided to them. Tax authorities should inform the taxpayers about the options available for resolving disagreements, and they will reach out to the taxpayers to reach an outcome quickly.

- **Right to have the costs of compliance considered when administering tax legislation**

  Tax authorities should consider the cost of compliance of taxpayers while administering the tax legislation. They should make honest efforts to keep the compliance cost at the minimum.

- **Right to get access to the information the authorities hold about the taxpayers**

  Taxpayers are entitled to access their own information, which is held by the tax authorities as authorized by the law.

- **Right to tackle those who bend and break rules**

  The tax administration should identify those who are not paying taxes to the extent they owe or are claiming more than they should, and recover the money and differentiate them from those who are prompt in discharging their tax liability. The tax administration should charge interest and penalties where appropriate, and it should be fair and reasonable on how they use their powers. Specifically, there can be no bias in applying the same.

## 3.2. Rights in Taxpayers' Charter – Country-wise Analysis

### *3.2.1. Canada*

- **Right of not paying the disputed amount of income tax before having an impartial review**

  The taxpayer can object to the assessment and reassessment if he feels that the law was applied incorrectly. He can do so by providing proper explanation to the authorities and evidence to prove that such assessment or reassessment was not done properly. In such cases, the assessee will have to pay only the disputed amount of taxes.

- **Right to lodge a service complaint and to be provided with an explanation by tax authorities on findings**

  The taxpayers have the right to raise a service complaint if they encounter difficulties, such as misleading information, staff behaviour, undue delays, mistakes, etc. They will be heard and provided with a proper solution by the authorities.

- **Right to expect tax authorities to be accountable**

  The taxpayers have the right to expect the tax authorities to be accountable for their actions and decisions regarding the taxpayers and their service commitment towards the taxpayers.

- **Right to relief from penalties and interest under tax legislation because of extraordinary circumstances**

  The taxpayers should be given relief from payment of penalties and interest under tax legislation where the default by the taxpayers was on account of extraordinary circumstances, which was beyond the control of the taxpayers.

- **Right to expect tax authorities to publish service standards and report annually**

  Service standards serve as a basis to measure the performance of tax authorities towards their commitment to the public. The tax authorities should set the service standards and measure their performance and publish such reports annually in the public domain.

- **Right to expect to be warned about questionable tax schemes in a timely manner**

  The taxpayers can expect the tax authorities to provide the information about the questionable schemes of the tax administration, which are under their strict scrutiny.

- **Right to request a formal review without fear of reprisal**

  If the taxpayer wants a decision or action to be reviewed including, legal review. He can lodge a complaint and get it reviewed.

*3.2.2. United States of America*

- **Right to be informed**

  The taxpayers are entitled to know the procedures and be provided with clear explanations, which will help them in complying with the tax laws.

- **Right to quality service**

  The taxpayers can expect courteous, prompt, and professional assistance from the tax authorities.

- **Right to challenge tax authorities position and be heard**

  The taxpayers can provide additional information and documentation to the tax authorities and expect the tax authorities to consider them in dealing with their tax matters.

- **Right to finality**

  The taxpayers have the right to know the maximum period of time within which they must challenge the tax authority's position. They should also be informed of maximum time period until which the tax authorities must complete audit of a tax year or collect tax debt.

### 3.2.3. *United Kingdom*

- **Right to be deal with complaints quickly and fairly**

  The tax authorities should resolve the taxpayers' complaints quickly and in a timely manner. If the authorities fail to do so, the taxpayer can ask a third party to look into the issue. In which case, the tax authorities will have to work with this third party to resolve the dispute.

### 3.2.4. *Australia*

- **Right to get the things right**

  Tax authorities must help the taxpayers to understand taxpayers' rights and obligations by providing accurate, consistent and clear information to taxpayers.

- **Right to get the explanation regarding decisions made about the taxpayers**

  Tax authorities should explain the decisions taken regarding affairs of the taxpayers along with adequate reasons. Contact details of the tax officials dealing with the taxpayers' case should also be shared.

- **Make it easier for taxpayers to comply**

  The tax authorities will make it easier for the taxpayers to understand their obligations and cheaper for them to comply with it.

### 3.2.5. *Qatar*

- **Providing helpful and efficient service**

  The tax authorities should help the taxpayers in understanding and meeting their obligations. They should also provide the taxpayers with updated information in clear and plain language. They should also resolve the taxpayers' concerns, problems, or complaints in a timely manner.

### 3.2.6. *Kenya*

- **Right to information**

  The taxpayers are entitled to complete and accurate information on their rights and obligations under the various statute.

- **Right to identification**

  The taxpayer has the right to demand from the official of the tax authority the identification card while visiting or serving the taxpayer on official duties.

- If the taxpayer is selected for an audit, he has the right to be notified in advance.

- He has the right to dispute an assessment or object to the concerned authority's decision as specified by law.

*3.2.7. New Zealand*

- **Reliable advice and information**

  Tax authorities should provide the taxpayers with reliable and proper information about their rights and obligations. They should also make sure that the staff of the tax authorities are well trained and cater to the needs of the taxpayers in providing updated and timely information.

*3.2.8. Ireland*

- **Right to make complaint**

  Tax authorities should deal with the complaints of taxpayers promptly and in an impartial way, and assure the taxpayers that availing of this procedure will never prejudice their rights to raise issues with:

  - Ombudsman
  - The Workplace Relations Commission under the Disability Act or
  - Make an appeal to the Independent Appeal Commissioner, where appropriate.

*3.2.9. Mexico*

- Right to the available public information and prompt and courteous tax assistance.
- Right to have audits, inspections of records, and meetings take place at a reasonable time and place.
- The right to have the Department conduct its audits in a timely and efficient manner and be entitled to the correct calculation of interest as provided in the Tax Administration Act.
- The right to simple, non-technical information explaining procedures, remedies and rights during audit, protest, appeals and collection proceedings under the Tax Administration Act.
- The right to an explanation of audit results and the basis for audits, assessments or denials of refund that identify tax, interest, or penalty due.
- The right to seek review, through formal or informal proceedings, of findings or unfavourable decisions that occur during audit or protest procedures.
- The right to abatement (forgiveness) of an assessment of taxes that has been incorrectly, erroneously, or illegally made and a right to seek a compromise

of a stated tax liability. When the Secretary of Taxation and Revenue in good faith doubts that you owe us the amount of claim, you have the right to seek compromise if a way exists in taxpayers' particular case.

- The right to clear information about penalties if a tax assessment is not paid, secured, protested, or otherwise provided for
- The right to timely notice of collection actions that require sale or seizure of your property under the Tax Administration Act, and
- The right to ask to pay your tax obligations by instalment agreements.

It can be noticed that different types of rights are provided in taxpayers' charter, which can be broadly classified as rights, which are *protected by the legislature*, and rights that are provided in the *administrative guidelines*.

Each country has its customised taxpayer charter providing those rights and obligations, which they believe are necessary for their tax system. One of the most important administrative rights to a taxpayer is 'presumption of honesty'. Curiously, certain countries do not have 'presumption of honesty' in the rights prescribed for taxpayer, the. Canadian Taxpayer Bill of Rights is a typical example.

Right to appeal, right to review, right to be represented by someone else on our behalf, right to be heard, etc. are protected both by legislative and administrative guidelines and are enforceable under law. Whereas, right to information in taking the decision, right to quality service, right to expect the tax authorities to be accountable are the rights, which are not provided in the legislation but are expressly provided in t certain taxpayers' charters. Enforcement of such rights will be possible if the taxpayers' charter of such country is not in the form of administrative measures but has the protection of statute.

The disadvantage when taxpayers' rights are not protected by law is that the taxpayer cannot appeal in court in case of violation of such right, however, such violation can be reviewed based on principles of natural justice. tax authorities may provide protection of such rights to taxpayers, but usually, exercise of protection and the existence of that protection remain at the discretion of the tax authorities.[8]

Another vital right provided by most countries is the *right to privacy*. Off late, there is an increasing requirement for transparency, and this has resulted in privacy concern for taxpayers. A balance needs to be obtained between the right to privacy and the requirement for transparency. More requirement for international co-operation is expected considering the nature of activities of taxpayers -like country of residence, country of source, country of market, and country where assets are held.

---

8. A Model of Taxpayers' Rights as a Guide to Best Practice in Tax Administration by Bently, Robert (https://pure.bond.edu.au/ws/portalfiles/portal/28897742/bentleyd1_Full.pdf).

There are no boundaries to taxpayers, and this has resulted in increased challenges to taxpayers as well as tax authorities.

It is important that the taxpayers' rights should be protected even when the information of such taxpayers is exchanged between the countries under various agreements and arrangements. To curb tax evasion and tax avoidance, several agreements are entered between the countries to exchange the taxpayers' information, some of the measures are listed below.[9]

- Tax Information Exchange Agreements (TIEA) - Aims at achieving international co-operation through exchange of information (i.e., taxpayers' information)
- Exchange of Information on request - Under this scheme the tax authorities of one jurisdiction requests for information of specific person or the specific case from another jurisdiction. It is to be noted that under this arrangement only the specific detail regarding the taxpayer for an investigation is asked for.
- Automatic exchange of information - Under this arrangement, bulk taxpayers' information in general is transmitted from the source country to the residence country periodically.
- Foreign Exchange and Tax Compliance Act - Reporting obligation of information in respect of offshore financial accounts maintained by the US residents and citizens.

The main concern of taxpayer under such arrangements is maintenance of privacy and confidentiality of the data that is been shared with the tax authorities of the other jurisdiction. It is the responsibility of each Country to ensure that the information held by the authorities relating to the taxpayers are treated confidential by the tax authorities of such country where the taxpayer is residing. The information should be strictly protected from unauthorised use and should be used only for the purpose it is obtained and to the extent allowed under the specific law of the country.

However, there are no such rules or regulations provided under the Act or the relevant DTAAs, TIEAs, which protects the secrecy and the confidentiality of the data that is exchanged between the countries. They do not mostly contain participation rights for taxpayers, such as the right to be notified or object to the Exchange of Information procedure. Globally, there is no general practice in informing the taxpayers that their information is sent to a different jurisdiction – only limited countries like Germany, France, Switzerland, etc. notify taxpayers.

9. H. Padamchand Khincha, Neha P. Khincha, and Priya Kothari. 2018. Taxpayer Rights in International Exchange of Information, in Parthasarathi Shome edited, *Challenges in Domestic and International Taxation: Emerging Indian Experience,* OakBridge, Gurugram.

Even Article 4(3) of the Multilateral Convention on mutual administrative assistance in tax matter merely states that: 'any Party may indicate that, according to its internal legislation, its authorities may inform its resident or national before transmitting information concerning him'. This is supported even by the OECD commentary which says that even if such procedures are present in the legislation of such countries, exchanging the information should not create a problem for the requesting country to carry the investigation effectively.[10]

OECD recommends that the taxpayers are informed so that the taxpayers can grant their support and also, any confusion can be avoided.[11] Article 26 of the OECD Model Tax Convention requires the requesting state to demonstrate the foreseeable relevance. Foreseeable relevance requires the requesting state to explain how the information requested would help in collecting taxes, investigation and assessment, and the information asked should be relevant for such purposes at the time when such request was made. This helps in preventing the tax authorities of the other jurisdiction from engaging in a fishing expedition (i.e., speculative requests that have no apparent nexus to an open enquiry or investigation).

Where there is no provision under the exchange of information arrangements (International framework) to protect the taxpayers' rights, the taxpayers have to resort to the provisions available under the domestic laws of the country. However, as the purpose of such arrangements is exchange of information to curb tax avoidance and tax evasion, domestic laws also do not contain any provision to protect the taxpayers' rights of privacy and confidentiality.

It is to be noted that for the juridical balance, protection of taxpayers' rights and procedures and sanctions under the TIEAs should go hand-in-hand. In this respect, it is in the good interest of the tax authorities and the taxpayers that the taxpayers' charter provides specific provisions, which are not present in the domestic laws to protect the taxpayers' confidentiality and privacy under such agreements.

The main intention of proving specific rights in the taxpayers' charter is to protect the taxpayers from unnecessary harassment by the tax authorities, and hence, the tax authorities should respect the rights of taxpayers and increase the mutual trust between them, which will contribute to a better tax administration system. It is to be ensured that protection of taxpayers' rights is not only limited to the tax laws but also extends to the various information exchange arrangements entered into between different countries.

---

10. The Evolution of the Exchange of Information in Direct Tax Matters: The Taxpayers' Rights under Pressure by Niels Diepvens & Filip Debelva. https://www.researchgate.net/publication/304015469_The_Evolution_of_the_Exchange_of_Information_in_Direct_Tax_Matters_The_Taxpayers'_Rights_under_Pressure.
11. OECD, "Commentaries on the Articles of the Model Tax Convention," at 404 (2010) https://www.oecd.org/berlin/publikationen/43324465.pdf.

In addition to rights, taxpayers should also fulfil certain obligations set out in the taxpayers' charter. This will help the tax authorities in discharging their duties in effective and efficient manner.

Out of the countries that are selected for the comparative study, countries such as United Kingdom, Australia, Qatar, Hongkong, Kenya, Ireland along with the rights provided in the charter also entrust the taxpayers with certain obligations.

An overall list of obligations, which are entrusted to the taxpayers in the taxpayers' charter mentioned above are listed here under:

## 3.3. General Obligations Seen in Most Countries' Taxpayers' Charter

- **Be honest and truthful**

  Taxpayers should disclose proper details and the correct amount of income in their tax return and all the other correspondences required with the tax authorities. They should be honest in their communication with the tax authorities.

- **Keep accurate and required records**

  Taxpayers should keep accurate records, which are required under law and should produce them as and when called for by the tax authorities.

- **Take reasonable care to avoid mistakes**

  Taxpayers should take reasonable care to avoid mistakes when they send information to the tax authorities regarding payments of their taxes, claims or reliefs and provide complete and accurate information in their tax returns, activity statements and other documents they provide.

- **Lodging by the due date**

  The documents such as tax returns, activity statements, and other information must be lodged or returned by certain dates. If taxpayers are having difficulty complying with these dates, they should contact the authorities before the document or information is due. Depending on the circumstances, the tax authorities will allow them to lodge it beyond due date with applicable charges.

- **Paying by the due date**

  The taxpayers should pay taxes by the due date. However, if they have difficulty in paying the same, they should inform the concerned authorities preferably before the due date. In such case the authorities may extend the time to pay such amount without charging interest or negotiate to pay in installments.

- **Being cooperative**

  Taxpayers should cooperate in all communications and dealings with the tax authorities. They should provide them with all the relevant information and details asked for and should help the tax authorities in discharging their duties.

## 3.4. Obligations Specific to Certain Countries' Taxpayers' Charter

### *3.4.1. United Kingdom*

- **Work with the authorities to get things right**

  The taxpayers should make sure that they are paying the right amount of tax and claiming the correct amount of money. If they are doubtful regarding the same, they should communicate with the tax authorities and get the right information.

- **Find out what you need to do and keep us informed**

  The taxpayers should make sure that they know how to pay tax and claim payments and get in touch with the authorities as soon as possible if they need any help.

- **Know what your representative does on your behalf**

  The taxpayers should make sure that they know what information and payments their representative sends to the tax authorities. Make sure that the information and payments are accurate and provided on time.

- **Respond in good time**

  Taxpayers should send the returns and pay any amounts they owe on time and pay any interest on late payments or penalties promptly to the tax authorities.

### *3.4.2. Qatar*

- **Know the responsibilities**

  Taxpayers are expected to know their compliance requirements under the law. They should know how to register themselves in the tax system, file the tax return, pay the tax, and claim the refund on time.

### *3.4.3. Hong Kong*

- **Keeping the tax authorities informed**

  Taxpayer should inform the tax authorities if there are any changes in business or correspondence address.

*3.4.4. Kenya*

- **Claims and refunds**

  Taxpayers have the obligation to make the refund claim within the time stipulated failure of which will not be processed as stipulated in the law.

- **Objections**

  In case of any objections, the taxpayer is required to pay the undisputed amount of tax to the tax authorities.

*3.4.5. Ireland*

- **Courtesy and consideration**

  Taxpayers should treat the Revenue officials with courtesy and should provide them with all the required information for discharging their duties.

- **Information and assistance**

  The taxpayers should provide the tax authorities with an accurate and complete information and should inform them of the developments that are relevant to their taxes.

Though all the countries have not expressly mentioned the obligations, the taxpayers should consider them in discharging their duties under the respective tax laws. This will assist the taxpayers in better administration.

Having a balance between rights and obligations is important for an effective implementation of taxpayers' charter. For example, taxpayers' right to presumption of honesty is the basic right of the taxpayer. However, considering the practical scenario, such as the increase in tax evasion, a balance is required by affixing obligation on the taxpayer to be honest as well.

## 4. Impact of Taxpayers' Charter Introduced by Various Countries

While implementing taxpayers' charter various countries have had several thoughts on whether to implement it as legally enforceable or merely administrative guidance.

Let us understand peculiarities of taxpayers' charter introduced by some of the countries like – The United Kingdom, The United States of America, Australia, Canada, etc.

### 4.1. The United Kingdom

At first, UK drafted its taxpayer rights in 1986. It was finally introduced in 2009 and amended/ updated in the year 2016. It specifies rights of a taxpayer, the level of fairness to expect from Her Majesty's Revenue & Customs (HMRC) and the obligations of the taxpayer. It has also taken elaborate grievance redressal measures with judicial review procedures, adjudicators, ombudsman, etc.

One of the major highlights about UK's taxpayers' charter is that it has an efficient mechanism in place for compensating those taxpayers who suffer damage as a result of inappropriate or wrongful action taken by tax officers.

### 4.2. The United States of America

The US Internal Revenue Service (IRS) introduced the concept of Taxpayer Bill of Rights in 1988 and later adopted the same in 2014. The Federal Charter provided rights of taxpayers who are dealing with the IRS. These rights are codified in the IRS code, thereby ensuring compliance of the same. However, effectiveness of these provisions may not be as anticipated, as the code does not specify legal remedies against actions that violates taxpayer rights.

Resistance to codify legal actions against IRS could be a major reason why such provisions were not codified.

As per the US Taxpayer Bill of Rights, the onus of proving against a taxpayer lies with the IRS, else taxpayer is eligible for refund of attorney's fees, among other requirements.

### 4.3. Canada

Taxpayer Bill of Rights introduced in Canada in 2007 lists 16 rights of a taxpayer while dealing with Canada's Revenue Agency (CRA) – both legislative and administrative in nature. These rights are administrative in the nature, internally adopted by the CRA and not an enforceable law.

Grievance redressal for legislative rights is provided in the country's Income-tax Act, whereas grievance redressal of administrative rights is provided through services like service complaints process and taxpayers' Ombudsman.

The Canadian Taxpayer Bill has a peculiar, but well appreciated right that helps reduce compliance cost, especially for small businesses. This right aims at letting small businesses focus their energy and resources on growth of their business and the economy.

### 4.4. Australia

Australian taxpayers' charter has listed rights of taxpayer, services expected from Australian Tax Office (ATO) and obligations of a taxpayer. Unlike US, Australian taxpayer charter does not create legal rights as the same is not incorporated in the legislation. Although, Australia has introduced taxpayers' charter as administrative guidelines, but the basic legal rights are protected by the Law.

Australia is one of those countries, which has successfully implemented taxpayers' charter and as on date, has achieved great results in improving tax administration. Post implementation, results of taxpayers' charter are released by Australia annually unlike the other countries who have adopted the taxpayers' charter. This will give a clear understanding of the success in implementing taxpayers' charter.

Australian taxpayers' charter was introduced in the year 1997 and revised later in November 2003. The country has seen significant increase in the rate of voluntary compliance made by the taxpayers due to the increased value provided by the tax authorities as provided in taxpayers' charter. As per the Commissioner of Taxation annual report for the year 2018-2019, out of the total tax collection, 96% of the total tax collection was through voluntary compliance and only 4% of the collection was through the compliance activities undertaken by the tax authorities, which is an evident sign for high level of trust the taxpayers have in the tax authorities.[12]

As per the survey conducted[13], out of the respondents selected for the survey, majority of the people believed that the tax office adheres to the obligations set out in taxpayers' charter. ATO consistently reviews the performance of the taxpayers' charter and updates it based on the reviews received from public. This helps to build mutual trust and increases mutual co-operation between the taxpayers and the tax administration, which is especially an important aspect for the success of taxpayers' charter.

## 5. Taxpayers' Charter Introduced in India

India is known for its aggressive tax practices, be it from the taxpayer or tax administration - given historically its high tax rates. Multiple tax positions, interpretations, aggressive assessments, etc., created uncertainty in the minds of business. Working under the presumption that all taxpayers are tax evaders and levying unreasonable tax demand is one of the major criticisms received by Indian tax authorities. Further, long drawn litigation process adds on to the delay in settling tax disputes, and there is no tax certainty.

Many a times, to avoid spending time on tax litigation, taxpayers resolve the dispute by paying tax even if they do not agree with the demand raised on them.

---

12. Taxpayers rights in Australia twenty years after the introduction taxpayers' charter by Duncan Bently (https://www.researchgate.net/publication/316506870_Taxpayer_rights_in_Australia_twenty_years_after_the_introduction_of_the_Taxpayers'_Charter).
13. The Taxpayers' Charter: Does the Australian Tax Office comply and who benefits by Valerie Braithwaite and Monika Reinhart (https://www.researchgate.net/publication/240637923_The_Taxpayers'_Charter_Does_the_Australian_Tax_Office_Comply_and_Who_Benefits).

Some of the major contributors to this thought process is the frequently amended tax laws that create unpredictable tax environment and the aggressive approach adopted by the tax authorities further aggravates the situation. Both resident taxpayers and non-residents are hesitant when it comes to dealing with the taxation regime and the tax authorities in India.

In India though taxpayers' charter was not in place until the year 2020, the rights of the taxpayers were protected through the administrative guidelines since 1997. Central Board of Direct Taxes (CBDT) in the year 2010, introduced the Citizen's Charter which was later revised in 2014. The Citizen's Charter included some of the service delivery standards, explained the expectations from the taxpayers, obligations of the taxpayer, and provided a grievance redressal mechanism.

Some of the service standards included in the Citizen's Charter are discussed in Table 2.[14]

**Table 2. Service Standard in Citizen's Charter**

| Sl. No | Services | Time limit |
|---|---|---|
| 1 | Issue of refund along with interest under Section 143(1)<br>-For electronically filed returns<br>-others | <br>6 Months<br>9 Months |
| 2 | Issue of refunds including interest for proceedings other than under Section 143(1) of the Act | 1 Month |
| 3 | Decision on application of rectification | 2 Months |
| 4 | Giving effect to appellate/ revision order | 1 Month |
| 5 | Acknowledgement of communication received through electronic media or by hand | Immediate |
| 6 | Decision on application seeking extension of time for tax payment or grant of instalment | 1 Month |
| 7 | Issue of tax clearance certificate under Section 230 of the Income-tax Act | Within 3 working days from the date of receipt of the application. |
| 8 | Decision on application for recognition/approval to provident fund/superannuation fund/gratuity fund | 3 Months |

14. See Citizen's charter declaration (https://www.incometaxindia.gov.in/Documents/citizen-charter-declaration.pdf).

| Sl. No | Services | Time limit |
|---|---|---|
| 9 | Decision on application for grant of exemption or continuance thereof to institutions (University, School, Hospital etc.) under Section 10(23C) of the IT Act | 12 Months |
| 10 | Decision on application for approval to a fund under Section 10(23AAA) of the IT Act | 3 Months |
| 11 | Decision on application for registration of charitable or religious trust or institution | 4 Months |
| 12 | Decision on application for approval of hospitals in respect of medical treatment of prescribed diseases | 3 Months |
| 13 | Decision on application for grant of approval to institution or fund under Section 80G(5)(vi) of the IT Act, 1961. | 4 Months |
| 14 | Decision on application for no deduction of tax or deduction of tax at lower rate | 1 Month |
| 15 | Grievance redressal | 2 Months |
| 16 | Decision on application for transfer in case from one charge to another | 2 Months |

Citizen's Charter did not have the legal protection and did not bring out the major change in the tax administration. Even with the Citizen's Charter in place, a fulfilling tax administration was only a dream of the taxpayers.

Later, the Tax Administration Reform Commission (TARC) provided its first report under the chairmanship of Dr Parthasarathi Shome in 2014[15] pointing out the following on Indian tax administration procedure:

- 'Officers and staff at all levels of tax administration should be trained for customer orientation. Further for people posted in this vertical, the training in customer focus need to be more specialized and intensive. This training should be appropriate to the areas in which such officers are deployed such as customer relationship, measurement of customer satisfaction, taxpayer education, etc.
- In line with the international practice of spending 10-15 percent of the administration's budget, a minimum of 10 percent of the tax administration's budget must be spent on taxpayer services.

15. TARC. 2014. *Tax Administration reform in India -Spirit, Purpose and Empowerment (First Report)*, Government of India, New Delhi. (http://www.nadt.gov.in/writereaddata/MenuContentImages/First_report_TARC63548025 4365343004.pdf).

- In redressing taxpayer grievances, the decision of the Ombudsman should be binding on tax officers. To bring independence and effectiveness to the office of the Ombudsman, non-government professionals should also be inducted in the post.
- There is an urgent need to revisit the present citizen's charter to make it more meaningful and customer focused. The citizen's charter should be renamed the taxpayers' charter to focus on all categories of taxpayers.
- Continuous benchmarking of the tax administration, particularly in relation to delivery of taxpayer services, with that of other tax administrations should be done to highlight the area of focus'.

Despite numerous efforts taken by the government in this aspect, like e-assessment, steps initiated to monitor tax officials, tax administration system, etc. the taxpayers still face harassment to a certain extent.

The Union Finance Minister highlighted the requirement to create a trust-based tax environment in Financial Year 2020-2021 budget proposals. Accordingly, an introduction to taxpayers' charter was made in the Union Budget. The budget speech mentioned that, 'Any tax system requires trust between taxpayers and the administration. This will be possible only when taxpayers' rights are clearly enumerated. Towards this end, and with the objective of enhancing the efficiency of the delivery system of the Income Tax Department, I propose to amend the provisions of the Income-tax Act to mandate the CBDT to adopt a Taxpayers' Charter'.

The Finance Minister explained that fairness and efficiency of tax administration are important aspects of ease of living and ease of doing business. Therefore, the intent of bringing taxpayers' charter in the statutes was announced, where it was mentioned that the CBDT would adopt taxpayers' charter and issue necessary directions for implementation of the same.

With the above intention, India introduced taxpayers' charter to boost trust between the citizens and the authorities. Through insertion of new Section 119A in the Income-tax Act, 1961, CBDT was empowered to adopt and declare taxpayers' charter and issue such orders, instructions, directions or guidelines to other Income-tax authorities as it may deem fit for the administration of the charter.

Prime Minister of India on August 13, 2020, launched *Transparent Taxation - honouring the honest, platform encompassing faceless assessments, faceless appeals, and Taxpayers' Charter*. In his speech, he emphasised that the focus of this initiative is moving away from *power centric administration to people centric administration*. He assured that the taxpayers can expect fearlessness and fairness in tax administration at the same time, he emphasised on the point that it is the duty of the taxpayers to make prompt tax payments indicating the importance of two-way co-operation from tax administration as well as the taxpayers for an improved and better tax administration.

A list of 14 obligations of the revenue gives a broad understanding of the level of services the taxpayers can expect from the revenue/ rights of the taxpayers:

1. To provide fair, courteous, and reasonable treatment.
2. To treat taxpayer as honest: The tax administration should treat the taxpayer as honest unless there is evidence to the contrary
3. To provide a mechanism for appeal and review.
4. To provide complete and accurate information: The tax administration should provide the taxpayers with accurate information for fulfilling the compliance obligations under the law.
5. To provide timely decisions: The tax administration shall take decisions in every income-tax proceeding within the time prescribed under law.
6. To collect the correct amount of tax.
7. To respect privacy of taxpayer: The tax administration shall follow due process of law and be no more intrusive than necessary in any inquiry, examination, or enforcement action.
8. To maintain confidentiality: The tax administration shall not disclose any information provided by the taxpayer to the department unless authorized by law.
9. To hold the authorities accountable: The tax administration shall hold its authorities accountable for their actions.
10. To enable representative of choice.
11. To provide a mechanism to lodge complaints: The tax administration shall provide a mechanism for lodging a complaints and prompt disposal thereof.
12. To provide a fair and just system: The tax administration shall provide a fair and impartial system and resolve the tax issues in a time-bound manner.
13. To publish service standards and report periodically: The tax administration shall publish standards for service delivery in a periodic manner.
14. To reduce cost of compliance: The tax administration shall duly take into account the cost of compliance when administering tax legislation.

Most of the rights provided in taxpayers' charter of India is a combination of rights present in the taxpayers' charter of different countries (right to be treated honest, right to certainty, right to pay no more than the amount of tax required etc), but needless to say, it is very well amended to make it suitable to the Indian scenario – like the right to not to be subject to retrospective taxation, the right to request to a payment plan, etc. But what is missing in the Indian charter is the right of tax certainty.

Rights such as the right to be treated honest, the right to minimize compliance cost, the right to hold the tax administration accountable for their actions, the right to privacy and confidentiality of the taxpayers provide solutions to several problems faced by taxpayers such as unnecessary litigations, high compliance cost, etc., resulting in harassment and reduction in voluntary compliance by the taxpayers. The right to complain about the service of the tax administration holds the department accountable for their actions which helps in improving the service that is provided to the taxpayers.

The aim of the tax law should be to collect taxes legally due from the taxpayers and not the potential maximum amount.. In this respect, the right which is provided in the charter "right to pay no more than the correct amount of tax" is a welcome move. It is a practice for the tax authorities to not allow deductions or exemptions when it is not claimed in the original return. – this is a mistake apparent from the record, resulting in unnecessary litigations, which should now reduce. With this right now in place, at least there should be a reduction in the trend of only collecting taxpayer information and not effectively utilizing the information to determine the correct amount of tax payable by them. Paying tax is a civic duty. However, collecting the right amount of tax and protecting the interest of genuine taxpayers are the civic responsibilities of the tax authorities.

The right to request a payment plan and the right for licit arrangement of tax affairs of the taxpayers help to reduce the compliance cost of the taxpayers and also reduce unnecessary harassment by the tax officers even in situations that are beyond the control of the taxpayers.

Emphasis on protection of the right to privacy and confidentiality, helps to protect individuals and the corporates from any damage to their goodwill and reputation due to speculation in the media and other mediums. Media plays an important role, especially with regard to confidentiality of tax systems around the world. With a major role being played by the tax authorities in collecting information and the media in unearthing them, a balance should be maintained between transparency and privacy.

However, the taxpayers' charter of India, like many other country's charter, does not provide the right of confidentiality and privacy relating to the agreements between the countries for the exchange of information of the taxpayers. Rather, it provides an exception to the right of confidentiality of taxpayers' information by mentioning in the charter that the tax administration might have to share the taxpayers' information with other jurisdictions under various agreements. Transparency is such factor that is directly proportional to voluntary compliance.

The right to minimize compliance cost strives to achieve its objective by making the interactions with the tax authorities easier, by way of reducing the workload of taxpayers in complying with the provisions of the Act, etc. However, in practice, this seems difficult as the reduction of compliance cost is directly proportional to the complexity of the tax laws. Hence, the government should give importance to drafting tax laws, that are not complex in nature, easy to understand, and comply with by the taxpayers.

It is to be very well noted that taxpayers' charter is no substitute for having the rights of the taxpayers enshrined in the statute. Rights such as the right to appeal, time limits, protection against disclosure of confidential information should always be given proper statutory form. However, there are certain general and broader rights for which taxpayers' charter is a more suitable instrument (For example, the revenue authorities should collect the right amount of tax, not necessarily the maximum amount of tax which could be levied; taxpayers have the right to be represented at a meeting with the revenue authorities by a person of their choice.)[16]. Hence, the introduction of taxpayers' charter in India and the inclusion of such rights is an appreciable effort by the government to provide the taxpayers with necessary legal rights.

It is needless to say that only when the protection of rights by the tax administration and observance of obligations by the taxpayers go hand-in-hand, the system will become successful. Though the obligations of the taxpayers are provided in different parts of the legislation, providing them in a separate document makes it easier to access and refer. The taxpayers' charter of India expects the taxpayers to meet the following obligations, which are listed below:

1. The obligation to be honest, and compliant: The taxpayer is expected to honestly disclose full information and fulfil his compliance obligations honestly.
2. The obligation to be informed: The taxpayer is expected to be aware of his compliance obligations under tax law and seek the help of the department if needed.
3. The obligation to keep accurate records in accordance with the law.
4. The obligation to know what the representative does on his behalf: The taxpayer is expected to know what information and submissions are made by his authorised representative.
5. The obligation to respond in time: The taxpayer is expected to make submissions as per tax law in a timely manner.
6. The obligation to pay in time: The taxpayer is expected to pay the amount due as per law in a timely manner.

16. Get Charter by Philip Baker - https://www.taxation.co.uk/articles/2006-09-28-4403-get-charter.

It is the duty of both taxpayers and the tax administration to adhere to the provisions of the Act and the charter. This helps in promoting a healthy relationship between them, which is the basic motive of introducing the taxpayers' charter.

Recently, there has been a significant shift in digitization of compliance procedures - from online filing of tax returns/ forms, online payment of taxes, prefilling of returns, etc. The collection of data from various means, including other departments of the tax administration team, third parties, etc., are now effectively integrated to provide a seamless service to the taxpayers. Such improved signs of tax administration coupled with taxpayers' charter should have a holistic and integrated approach.

The taxpayers' charter in India is expected to improve the relationship between the tax authorities and the taxpayers, reduce unnecessary harassments through long drawn litigations, even in the case of honest taxpayers who are mostly victims of the perception of the tax authorities that most taxpayers are dishonest. It will also help the tax authorities to shift the focus to better administration rather than unnecessary litigations.

Further, with the tax regulations, taxpayers' rights and obligations in place, it is recommended that an effective *Compliance Program* is made available for taxpayers' education. This program should be a single document that provides all the details that a taxpayer should be aware of. In addition to this, simple and easy to understand tax laws and procedures will add to motivating the taxpayers in complying with them.

Also, post introduction of taxpayers' charter, the tax compliance pattern should be studied at regular intervals. 360-degree feedback should also be taken for its effective implementation, and if need be, required amendments should also be made to the tax regulations and taxpayers' charter based on the feedback.

Many countries across the world have introduced taxpayers' charter, keeping in mind the importance of protection of taxpayers' rights and interest. Introduction of taxpayers' charter in India in the statute itself is a welcome move for the common good and a positive step towards reforming the tax administration.

## 6. Concluding Remarks

Taxpayers' charter is nothing, but a consolidated set of behaviors expected from the taxpayer and the tax administration. Not many countries had taxpayers' rights and obligations separately spelt out and given legislative sanction. Many countries have certain rights and obligations incorporated as part of their tax provisions like certain countries already provide certain rights to the taxpayers such as the right to appeal, the right to be represented by someone else on taxpayers' behalf, the right to pay only taxes due under the law, etc. Even countries without taxpayers' charter attach equal responsibility to the taxpayers' rights and obligations.

The success of the tax system is always based on mutual co-operation between the taxpayer and the tax authorities. The taxpayers' charter will surely increase the accountability of the tax administration towards taxpayers, which will promote transparent proceedings and communication between the taxpayers and the tax authorities. It also helps in improving voluntary compliance that improves tax administration and increases collection of taxes – this being one of the important motives behind introducing a taxpayers' charter.

***Should there be a model taxpayers' charter applicable to all?***

Having understood the fact that there could be certain expectations that differ between a developed economy and an emerging economy when it comes to taxpayers' charter, the question really is – should a blanket set of rights and obligations be charted that are applicable globally? Or should there be a separate set for developed economies and a separate set for emerging economies? Or should each country draft its own taxpayers' charter based on a study conducted within?

There are no set of hard and fast rules to answer this. However, each country will require a set of rights and obligations based on the mutual experience of the tax administration and taxpayers. Say for example, in a country that lacks 'intrinsic motivation', the focus should be more on protecting the interest of the taxpayers without compromising tax revenue.

Also, reforms, prioritizing improving tax administration experience, including adherence to tax policies and compliances differ across countries – depending on the current stage of development, level of tax abuse, capacity of the tax administration, etc. It is difficult to draft a taxpayer charter with one size fits all approach. Developing and emerging economies usually face larger tax gaps, and therefore, prefer that their regulations ensure increased revenue yields from effective compliance. For these economies, the primary focus should be to ensure the collection of the basic revenue due without any tax leakage.

## REJOINDER

**Rohitash Chaudhary**

## 1. Introduction

In this Chapter, Girish has elaborated on the challenges faced by tax authorities and taxpayers to comply with tax laws. Such challenges have, in many cases, led to the designing of procedures acceptable for both tax administration and taxpayers to encourage voluntary compliance. A good tax system should have a balance between taxpayers' rights and obligations. These thoughts also facilitated the introduction of taxpayers' charters in several countries as taxpayers' rights and charters are inextricably linked.

However, Girish points out that a taxpayers' charter is not a substitute for having the rights of taxpayers enshrined in the statute. The basic motive of introducing a taxpayers' charter is promoting a healthy relationship between taxpayers and tax authorities and both should adhere to the provisions of the Act and the charter. A taxpayers' charter will help tax officers to shift their focus to a better tax administration rather than indulging in unnecessary litigation.

## 2. Cross-country Taxpayers' Rights and Ombudsman Experiences

In 2014, India's Tax Administration Reform Commission (TARC) discussed that:

> The recognition of the 'rights' of the taxpayer is an emerging trend. In a number of countries, such as the Netherlands and Russia, these rights have been codified in tax laws, while in others, for example, in Australia, Ireland, New Zealand, Singapore, and South Africa, they have been elaborated upon in tax administration documents, sometimes referred to as taxpayer's charter or service charter.
>
> Many tax administrations have special institutional arrangements to deal with taxpayers' complaints. Dedicated bodies like the Ombudsman in Australia, Canada, UK, Brazil, South Africa and tax mediators in Belgium and France look into tax related complaints. These bodies are independent of the tax administration. In many countries, they have been set up under a specific law. The primary purpose of this arrangement is to ensure that taxpayers have an opportunity to raise matters when they feel they have been treated in an unfair manner. India too has set up the office of the Ombudsman at different places. However, by and large, taxpayers appear to be afraid to file formal complaints for fear of retaliation, whether unfounded or not, from the tax administration.[17]

17. TARC. 2014. *Tax Administration Reform in India: Spirit, Purpose and Empowerment (First Report)*, Government of India, New Delhi, p 55.

## 3. Indian Experience

In 2010, India introduced a citizen's charter in the form of administrative guidelines. Experience with the charter shows that due to the lack of legal protection, it was not effective to bring out a major change in the tax administration.[18] In 2014, TARC recommended that there is an urgent need to revisit the present citizen's charter to make it more meaningful and customer focused. The citizen's charter should be renamed the taxpayer's charter to focus on all categories of taxpayers.[19]

The Indian government introduced a law on tax charter in 2020. Unlike the earlier citizen's charter this time the taxpayers' charter has the backing of law.

Girish emphasized that tax authorities collect a lot of information from taxpayers, and it should be kept confidential to maintain a balance between transparency and privacy. Unlike other countries, India's taxpayers' charter does not provide the right to confidentiality and privacy in agreements between India and other countries for the exchange of taxpayer information. The right to taxpayer privacy was brought out forcefully by Khincha et al. in an earlier ITRAF volume. They discussed a taxpayer's privacy and confidentiality rights in the context of information exchange:

> Increased cross-border opportunities pose a challenge for a government in maintaining investment flows and simultaneously ensuring effective collection of taxes. At the same time, the need to focus on the challenges to a taxpayer's privacy rights and interests presented by tax information exchange (TIE) assumes importance. International agreements need to help protect taxpayer privacy rights while at the same time encouraging more effective sharing of taxpayer information across borders. The implementation of TIE should be accompanied by assurance to governments that the rights of their citizens and residents will be respected.[20]
>
> ...The Global Forum guide on the protection of confidentiality of information exchanged for tax purposes published in 2012 sets out the best practices related to confidentiality. It also provides practical guidance, including recommendations and a checklist, on how to meet an adequate level of protection. This is after due consideration to the fact that different tax administrations may have different approaches to ensuring that in practice, they achieve required level of effective protection of confidentiality.[21]

---

18. Mukesh Butani and Shreyash Shah. 2020. Taxpayer Charter: A Roadmap for Mutual Trust and Respect, *Financial Express,* August 21. https://www.financialexpress.com/opinion/taxpayer-charter-a-roadmap-for-mutual-trust-and-respect/2061181/, (last accessed on January 9, 2021).
19. TARC (2014), First Report, op. cit., p 92.
20. H. Padamchand Khincha, Neha P. Khincha, and Priya Kothari. 2018. Taxpayer Rights in International Exchange of Information, in Parthasarathi Shome edited, *Challenges in Domestic and International Taxation: Emerging Indian Experience,* OakBridge, Gurugram, pp 279-80.
21. Khincha et al. (2018), op. cit., p 287.

In India's taxpayers' charter a unique clause is the tax department's promise "to hold its authorities accountable for their actions". The taxpayers' charters in other countries reveal that accountability is included in it, but there is no specific focus on holding their authorities accountable for their actions. In India, taxpayers sometimes may be obliged to pay what may be perceived as unjust tax demands to meet the administration's revenue targets for a fiscal year.

In 2014, TARC pointed that

> India does not specify what the taxpayer can do if not satisfied, nor is there any indicator of accountability on the part of the tax officer or time limits for responses to categories of taxpayer queries. The tone is set, instead, with respect to the tax officer's voluntary service orientation.[22]

It is not clear how accountability will work, for example, would taxpayers request courts to instruct the tax administration to publish clear guidelines on ensuring accountability[23]?

## 4. Success is Not Built-in

Shome commented in 2020[24]:

> A taxpayers' charter was introduced in India primarily because country after country were adopting it. At that time officers did not take it too seriously because they knew that there was a certain limited objective to the whole exercise. The Ombudsman was powerless and taxpayers complained that they will be thrashed by assessment officers if they reach out to Ombudsman.
>
> (However), it is observed that, from a policy making level, the taxpayers' charter appears to carry some seriousness. This is because, for the first time, it has legislative backing while the earlier citizen's charter was merely administrative in nature. It seems that the administration is willing to take in comments from taxpayers. So, it depends on what taxpayers feel. Can they really bite the bullet and bring matters to the attention of the policy making authorities through industry associations?
>
> Taxpayers should hold the hand and support the efforts made by the authorities because the legislation process has shown that there is some meaning to it; otherwise, authorities would not go to this extent to legislate a

22. TARC (2014), First Report, op. cit., p 55.
23. Harsh Roongta. 2020. Taxpayers' Charter: Expected More Fairness, *Business Standard*, August 30. https://www.business-standard.com/article/opinion/taxpayers-charter-expect-more-fairness-120083000897_1.html, (last accessed on January 12, 2021).
24. ITRAF Annual Conference (Webinar), 4-5 December, 2020 (recording). For more details see, http://www.itraf.org/itraf-annual-conference-webinar/.

taxpayers' charter. All the rights and obligations cited in the taxpayers' charter is important and carry weight but it cannot be successful without complete bravery and courage of taxpayers. They have to approach and access the policy makers as opposed merely the administration so that implementation of the charter actually becomes successful.

In, 2014, TARC discussed the formation of a Feedback Analysis, Programme Evaluation and Taxpayers' Charter Division:

> This division would also be responsible for designing the taxpayer's charter and evaluating the performance of the department vis-à-vis the timelines committed in the charter. Based upon analysis and feedback, timelines provided for existing services could be amended and more services could be included in the charter. The taxpayer's charter designed here would be implemented by the service delivery and grievance redressal setup in the field formation.[25]

Girish adds to the TARC's proposal that, with taxpayer's rights and obligations in place, an effective compliance programme could be structured for taxpayer education. It must include important details for taxpayer's awareness, simple and easy-to-understand tax laws, and procedures to comply with these laws. Post implementation of charter, the tax compliance pattern should be analysed at regular intervals. Feedbacks should be collected at regular intervals from taxpayers, and required changes must be introduced in tax regulations and the taxpayers' charter.

Girish also suggests that an effective redressal mechanism should be introduced to address the taxpayer's grievance and make tax officials accountable for their wrong actions. Seth (2020) has elaborated on this matter:

> Some tax officers found that the taxpayers' charter is weak and unclear compared to the existing citizen's charter that specifies stiff timelines for delivery of services. This has created confusion among officers whether to abide by the timelines mentioned in the citizen's charter or go by the taxpayers' charter. The taxpayers' charter only talks about 'providing timely decisions' and 'resolve tax issues in a time-bound manner'. However, the citizen's charter specifies timelines for 16 services, including issue of refunds, acknowledgement of communication received, redress of grievances, and so on. There was expectation from the present charter that taxpayers will get compensated for delays in issuance of refunds or other services.[26]

---

25. TARC (2014), First Report, op. cit., p 83.
26. Dilasha Seth. 2020. Experts Give Taxpayers' Charter a Thumbs Up, Want Govt to Walk the Talk, *Business Standard*, August 13. https://www.business-standard.com/article/economy-policy/experts-give-taxpayers-charter-a-thumbs-up-want-govt-to-walk-the-talk-120081301888_1.html, (last accessed on January 12, 2021).

Other experts have also viewed the taxpayers' charter to possess an impulse to generate trust since it provides an opportunity to build trust between the taxpayer and the administration. If so, it should carry the potential for the protection of taxpayers by making tax law predictable and compliable. While difficult to balance, it would combine the obligations of the tax administration to enforce the law, and meeting the legitimate expectations of taxpayers.[27]

Baker (2018) has made forceful comments on the protection of taxpayers' rights in the context of international taxation:

> Many people believe that protection of taxpayers' rights was the 16th, missing Action point in the BEPS Project. It was a vital issue which the OECD and the countries engaged in the Project should not have ignored; the fact that it was not included as an Action Point speaks volumes about the need to reconsider the international tax architecture to ensure that bodies with a specific human rights agenda play a greater role in the development of rules of international taxation.[28]

It is interesting that Baker's chapter in this volume addresses the issue of a new international taxation architecture (See Chapter 3).

## 5. Conclusion

To conclude, the success of a tax system is based on mutual trust and co-operation between the taxpayer and the tax administration. The objective of a taxpayers' charter should be to provide taxpayer's rights and obligations in a transparent and self-explanatory manner to help both groups to exercise their rights and responsibilities. The focus of a taxpayers' charter should be to expedite voluntary compliance, and taxpayers should not be afraid of any adverse action for approaching the tax authorities. The right to privacy and confidentiality of taxpayer's data under cross-country information exchange should be specifically included in a taxpayers' charter. A taxpayers' charter should improve revenue collection through voluntary compliance while protecting taxpayers from any unjust tax demand by authorities.

Surveying the literature by Baker, Butani and Shome, the view about a taxpayers' charter is very similar, that is, to have it included in the legislation. The success of a taxpayers' charter also lies on taxpayers by supporting the authorities in providing valuable inputs—through focus groups—on legislation, administration, and policy aspects of the implementation of a taxpayers' charter. In line with TARC recommendations, a taxpayers' charter division could be created within the tax

27. Butani and Shah (2020), op. cit.
28. Philip Baker. 2018. Foreword, in P. Shome edited, *Challenges in Domestic and International Taxation: Emerging Indian Experience*, OakBridge, Gurugram, pp vi-vii.

administration for the designing of and continual improving of the taxpayers' charter, dissemination of information, drafting of simple laws, and grievance redressal.

A final point is to point out that the earlier citizen's charter that had not been legislated did stipulate timelines in imparting services. Yet the subsequent taxpayers' charter, which has been legislated recently, skirts around timelines without specifying them. Timelines are essential for taxpayer trust and should be specified. In total, the measures should help in reducing tax litigation in India where tax uncertainty is not a new thing. Having legislated on the matter, the Indian tax administration should not miss the opportunity of earnestly providing the services that should follow the legislation for the policymakers' objective to be realized.

# Subject Index

## A

**D**

G

**N**

## T